LYNCHINGS
IN MISSISSIPPI

ALSO BY JULIUS E. THOMPSON
AND FROM MCFARLAND

*Dudley Randall, Broadside Press, and the Black Arts Movement
in Detroit, 1960–1995* (1999; paperback 2005)

*Percy Greene and the Jackson Advocate:
The Life and Times of a Radical Conservative
Black Newspaperman, 1897–1977* (1994)

1005333612

LYNCHINGS IN MISSISSIPPI

A History, 1865–1965

Julius E. Thompson

McFarland & Company, Inc., Publishers
Jefferson, North Carolina, and London

Excerpts from *Vernon Can Read* by Vernon E. Jordan, Jr., ©2001 by
Vernon E. Jordan, Jr., and Annette Gordon-Reed, Perseus Books, LLC.

The poem "Emmett Till" used by permission of James A. Emanuel.
"In 1955, Till, a fourteen-year-old from Chicago, for allegedly whistling
at a white woman in Mississippi, was murdered by white men who tied a
gin mill fan around his neck and threw his body into the Tallahatchie River."

LIBRARY OF CONGRESS CATALOGUING-IN-PUBLICATION DATA

Thompson, Julius Eric.
Lynchings in Mississippi : a history, 1865–1965 / Julius E. Thompson.
p.   cm.
Includes bibliographical references and index.

ISBN-13: 978-0-7864-2722-2
ISBN-10: 0-7864-2722-1
(illustrated case binding : 50# alkaline paper) ∞

1. Lynching—Mississippi—History.   2. Mississippi—Race relations.   I. Title.
HV6465.M7T46 2007   364.1'34—dc22   2006024511

British Library cataloguing data are available

On the cover: Art by Kate Irwin;
background map of Mississippi from
Harper's Weekly, Jan. 6, 1866 (Library of Congress)

Manufactured in the United States of America

*McFarland & Company, Inc., Publishers
Box 611, Jefferson, North Carolina 28640
www.mcfarlandpub.com*

Contents

Preface

Lynchings in Mississippi: A History, 1865–1965 explores a topic of major significance in American history that greatly impacted the American people in the late nineteenth through the mid-twentieth century. During this era, thousands of Americans were killed by lynch mobs, but this plight especially became a burden for African Americans. No state was more severe in terms of lynching than Mississippi, which holds the record for the highest number of lynching victims in the United States from 1865 to 1965, at more than 500 out of a total of at least 5,000 victims since Reconstruction. Lynchings were terror-filled events and are generally defined as illegal actions by a mob of three or more persons who kidnap a person or persons for vigilante justice for an accused crime against economic interests, such as property, murder, rape, or attempted rape, and minor offenses, including being a well-off black, or for some kind of insult to a white person.

The national response to lynching was mixed. Many individuals and groups were opposed to lynching, but large segments of society and government remained quiet for long periods. Black Americans were especially active in the anti-lynching struggle, and no single individual was more active in this case than Mississippian Ida B. Wells-Barnett (1862–1931), who emerged in the 1890s as an important advocate for black rights and a leader in the anti-lynching crusade. Barnett wrote widely and lectured extensively in the United States and Europe on the lynching problem. No central African American organization has been more historically active as the National Association for the Advancement of Colored People (NAACP) in the struggle against U.S. lynchings.

From its origins in 1909–1910 to the 1950s, the NAACP waged a relentless campaign to challenge the nation to deal with the lynching issue and especially to promote the passage in Congress of an anti-lynching bill that, unfortunately, never became a law between the 1910s and 1960s. Although black Americans were very active against lynching, many white Americans were silent or not active enough in this human rights struggle. This was especially true of the U.S. government, including various presidents, Congress, and the courts. However, some white individuals and groups were anti-lynching supporters. A major force in the South in this regard was Jessie Daniel Ames and the Association of Southern Women for the Prevention of Lynching, organized in Atlanta, Georgia, in 1930; this group also had supporters and branches in Mississippi. Other whites opposed to lynching were various unions, teachers' groups, and liberal thinkers among artists, writers, and scholars. Still, many groups such as the Ku Klux Klan supported lynching, and the phenomenon of lynching survived for more that 100 years as a major challenge to the American justice system.

Mississippi represents the most extreme cases of lynching, and an understanding of how the crisis unfolded and grew there may help contemporary readers to place the national issues in better historical perspective. These issues include: the range of the lynching volume; the reasons for lynching; the distribution by counties, cities, and rural locations of lynchings; and the response of Americans to the lynching crisis over time.

Although this book seeks to explore the historical nature of lynching in Mississippi this is not a sociological or psychological study of the phenomenon. Rather, it is an effort by a black historian to explore the full range of the lynching problem in its social, cultural, and political significance in a key state. The author employs a black perspective to underline the importance of the lynching theme within the context of African-American life and history from the nineteenth century to the present. This is the first attempt by a black scholar to focus a scholarly book on lynching in Mississippi.

A number of colleagues and former students have been helpful. Scholars who have impacted my work across the years include: Jerry W. Ward and Dorothy V. Smith of Dillard University, New Orleans, Louisiana; Wendell P. Holbrook of Rutgers University, Newark, New Jersey; H. Lewis Suggs, formerly of Clemson University, Clemson, South Carolina; James L. Conyers, Jr., and Ahati Toure of the University of Houston, Houston, Texas; Colia L. Clark, Philadelphia; Camille A. Jones, Carbondale, Illinois; and Deborah LeSure-Wilbourn of Coldwater, Mississippi provided research assistance. For typing assistance, I wish to thank Linda Hudson; Candance Benton of Columbia, Missouri; Janet Howard of Hannibal, Missouri; and Jamie Ward and Jeannie Cook of Carbondale, Illinois.

Lynching in Mississippi remains a topic of deep concern and interest to the American people, and it is hoped that future generations will also learn from the errors and terror of the past.

Columbia, Missouri
Fall 2006

1

The Emancipation Era, 1865–1869

After a long period of enslavement, the African American population of Mississippi emerged in 1865 to face the challenges of a new world. Blacks had lived in a state that was one of the major cotton-producing areas in the world, with the wealth created going to white people. The black population in Mississippi had grown from 3,454 in 1800 to 437,406 in 1860, or 55.2 percent of the state's total population.[1] The state's free black population in this group consisted of only 773 individuals, while the white population of Mississippi stood at 353,899.[2] By this date the state also had a very small Native American population.

In the five-year period under discussion, black Mississippians were faced with the tasks of overcoming centuries of the impact of American slavery and of organizing institutions to promote the equality, justice and freedom of opportunity for the community in the various spheres of economic, social and political life in the state.[3] On the opposite side of blacks stood the former Confederates who had lost the Civil War and their cherished institution of slavery. Indeed, after the war Mississippi was in a poor state of existence.[4] Too many white Mississippians still viewed blacks as a cheap source of labor and as a group that should still be under the political, economic and social domination of white Mississippians. How was this goal to be achieved by white people in the state?

The first order of business was to regain political control of Mississippi, but it would take whites 10 years to achieve this objective. A more immediate task at hand was an expressed need to control the black community. At first, white Mississippians tried to do so with the Black Codes, new laws passed by the Mississippi legislature in late 1865 to control black activity in the state. One study notes:

> Black people faced serious controls under the code. The law provided for the "binding out" of young black children as apprentices. Former owners of the children were given first choice. Blacks had to have a home or job by January 1, 1866, or be fined as vagrants. If they could not pay the fine, they were "hired out," with former owners given the first option. Blacks had to have licenses to do certain jobs, they could not own guns, and they could not rent land except in towns. It was illegal for blacks and whites to marry each other.[5]

3

The counties of the state of Mississippi (COURTESY MISSISSIPPI DEPARTMENT OF ARCHIVES AND HISTORY, JACKSON, MISSISSIPPI).

Northern reactions and black residents were pressed into action against the Black Codes, and some relief came with Congressional Reconstruction and the work of the Freedmen's Bureau in Mississippi.[6] Nonetheless, blacks were also faced with a situation where the customs of race relations restricted their rights in Mississippi. They were also faced with the actions of anti-black groups such as the Ku Klux Klan, first organized in Pulaski, Tennessee, in 1865 and very active in Mississippi during the 1860s.[7] The Klan and other white terrorist groups used intimidation and violence to suppress black political, social and economic rights in the state.[8]

In spite of the oppression of such forces on the local and state level, black Mississippians were able to forge ahead with a program to increase the life changes of the community in the state. One scholar notes that focus was especially concentrated on bringing improvements for blacks in the areas of "the church, education, farming, government, and the emerging press."[9] Black Mississippians were an essential part of bringing reforms to the state and promoting the Republican party—the instrument of their freedom—and creating new leaders to advance black political concerns to the nation. Mississippi produced 226 political leaders who served the state on the federal, state and local levels of government during Reconstruction.[10] Three of the most famous national black leaders during Reconstruction came from Mississippi. Serving in the Senate were Hiram R. Revels (1827–1901) and Blanche K. Bruce (1847–1898), and John Roy Lynch (1847–1939) served in the House of Representatives.[11]

Thus, although the black community was faced with a host of ills in the late 1860s, the group had begun to gain some degree of independence from the daily controls of the white community they had suffered under during slavery. They had to achieve progress, however, in spite of aid from the Freedman's Bureau and some religious groups whose provision was largely at the expense of these black groups. Reparations for previous black slave labor were not paid in the 1860s, and now the black community had to wage a life and death struggle to overcome the lynching crisis that loomed before them. The period ahead would test their courage, faith, and future hopes.

During the period 1865–1869, the state criminal justice system must be viewed as an agency that represented white Mississippians who wished to continue to control the black population. In essence Mississippi represented the defeated South after the Civil War, and the major goal of the state's white leaders was to maintain order (the older order!) and to control black labor and rights.[12]

On a daily basis blacks in the state were faced with a system that attempted to use the laws and customs of Mississippi to keep the black community in its historical place. Clearly the Mississippi Black Code, as previously noted, sought to prescribe the freedoms of blacks as Reconstruction opened in the mid-1860s.[13] For many blacks, however, the terror of the times was still focused on such groups as the Ku Klux Klan, a white supremacy organization that, according to scholar Allen W. Trelease was a major factor in spreading terror and oppression against the black community in the last quarter of the nineteenth century.[14] The greatest criminal justice issue and crisis facing blacks in Mississippi, however, would come with terror associated with lynching and its assorted horrors from the 1860s through the next 100 years.

The struggle of the African American people in Mississippi for economic, political and social equality lay in the background efforts of elements within the defeated Confederates to gain special advantages and control over the black community in the state. Lynching and violence against blacks must be considered one element in the arsenal of whites to do so. The problem of lynching is generally defined as "an extralegal means of social control in which individuals take the law into their own hands to inflict corporal punishment and/or death upon persons who violate local customs and more."[15]

In Mississippi, as elsewhere in the South, white men justified lynching in cases of rape "to protect the white women from the agony of testifying in court."[16] The evidence from all periods under study, however, reveals that this factor was more in the imagination of Southern white men than in the actual occurrence of such events. From the earliest periods onward, lynchings were especially focused on the alleged crimes of blacks against white men, including murder, assault or robbery, or insulting whites with a prime consideration of such "attacks" on white women.[17]

The lynching phenomenon was also used to intimidate black voters and political leaders in the 1860s in Mississippi. One scholar notes that "in Mississippi, whites applied the lessons of lynching most severely in the Republican counties and regions of the state." In fact, the Republican counties "had a higher incidence of lynching than their non–Republican counterparts and ... Republican regions had over 60 percent more lynchings than non-Republican regions before disfranchisement."[18] Many scholars now agree with the assessment of the period of scholar W. Fitzhugh Brundage that often lynchings took place as a signal of white masculine authority. A part of this problem for some white males was the issue of economic domination over blacks and other groups and fear of labor troubles or loss of property to non-whites. Other white males were very fearful of alleged sexual transgressions against white women,[19] so there were many cases for lynching in Mississippi during and after the 1860s. Always the central problem for the black community in the state was that lynching could happen every day and often did.[20]

Scholars have long noted the violent nature of Mississippi society.[21] For the black Mississippi community this fact took on a special emphasis in the Emancipation Era of the late 1860s, when the lynching phenomenon really began in the state. Historian Neil R. McMillen even traces the problem to an earlier period during the antebellum stage of Mississippi's history, when the state first gained a national reputation for mob violence.[22] Even though many scholars agree that the years 1865–1869 were very violent ones for blacks in Mississippi, they generally note that the exact number of blacks killed during the period remains a mystery. Table 1.1, Lynchings in Mississippi, 1865–1869, gives a summary of the range of the problem with the known data from the period.[23]

Historian Vernon Lane Wharton believes that the first lynching of a black Mississippian after the Civil War took place in Oktibbeha County in northeast Mississippi for the alleged rape of a white woman.[24] Other incidents of violence against black people, generally males, seem to have taken place statewide in 1866–1869. The Ku Klux Klan and other white Mississippi regulators were major instigators in the campaign to keep blacks in their place and to control the black population in the state with lynching as a significant tool of oppression. The data suggest that perhaps hundreds of blacks were lynched in Mississippi during this era, with many of the victims remaining unknown to history. If we accept Charles Summers's estimate that "2 or 3 per week" were lynched in Mississippi in the late 1860s, then we can probably assume that hundreds were in fact killed, and this may not be an exaggeration of the problem.[25] In any event, it was a period of stress for the African American community in Mississippi, but a greater challenge yet lay ahead in the coming decades, when lynching would become a larger phenomenon in the daily lives and struggles of black Americans. Over time, Mississippi would come to carry the undesirable label as the state with the most lynching victims. As historian James Silver has observed, Mississippi was a "closed society," one in which lynching became accepted as an ordinary everyday occurrence, with most of its victims being black males.[26] Lynching became a statewide tradition. Two scholars

TABLE 1.1: LYNCHINGS IN MISSISSIPPI, 1865–1869

Year	Number of Lynchings	Names of Lynching Victims	Location of Lynchings
Summer of 1865	1	Unknown	Oktibbeha County
1865–1866	A number of white men were lynched for stealing horses	Unknown	By regulators in Eastern Mississippi
1868	The Ku Klux Klan boasted of lynching 291 blacks throughout the South; some of these must have been in Mississippi	Unknown	The South
1867–1868	Two to three blacks were lynched in Mississippi every week	Unknown	Statewide in Mississippi
1869	Thirty-five blacks were lynched during this period (1869–1871)	Unknown	Kemper County
	Thirty-one victims were lynched in the South; some of which must have been killed in Mississippi.		The South

on the period wrote that "lynching was community-sanctioned murder. Crimes were alleged; trials were summary; death, often accompanied by torture and mutilation, came by hanging, shooting, burning, stabbing, dragging, and combinations thereof."[27]

The response to lynching in Mississippi in the years 1865–1869 depended upon the circumstances of one's background. For the black community, lynching was a crime against black people that they had to struggle to overcome. Yet the crisis facing black Mississippians in the 1860s included not only physical violence but also economic, political, and social oppression. The black community had to face threats from white Mississippi against all aspects of black freedom in the state. However, as a group of Mississippi scholars have observed, "Black Mississippians did not meekly accept being disfranchised and forced into second-class citizenship. They developed a 'mask' to wear for white society. A black minister might, for example, advise his congregation on ways to outwit the white man. But if the preacher met that man on the street, he would be outwardly polite and respond with 'Yes, sir' and 'No, sir.' There was one social self for whites and a real self shared only with other blacks. Resentment, however, ran deep among many blacks."[28] This state of affairs would run deep in the black Mississippi psychological state of consciousness for many years to come.

2

Terror in the Day and Night, 1870–1879

The decade of the 1870s was a time of continued changes, reforms, and setbacks for black people in Mississippi. By 1870 the black population in the state stood at 444,201 compared to 283,896 for white Mississippians.[1] Thus, blacks held a majority (60 percent) of the population of Mississippi, but they did not control the political, economic, or social affairs of the state; white Mississippians continued to hold the spheres of influence in all aspects of life. Nonetheless, blacks continued to struggle for a political voice in Mississippi. Only black males could vote, and so the increasing number of black leaders who emerged in Mississippi government included men such as Hiram R. Revels (1827–1901), Blanche K. Bruce (1841–1898), John Roy Lynch (1847–1939), James Hill (1846–1901), and James Lynch (1838–1872), an outstanding minister and orator and Mississippi Secretary of State 1870–1872 (no relation to John Roy Lynch), among others.[2]

Such men were influential in Mississippi in helping organize the Republican party in the state, creating the Union Leagues, spreading political consciousness, promoting black political organization, stressing education for the black community, and bringing other reforms to Mississippi.[3] Therefore, when Mississippi was admitted to the Union on February 23, 1870, black leaders were in a position to help determine the future of the state.[4] However, as Esmond Wright has observed, "Blacks were segregated into all social and cultural spheres. They lived in sections of towns and cities set apart for them. They went to a separate school, if they went to school at all."[5] Nevertheless, the black community was able to forge a better tomorrow by stressing and strengthening the black family, creating hundreds of black churches (a majority of which were Baptist and Methodist), aiding in the establishment of black schools, and placing some attention on the special concerns of black women, mainly observed in the creation of black women's clubs and church work.[6]

Four black colleges were active in Mississippi during the 1870s: Rust College (formerly Shaw University), established at Holly Springs in 1866 by the United Methodist Church; Tougaloo College, established near Jackson in 1869 by the American Missionary Association; Alcorn University, created near Lorman in 1871 by the State of Mississippi; and Jackson State University (formerly Natchez Seminary for Freemen, Jackson College), established at Natchez in 1877 by the American Baptist Home Mission Society.[7] These institutions played an important part in the educational advances of black Mississippians during and after the Reconstruction Era.

On the economic front, black Mississippians found it rough going in the 1870s. For one thing, they were faced with a general situation where white Mississippi groups such as the White Liners sought to combine many Ku Klux Klan tactics with social ostracism and economic pressure as more subtle methods of intimidation. In fact, many blacks became trapped in the tenant and sharecropping systems of agriculture developed in the South during Reconstruction. As one scholar notes, under this system, "The tenant was a worker [and often whole families] who farmed the plantation owner's land, kept part of the crop for himself, and paid the plantation owner with money or the rest of the crop."[8] Cotton remained "king" in Mississippi during the 1870s.

Against this background a small black middle class began to emerge in the 1870s to serve the needs of the black community. There were 11 lawyers in this group who practiced law in Mississippi. They were Abraham W. Shadd (1844–1878), John F. Harris (b. 1830/1), John Werles (d. 1880s); J.D. Ferrie, William Smallwood, Lewis J. Winston (b. 1847/8), Josiah T. Settle (1850–1915), M.M. McLeod (d. 1895), Col. George F. Bowles (b. 1844), L. K. Atwood, and John D. Webster.[9] Other early members of the black middle class in Mississippi included teachers, medical doctors and dentists, religious figures, and business persons. By 1870 black Mississippi had produced 200 artisans, 44 manufacturing businesses, 149 service establishments, 66 retail businesses, and 181 farmers of note, for a total of 640 black businesses in the state. Black Mississippians engaged in a "broad range of economic activities as shopkeepers, storekeepers, skilled artisans, haulers and draymen, and restaurant owners."[10] By 1874 black Mississippians had made deposits in Freemen's Banks of Mississippi at Columbus ($18,857), Natchez ($22,195), and Vicksburg ($104,348).[11] Such efforts were a major achievement for a people only removed from slavery for less than 10 years.

The economic crisis facing most black Mississippians during Reconstruction, however, was a story of hardship. One scholar on the period observed, "The truth is that blacks were unable to buy their own land not because they lacked the will to save, but because the wages they received were so pitiably small. Typical pay for a full field hand in Mississippi in 1866 was something less than $15 per month, plus Food and quarters."[12]

Thus, the political, social, and economic position of blacks in Mississippi was a mixed one during the decade of the 1870s. Some progress had been made since the 1860s, yet the average black person and family in Mississippi could only look to the future for the hope of continued progress and advancement for all of the black citizens of the state.[13] Like their political, social and economic positions in Mississippi during the 1870s, blacks found that the criminal justice climate for the period was a mixed blessing. As scholar James T. Currie has noted on the Emancipation period in the state, "Unequality in the criminal justice system was the norm for the white community's response to blacks."[14]

Clearly more blacks than whites in Mississippi were forced to experience prison life. As late as 1869 "Mississippi locked up 259 blacks and 105 whites."[15] Scholars have noted that conditions in Mississippi were more difficult for blacks after the whites of the state were able to recapture political power with the Revolution of 1875, which brought an end to effective Reconstruction in Mississippi. Two scholars describe this complex situation in Mississippi as involving white democratic efforts in 1876 to pass a new bill, the Pig Law, "which vastly expanded the number of crimes classified as grand larceny, thereby causing the number of prison convicts (mostly black) to skyrocket."[16] Such actions now meant that a black person convicted under the Pig Law for stealing a piece of property worth more than $10 could receive a prison sentence of five years at hard labor.[17] The end result of Mississippi's new legal system of the late 1870s was that "these laws increased the size of the prison labor pool. In Mississippi it increased nearly 300 percent in less than four years, from 272 convicts in 1874 to 1,072 by the end of 1887."[18]

Black and white Mississippians lived in two different worlds, as Christopher R. Adamson makes clear. "There was almost complete segregation of white and black prisoners. While black felons in Mississippi worked on plantations and railroads, not a single white left the penitentiary.... Local sheriffs in Mississippi made sure that whites were never put in chaingangs."[19]

Furthermore, this was a period under Mississippi's criminal justice system in which "the life conditions for Southern blacks became highly unstable, as that instability increased, the plea for protection accelerated and shifted forms as African Americans worried less about equal protection and more about the simple protection of life, liberty, and property."[20] It was a trying time for blacks in Mississippi.

As in the 1860s, there were many background reasons for the lynching of people in Mississippi during the years 1870–1879. The negative work of such organizations as the Ku Klux Klan must be viewed as a major cause of lynching in the state. Such groups tried to use terror to control the black population in Mississippi and, of course, in their never-ending campaign to support white supremacy.[21] Many white Mississippians also viewed lynching, or the threat of this terror form, as an effective method to prevent or control black voting and political activities in Mississippi.[22] One scholar wrote of this period, "To reinforce such threats of economic lynching of every black who dared vote Republican, lists were prepared and published of those who were known Republicans, and alongside these were printed lists of blacks who had promised to vote the Democratic ticket."[23]

Such "conservative attitudes" increased the difficulties of blacks performing their political freedoms in the late 1870s and left some of them victims of lynch mobs in Mississippi.[24] This problem was especially acute in the Delta region, an area where, as one scholar notes, "at least 80 percent of the potential electorate was black."[25]

Ill feelings toward blacks by Southern whites must not be underestimated as a cause of lynching in Mississippi during the 1870s for, in fact, as Allen D. Grimshaw wrote, "The bitterness of white Southerners at losing the war was hardly assuaged by events of the immediate post-war-years."[26] In other words, the fact that blacks had secured their freedom and appeared to be making advances in the South left a sense of "revenge" against blacks by many whites. Other whites turned their anger during the period against black schools and the supporters of black education, especially Northerners who taught in such institutions.[27]

Some scholars point to the economic crisis of the 1870s and especially to the year 1874 to denote tensions and conflicts between blacks and whites in the state. Some poor white Mississippians may have blamed blacks for their own hardships and viewed lynching as one means of receiving satisfaction for their own general plight in society (i.e., using blacks as a scapegoat for white economic disturbance during this period). More upscale whites may have viewed lynching as a method to aid in the control of blacks as a labor resource on white-owned plantations, farms and other businesses to keep blacks on the land, working, and always available for white use.[28]

The African American exodus to Kansas in the 1870s must also be viewed as another significant factor in influencing white Mississippians to try to convince black labor to remain in the state. Blacks in Mississippi and other states viewed the migration to Kansas as offering them hope against their mistreatment in the South; they also wished to improve their general economic, social and political condition. In all, 25,000 blacks left the South for Kansas; 5,000 to 10,000 of them departed from Mississippi and Louisiana by 1879.[29]

A final cause of lynching in Mississippi during the 1870s revolves around the sexual fears and racism of many Southern whites, especially when it came to the issue of the rape or attempted rape of white women by black men. One study interpreted this phenomenon to mean that "The white man's fear of black male sexual aggression manifested itself in the use of lynching as 'punishment' and social control ... the most socially compelling 'rationale' for the murders was to avenge black men's alleged sexual assaults upon white women."[30]

Many contemporary scholars view such charges as mythmaking on the part of many Southern whites.[31] Yet the reality for many black males in Mississippi and elsewhere was that even the charge of raping a white woman could lead to death. Although many Southerners claimed, even during this early period, that blacks were lynched largely because of the rape of white women or for the protection of white women, this reasoning does not appear to have been accurate. As Allen D. Grimshaw noted, "Failure to show the proper respect to a white man was equally important, and a cause which includes a variety of offenses ranging from a demand for an explanation of financial transactions to the more heinous crime of engaging in political activity."[32]

Estimating the number of lynchings in Mississippi for the years 1870–1879 remains a difficult task for the historian. Records for this period were poorly kept, and many lynching victims remain unknown. Nevertheless some data are available. Table 2.1 on the following page notes the significance of this problem for the state.[33] At least 769 persons were lynched in Mississippi during the 1870s. The worst years were 1874–1875 when the white Democrats in Mississippi were successful in overthrowing the Reconstruction government in the state and replacing it with the old order. Their campaign included political and economic intimidation and, of course, race riots and lynchings to force blacks out of politics or to vote for the Democratic ticket. W.E.B. Du Bois described the scope of this disaster. "On the whole, one cannot escape the impression that what the whites in Mississippi feared was that the experiment of Negro suffrage might succeed. At any rate, they began a revolution known as the 'Mississippi plan.' Here was no labor dictatorship or dream of one. White labor took up arms to subdue black labor and to make it helpless economically and political through the power of property."[34]

Thus, political participation by black Mississippians seems to have been a major reason for whites lynching blacks in Mississippi during the 1870s. However, Vernon Lane Wharton suggested that the murder of a white person by a black Mississippian was settled by the lynching of an African American. The scholar noted that "there also seems to have been a general understanding that a Negro who murdered a white was to be lynched; to this rule there were few, if any, exceptions."[35] Yet blacks as well as whites were lynched for a varied list of other reasons. These will be discussed in due time throughout this book.

The surviving data from this period suggest that 83 percent of the lynching victims (686 individuals) in Mississippi were killed for political participation in the 1870s. This leaves 17 percent for all other causes, including at least two people who were lynched for the charge of murder.

White mobs in Mississippi seem to have singled out black leaders for death by lynching; at least this is what a reading of Table 1 denotes. The death list includes two county commissioners in Meridian (1871); Warren Tyler and William Dennis, also in Meridian (1871); many black leaders including James Mason in Vicksburg (1874); Jack Dupree in Monroe County (1871); and Charles Caldwell and his brother, Sam Caldwell, in Clinton (1875). This is just the top of the list. How many other blacks were killed for being leaders? This question remains an unknown factor in the history of the period.[36]

How were black Mississippians able to respond to the deaths by lynching of so many

of their fellow citizens between 1870 and 1879 at the hands of the White Liners, the Ku
Klux Klan, white Democrats, and common white people from Mississippi and other states?[37]
Indeed, how were a people only 5 to 15 years removed from chattel slavery supposed to deal
with a central problem that scholar Eric Foner has labeled "revolutionary terror"?[38] They
had to organize themselves to fight back when they could. From the previous decade (the
1860s), they could muster courage from the fact that more than 18,000 African Americans

TABLE 2.1: LYNCHINGS IN MISSISSIPPI, 1870–1879

Year	Number of Lynchings	Names of Lynching Victims	Location of Events	Accusations Against the Victims
(April 1869) to March, 1871	174	?	Meridian (Massacre)	Political Activity
1870–1871	Dozens	?	Kemper County	Political Activity
1874 (Dec.)	300? 59? 29? (Black men)	?	Vicksburg (Warren Co.)	Political Activity
1875	?	?	Vicksburg	Political Activity
1875	1 (White male)	?	Yazoo Co.	Political Activity
1875	Dozens (Black men)	?	Rose Hill	Political Activity
1875	Dozens (Black men)	?	Satartia	Political Activity
1875	4 (Black men)	?	Columbus	Political Activity
1875	Dozens (Black men)	?	Drew	Political Activity
1875	? (Blacks)	?	Pike Co.	Political Activity
1875 (Sept.)	35–50 (Blacks)	?	Clinton (Hinds Co.)	Political Activity
1875	1 (White Republican)	?	Yazoo City	Political Activity
1875	80 (many black leaders)	?	Yazoo City/Co.	Political Activity
1875	1 (White Republican)	?	Clinton	Political Activity
1875	(many black leaders)	?	Clinton	Political Activity
1875	1 (black leader)	Charles Caldwell	Clinton	Political Activity
1875	1 (black)	Sam Caldwell (brother of Charles Caldwell)	Clinton	Political Activity
1875	?	?	Friars Point	Political Activity
1875	?	?	Rolling Fork	Political Activity
1875	1 (black leader)	Jesse Mason	Vicksburg	Political Activity
1875	12 (blacks)	?	Macon	Political Activity
1877	Dozens? (blacks)	?	Kemper Co.	Political Activity

from Mississippi had fought on the side of the Union for black freedom and a United States of America.[39] As late as January 1866, as Du Bois noted, "there were 8,784 Negro troops and 338 Negro officers" in Mississippi. However, "by the 20th of May, 1866, all black troops had been mustered out and removed from Mississippi."[40] Yet the memory of their presence and the skills they had achieved in the Civil War remained a part of the collective strengths of black Mississippians. So, in some circumstances and because they had weapons, local blacks were able to offer some defense of their lives, property and humanity against the terrorist tactics of some white Mississipians.[41] Overall, blacks in the state were outgunned and in a weakened economic, social and political state due to centuries of enslavement they had suffered and reparations they did not receive in the 1860s or 1870s.[42]

Black Mississippians were also blessed that they had a group of experienced leaders who emerged during the Emancipation Era to aid their growth and development. This group included 31 blacks in the Mississippi House and 5 members in the state Senate. Overall, blacks in Mississippi produced 226 officers in Reconstruction Mississippi. Only South Carolina had more (314).[43] Black Mississippi also produced three of the leading national voices in Congress during Reconstruction: Blanche K. Bruce and Hiram R. Revels in the U.S. Senate and John Roy Lynch in the U.S. House of Representatives. These leaders helped to tell the black Mississippi story to the world and to aid reform in society, especially during Reconstruction.[44] These leaders, along with black males in Mississippi, made the first efforts to promote black political rights including encouraging blacks to vote on all levels of political activity in the state. This work on the part of the blacks must be viewed as part of their struggle against the general oppression of their 1870s community.

Leaders such as James Lynch, J.J. Spelman, J. Garrett Johnson, Blanche K. Bruce, and Hiram R. Revels helped to develop the black press in Mississippi during the 1870s. They produced a black press that included the *Colored Citizen's Monthly* in Jackson (1870), the *Baptist Signal* (1879), the *People's Journal* in Jackson (1877), the *Reflector* in Jackson (1870s), the *Jackson Field Hand*, the *Floreyville Star* in Rosedale (1874), and the *Mississippi Republican* in Vicksburg (1877–1879).[45] Such papers began the long journey by blacks in Mississippi to develop the press as a medium of expression to carry the black voice out to the world. It was a tremendous challenge that black Mississippians took up in earnest in the 1870s.

The black church in Mississippi also served as a vehicle for black protest and uplift during this period and especially as an agency for the spiritual needs of blacks. In the late 1860s the total number of black churches increased in Mississippi from 105 to 283.[46] Along with the black family, schools, and the press, the black church served as a solid foundation to aid the black struggle in Mississippi for continued progress in spite of white oppression and the burden of lynching. These institutions also helped blacks in Mississippi to "keep the faith" for the long struggle ahead that the people knew they had to face as the 1870s grew to a close.

Finally, black Mississippians responded to the lynching crisis and their economic, political and social oppression by "voting with their feet" to migrate out of Mississippi. By 1879, when the Kansas Exodus was underway, at least 5,000 to 6,000 black Mississippians had escaped from Mississippi to settle in the Midwest. One scholar noted that others tried to move even further afield with an effort in 1877 by "a group of Mississippi freedmen...to move en masse to New Mexico or Arizona."[47] This task was achieved at great cost to blacks by the opposition of white Southerners.[48] A scholar noted, "At Greenville, Mississippi, the mayor frequently ordered the dispersal of Negroes who gathered to plan for, or to participate in, the exodus."[49] Still, many thousands of blacks left Mississippi to take their chances for more freedom—and less risk of lynching—in other states.

H R Revels

HON. HIRAM R. REVELS
SENATOR FROM MISSISSIPPI

Hiram Rhodes Revels (1827–1901) was born in North Carolina but lived and worked in many other states as an educator, journalist, and minister. During Reconstruction, he emerged as one of the big three among black leaders in Mississippi, including Blanche K. Bruce (1841–1898) and John Roy Lynch (1847–1939); Revels served as the first African American senator (representing Mississippi) in Congress during 1870 and 1871. He also became the first black president of Alcorn State University in 1871 (COURTESY OF THE ROBERT W. WOODRUFF LIBRARY OF THE ATLANTA UNIVERSITY CENTER).

In general, during the 1870s the white response to lynching in Mississippi settled on regaining white political control in the state and keeping blacks in a weak economic and social position—and exploiting their labor resource. In essence, as Mary Frances Berry noted on the period, "Congress and the president took no action to prevent lynchings, and state governments did not prosecute the perpetrators, even when the event was publicized at least a day in advance."[50]

John Roy Lynch (1847–1939) was born a slave in Concordia Parish, Louisiana. After the Civil War, he became a photographer in Natchez, Mississippi, and an active Republican politician. He served as a justice of the peace (1869); a representative of Adams County in the state legislature (1870–73), and Speaker of the House (1872–73), followed by three terms (1873–77 and 1882–83) in the U.S. House of Representatives. Lynch was one of the best known of the black Reconstruction leaders (COURTESY OF MISSISSIPPI DEPARTMENT OF ARCHIVES AND HISTORY).

Indeed, according to Lerone Bennett, Jr., this was a period in which "the South looked back in anger. Hundreds of freemen were massacred in 'riots' staged and directed by policemen and other government officials."[51] Many white Mississippians viewed lynching and the general oppression of blacks as an effort to increase their own power and white supremacy in Mississippi. This is a central theme in the Revolution of 1875 in the state. It was a period whereby:

The Mississippi campaign united the white population as never before, mobilizing thousands who had not cast ballots during Reconstruction and all but eliminating the Scalawags vote, estimated at over 6,000 as late as 1873. Wherever possible, however, blacks remained steadfast; indeed in some plantation counties, the Republic vote actually increased. But where violence had devastated the party's infrastructure and blacks "feared for their lives" if they presented themselves at the polls, the return constituted a political revolution.[52]

White Mississippians were determined to crush "black power" and the majority population—black—in Mississippi with violence. Yet they did not count on the strength of the black opposition to their violence and tactics. As one scholar noted, "So determined [was] black resistance, in fact, that the [Mississippi] plan was obliged to resort to even more strin-gent measures in order to put it down."[53]

The 1870s was an era that witnessed the end of Reconstruction and the submission of black freedom in Mississippi and the South. The costs were extreme for the black commu-nity. One study observed that, "economically as well as politically, the black man who showed the greatest initiative and independence was the most liable to suffer attack. In Noxubee and Winston counties where there was a concerted effort by the Klan to drive off [or] despoil Negroes who owned or even rented the land they worked, and a white man who sold land to Negroes was threatened with death."[54]

Black resistance continued, and "the most common course of resistance was simply to move away. An emigration meeting was held in Aberdeen and many blacks departed singly or in groups for Louisiana and elsewhere to escape the terror. One effect of Klan activity, therefore, was to create a severe labor shortage in much of the area."[55]

The end of the 1870s brought the "old regime" back to power in Mississippi and left black Mississippians in a weakened position. As Lerone Bennett, Jr., noted, black Mississip-pians had demonstrated their interest in government and commitment to reforming soci-ety.[56] In other words, black Mississippians never attempted to dominate the political situation in Mississippi but tried to share the political power of the state with other citizens. For the positive outlook they had to suffer Mississippi being "redeemed" by and for the benefit of its white minority. The federal government accepted the result. "The 'Mississippi Plan' was quickly adopted by Democratic leaders in Louisiana, Florida, and South Carolina. All three states elected governors and legislatures in 1876, as well as sharing the Presidential vote for that year."[57]

Thus, Reconstruction ended in Mississippi with a period of escalating violence against blacks. This condition would remain the focus of the white community in Mississippi for many decades to come. Meanwhile, the black community in Mississippi was faced with a never-ending challenge to advance the political, economic and social interests of blacks while trying to successfully decrease the problem of lynching and other oppressive meas-ures.[58] These critical problems and issues would only become more severe in the 1880s.

3

Hope in a Time of Despair,
1880–1889

Black Mississippians entered the 1880s in a sorrowful mood: Reconstruction had ended, black rights and freedoms were being proscribed at every turn, and life was a bitter struggle for most people from day to day. In the rural areas and on the farms, Mississippi blacks were in trouble. Scholar Pete Daniel describes the economic period as one in which blacks had moved from slavery only to continue suffering under a new agricultural system of share-cropping.[1]

The state of Mississippi still contained a predominately black population with 650,291 blacks in 1880, in comparison to 479,398 whites,[2] but the power relationship between blacks and whites was definitely to the advantage of the white Mississippians. In the 1880s, some blacks still attempted to flee Mississippi for more promising lands elsewhere, but this process was never an easy one. Scholars such as Jonathan M. Weiner have observed that many white southerners used violence and even death threats or assassination of black migration leaders who encouraged African Americans to leave Mississippi and other southern states for more secure opportunities in the Midwest.[3] In general, Mississippians were poor people. A key study of the period observes, "Mississippi's per capita income in 1880 was only $82, among the lowest in the nation. Cotton prices fell from twelve cents per pound in 1870 to nine cents in 1884...."[4] Black Mississippians were caught in a straitjacket of poverty on the farm and in Mississippi's small towns and cities. If fact, by 1880, only 5,827 Mississippians made a living by earning wages, the majority of whom lived in, or near, Mississippi towns and cities.[5]

In spite of great suffering, a small black middle class continued to exist in Mississippi during the 1880s. One study notes that during this era, "The major achievements of the blacks in business were in banking, insurance, and publishing. The first banks began as depositories for black benevolent societies in the last decades of the nineteenth century."[6] In the 1880s black Mississippians did not operate any banks in the state.[7] The first to appear was at Vicksburg, the Knights of Honor Savings Bank, in 1892.[8] Black leaders were also very influential in the black Mississippi insurance industry, as were black lawyers in Mississippi. A small group continued to operate in the state during the 1880s, with eleven individuals active from the 1870s and five new lawyers in the 1880s, including Willis E. Mollison, Wilford H. Smith, Samuel A. Beadle, A.B. Grimes, and Dave Temple.[9]

Black leaders in Mississippi also continued their efforts to produce a black press for the state. One study notes, "Mississippi boasted seventeen black newspapers during the 1880s, for the most part religious-oriented journals. The growth reflected, in part, the hardening economic, political, and social conditions after the Civil War, when the state's Confederates had attempted by whatever means possible to deny black progress and humanity."[10] Black Mississippi bankers, doctors, dentists, businesspersons, and others helped to keep the black economic dream for freedom alive in the state during a very harsh period.

The 1880s were also a period of social and cultural developments among blacks in Mississippi. Jesse O. McKee wrote "Black Mississippians also maintained their own churches, lodges, and private educational institutions. Most of their social life revolved around their churches, just as [that of] white Mississippians did. Dinners on church grounds, gospel singing, and preaching enlivened Sundays for black Mississippians. Sometimes ballgames and dances provided additional entertainment."[11]

The realities of daily life were another matter. Education was a key theme to black Mississippians, yet they received major opposition from whites on this matter. A scholar of the period points out, "Southern white Americans imposed segregated but unequal education upon African Americans."[12] This negative attitude toward black social/educational progress is revealed in even the salaries for black and white teachers in Mississippi. Zhang Juguo notes, "In 1881 in Mississippi, black teacher[s] earned $27.40 monthly, while white teachers' monthly salary was $31.37."[13] Nevertheless, black people continued to make a way out of little resources. This is clear in the efforts of black women in Mississippi in the 1880s to promote their own interests and those of their families and communities by establishing women's clubs and literacy and cultural circles, and advancing the growth and development of black churches and schools.[14]

Black women and men were faced with a social climate that was becoming unbearable for many in the community in the 1880s. Not that complete segregation came all at once during this decade; however, the custom of segregation and soon Mississippi law made the process another reality for black Mississippians.[15] For example, scholar Edward L. Ayers observed, "Mississippi's legislature of 1888 ... [created] its first railroad segregation law in the context of an act that created a railroad commission. The focus of the language now shifted from the rights and comforts of blacks to the power of railroad officials to make the law operate smoothly."[16] Due to such oppressive methods as these, black Mississippians such as Charles Banks and Isaiah Montgomery of Mound Bayou (incorporated in 1877) "were leaders in efforts to establish and promote economically viable and politically independent all-black towns and agriculture settlements as the solution to the black dilemma. Most of these ventures were abject failures."[17] They did, however, point the way for some blacks, if only a small minority, to escape the constant tensions of contact with the white community, thus perhaps giving some blacks a psychological release from the daily oppression of whites in Mississippi.

The struggles to promote black freedom were also negatively impacted politically by the events that occurred in the 1880s. White Mississippi began an effort to disenfranchise black voters in the state. However, this goal would take years to effectively put in place. Meanwhile, during the 1880s, black Mississippians continued their efforts to work within the system. According to August Meir, during this period "there appeared the practice known as fusion of dividing the offices between Negro Republicans and white Democrats, so that the former held a seat or so in the legislature and a share of the less important local positions."[18] However, Mississippi and the South eventually received some national support in their drive to decrease black rights when, "In 1883 the Supreme Court had struck down the Civil Rights

Act of 1875, which had outlawed racial discriminations in public accommodations."[19] Soon the doctrine was expanded to include black political, economic and social rights. It was a heartless era. John Roy Lynch, the last black congressman from Mississippi, told his House colleagues in 1882 that Negroes

> have bravely refused to surrender their honest convictions, even upon the altar of their personal necessities. They have said to those upon whom they were dependant, you may deprive me for the time being of the opportunity of making an honest living. You may take the bread out of the mouths of my hungry and dependent families. You may close the schoolhouse door in the face of my children. Yes, more, you may take that which no man can give[,] my life. But my manhood, my principles, you cannot have.[20]

The 1800s were a decade of ups and downs for the political interests of black Mississippi. By the end of the decade, blacks were still fighting for their political rights in the state.[21] White Mississippians continued to argue among themselves over "the Negro Problem" and black voting, but it would take another year (1890), before they could call a Mississippi Constitutional Convention and begin the major push to destroy the black vote in Mississippi. Meanwhile, the white custom of discrimination and oppression of blacks would remain in force.

Black Mississippians looked upon a criminal justice system in the 1880s that also negatively impacted their community in the state. If they were arrested and convicted of a crime in Mississippi, then death was a real possibility while they were confined in a Mississippi prison. One scholar noted about the era, "Because of overwork, cruel torture and unsanitary living conditions, the death rate among African American convicts was horribly high. From 1880 to 1885 almost 11 percent of African American convicts in Mississippi died annually: and in 1887, 16 percent died."[22] David M. Oshinsky also made clear just how severe the death rate was for black prisoners in 1882, "126 of 735 black state convicts perished, as opposed to 2 of 83 whites."[23] He also noted that Mississippi had a high rate of children as convicts (one in four) in some Mississippi prisons.[24]

Although the blacks were successful in securing appointments to some Reconstruction Era police departments in Mississippi, many whites were not happy about this situation. For example, "In 1884 seven African-American police officers in Vicksburg, Mississippi, were forced to resign because white citizens resented being policed by them. White citizens stated that being arrested 'by colored policemen' was 'humiliating and degrading in the extreme,' and they pledged to resist 'hereafter the arrest of any white persons by a colored policeman.'" The animosity of whites toward Reconstruction-era African American police officers was best expressed by Mississippi Whig politician Ethelbert Barksdale, who said, "Law enforcement means domination, and the white man is not used to being dominated by Negroes."[25] Yet Vicksburg, as early as 1870, was a city where blacks composed 55 percent of the local population and 50 percent of the police force. By 1880, however, blacks were 49 percent of Vicksburg's population and represented only 15 percent of the city's police department.[26]

For the average black Mississippian, the state's cruel criminal justice system was best expressed in its convict-lease system. Gilbert Osofsky's work describes this institution as an inhumane burden on prisoners, but especially so on blacks, who were generally a majority of convicts in Mississippi and the South.[27] White Mississippi's attitudes toward the state's responsibility to prisoners was expressed in 1886 when the state's "penitentiary was leased to the Gulf and Ship Island Railroad Company. The first two Redeemer governors in this state were both railroad attorneys."[28] Finally, the tone and mood in Mississippi in the 1880s is reflected in Christopher R. Adamson's observation that the convict-lease system was an

TABLE 3.1: NATIONAL LYNCHING VICTIMS, 1880–1889

Year	Total	Black	White
1880*	37		
1881*	43		
1882	113	49	64
1883	130	53	77
1884	211	51	160
1885	184	74	110
1886	138	74	64
1887	122		
1888	142		
1889	176	95	81
TOTALS	1296	396	556

*estimated

economic and political replacement for the cotton era's slavery system. The goals of the convict-lease policy in Mississippi were to create a continuing condition of African American subservience—economic and political—in the state's society.[29] Thus, black Mississippians in the 1880s were harshly impacted by a criminal justice system that attempted to limit black rights and promote white supremacy.

Scholars have generally listed six crimes that allegedly justified lynching in the United States. In descending order of importance they are: (1) homicides, (2) felonious assault, (3) rape, (4) attempted rape, (5) robbery and theft, and (6) insult to white persons. All other causes would follow the six listed above.[30] In the 1860s and 1870s in Mississippi, a large number of blacks clearly were lynched for political participation, which is not noted on the above list.[31] The national list of the causes of lynchings certainly also applies to Mississippi in the 1880s and later decades. Thus, although many Southern whites tied the lynching events of the period to the charge of rape or attempted rape of white women, this justification was not based on reality.[32] Perhaps the lynching phenomenon had to do more with white male power in Mississippi and the South than with really protecting the white women.[33]

Both black and white Mississippians lived in a state where "A Mississippi editor declared [as late as] in 1879 that there was an average of a murder a day in the state."[34] Thus violence was a major problem of society and made doubly so by the lynching crisis. For most black Mississippians, the special dangers in this period lay in the fact that "in most cases, lynching victims were summarily executed before receiving any trial. Their guilt was never established at all, let alone beyond a reasonable doubt."[35] In addition, as in the 1860s and 1870s, if a black person was successful in a financial sense, he was greatly at risk of lynching, especially in rural areas.[36] Finally, some scholars have also suggested that lynching must be viewed as an expression of religious phenomenon for some whites.[37] Some whites used the symbols of Christianity to justify the terrible acts of lynching and as a way of dominating blacks in

Mississippi and the South. In other words, Southerners attempted to use religion and ceremony as additional areas of justification for the violence (lynching) of blacks, and this process made them feel better and feel less guilty at the conclusion of the lynching events.

Whatever the cause of lynchings in Mississippi during the 1880s and later, the end results were always the same. Katheryn K. Russell describes the lynching ritual:

> Those people who were selected to conduct the lynching selected a site based upon the location. This included finding a venue that would accommodate the expected onlookers and location [of] an appropriate tree. Following this, ritual instruments were gathered including rope, wood, guns, kerosene, tar and feathers. Lynchings had many characteristics of a sporting event. Entire families, including children, participated. Families packed food, drink, and spirits for the event.
> White mobs, which sometimes included police officers, gathered to take part in the hanging, burning, or shooting. After the tools were selected, the Black victim was required to strip naked. Black men were usually castrated and sometimes their bodies were used as target practice. The murderous assault ceremoniously concluded with whites parceling out the remains of the Black victim. Teeth and other body parts were collected as souvenirs. In notorious cases, newspaper advertisements announced upcoming lynchings.[38]

Such spectacles were a weekly or monthly occurrence in Mississippi and the South in the 1880s. As such they made living in Mississippi especially difficult for blacks and other progressive citizens.

The lynching data on the period 1880–1889 give a harsh picture of life for blacks in Mississippi. However, one author suggested that more whites than blacks died by lynching in the early 1880s. He wrote, "It is a curious fact that in the early years of the 1880s—when statistics on lynching began to be kept—considerably more whites were lynched than Negroes. Between 1882 and 1888, 595 whites and 440 Negroes were lynched in the United States. But inexorably the figure changed. In 1889, 76 whites and 94 Negroes were lynched."[39]

The story in Mississippi was much more complex. Table 3.2, Mississippi Lynching Victims, 1882–1889 (on page 22), denotes that at least 257 blacks, 20 whites, one Chinese and two unknown victims were lynched for a total of 280.[40] Thus, Mississippi does not fit the national model for the 1880s. The state was a much more violent residence for African Americans than for whites. Table 3.2 outlines the lynching totals for the state by year and race. Years in which 20 or more blacks were lynched in the 1880s include: 1885, 21 victims; 1886, 24 victims; and 1889, 144 victims. These were years when tensions ran high in Mississippi, as the older order consolidated its power and hold over Mississippi political, economic and social institutions, including controlling black people in the state. The lynching phenomenon represented one area of this control. William Cohen notes, "The second half of the decade [1880s] witnessed a massive increase in the frequency with which the crime [lynching] occurred. In the years from 1885–1889, the number of lynchings of blacks increased by about 63.5 percent over what it had been in the previous five-year period."[41]

At this point it might be best to ask what a Mississippi lynching was in the late nineteenth century. One answer comes from Maurice S. Evans, who described the period as "Blood Guiltness." He wrote:

> A Negro man in Mississippi became involved in a quarrel with a white man who was on the point of shooting him when the Negro fired and fatally wounded him. He fled into the woods along with his wife. Bloodhounds were put on the trail, and after a long chase they were Captured. According to an eye-witness they were tied to trees and forced to hold out their hands while one finger after another was severed. Their ears were then cut off, and both fingers and ears were distributed as souvenirs. A large corkscrew was next bored into

TABLE 3.2: MISSISSIPPI LYNCHING VICTIMS, 1882–1889

Year	Total	Black	White	Other
1882	6	5	1	
1883	20	17	2	1 Unknown
1884	19	15	4	
1885	28	21	6	1 Chinese
1886	27	24	3	
1887	16	14	1	1 Unknown
1888	18	17	1	
1889	146	144	2	
TOTALS	280	257	20	3

their arms, legs, and body, the spiral tearing out large pieces of quivering flesh. Neither man nor women begged for mercy nor uttered a cry. They were finally roasted alive.[42]

These events took place across the South, but Mississippi became a major center for such terror. As a scholar on the era declares, "The epidemic of extralegal executions which began during Reconstruction grew worse in the 1880s."[43] In fact, during the decade of the 1880s, lynchings are known to have taken place in 49 of Mississippi's 82 counties.

Table 3.3, Mississippi Counties with Largest Number of Lynching Victims, 1882–1889, notes the counties with three or more lynchings during this period—19 of the 82 counties of the state. Mississippi counties with three lynchings in the 1880s are Claiborne, Madison, Panola, and Tallahatchie; with four lynchings are Desoto, Issaquena, Lafayette, Sharkey, and Smith; with five lynchings are Copiah, Kemper, and Warren; 6 lynchings, Yazoo; 12 lynchings, Hinds; 13 lynchings, Franklin; and 111, Leflore. The data suggest that lynchings occurred in all parts of Mississippi except for the Gulf Coast area. When Mississippi is divided into six major regions, the division of the lynching data by county and region shows the following pattern: (1) The Delta contained the most counties with 3 or more lynchings, 7 counties (Desoto, Issaquena, Leflore, Panola, Sharkey, Tallahatchie, and Yazoo) with 138 lynchings; (2) Southwest Mississippi is second with 5 counties (Claiborne, Copiah, Franklin, Pike, and Warren) with 34 victims; (3) Central Mississippi is third with 3 counties (Hinds, Madison, and Smith) and a count of 19 lynching victims; (4) Eastern Mississippi is fourth with 2 counties (Kemper and Lowndes) and 11 victims; and (5) Northern Mississippi is fifth with 2 counties (Grenada and Lafayette) and 10 lynching victims. Areas of counties with large black populations such as the Delta and Southwest Mississippi placed blacks at greater risk of lynchings, but lynching took place even in counties such as Lafayette in northern Mississippi and Lowndes in eastern Mississippi where there was a smaller black population. In terms of the five counties with the highest lynching totals during the 1880s, the Delta stands out again, with Leflore and Yazoo counties (120 victims), Southwest Mississippi with Franklin and Pike counties (21 victims), and Northern Mississippi with Grenada County (6 victims).[44]

The work of journalist Ida B. Wells-Barnett (1862–1931) is noted during the last

TABLE 3.3: MISSISSIPPI COUNTIES WITH
LARGEST NUMBER OF LYNCHING VICTIMS, 1882–1889

County	Number of Victims	County	Number of Victims	County	Number of Victims
Claiborne	3	Kemper	5	Sharkey	4
Copiah	5	Lafayette	4	Smith	4
DeSoto	4	Leflore	111	Tallahatchie	3
Franklin	13	Lowndes	6	Warren	5
Grenada	6	Madison	3	Yazoo	9
Hinds	12	Panola	3		
Issaquena	4	Pike	8	TOTAL	212

quarter of the nineteenth century. Born in Mississippi and educated in the state at Rust University, she was a major voice in bringing public attention and stressing reform efforts to end lynching in the United States. Her reports note two Mississippi lynchings of this period and help to describe the tone of the period. On a lynching in 1885 she writes, "Ebenzer Fowler, the wealthiest colored man in Issaquena County, Miss., was shot down on the street in Mayersville, January 30, 1885, just before dark by an armed body of white men who filled his body with bullets. They charged him with writing a note to a white woman of the place, Which they intercepted and which proved there was an intimacy existing between them."

On an event in 1889 she noted, "Oct. 19, 1889, at Canton, Miss., Joseph Leflore was burned to death. A house had been entered and its occupants murdered during the absence of the husband and father. When the discovery was made, it was immediately supposed that the crime was the work of a Negro, and the motive that of assaulting white women."[45] Ida B. Wells-Barnett's pen and work against lynchings would continue long into the future.

Mississippi justified lynching as a necessary evil in society. Perhaps L. Ray Gunn best noted how the lynching era promoted its reasons for this crime against humanity, "Southern whites justified lynching as a necessary response to black crime and an inefficient legal system, but virtually any perceived transgression of the racial boundaries or threat to the system of white supremacy could provoke mob action."[46]

A myth emerged in Mississippi and the South that most lynchings of black men were undertaken because of "the charge of rape or sexual assault of white women by black men."[47] Of course this charge was not true. Table 3.4, Mississippi Lynching Victims, Range and Percentage of Offenses Alleged, 1880s (on page 24), indicates very clearly that only 45 cases represented the alleged charge of rape or attempted rape of women in Mississippi in the 1880s, while the number for murder was 67. In 1889, during the Leflore County crisis, an even greater number of Mississippi blacks were killed (117) for their political activity and alleged "rebellion" against white control in the county. Economic crimes were also highly represented on the list of causes for lynchings in the 1880s. For example, thirteen Mississippi victims were lynched for arson, two for cutting a levee, one as a horse thief, and one for wrecking a train. Table 3.5, White Mississippi Lynching Victims by Year and County, 1882–1889 (on page 25), notes that, like black victims of lynching in Mississippi, white male

Table 3.4: Mississippi Lynching Victims, Range and Percentages of Offenses Alleged* (1880s)

Causes	Number	Percentage
Murder	67	25.2%
Rape/attempted rape	45	16.9%
Arson	13	4.9%
Political participation	117	44.0%
Grave robbery	2	0.8%
Cutting a levee	2	0.8%
Self defense	1	0.4%
Insulting a white woman	2	0.8%
Horse thief	1	0.4%
Train wrecker	1	0.4%
Unknown	15	5.6%
Total	266	100.0%

*Research data by the author

victims were generally killed for the crime of murder—eleven cases out of the twenty white lynchings for the period. The rest of the white males were lynched for basically economic crimes—two for cutting a levee; one each as horse thief, train wrecker, and burglar; and one for unknown reasons.

Between 1880 and 1889, blacks in Mississippi were hard pressed to establish an effective anti-lynching method or system to respond to the continuing lynching attacks against the black community. White Mississippians were attempting to decrease their political, economic and social rights, and events and forces outside of Mississippi were not that supportive of major black issues in the South. Some blacks in Mississippi continued to vote (about 34 percent of eligible blacks) and to try to influence political developments in the state; however, whites maintained control of the political system.[48] Some blacks tried to focus their energies on economic development, but they, too, were at risk for lynching or economic intimidation if some whites believed they were too successful. As in the 1870s, some black Mississippians could try self-defense against white attacks, but generally, as in the earlier periods, whites had more weapons than blacks and controlled the criminal justice system and the police forces of the state. So what could blacks do to challenge the lynching status quo in Mississippi during the 1880s? They could still "vote with their feet" to migrate from Mississippi to other states. During 1880–1890, Mississippi suffered a loss of 17 percent of its black population and thousands of blacks moved out of the state.[49]

In general, the white Mississippi response to lynching can be summed up with a few words: Control the black population of Mississippi at all cost.[50] What better "underground" system to add to the above goals than lynching? Then, too, as authors have long noted in

TABLE 3.5: WHITE MISSISSIPPI LYNCHING VICTIMS BY YEAR AND COUNTY, 1882–1889

1882
Name and county unknown.

1883
Mack Marsden, for murder, DeSoto County
D. W. Powell, for rape, Issaquena County

1884
Samuel T. Wilson, for murder, Issaquena County
Mark Moore, for murder, Kemper County
___ Scott, for horse thief, Lafayette County
Jordan Parker, for train wrecker, Lamar County

1885
Robert Doxey, for murder, Marshall County
Perry McChristian, for murder, Grenada County
James Farthley, for murder, Grenada County
Felix Williams, for murder, Grenada County
John Campbell, for murder, Grenada County
David Fairly, for murder, Green County

1886
Unknown name, for cutting a levee, Coahoma County
Unknown name, for cutting a levee, Coahoma County
Frederick Villarose, for rape, Warren County

1887
James M. Webb, for murder, Attala County

1888
___ Morley, for murder, Warren County

1889
Thomas Talbout, for rape, Kemper County
Thomas Harris, for burglary, Monroe County

Mississippi, "Tragically, the culture was deeply imbued with racist ideas," and the justification for lynchings in the state proved this point over and over.[51] Scholar Neil R. McMillen, writing on this period, highlights the white attitude toward lynching:

> During the 1870s and 1880s, mob executions of blacks were so common that they excited interest only in the black community. State and local authorities kept no records and never sought the arrest of vigilantes. Most of what was known about mob violence appeared in the highly sectarian pages of the white press, where the subject was typically covered, when it was covered at all, among the "Mississippi Brevities" or "Miscellaneous Items." In fairly typical fashion, an 1885 issue of the *Raymond Gazette* noted in a single line of small type: "Four negroes were lynched in Grenada last week; also one at Oxford."[52]

It was a sad period in the history of Mississippi.

Nationally, the black community followed events very closely in Mississippi and the South. This was especially true of the black press and black leaders in the Northern states.

Nationally, black newspapers that covered the South included *The New York Age*, *The Washington Bee*, and the *Indianapolis Freeman*, among others. The editors, T. Thomas Fortune, William Calvin Chase, and Edward Elder Cooper, called for an end to lynchings and for equal rights for all Americans.[53] Black leaders from all walks of life in the 1880s, with differing degrees of emphasis, suggested that lynchings were wrong and a strain on American democracy. Among the national leaders who called for change in society were Booker T. Washington (1856–1915), principal of Tuskegee Institute and one of the most powerful black men in America; William E.B. Du Bois (1865–1963), a foremost scholar of the period; Frederick Douglass (1817–1895), the most important black abolitionist leader still alive in the 1880s; Frances E.W. Harper (1825–1911), a noted black woman abolitionist and writer; and Ida B. Wells-Barnett, a noted teacher and journalist of the period and one-third owner of the Memphis, Tennessee *Free Speech and Headlight* newspaper in 1889.[54] Certainly, all of their efforts helped to bring public attention to the problem of lynching, if not the absolution of this painful system of terror in the 1880s.

National white leaders, such as those who held the office of president of the United States in the 1880s, knew of the lynching problem in Mississippi and the South, but when taken as a group, James A. Garfield (Rep. 1880–1881) and Chester A. Arthur (Rep. 1881–1884) did nothing to solve the lynching problem. Garfield, according to one scholar, believed "education as the solution to [black] hardship was simplistic, but it surely was an essential step in advancement for blacks."[55] Except, one could argue, in the case of lynching victims? Other presidents of the period were just as ineffective as Garfield, but at least Harrison's voice was raised against lynching.[56] A scholar of the era also noted that: "In 1883, the endeavor of President Chester A. Arthur to develop the Republican Party in the South at the expense of blacks and the increase in lynching were factors which led to a revival of the Black Convention Movement."[57] Some support for the anti-lynching movement in the 1880s did come from the Northern white press, especially from such newspapers as the *Chicago Tribune* which, in 1882, became the first major national newspaper to collect data on the lynching problem in this nation.[58] Other papers that covered the lynching crisis include the *New York Times*, the *New York Post*, and the *Pittsburgh Dispatch*, among others.[59] Yet the white press, both North and South, could be brutal on the lynching problem and prejudicial against blacks. For example:

> An 1889 Mississippi case illustrates this routine distortion by the white press. When two wagons met on a road, the one driven by a Black did not get out of the way of the white driver quickly enough. The white threatened to lynch the Black, who gathered his friends and resisted the mob when it came. Some of the whites were shot and the Blacks escaped, but the mob destroyed the property of the Blacks, including buildings and cattle. This was reported as an occasion where Blacks made a sudden, unprovoked, and murderous attack on innocent whites.[60]

Such conditions would remain a staple of some parts of the American press long into the next century.

Many scholars have commented on the fact that "apart from slavery, lynching is perhaps the most horrific chapter in the history of African Americans."[61] The national totals for this crime against humanity stood at 1,203 for the period 1882–89, including 534 black victims and 669 whites.[62] Yet the research for this chapter indicates that Mississippi alone accounted for 257 black and 20 white lynching victims. Such facts suggest that Mississippi became an early leader in the lynching terror of America. Thus, the impact of lynching on Mississippi society remains a compelling one for the decade of the 1880s. Scholars have also noted that the known lynching totals for Mississippi for this period may be too low. One study suggests that "one Mississippi historian has declared that it was impossible to make any reliable estimate of the number of Negroes lynched by whites in that state because 'such matters attracted little or no attention in the press.'"[63] Indeed, Mississippi and the South were a strange world for black people, yet also their home places. Their plight, as would soon be evident, would only grow more intensive in the years ahead.[64]

Thus, lynching impacted every black community in Mississippi.[65] A noted scholar observed, "The most effective black opposition to lynching was the nonviolent tactic by which blacks sought to mobilize public opinion against lynching." This call was a tall order for blacks to respond to, but the crisis of lynching would continue for many years in Mississippi and the South, and thousands of American citizens would die at the hands of lynch mobs before the terror would end. An old black spiritual from the slavery era best sums up the mood of black America at this point in their history and as they faced the challenges of an unknown future:

> See these poor souls from Africa
> Transported to America;
> We are stolen, and sold in Georgia,
> Will you go along with me?
> We are stolen, and sold in Georgia,
> Come sound the jubilee!
> See wives and husbands sold apart,
> Their children's screams will break my heart—
> There's a better day a coming,
> Will you go along with me?
> There's a better day a coming.
> Go sound the jubilee![66]

4

Faith During the Years of Nadir, 1890–1899

The decade of the 1890s was a time of testing the endurance of the African-American people in Mississippi. It was an era of cruelty toward blacks. The lynching phenomenon increased in its ferociousness, with hundreds of blacks killed in the South, and Mississippi remained a leader among the lynching states. Poet Paul Laurence Dunbar (1872–1906) seems to have captured the tone of the period in his classic poem, "We Wear the Mask."

> We wear the mask that grins and lies,
> It hides our cheeks and shades our eyes,—
> This debt we pay to human guile;
> With torn and bleeding hearts we smile,
> And mouth with myriad subtleties
>
> Why should the world be overwise,
> In counting all our tears and sighs?
> Nay, let them only see us, while
> We wear the mask.
>
> We smile, but, O great Christ, our cries
> To Thee from tortured souls arise.
> We sing, but oh, the clay is vile
> Beneath our feet, and long the mile;
> But let the world dream otherwise,
> We wear the mask.[1]

The economic fortunes of blacks in Mississippi during the 1890s were a mixed picture. Blacks were still the majority population in Mississippi in 1890, with a count of 744,749, compared to 544,851 whites and 2,190 other groups, including Native Americans and Chinese-Americans.[2] Mississippians remained a largely rural people in the 1890s with 94.6 percent of them living in rural areas and only 5.4 percent (69,966) in cities.[3] Yet, where possible, thousands of blacks still sought to migrate away from Mississippi during this period.[4] They needed relief from the economic oppression and daily insults which black people experienced in the state during the years 1890–1899.

In general, Mississippi experienced hard times economically in the 1890s. But the period was a depression for blacks. Dewey W. Grantham writes, "Another basic influence in shaping Mississippi politics during these years was the state's overwhelming ruralism and its predominantly agricultural economy. A large part of the state still resembled a frontier, as was evident in the loneliness of the far-flung plantations, isolated hill farms, and vast timber tracts."[5] Indeed, most blacks in Mississippi were farmers. In 1900, there were 128,351 of them in the state.[6] Kelly Miller observes that as late as 1899, 58.3 percent of the farms were operated by blacks.[7] But, what was the economic world like for black farmers? Manning Marable describes their world:

> The rural Black peasantry was caught in an almost impossible cycle of penury. Sixty-five percent of them were illiterate in 1890. They had scant knowledge of modern agricultural techniques, such as soil erosion prevention, crop rotation, and the use of complex farm machinery. Barely one-fifth of them could even afford fertilizers. As sharecroppers, they were forced to give half of their annual crop to their landlords. But most had accumulated little capital after selling their cotton and corn crops.... Although the data is not conclusive, there is even some evidence that Black life expectancy at birth actually fell slightly, from an average of 35 years in 1850 to less than 34 years in 1900. During the same period, whites' life expectancies increased from 40 to about 50 years.[8]

A central problem lay in the focus on cotton production. From a high of 83 cents per pound in 1865, "the price of cotton plunged to a low of 6 cents per pound in 1899."[9] And many blacks were forced to work in a system where sharecropping was the norm; yet, "By 1890 many farmers could no longer make a living from cotton."[10] It was an economic position from which many blacks could not escape. At the bottom were blacks who existed under the convict lease system which existed in Mississippi prisons, or those forced to labor for whites in order to secure their freedom at some future date. Edward L. Ayers notes that the vast majority of the prisoners were African Americans.[11] Many blacks also found themselves trapped in a world where peonage became a burden to oppress them economically in the late nineteenth century.[12]

From such a poor economic position, the small black middle class in Mississippi continued its fight for survival and growth. This was a world composed of "small businesses, drug firms, cafes, and even theatres and banks. Black people also worked in skilled trades, as bakers, masons, smiths, and carpenters. It was the Age of Booker T. Washington, who emphasized vocational education and economic self-help."[13] At least twelve black Mississippians in 1890 held wealth and property at or above $10,000.[14] Jackson, Mississippi, the capital city, held important black businesses. Two early studies note this fact. In 1908, D. W. Woodward observed that "the 8000 or more Negroes own one-third of the area of the town."[15] In 1909, Booker T. Washington found that the best known black business leader in the city was Dr. Sidney D. Redmond.

> Dr. Redmond received his medical training at the Illinois Medical College and the Harvard Medical College. When he settled in Jackson ten years ago he had practically nothing. At the time this is written he is president of the American Trust and Savings bank, the oldest of the Negro banks in Jackson and a stockholder in three banks controlled by the white people, as well as in the electric power and light company which lights the city streets. He owns two drug stores, one of which is situated on the chief business street of the town. He receives rent from more than one hundred houses.[16]

The black Mississippi middle class world also consisted of black doctors, lawyers, bankers, and newspaper publishers, among other occupations. A handful of black doctors served the black community, including: Dr. E. P. Brown of Utica; Dr. Banks and Dr. Woods

Dumas (d. 1944) of Natchez; Dr. Percy Sherrod of Port Gibson; and, as noted above, Dr. S. D. Redmond of Jackson, among others.[17] They worked against the odds to deliver health care to black Mississippians.

Mississippi also had a small group of black lawyers among the 431 black lawyers in the United States in 1890.[18] Members of this group included James Henry Piles of Panola County, John Roy Lynch of Natchez, Abram W. Shadd of Washington County and Issaquena County, John D. Werles Greenville (Leflore County), Colonel George F. Bowles of Natchez (Adams County), Willis E. Mollison of Mayerville, John H. Burris of Rodney (Claiborne County), Wilford Horace Smith of Leota, Cornelius J. Jones and Samuel A. Beadle of Brandon (Randin County) and Vicksburg (Warren County), M. D. Fleming of Vicksburg, and Julian Talbot Bailey, among others.[19] A talented group, black lawyers fought tirelessly to advance legal services to the black community of Mississippi, while living and working in a system where "virtually all aspects of the black historical experience in America have been influenced by the experience of racism."[20]

The first black-owned bank in Mississippi was the Lincoln Savings Bank, established at Vicksburg in 1892 by Robert Warsau Ware and Henry C. Wallace. W. E. Mollison later served as president. Other black banks would follow at the turn of the century.[21]

Black Mississippians also produced forty-six newspapers in the 1890s. The focus of the black press in the state was on "commercial, religious, fraternal, educational, and organizational" news and commentary.[22] Like all other elements among Mississippi's black middle class, black press publishers, editors and reporters left a rich legacy of struggle for future citizens to imitate and to advance the cause of liberty and justice for all of the American people.

Black Mississippians in the 1890s lived through a Jim Crow system with its origins in the state beginning in 1890. In fact, this was "a system of legalized segregation and political and economic disenfranchisement" that impacted every aspect of black social life in the South.[23] In this world of white supremacy in the late nineteenth century, whites were at the top of the system, and blacks were at the bottom.[24] Such an ideology was at home in white Mississippi. Its impact was felt on black education in the state. Stuart Grayson Noble described the situation in 1899:

> White schools in 1899 were enrolling 10.95 per cent more of the school population than in 1886, and the Negro schools but 5.3 percent more. Yet, the increase of enrollment in Negro schools was far in excess of the increases of the average daily attendance. In fact, the average daily attendance showed scarcely any increase. The number of teachers also failed to increase. In 1899, the average Negro teacher was required to teach sixty-three children, thirteen more than in 1886, and for this increase in his duties he received the sum of $19.39, or $8.01 less than he received in 1886.[25]

Yet, overall the black community was faced with a situation, as the following data indicates, that greatly depressed the community. For example, in 1894–1895, Mississippi contained:

White students:	162,830
Black students:	187,785
White teachers:	4,591
Black teachers:	3,264
(1895) Monthly salary for white teachers:	$33.04
Monthly salary for black teachers:	$21.53
(1890) Percentage of illiterates in Black Mississippi population at least 10 years of age:	60.8%[26]

Thus, blacks had to really fight for their rights to an education and an opportunity to uplift their own communities. One thing was for sure: nobody else would do it for them. And many white Mississippians disapproved of black education.

This problem was also experienced by Mississippi's public black colleges, in terms of state support. In the 1890s there were nine historically black schools of higher education in the state. All were private institutions except for Alcorn College, with 305 students in 1895. The other institutions were Jackson College (Baptist) in Jackson with 150 students in 1895; Rust University (Methodist) in Holly Springs with 230 students; Meridian Academic (Methodist) in Meridian with 169 students, Edward Walter's College (African Methodist Episcopal) in Jackson with 159 students; Southern Christian Institute (Christian) in Edwards with 95 students; Tougaloo University (Congregationalist) in Tougaloo with 377 students; Mount Herman Female Seminary (non-sectarian) in Clinton with 76 students; and State Colored Normal School in Holly Springs with 190 students.[27] But Mississippi supported its historically white institutions at much greater levels than it did Alcorn. For example, in 1890 the state's appropriations per student in Mississippi's institutions of higher learning were:

University of Mississippi	$136
A. & M. College	$103
Industrial Institute and College	$ 70
Alcorn A. & M. College	$ 45[28]

This unequal distribution of state funds for education would remain a special burden for the black community to bear for many years into the future.[29]

By the 1890s, the black church had emerged in Mississippi as the most powerful institution among African Americans in the state. W. E. B. Du Bois suggests that at the turn of the century there were 2,354 black churches in Mississippi, with a seating capacity of 614,681; with property worth $1,434,102; and membership of 224,404.[30] Out of the black Mississippi church came many black leaders, men and women who helped to make a difference in the life and progress of black Mississippians. Yet, even in this independent and strong black community asset, the white world looked on and tired to influence events. Many white Christians used religion to enforce segregation and to demand white supremacy and black inferiority. The gospel was viewed by many as just one more instrument to keep blacks in a low position.[31] Nevertheless, black Mississippians were able to maintain their independent churches, and to advance the common interests of the black community from one generation to the next.

Black Mississippians were also faced with many other social issues in the 1890s, including health care concerns, the status of black women and children, and cultural needs of the community. As in the long past, blacks of this era in the state were significant players in the development of the blues, work songs, gospel music, and jazz.[32] Such contributions helped the black community face the adversities of the period, enriched the lives of the people, and helped give them hope for the future. These achievements were produced by blacks in Mississippi in spite of white racism and opposition to black advancement in American life.

Politically speaking, the 1890s were a diabolic period in the history of blacks in Mississippi. Historian Rayford Logan refers to the era as "the Nadir" in the African American experience (one of the central low points in the journey of blacks in America since the Civil War).[33] Such was the case in Mississippi where blacks were fighting for their lives—and still trying to advance toward a new century which might offer them greater hope for freedom, equality and justice in their own country. But, for the present they were politically at a dead end. Political scientist Hanes Walton, Jr., notes that social scientists "have said that only three factors socialize the individual politically: the family, the school, and the peer group. But in reality the government itself socializes people."[34]

Black Mississippians were in a difficult situation. They had to continue to struggle—economically, socially, and politically—while faced with a harsh white community in Mississippi. It was a supreme challenge.[35]

Among the central political concerns of blacks in Mississippi in the 1890s were the necessities to keep the black vote alive (for black men) and to seek some political offices in the state. Both tasks were difficult to achieve. For one thing, beginning in 1890—after white Mississippi pushed through a new state constitution with one black delegate present, Isaiah T. Montgomery of Mound Bayou—a painful system of anti-black political methods were enacted to decrease the black vote and the role of blacks in state government.[36] The new suffrage restrictions in Mississippi included the payment of a $2.00 poll tax by voters—(covering two years before an election), a secret ballot, a literacy test for voters, and a requirement that the voter understand the state constitution at the time of registration.[37] These requirements became a prerequisite for voting in Mississippi. They were used effectively to block black voting rights and those of some poor whites.

The new order in Mississippi meant the following for black voters:

1. In 1872, there were 130,278 eligible black voters in Mississippi (22,024 more than white voters); by 1898, whites had a voting majority of 60,000.
2. In the 1890s, black Mississippians should have had a majority of 70,000 voters in the state.
3. Black voters in Mississippi were reduced during this period from 257,305 to 76,742, a two-thirds reduction.
4. By 1892, only 8,615 blacks were registered to vote in Mississippi.[38]

Black leaders in Mississippi were thus faced with a major crisis, politically speaking. Most were Republicans now living and working in a Democratic controlled state and region. As one scholar of the period sees it, they were "stymied." Furthermore, "Only a few dozen in the whole state were permitted to vote and none held office, except in Mound Bayou, an all Black town. In the few cases where Blacks did vote, they were never allowed to watch the counting of the ballots; thus, their ballots could easily be thrown out, since they were in separate boxes."[39]

Significant black leaders from the past still lived in the state, such as John Roy Lynch, Blanche K. Bruce, Isaiah Montgomery, Hiram R. Revels and countless others, but most had to turn their attention to politics outside Mississippi and to national Republican concerns.[40] This period was also the Age of Booker T. Washington and his strategy of accommodating black interests to white supremacy in the South and nation. Washington's prominent position in the South only grew after his famous 1895 "Atlanta Compromise Speech." This philosophy also became a watchword among some black Mississippians. Why? Fear, perhaps, of the possible consequences of white reaction (and violence) against any "non-sensible" African Americans.[41] Yet, in spite of everything, by "1890 six blacks still served in the legislature" of Mississippi.[42] They were lonely voices still crying out for the plight of black Mississippians to be heard on the world stage.

Mississippi's criminal justice system in the 1890s was designed to serve one purpose—with blacks in mind—to keep them down, to guard against black activities, to protect at all costs white political, economic, and social interests and control of Mississippi. This was a world, according to historian Mary Frances Berry, where "segregation became the legal means of enforcement in a system devoted to the maintenance of white supremacy and black subordination."[43] Many Mississippi whites believed that a special goal of segregation demanded the removal of black policemen from Southern police departments. In fact, by the 1890s, most black policemen had been removed from police duty in the South.[44] Thus, another possible area of protection and aid for black legal safety was cut off from the black community.

Jackson, Mississippi, housed the state penitentiary. United States blacks in 1890 "comprised 12 percent of the national population and 25 percent of the prison population." In Mississippi, African Americans "comprised about 90 percent of the prison population."[45] And, to make matters worse, "living conditions for the predominantly black convict populations were inhuman."[46] Such conditions were appalling, but, with the lynching problem in the 1890s added, hope for black people seemed like a lost dream during and after this period.

The causes of lynching in Mississippi were as varied in the 1890s as they were in earlier periods. One contemporary student of lynching has observed in his study that at least 88 causes were established for lynchings. The list is instructive and appears as Table 4.1, Offenses for Which Blacks Were Lynched During This Period[47] (page 34). The offenses cover a wide range of charges, but as is evident from earlier and later periods of lynching in Mississippi and the nation, seven major categories can be defined as the major causes of lynching. As classified by most scholars for the last one hundred years, these seven areas are (1) homicides, (2) felonious assault, (3) rape, (4) attempted rape, (5) robbery and theft, (6) insult to a white person, and (7) all other causes.[48] In general the lynching problem in Mississippi operated along these same lines for this period. Clearly, rape and attempted rape are not the leading "causes" of lynching, even though many white Mississippians and other southerners claim that this was the case. Alleged social and economic crimes (often against white men) were among the leading causes of lynching in Mississippi.[49] A central theme that seems to come back often as one studies each decade of lynching in Mississippi is that white Mississippians viewed blacks as the origins of violence against whites rather than seeing the reality of their own violence against blacks. Edward L. Ayers brings this to our attention when he writes: "For their part, Southern whites were convinced that it was blacks who were dangerous, who bred the violence that hung over the South."[50] This state of affairs would run for several generations. Black Mississippians always had to be conscious of vigilante groups and historically the Ku Klux Klan was first on this list. They had to be aware of riots and mob actions and individual or small groups of hostile whites who could, on short notice, assemble a lynching party.[51]

During the long nightmare of the 1890s, Americans had to endure at least 1,709 lynchings in this country, of which 1,175 were of blacks, 517 whites, and 17 Mexican-Americans and Native Americans. These yearly totals are represented in Table 4.2, National Lynching Victims, 1890–1899[52] (page 35). In Mississippi there were at least 195 lynching victims for this period. Table 4.3, Mississippi Lynching Victims, 1890–1899 (page 35), observes this fact, although the national data figures (145) are somewhat lower than my own research findings. This portfolio of data indicates that the 1890s were one of the worst decades in American history of the lynching crisis facing the nation.[53] This was an era of great violence in American society. Scholar Gilbert Osofsky suggests that it was an era when "late-nineteenth-century statistics of lynching are unreliable. The 'Miscellaneous Items' sections of contemporary Southern newspapers carry sentences like these: 'Four negroes were lynched in Grenada last week; also one at Oxford.' Whatever the inadequacies of statistics, however, there is no doubt that the late nineteenth and early twentieth centuries were a heyday of Negro murder."[54]

TABLE 4.1: OFFENSES FOR WHICH BLACKS WERE LYNCHED DURING THIS PERIOD

Murder
Alleged Murder
Attempted Murder
Complicity in Murder
Murderous Assault
Threat to Kill
Aiding in Escape of Murderer

Robbery
Burglary
Thief
Larceny
Attempted Robbery
Passing Counterfeit Money
Hiwayman
Suspected Burglar
Fraud

Assault
Attempted Assault
Criminal Assault
Shooting Officer
Resisting Arrest
Kidnapping

Fire or Incendiarism
Barn Burning
Arson

Rape
Attempted Rape
Alleged Rape

Rape and Incendiarism
Robbery and Murder
Rape and Murder
Robbery and Arson
Robbery and Assault

Cause not given
Unknown Offense
Guilty of No Offense
Mistaken Identity
Mistaken for Another
By Mistake
No Offense

Gambling
Quarrel over Profit

Protecting a Negro

Racial Prejudice—Black against a White
Miscegenation
Insulting a White Woman
Testifying against Whites
Attention to White Women
Forcing White Boy to Commit Crime
Expressing Sympathy with Murder of White
    Man

Testifying for one of his own race
Assaulting a White man
Race Trouble
Entering a White Woman's Room

Insulting Women
Wife Beating

Political Causes
Refusing to Give Evidence
Turning State's Evidence
Prevented Evidence
Informing
Giving Information/Evidence

Desperado
Outlaw

Elopement
Threat
Being Disreputable
Vagrancy
Bad Language
Damage to Property
Bad Reputation
Insults
Accomplice
Writing Insulting Letters
Being Troublesome
Rioting

Lawlessness
Killing Animal
Self Defense
Various Crimes
Conjuring

Poisoning
Introducing Small Pox

Mob Indignation

TABLE 4.2: NATIONAL LYNCHING VICTIMS, 1890–1899*

Year	Total	Black	White	Mexican/ Native American
1890	127	90	37	0
1891	200	127	71	2
1892	262	162	100	0
1893	206	155	46	5
1894	195	134	58	3
1895	184	113	68	3
1896	133	80	51	2
1897	162	124	38	0
1898	130	103	25	2
1899	110	87	23	0
TOTALS	1709	1175	517	17

*National Data from all Sources

TABLE 4.3: MISSISSIPPI LYNCHING VICTIMS, 1890–1899

Year	National Data* Total	Authors Data Total
1890	10	13
1891	24	32
1892	12	23
1893	15	22
1894	25	19
1895	12	17
1896	4	11
1897	14	23
1898	12	15
1899	17	20
Totals	145	195

*National Data from all Sources

TABLE 4.4: DISTRIBUTION OF LYNCHING VICTIMS
IN MISSISSIPPI BY COUNTY, 1890–1899

2 Adams	3 Jefferson Davis	2 Pike
2 Alcorn	2 Jones	1 Quitman
6 Amite	4 Kemper	9 Rankin
2 Attala	4 Lafayette	6 Simpson
3 Bolivar	6 Lauderdale	1 Smith
2 Calhoun	1 Lawrence	4 Tallahatchie
5 Claiborne	2 Leake	1 Tate
1 Clay	3 Lee	3 Tippah
2 Coahoma	5 LeFlore	7 Warren
7 Copiah	4 Lincoln	8 Washington
4 Desoto	7 Lowndes	1 Wayne
4 Forrest	1 Madison	2 Wilkinson
3 Franklin	2 Marshall	3 Winston
4 Grenada	6 Monroe	3 Yalobusha
5 Harrison	2 Montgomery	5 Yazoo
17 Hinds	5 Neshoba	2 Unknown
1 Holmes	1 Newton	
2 Itawamba	1 Noxubee	
1 Jackson	1 Oktibbeha	195 TOTAL
1 Jasper	3 Panola	

Mississippi was indeed a land of contrasts. Its population base consisted of four groups: whites, blacks, Native Americans and Chinese-Americans. One scholar notes:

> Many of the white residents are descendants of settlers from states along the Atlantic Seaboard and the Northeast and are primarily of Scotch-Irish, English, and northern European ancestry. The black residents, also of old stock, are largely descendants of slaves who were brought to Mississippi before the Civil War.
>
> The only other minority groups of any size are the nearly 4,000 Choctaw Indians concentrated in three east central counties, and a lesser number of Chinese, who have maintained a strong cultural identity in the Delta since the 1870's.[55]

In such a world, blacks were at the bottom of the social system. They were faced with a special challenge of dealing with Mississippi's white elites, while also having to contend with the state's large number of poor whites. It was a situation whereby "white supremacy was so thoroughly entrenched by the 1890 constitution that the Negro no longer counted in Mississippi politics, except as an oratorical whipping boy, and other divisions could come to the fore."[56]

From such a background came the 195 known lynching events in Mississippi during the 1890s. Table 4.4 denotes the range of the problem by county for the ten-year period. Lynchings took place in 54 of the state's 82 counties.[57] Thirty Mississippi counties held three or more lynching events between 1890 and 1899. Fifteen counties had the highest lynching rates for the state during this period, including Claiborne, Harrison, Leflore, Neshoba and Yazoo with five each; Amite, Lauderdale, Monroe and Simpson with six each; Copiah, Lowndes and Warren with seven each; Washington with eight; Rankin with nine; and Hinds with seventeen, the highest total for any county during the decade. This data suggests that lynching was a state-wide phenomenon in Mississippi, but was especially concentrated in the Delta, central, east and south Mississippi counties. The Gulf Coast area was the only part of the state which did not have a high lynching volume for the 1890s. Perhaps the greater concentration of the state's black population outside of the Gulf Coast area helps to explain this.

The year 1892 is representative of the impact of the lynching problem in Mississippi. Ida B. Wells-Barnett notes an important case in which a black family of five persons was lynched at Quincy, Mississippi, on the charge of well poisoning. She writes:

Suspected, Innocent and Lynched

Five persons, Benjamin Jackson, his wife, Mahala Jackson, his mother in-law, Lou Carter, Rufus Bigley, were lynched near Quincy, Miss., the charge against them being suspicion of well poisoning. It appears from the newspaper dispatches at that time that a family by the name of Woodruff was taken ill in September of 1892. As a result of their illness one of more of the family are said to have died, though that matter is not stated definitely. It was suspected that the cause of their illness was the existence of poison in the water, some miscreant having placed poison in the well. Suspicion pointed to a colored man named Benjamin Jackson who was at once arrested. With him also were arrested his wife and mother-in-law and all were held on the same charge.

The matter came up for judicial investigation, but as might have been expected, the white people concluded it was unnecessary to [a]wait the result of the investigation—that it was preferable to hang the accused first and try him afterward. By this method of procedure, the desired result was always obtained—the accused was hanged.[58]

To the Parsons, Kansas, *Weekly Blade*, an African-American newspaper, the entire era represented "A Damnable Outrage."[59] One thing was obvious to the black press: the Age of Segregation, as reflected in the lynching crisis, would be a long and difficult journey for black Americans.

Three other lynching cases during the 1890s are illustrative of the problem in the state. The first case demonstrates the economic causes of lynching, when whites wanted the land of a successful black farmer or landowner:

On the eighteen[th] of February, 1897, about eight miles from Roxie, Mississippi, a murder was committed of the most dastardly nature. Ben Land, a coloured man, and his wife lived on a piece of United States land, which by hard, continuous labour they had improved. Late at night, when he and his wife were asleep, armed men surrounded his little home, sprinkled it with coal oil, set it on fire, and waited. Soon the place was enveloped in flames, and poor Land and his wife rushed out into the darkness to save their lives. She did escape; but he was shot down the moment he emerged from his burning home, and was found next morning "with all the top and back of his head shot off." His only offense was living on that particular piece of land, which was proven in the State's Court. He was known as a quiet, industrious man, and lived on terms of peace and good-will with everybody. The fact is, a white family wanted the property and had approached Land in respect of it, who, having consulted Hon. S. A. Beadle, an attorney-at-law, intended compromising with them, because he knew that henceforth his life would not be safe. He was not allowed to live long enough to carry out his purpose. He was murdered, and his wife was turned out to do as best she could, and white men saw the deed done,—did it—and went on their way in a Christian country.[60]

Sociologists Stewart Tolnay and E. M. Beck describe a very interesting lynching during 1899. The case is illustrative of the complex nature of Mississippi lynchings:

The last lynching incident of the nineteenth century in Yazoo County occurred on March 18, 1899. There had been seven previous lynching victims in the county, and there would be nine more before 1930. In the days preceding March 18, there had been a racial confrontation on The Midnight, a plantation near Silver City. During that encounter, shots were exchanged between blacks and whites, but no one was injured. Following the incident, three "ring leaders" of the black insurrection were arrested: Minor Wilson, C. C. Reed, and Willis Boyd. As so often happened, however, the wheels of formal justice were not allowed to grind this case to its natural completion. While being transported to Silver City, Wilson, Reed, and Boyd were taken away from law officers by a mob of determined whites. The three men were shot to death, then their bodies were weighted down and thrown in to the Yazoo river.[61]

Nevertheless, one single factor outweighed all others in the "Age of Lynching in Mississippi," and that was a concentration on lynching black males. Although black women were victims of lynching, their total numbers were much smaller than black males. Table 4.5, Black Women Lynching Victims in Mississippi, 1890–1899, lists only six known black women lynching victims for this period. White Mississippi males were also lynched during the 1890s, but like black women their numbers were small. Table 4.6 notes the known five examples of white male lynching victims in the decade for Mississippi. If we take 195 known

TABLE 4.5: BLACK WOMEN LYNCHING VICTIMS IN MISSISSIPPI, 1890–1899

Name	Town/County	Date	Causes
Louise Stevenson	Hollondale, Washington County	Sept. 28, 1891	Accessory to Murder
Mother of W. Lee	Lowden County	1891	Accomplice to Murder
Mahala Jackson	Jackson, Hinds County	Sept. 15, 1893	Alleged well poisoning
Louisa Carter	Jackson, Hinds County	Sept. 15, 1893	Alleged well poisoning
Unknown	Simpson County	July 24, 1894	Race prejudice (conspiracy)
Unknown	Tallahatchie County	1897	Robbery and arson

TABLE 4.6: WHITE MISSISSIPPI VICTIMS BY YEAR AND COUNTY, 1890–1899 (ALL MALES)

Name	Town/County	Date	Causes
F. Marsh Cook	Jasper County	July 1890	Politician Participation (Republican)
Sharp	Neshoba County	Jan. 2, 1891	Robbery
James Talbert	Fort Stephenson, Kemper County	Nov. 8, 1892	Murder
William Patterson	Westville, Claiborne County	July 19, 1898	Murder
Daniel Patrick	Scranton, Jones County	June 20, 1899	Rape and arson

lynching victims for the state as the total between 1890 and 1899, then 184 of this number were black males—a harsh situation, indeed.

Generally, in the 1890s, lynch victims in Mississippi were accused of five major offenses. There are outlined in Table 4.7 and include 61 cases (31 percent) of rape or attempted rape, 57 cases (29 percent) of murder, 19 cases (10 percent) of bad reputation, 18 cases (9 percent) of robbery, and 10 cases of arson (5 percent). As in previous periods, only a minority of lynching victims were charged with the crime of rape, while almost as many victims were accused of murder. Economic crimes, generally viewed as crimes against white males, total 24 percent of the victims (for having a bad reputation, robbery, and arson).[62]

Mississippi lynchings in the 1890s were especially high during the months of March, June, July, September and December. Table 4.8 on page 40 denotes, however, that the time of year for a number of cases (45) is not known. These data suggest that lynchings were more likely to take place in the warmer months of the year. But whiter months could also prove dangerous for lynching victims in Mississippi.[63]

The nightmare of the Age of Lynching in Mississippi between 1890–1899 forced the black community to use every possible strategy for the protection and advancement of the black community. As the 1890s were one of the harshest decades of the lynching crisis in America, blacks had to make an heroic effort to challenge white supremacy and prepare for

TABLE 4.7: MISSISSIPPI LYNCHING VICTIMS, RANGE AND PERCENTAGES OF OFFENSES ALLEGED, 1890–1899*

Causes	Number	Percent
Rape/attempted Rape	61	31%
Murder	57	29%
Bad Reputation	19	10%
Robbery	18	9%
Arson	10	5%
Unknown	9	5%
Insults to White People	6	3%
Well Poisoning	5	3%
Assault	4	2%
Miscegenation	2	1%
Political Participation	1	1%
Conjuring (voodooism)	1	1%
Mistaken Identity	1	1%
Land Dispute	1	1%
TOTAL	195	100%

*Research Data by the Author

the long future ahead. Deborah Gray White notes this valid point when she writes: "Black people dealt with the assault by turning inward. Locked out of most arenas of American life they accommodated racism by retreating to their own institutions."[64] The black masses seem to have turned to the black church for special comfort and aid during this period. Resistance to white oppression was generally out of reach of the white community and black men, women and children could all be active in the black church. This was also true of the development of the Black Women's Club Movement in late nineteenth century Mississippi.[65]

The 1890s also found continued development of the black press as an important medium for black expression. White censorship of the black press in Mississippi was a problem, but African-Americans in the state could turn to other press outlets in other states. For example, "In 1900 black Baptists at the local and state levels published forty-three newspapers, the great majority of which were located in the South."[66] And important national black newspapers did reach Mississippi blacks, often underground.[67] Blacks could also write letters and petitions to government officials, influential white and black leaders in Mississippi and elsewhere to address the wrongs which they suffered in their home state.

Black Mississippians still "voted with their feet" to migrate from Mississippi or to relocate to other sections of the state in the 1890s as a response to lynching and general discrimination of African Americans.[68] What black Mississippians sought in the 1890s was justice. One author asks: "What is justice, and what is the relation of justice to the idea of law?"[69] For black Mississippians during this period it seemed as if justice did not exist. Yet they lived in a society where "justice centers on the imperative that people are to receive

TABLE 4.8: MISSISSIPPI LYNCHINGS BY MONTH AND SECTION OF STATE, 1890–1899

Month	North	Delta	East	Central	South	Gulf Coast	Unknown Place	TOTAL
January	2	0	0	2	1	0		11
February	1	2	0	1	4	0		8
March	2	5	2	4	1	0		14
April	3	1	0	1	2	0		7
May	1	1	5	2	2	0		11
June	2	0	2	1	9	1		15
July	4	1	3	5	11	1		25
August	2	1	0	0	3	0		6
September	2	1	4	7	1	0		15
October	1	1	0	5	3	0		10
November	2	0	4	2	1	0		9
December	0	5	3	4	2	0		14
Unknown Date	10	6	8	10	8	3	2	47
TOTALS	32	24	37	44	48	5	2	192

what they are due. Justice can be a personal virtue: a settled disposition to consider and act on what others are due. But it is a virtue of institutions, not of persons, that justice connects most closely to the idea of law."[70]

But in the black Mississippi world of the 1890s, justice for blacks was a dream to be realized, hopefully, in the twentieth century, following years of struggle and hard work. For the present, black Mississippians had to struggle daily and reflect on a better tomorrow.

Black Americans in other states were acutely aware of the status of blacks in Mississippi during the 1890s. For many, "Mississippi became synonymous with the Jim Crow South" and lynching,[71] and represented the worst example of extralegality when it came to black freedom and the lynching crisis. This process meant that "essentially, these (white) individuals and groups question the legitimacy of government, and advocate some form of drastic action to cure the perceived inadequacies."[72] So blacks outside of Mississippi had to aid the struggle against lynching in the state and the South. Without a doubt, the leading black leader to protest the loudest on the lynching issue was Ida B. Wells-Barnett, a native of Mississippi. Scholars have long noted the primacy of her role in the anti-lynching crusade. She is especially noted for saying, "Emphasis on rape as a justification for lynching only served to reinforce racist stereotypes of black men as sexual predators and to put them 'beyond the pale of human sympathy.' The sexual excuse for lynching helped perpetuate both the racial and gender inequalities in American society."[73] Wells-Barnett's body of work on lynching helped to shape national and international thinking on the issue of American lynching, including her editorial work on the *Memphis Free Speech* newspaper, her pamphlet, "Southern Horrors, Lynch Law in All Its Phases" (1892), and her travels and public lectures in the United States and abroad, especially in Great Britain, to focus public opinion against the evils of lynching.[74]

Also of note in the early 1890s was the work of Frederick Douglass (d. 1895), who spoke out vigorously against lynching. One of Douglass' best known attempts in this regard was his article "Lynch Law in the South," published in 1892 in the *North American Review*. One scholar notes that in this important essay, "Douglass analyzes the race issue realistically, calls for social equality, but also sternly warns southerners that they may drive the Negro to acts of desperation; at the same time he offers a keen explanation of the charges against the Negro."[75] Douglass was also important in encouraging blacks to revitalize, in the 1890s, the Black Convention Movement (earlier conferences and meetings of blacks to deal with slavery between 1830 and 1860) to deal with lynching and the general discrimination which blacks faced in America.[76]

The dominant black leader in America in the 1890s, Booker T. Washington was something of an enigma to this historical period. Perhaps Lerone Bennett, Jr., best describes his attitude and influence: "A conservative man, shrewd, hard-working and, some say, devious, Washington essayed a program of conciliation and racial submission. He refused to attack Jim Crow directly and urged Negroes to subordinate their political, civil and social strivings to economic advancement. By implication anyway, he accepted segregation and concentrated on a program of industrial education."[77] These three key leaders, Wells-Barnett, Douglass, and Washington were representative of the scope of national black concerns in Mississippi on the lynching problem. Many other black leaders of religious groups, fraternal orders, social organizations and the black press were, as well. Such concerns were certainly needed, for at home in Mississippi blacks were in a real struggle for survival.

The black situation in Mississippi was revealed in the attitudes of most Mississippi whites in the 1890s. During this era "a different kind of conservation pervaded Southern constitutions in the last part of the century. Race relations were the key. These constitutions were obsessed with the preservation of white supremacy. Blacks had to be kept in their place, legally and socially. Law and terror made a most effective combination."[78] Blacks in Mississippi and the South were up against a harsh system of racism, one in which

> Southern white thinking on race was strongly influenced by the rise of what has been called the "Radical mentality" in the 1890s. It flourished between 1897 and 1907, and it remained powerful until the First World War. "Radicalism," according to Joel Williamson, "envisioned a 'new' Negro, freed from the necessarily very tight bounds of slavery and retrogressing rapidly toward his natural state of savagery and bestiality." The Darwinian concepts of racial degeneracy and extinction provided a "scientific" basis for Radicalism and other anti–Negro propaganda around the turn of the century. Energetically promoted by southern leaders such as Benjamin R. Tillman of South Carolina, James K. Vardaman of Mississippi, Thomas Dixon of North Carolina, and Rebecca Felton of Georgia, this form of white racism exerted great influence at the popular level. One reason was the work of southerners like Rebecca Felton, who became increasingly concerned in the 1890s about mounting attacks of black men on white women.[79]

A key to understanding white Mississippi during this period is to understand the rise of such leaders as James K. Vardaman (1861–1930), and Theodore G. Bilbo (1877–1947), among many others. Such men placed a high order on an "exalted view of southern women and [the] advocacy of lynch law." To such people, blacks were "an inferior race," while whites were a "superior race."[80] Such thinking carried lynching from the 1890s into a new century.

National leaders in the United States were indifferent to the lynching crisis in Mississippi at the end of the nineteenth century. This was especially the case with the office of the president of the country. While some presidents in the 1890s—Benjamin Harrison, Grover Cleveland and William McKinley—may have been personally against lynching, this did not help blacks and others in the country who were lynch victims. And, as indicated earlier, the 1890s were a leading decade in American history in the total number of lynch victims. William McKinley was just one American president who could not effectively deal with the lynching crisis facing the nation.[81] The silence of so many national leaders in the 1890s became a deadly consequence for the hundreds of people lynched in this country.[82]

And so at last the decade of the 1890s came to an end. It had been a long and tortuous journey for the several hundred Mississippi lynch victims of this period, and it must have evoked very sad memories for the family members and friends of the victims. Yet one voice above all others continued to fight in the crusade to end lynchings. Richard A. Couto captured the essence of Ida B. Wells-Barnett as she struggled endlessly to promote public outrage over American lynching: "Ida B. Wells-Barnett protested southern lynching over a lifetime and across the country and in Britain. She understood an early, if not the first, systematic study of lynching. She cited 197 lynchings in the Untied States in 1894, a number that exceeded by 65 the number of legal executions that year."[83] Mississippians ended the 1890s on the sour note of lynchings as a way of life in the deep South state. This perspective would remain active in Mississippi far at least another sixty-five years, if not longer. It was a very trying period in the history of the state.

5

The Search for Justice in a
New Century, 1900–1909

Mississippians entered the twentieth century on a hope and a prayer. Although rich as an agricultural state, Mississippi was poor in most other areas, and considered a backwoods area by most of the rest of the nation. A harsh era of Jim Crow stood across the land impacting all Mississippians, but especially the black majority in the state. The population of blacks in the opening decade of the new century stood at 910,070 (58.4 percent of the total population).[1] By 1900, ten percent of all United States blacks lived in Mississippi. Mississippi was basically still a rural state in 1900, with 92.3 percent of the residents living in rural areas.[2] The state had only ten cities with a population over 3,500 each. They were Vicksburg (14,834), Meridian (14,050), Natchez (12,210), Jackson (7,816), Greenville (7,642), Columbus (6,484), Biloxi (5,467), Yazoo City (4,944), Water Valley (3,813), and Corinth (3,661.)[3] It was a time of deep crisis in the state's history, made even more unbearable by the extent of the violent racism in Mississippi and a general climate of poor economic, political and social outlooks. Against this backdrop stood the black sharecropper, the other poor farmers, and those in extreme poverty. David Tyack, quoting W. E. B. Du Bois, notes the impact of this economic problem: "Whether sharecropper or tenant farmer, the average Negro peasant never seemed to be able to get ahead."[4]

Also by 1900, seven percent of blacks owned their own land in the Mississippi Delta, another indication of how the vast majority was tied to sharecropping.[5] Even when African Americans were successful, owned land, and had developed businesses, they were not safe from the arms of Mississippi's government and white citizens. Examples from the period will demonstrate this fact. One scholar notes: "In Meridian, Mississippi, authorities destroyed a black settlement on the edge of the city. Officials justified their actions on the pretext that it represented a public health hazard. Similarly, in Natchez, Mississippi, authorities removed blacks from their homes and destroyed the structures on the premise that they were contaminated with yellow fever."[6] Scholar Leon F. Litwack describes the situation in Bolivar County: "Even as [Booker T.] Washington articulated his self-improvement creed, the violence inflicted upon his people was often selective, aimed at those who had succeeded, those in positions of leadership, those who owned the best farm in the county and the largest store in town, those perceived as having stepped out of their place."[7]

Yet the complexity of the black experience in America, even in Mississippi, is borne

Most lynching victims in the United States were African American men, as demonstrated in this photo of a triple lynching in Mississippi. Pictures of such events denote the horror of these issues for American society (COURTESY OF THE JACKSON ADVOCATE).

out by the fact that in spite of white racism and oppression, blacks continued to strive, individually and collectively, during this decade of hardship to advance themselves economically. Take the area of black banks. By 1909, black Mississippians had established eleven such institutions in the state, with resources of $602,000.[8] One of the major supporters of black banks, according to Booker T. Washington, was the aid that they received from black fraternal organizations. He writes that in 1908:

> Not infrequently I have found that Negro banks owe their existence to the secret and fraternal organizations. There are forty-two of these organizations, for example, in the State of Mississippi, and they collected $708,670 last year, and paid losses to the amount of $522,757. Frequently the banks have been established to serve as depositories for the funds of these institutions. They have then added a savings department, and have done banking business for an increasing number of stores and shops of various kinds that have been established within the last ten years by Negro business men.[9]

Theodore Hemmingway observes that blacks in Jackson, Mississippi, had achieved remarkable economic success by 1908. He writes:

> Jackson, a city of 16,000, half of which was black, was the center of black commercial and industrial life in Mississippi. Black Jacksonians owned one third of the city's municipal property. One half of Jackson's Negroes owned their own homes, and others rented largely from people of their own race. Two black banks operated in Jackson and financed the construction of homes on the easy payment plan. Overall, Jackson blacks had $200,000

The Mississippi Medical and Surgical Association was established in 1900 by thirteen African American physicians to "promote the collective interest of physicians and patients of African American descent." The first members of this association are pictured, ca. 1900 (COURTESY OF THE JACKSON ADVOCATE).

on deposit in white-controlled banks and owned $1,250,000 in property. Additionally, the town had several blacks of exceptional wealth. Among these were Dr. L. M. Ganaway, attorney L. K. Atwood, and a baker, H. K. Risher, who grossed $30,000 per year. He established his shop in 1861.[10]

Against this very interesting background was the fact that "in 1900 the riches 1% of America's population owned over 80% of America's wealth; while 80% of the United States population worked at subsistence levels."[11] Such were the challenges of the age for Americans of all walks of life.

The social nature of Mississippi society between 1900 and 1909 was also one of extremes. Blacks faced segregation (by law and by custom) in all segments of their lives. According to Scott L. Malcomson: "Formal segregation not only focused one's daily attention on race in general, it specifically brought attention to the racial body. In a sense, it heightened racial intimacy, one's awareness of the tactile bodies of others, and of one's own."[12]

A central distinction of the period for blacks was their short life spans due to their economic, social, political and psychological conditions in life. David L. Lewis has suggested that as late as "1900, a Negro boy baby at birth had a life expectation of thirty-two years."[13] Although Mississippi had black doctors their numbers were small and concentrated in the state's largest cities. To aid and "promote the collective interest of physicians and patients of African American descent," the Mississippi Medical and Surgical Association was established in 1900 by thirteen black doctors including Drs. S. A. Miller, Canton; A. W. Dumas,

Natchez; S. D. Remond, Jackson; L. T. Miller, Yazoo City; E. W. Moore, Edwards; J. E. Beall, Jackson; H. E. Conner, Brookhaven; J. C. Mazique Sibly, Natchez; B. F. Fulton, Greenville; James May, Natchez; D. W. Sherrod, Macon-Meridian; J. A. Miller, Vicksburg; and C. H. Woods, Vicksburg.[14] Such physicians were pioneering in the struggle to advance the health status of black Mississippians.

Black Mississippi women were active during this period, especially on matters relating to the family, health care, church, education, political concerns (securing the right to vote and hold office), and issues of discrimination against any group of Americans. Black women were effective in organizing a major organization to address the above concerns in 1908. In that year, they formed the Mississippi Federation of Colored Women's Clubs, and it has been active in advancing black women and the black community across the years.[15]

On the issue of education, blacks found the decade to be a difficult one. For one thing, official Mississippi had a disdain for black education. No one in Mississippi represented this negative position more than Governor James K. Vardaman. In 1900 he noted that expenditure of funds (state or private) on schools for African-Americans was a "positive unkindness to him." Education for African-Americans made them "unfit for the work which the white man has prescribed, and which he will be forced to perform." Vardaman also believed that "this education is ruining our negroes. They're demanding equality."[16] Against this attitude, according to Thomas E. Gossett, were the consequences which blacks faced: "When [Vardaman] became governor in 1900, he drastically reduced the amount of state money spent for Negro schools. The only kind of education he thought suitable for the Negroes was vocational education and not much of that."[17] Yet blacks endured. And nationally, by 1910, there were 5,000 African-Americans in college and several hundred of this number were in Mississippi institutions.[18] Added to the significance of the above factors were the special challenges and obstacles that blacks had overcome in reducing their national and state rates of illiteracy. A study of the period remarks on the national progress that blacks had made in this area: "The illiteracy rate among Negroes 10 years of age and over declined to 30.4 percent in 1910, while illiteracy among Negro children 10 to 14 years of age declined from 30.1 percent in 1900 to 18.9 percent in 1910."[19]

Black Mississippians could also turn to their religious institutions for support and strength during the bleak years of 1900–1909. Black churches gave Afro-Mississippians a refuge from the hostility of white Mississippi, a place where their spirituality could grow and develop, their leadership skills could be enhanced, and where black creativity could be expressed—especially in the development of religious music such as gospel. C. Eric Lincoln reminds us that:

> Black Christians draw upon four principal traditions: (1) the more formal and less expressive service of the Presbyterians, Episcopalians, Congregationalists, etc.; (2) the less restrained worship of the Baptists and Methodists; (3) the exuberant camp meeting tradition with its extensive lay involvement; and (4) the vestigial African ritual traditions like the "ring dance," which lingered in isolated slave communities such as the Sea Islands of the South Atlantic Coast. All these traditions found their expression in the black church. In consequence, long after the Civil War the ring dance was still a feature of some black churches.[20]

In one last area, political interests, they also faced special burdens and challenges in the decade under study.

Black Mississippians suffered many insults during the Age of Segregation. In the political arena they were faced with a situation whereby "the Mississippi legislature led the way in writing blacks out of power; it embodies the radical spirit."[21] This meant, in reality, keeping blacks down politically. It was a trying situation. A central white Mississippian who seemed to reflect the political position of many whites in the state was James K. Vardaman. One study notes:

> [When he] campaigned—successfully—for the governorship of Mississippi in 1900, on an eight-wheeled lumber wagon pulled by eight yoke of oxen, [he would] excite the passions of back-country yokels by screaming that "we would be justified in slaughtering every Ethiop on earth to preserve unsullied the honor of one Caucasian home." The Negro, said he, is a "lazy, lying, lustful animal which no conceivable amount of training can transform into a tolerable citizen." And again, "Anything that causes the negro to aspire above ... the functions of a servant, will be the worst thing for [him]." On another occasion he thundered, "I am opposed to negro voting.... I am just as much opposed to Booker Washington as a voter, with all his Anglo-Saxon reinforcements, as I am to the coconut-headed, chocolate-colored, typical little coon, Andy Dotson, who blacks my shoes every morning. Neither is fit to perform the supreme function of citizenship."[22]

This "radical spirit" of white Mississippians, as with other southerners throughout the South, resulted in a great reduction of black voters after the Plessy v. Ferguson decision of 1896. The example of Louisiana is illustrative of the South. In that state, "The number of blacks registered to vote fell from 127,000 in 1896 to 3,300 in 1900."[23] The reduction of black voters was just as great in Mississippi.[24]

Black Mississippi women could not vote at all during the years 1900–1909, but they continued their proactive programs to gain suffrage and to end other areas of discrimination against African-American women and other groups.[25] However, at this time, in terms of political interests, the best that African-American women could hope for was to encourage black male voting in order to help safeguard the political concerns of the black community.

In essence the period was a dead one politically for blacks, but also one of fear and treachery. Perhaps George Coleman Osborn captures this mood best when he notes that in 1903 "persistent rumors circulated that thousands of Negroes, terrified by Vardaman's threats and intimidations, were actually leaving the state. The Jackson *Weekly Clarion-Ledger* foretold a great exodus of Negro laborers to Arkansas, Louisiana, and Tennessee."[26] This was one aspect of the daily lives of black Mississippians that had not changed for over twenty-five years. Yet the struggle for them was not nearly over. They still had the daily challenge of dealing with Mississippi's criminal justice system.

Mississippi's criminal justice system during this period reflected the worst of southern traditions in keeping blacks by law and by custom in their proper places. In talking about "the good old days," Oscar T. Barack, Jr., and Nelson M. Blake remark: "The two races did not enjoy the equal protection of the laws. By tacit consent of Southern authorities, blacks were kept off the jury lists. The courts dealt severely with blacks accused of killing or assaulting whites, whatever the provocation, but were singularly indulgent toward whites accused of similar crimes against blacks."[27] Mississippi blacks, once arrested and convicted, were confronted with the state's convict leasing system. The central problem lay in the fact that Mississippi prisoners, "men, women and children alike—were compelled to toil under threat of violence, and since their ... ranks were in ample supply, they became an expendable resource. As one lessee recalled, 'Before the war, we owned the Negroes.... But these convicts, we don't own 'em. One dies, get another.'"[28]

Such harsh conditions made the Mississippi criminal justice system a very hard place

Table 5.1: Lynching Victims, 1900–1909*

Year	National	Black	White	Mississippi
1900	101	89	12	20
1901	135	108	27	18
1902	94	84	10	11
1903	104	87	17	18
1904	86	79	7	16
1905	65	60	5	14
1906	68	64	4	11
1907	62	59	3	13
1908	100	92	8	20
1909	89	75	14	11
Totals	904	797	107	152

*National data from all sources

for blacks and also for many whites to survive. One author notes: "It was this structural propensity for neglect and mistreatment that characterized convict leasing in every state. Because the upkeep of prisoners as well as idleness cut into lessees' profits, conditions tended to be Spartan and the hours long."[29] Events in the state moved swiftly in the official government position of Mississippi toward convict leasing early in the twentieth century. A major study of the period reveals, "Like other states, Mississippi began hiring out its convicts as a temporary solution to fiscal crisis, but the practice soon became entrenched."[30] Thus, Mississippi blacks lived in a state where "Southern justice made the Negro consider the courts places of punishment rather than protection...."[31] And when blacks looked out across Mississippi for the years 1900–1909, they were still confronted with the age-old problem of lynching.

As in previous decades, Mississippians gave many political, economic, and social reasons to justify lynching their fellow citizens. Stewart E. Tolnay and E. M. Beck, in A Festival of Violence: An Analysis of Southern Lynchings, 1882–1930 (1995), list eighty-one reasons given for black lynchings in the South.[32] For the period 1900–1909, my research uncovers thirteen leading alleged causes of Mississippi lynching, including rape or attempted rape, murder, burglary, robbery, arson, insults to white people, assault, race prejudice, informing, threats to kill, race rioting, lawlessness, and killing a horse; the total is 135 lynching victims, with data missing on 17 cases.[33] Both sets of data are indicative of one important fact—"that a broad spectrum of alleged behavior could lead to mob violence" in Mississippi and throughout the South.[34] Furthermore, many individuals were at risk for a lynching, regardless of where they lived in Mississippi, yet some areas of the state, as will be demonstrated, were more dangerous, especially for blacks, than other regions.

The violent period of American lynchings continued in the first decade of the twentieth century, with at least 904 victims killed between 1900 and 1909. Of this number, 797

TABLE 5.2: DISTRIBUTION OF LYNCHING VICTIMS IN MISSISSIPPI BY COUNTY, 1900–1909

County	Number of Victims	County	Number of Victims	County	Number of Victims
Alcorn	3	Jones	3	Rankin	1
Amite	4	Kemper	5	Smith	6
Bolivar	5	Lafayette	1	Stone	2
Carroll	5	Lauderdale	2	Sunflower	6
Chickasaw	3	Leake	1	Tallahatchie	6
Coahoma	5	Lee	1	Tunica	11
Copiah	2	LeFlore	3	Warren	3
Desoto	4	Lincoln	3	Washington	8
Forrest	3	Lowndes	1	Webster	1
George	1	Neshoba	1	Wilkinson	5
Harrison	5	Newton	4	Yazoo	4
Hinds	3	Noxubee	2	Unknown	9
Issaquena	4	Pearl River	1		
Itawamba	3	Perry	2		
Jackson	5	Pike	2	TOTAL	152
Jefferson Davis	1	Quitman	2		

were blacks and 107 were white. In Mississippi, 152 people were lynched during the decade, 141 blacks and 11 whites.[35] See Table 5.1, Lynching Victims, 1900–1909, for a year-by-year account of the victims. Four years stand out in the early century for the largest numbers of lynch victims nationwide. In 1901, 135 victims were killed; in 1903, 104 victims; in 1900, 101 victims; and in 1908, 100 victims. The year 1901 was also the worst for the killing of white victims, with 27 lynchings known to have taken place. One hundred and eight black victims were lynched that same year. Meanwhile, in Mississippi, the highest numbers of lynch victims were killed in 1900 and 1908 (20 victims for each year), followed by 1901 and 1903 (18 victims each year). Most of the Mississippi lynch victims were young black males from the age of fifteen to thirty-five.[36]

The range of Mississippi's lynchings by county for the decade are listed on Table 5.2. Lynchings took place in 43 Mississippi counties, well over half of the 75 counties existing in the state in 1900. Twenty-six counties had at least three or more lynchings during the decade, but 12 counties had the highest lynching totals for this ten-year period: Tunica (11); Washington (8), Smith, Sunflower, and Tallahatchie (6 each), Bolivar, Carroll, Coahoma, Harrison, Jackson, Kemper and Wilkinson (5 each).[37] The greatest majority (7) of these counties are in the Delta—Tunica, Washington, Sunflower, Tallahatchie, Bolivar, Carroll, and Coahoma—and were home to some of the largest concentrations of black people in Mississippi.

While the vast majority of black lynching victims were males, Table 5.3 (page 50) reveals that four black women (of 141 total black victims) were lynched in Mississippi during 1900–

TABLE 5.3: BLACK WOMEN LYNCHING VICTIMS IN MISSISSIPPI, 1900–1909

Name	Town/County	Date	Causes
Ida McCray	Carrolton/Carroll	8/1/1901	Implicated in murder
Betsy McCray	Carrolton/Carroll	8/1/1901	Implicated in murder
Unknown	Smith County	6/8/1903	Complicity in murder
Mrs. Luther Holbert	Doddsville/Sunflower	2/7/1904	Murder

TABLE 5.4: WHITE MISSISSIPPI LYNCHING VICTIMS BY YEAR AND COUNTY, 1900–1909

Name	Town/County	Date	Causes
Kit Nabors	Coahoma/Coahoma	11/18/1900	Murder
John Knox	Scranton/Jackson	2/26/1901	Murder
Milt Calvert	Griffith	5/22/1901	Attempted rape
Unknown	Erwin/Washington	7/11/1901	Suspected cattle thief
Unknown	Erwin/Washington	7/11/1901	Suspected cattle thief
Unknown	Erwin/Washington	7/11/1901	Suspected cattle thief
John Ameo	Erwin/Washington	7/11/1901	Suspected cattle thief
Victor -	Erwin/Washington	7/11/1901	Suspected cattle thief
Jesse P. Philips	Cleveland/Bolivar	7/20/1901	Murder
William McAlpin	Smith County	10/27/1903	Murder
Morgan Chambers	Meridian/Lauderdale	11/25/1900	Robbery

1909. Two were lynched in 1901 and one each in 1903 and 1904. All were alleged to have been involved in a murder.[38]

Eleven white males were also lynched during the decade (see Table 5.4). These events took place in seven counties: Coahoma, Jackson, Washington, Bolivar, Smith, and Lauderdale, and one unknown county. The county with the most cases was Washington (5). The eleven victims were charged with suspected cattle theft (5), murder (4), rape (1) and robbery (1).[39]

Mississippi's lynching victims were killed during all of the months of the year, however, the deadliest months occurred in October (23 events), June (16 events), March (12 events), July (12 events) and August (12 events) between 1900 and 1909.[40] The summer months were especially severe for Mississippi lynchings. But October, during this decade, was also bad. October represents a month that falls between the end of summer and the beginning of the fall and winter—a period that generally is not very cold in most of Mississippi. Table 5.6 also indicates that most lynch mobs did not like to conduct lynching parties during cold

TABLE 5.5: MISSISSIPPI LYNCHING VICTIMS, RANGE AND
PERCENTAGE OF OFFENSES ALLEGED, 1900–1909*

Causes	Number	Percent
Murder	73	48.03%
Rape/Attempted Rape	29	19.08%
Unknown	17	11.18%
Arson	8	5.26%
Robbery	5	3.29%
Assault	4	2.63%
Burglary	3	1.97%
Insults to White People	3	1.97%
Race Prejudice	3	1.97%
Race Rioter	3	1.97%
Informing	1	0.66%
Threats to Kill	1	0.66%
Lawlessness	1	0.66%
Killing a Horse	1	0.66%
TOTAL	152	

*Research data by the author

periods. For example, only eight lynchings each are represented for January and February during the decade, a very cold period indeed in Mississippi.[41]

Scholars have long been able to capture the essence of a lynching event in American society. The story is a sad one. William Z. Foster notes this fact in his study and observes:

> Here is a picture of a typical Southern lynching: "The sheriff along with the accused Negro was seized by the mob, and the two carried to the scene of the crime. Here quickly assembled a thousand or more men, women, and children. The accused Negro was hung up in a sweet-gum tree by his arms, just high enough to keep his feet off the ground. Members of the mob tortured him for more than an hour. A pole was jabbed in his mouth. His toes were cut off joint by joint. His fingers were similarly removed, and members of the mob extracted his teeth with wire pliers. After further unmentionable mutilations, the Negro's still living body was saturated with gasoline and a lighted match was applied. As the flames leaped up, hundreds of shots were fired into the dying victim. During the day, thousands of people from miles around rode out to see the sight. Not till nightfall did the officers remove the body and bury it.[42]

Case after case of such tragedy took place in Mississippi during the Age of Lynching. Such was the matter of fact for the years 1900–1909. A few examples from this period will now illustrate this burden on the backs of Mississippians, especially African-Americans.

TABLE 5.6: MISSISSIPPI LYNCHINGS BY MONTH AND SECTION OF THE STATE, 1900–1909

Month	North	Delta	East	Central	South	Gulf	Total
January	1	5	0	0	1	1	8
February	0	2	3	0	1	2	8
March	1	5	0	1	1	4	12
April	1	1	0	1	1	0	4
May	1	1	1	1	6	0	10
June	3	3	3	5	1	1	16
July	1	9	1	0	1	0	12
August	2	6	0	1	3	0	12
September	2	6	0	3	4	0	15
October	1	7	8	1	5	1	23
November	1	3	2	0	3	2	11
December	0	3	0	0	1	2	6
Totals	14	51	18	13	28	13	137

Case one describes a September 28, 1902, lynching of William Gibson, a black, at Corinth, Mississippi, accused of killing a local white woman, Mrs. Minnie Whitfield. The story, "Five Thousand People Witness the Lynching," ran in the *Fayette* (Mississippi) *Chronicle*.

Under the bright blue vault of the heavens and in the soft, warm summer sunshine, and in an amphitheater as natural as though planned by an architect, Mississippi vengeance took the place of Mississippi justice this afternoon, and William Gibson, the negro who confessed to the crime of criminally assaulting and murdering Mrs. Minnie Whitfield on Friday afternoon, August 29, at Corinth, Miss., was burned at the stake.

No one was prepared for what the day had in store for them, and the suddenness of the awful vengeance handed out to Will Gibson, the negro fiend, was all the more terrible to those who witnessed it.

The people of Corinth themselves learned at a late hour Saturday night that Gibson had been captured and had confessed to being the brute who assaulted and killed Mrs. Minnie Whitfield of one of the most highly respected families in this section. Gibson was captured about 7 o'clock in the evening, but it was not until about 11 o'clock that he confessed to the crime for which he had been arrested....

It was at this time the first report of a burning was spread about the city. On all hands it was passed from mouth to mouth that the hanging which had been planned would be changed to a burning at the stake, and that crowds were hauling boxes and wood to the scene of the affair, which was planned to take place about a half mile outside of the city....

[N]egro Gibson, who was pulled up by the rope about his neck, and punched up from the rear with the barrels of shotguns. Then Mich McCann also mounted the scaffold, and in a loud voice he announced, "The Ethiopian wants to say something."

Gibson was stood up on the scaffold and securely bound to the cross-beams of iron by heavy chains. Then wire was also wrapped about him and the iron, and in this condition he was told to go ahead and make his final talk. Gibson, speaking with a quiver in his voice, said: [Says he is guilty and deserves punishment, etc., etc. Story says the brother of the murdered woman would set the fire, etc.].[43]

Case two is noted in the diary of Henry Waring Ball, and appears to have taken place in the Delta, perhaps at Greenville, Mississippi, on June 5, 1903. Ball wrote in his diary of the event:

Today there was a lynching in town; a miserable negro beast attacked a telephone girl as she was going home at night, and choked her. She screamed and Hankins heard her and ran to her rescue. Bloodhounds were put on the trail, and a negro captured in bed. This morning the jail was stormed and the wretched creature carried down Washington Ave to the telephone exchange, where he was hung up in front of it, while the girls looked on and applauded. Everything was very orderly; there was not a shot, but much laughing and hilarious excitement—Webb was one of the most ardent lynchers. Nothing would satisfy him but that I must go with him to see the negro after he had been hanged, and I did. It was quite a gala occasion, and as soon as the corpse was cut down all the crowd betook themselves to the park to see a game of baseball. Good Lord! I am 20 degrees out of my latitude.[44]

In case three, Mary Church Terrell, a black woman leader, notes the killing of Luther Holbert and his wife, who suffered a double lynching in 1904, near Doddsville, accused of murdering a white planter and two black men. Terrell notes:

The prevailing belief that negroes are not tortured by mobs unless they are charged with the "usual" crime does not tally with the facts. The savagery which attended the lynching of a man and his wife the first week in March of the present year was probably never exceeded in this country or anywhere else in the civilized world. A white planter was murdered at Doddsville, Miss., and a negro was charged with the crime. The negro fled, and his wife, who was known to be innocent, fled with him to escape the fate which she knew awaited her, if she remained. The two Negroes were pursued and captured, and the following account of the tragedy by an eye-witness appeared in the "Evening Post," a Democratic daily of Vicksburg, Miss.
"When the two negroes were captured, they were tied to trees, and while the funeral pyres were being prepared they were forced to suffer the most fiendish tortures. The blacks were forced to hold out their hands while one finger at a time was chopped off. The fingers were distributed as souvenirs. The ears of the murderers were cut off. Holbert was beaten severely, his skull was fractured, and one of his eyes, knocked out with a stick, hung by a shred from the socket. Neither the man nor the woman begged for mercy, nor made a groan or plea. When the executioner came forward to lop off fingers, Holbert extended his hand without being asked. The most excruciating form of punishment consisted in the use of a large corkscrew in the hands of some of the mob. This instrument was bored into the flesh of the man and the woman, in the arms, legs and body, and then pulled out, the spirals tearing out big pieces of raw, quivering flesh every time it was withdrawn. Even this devilish torture did not make the poor brutes cry out. When finally they were thrown on the fire and allowed to be burned to death, this came as a relief to the maimed and suffering victims."[45]

Finally, the Collins Commercial, a Mississippi newspaper, tells of a lynching of a black man near Centerville for murder in October 1906.

"Lynched for Foul Crime"
Thomas Crompton, a Negro, was lynched near Centerville by a posse of several hundred citizens, to whom he confessed the murder of Eli Whitaker.

M. Whitaker had some trouble with the negro about rent cotton. The next day, Mr. Whitaker had occasion to ride through the negro's field and caught him stealing corn. He attempted to interfere, when the Negro stuck him, knocking him down and then killed him with a chunk of wood. After killing him the negro dragged his body out into the woods and hid it. That night the negro went into the woods, where he had the remains hidden, and taking an ax and mule with him, cut off both the dead man's legs, stuffed the body in a sack and carried it off several miles on the mule into the woods and buried it in a sink hole, covering it up and placing brush over the place.

Being suspected, the Negro was placed under examination and cross-questioned. After some evidence was found at his house he broke down and confessed the whole crime, telling the horrible story from beginning to end and telling where the remains were hidden.

The community was shocked and horrified as it was never before, and men gathered from miles around. The negro was quietly taken to the scene of his crime, where he was lynched by several hundred determined men.[46]

Collectively, it should be observed that of the 152 Mississippi lynchings of the decade, and of the four cases examined here, these are but a short summary of the hundreds of lynching events, across the state of Mississippi from the 1860s to 1909, and after. The events suggest, as the work of Ida B. Wells-Barnett demonstrates, "that most victims were successful small businessmen whose only crime was to challenge the social order; rape was alleged only against a third of them."[47]

In addition to the lynching events mentioned in this chapter, Mississippi blacks also had to contend, during this period, with the whitecapping violence which plagued several counties, most noticeably Amite, Franklin, and Lincoln, in Southwestern Mississippi, between 1902 and 1906.[48] One scholar describes this period:

Because they were bitter against lien merchants and absentee landowners who rented to and financed black tenant farmers, whites took to "whitecapping"—a Lower South term for nightriding violence. The Whitecappers wanted to control the blacks and strike out at town businessmen who seemed to manipulate rural affairs. County whites were frightened by the very presence of black landholders and renters without local white "supervision," and they were also angry when merchant-planters used black laborers on their plantations, "depriving" resident white farmers of labor. James K. Vardaman probably encouraged Whitecapper vengeance by his virulent 1903 gubernatorial campaign but, once in the seat of power, he hired Pinkerton detectives and helped to subvert and destroy the movement.[49]

In 1904 the *Voice of the Negro* noted a special event in Mississippi: a black man was saved from a lynching in the state. The *Voice of the Negro* reported:

A lynching was on the program at Batesville, Miss., February 27, for the evening's entertainment of the rabble. Invitations had been sent out freely and it appeared that His Excellence, the Governor, who had hitherto openly sanctioned lynchings, was semi-officially notified of the occasion and probably invited to participate. The matter was made so public, New York and London being notified hours ahead of time, that Vardaman decided to prevent the lynching and thereby earned the plaudits from civilization for one decent act. He ordered out a company of militia and taking a special train, saved the Negro. This ought to make Governor Herrick of Ohio feel like voluntarily going to jail for five years. There is nothing to make us believe that Vardaman values a Negro's life at all. Either his conscious smote him when he thought of the mischief his vile campaign speeches had stirred up or he was tired of such severe criticisms both north and south and wanted some praise. But whether it was a side show or a pricking conscience, the result is very commendable. It saved Mississippi from another exhibition of savagery. But a governor who can, during his canvass for election, promise the poor whites if elected to close the school house doors against Negro children, take away the horses and top buggies from Negro citizens and degrade the Negroes in every way possible, and who even now vetoes a bill to give a Negro school at Holly Springs a little appropriation, sending the bill back with the mendacious assertion that education does the Negro no good—such a man ought to be willing to have one decent act recorded to his credit while he lives.[50]

Such events were rare indeed in Mississippi.[51]

People during this period were surprised to discover that black lynch mobs completed a few lynchings in Mississippi. The following article notes this fact:

"Negro Necktie Party—Blacks Lynch One of Their Own Color for Usual Offense"
Cleveland, Miss., December 11
One of the most quiet and unique little necktie parties every pulled off in the Delta occurred at Boyle at an early hour last night, when Jim Green, a laborer on the Starkey Taylor plantation, was strung up by men of his own race. The crime for which he paid the penalty with his life was the criminal assault of a little girl about 8 years old, living on the same place. The assault of the child took place on the 8th, the brute making his escape.

He was captured by Negroes at Shaw, Miss., and was being brought to Cleveland for the purpose of being lodged in jail when they were met by a quiet and orderly posse of negroes. The prisoner was taken away from them and hanged to a tree limb, within a few hundred feet of where Negro Lewis Scott was strung up on the night of the 6th.[52]

Mississippi blacks seem to have been especially upset over the abuse of children, or extremely disturbing murders committed by blacks on other blacks, or of whites on blacks.

The responses to the lynching crisis in Mississippi for the period 1900–1909 were varied, depending on whether or not one was a resident of Mississippi or lived outside of the state. I. A. Newby reminds us, however, just what black Mississippians—for that matter, blacks elsewhere in the United States—were up against in the early twentieth century:

The summary of Southern attitudes published in 1914 by Dr. Thomas Pearce Bailey, Dean of the Department of Education and professor of psychology and education in the University of Mississippi, is illustrative. In one of the racists' best and most literate commentaries on Negroes and racial problems, Race Orthodoxy in the South, Bailey offered a succinct and comprehensive statement of his section's racial creed. Included were the following points: "blood will tell"; "the negro is inferior and will remain so"; "this is a white man's country"; "no social equality"; "no political equality"; "in matters of civil rights and legal adjustments give the white man, as opposed to the colored man, the benefit of the doubt, and under no circumstances interfere with the prestige of the white race"; "in educational policy let the negro have the crumbs that fall from the white man's table"; "let there be such industrial education of the negro as will best fit him to serve the white man"; "only Southerners understand the negro question"; "the status of peasantry is all the negro may hope for, if the races are to live together in peace"; "let the lowest white man count for more than the highest negro"; and "the above statements indicate the leanings of Providence."

These ideas, stated above in their simplest form, constituted the core of anti–Negro thought in the South and motivated the Southerner's determination to preserve white supremacy. But, and this is equally important, it was a core of ideas to which non–Southerners also generally subscribed.

Non-Southerners, of course, never gave the Negro as much attention as did Southerners, and they never so readily took action against the race. Yet they generally accepted the South's racial views, acquiesced in its racial policies, and shared its determination that white supremacy be maintained. They also did much to develop, elucidate, and reinforce anti–Negro thought. Without this, the rigid subordination of Negroes could never have occurred or endured so tenaciously.[53]

For Mississippi and the South, lynching was this region's business. Of course most black Mississippians did not view the issue this way—especially since most of the lynching victims were black. Many African-Americans in Mississippi turned to their own churches for support against this crime and called upon the governors of Mississippi and other state leaders, including white Christians and ministers, to aid them in helping to end lynchings. Such efforts by blacks largely brought only silence from the white community—and more lynchings continued to occur in Mississippi.[54]

Black women of this period continued their efforts to promote public discussion of lynchings, and to advance the rights of black women in Mississippi and America. But, like black men, they were up against not only white men, but many white women and their organizations as well, including white women's suffrage societies. As Marjorie Spruill Wheeler observes, this was a negative period as far as black rights and needs were appreciated by both white men and women.[55] Thus, black Mississippians had to fight on, against the odds, and take the long view—that a better day for blacks would come in the future, after years of struggle and hard work.[56]

During the years 1900–1909 black Mississippians had to turn their attention outside of Mississippi for any real support to address the lynching crisis in the state. The historical record reveals one name that stands above all others during these years in the struggle to end American lynching: Ida B. Wells-Barnett. No one was more active than Barnett in raising hell about the lynching problem in Mississippi, the South, and the nation. She continued to write about lynching in American publications, to lecture, and to organize and serve in black organizations. Her service included aid in the organization of the NAACP in 1909; an international anti-lynching campaign to bring world-wide attention (and pressure to bear on the United States) on lynching; aid in establishing in 1896 of the National Association of Colored Women; work in the Chicago black women's clubs (Alpha Suffrage Club, 1913; and in Chicago's Negro Fellowship League).[57] According to Gail Bederman, Wells was a success in the anti-lynching campaign because of her ability to correctly analyze the lynching phenomenon, based on a study of race, gender, and class issues among the American people.[58]

National American opinion on the problem of lynching was mixed in the years 1900–1909. At the presidential level, William McKinley and Theodore Roosevelt served for most of this period as the leaders of the country. While McKinley was less active on black issues than Theodore Roosevelt, a historical consciousness emerged that Theodore Roosevelt's policy on blacks was based on "political necessity,"[59] in other words to secure the president's re-election to office in 1904. Yet lynching remained a national problem. Many blacks believed that President McKinley was too silent on the problem of lynching, and did not offer Americans an effective response, either in Mississippi or the rest of the nation.[60]

President Theodore Roosevelt was forced by the press of national and international events to deal more with black concerns. For one thing, this period brought a major growth in United States colonies and expansion abroad, while worsening race relations continued to occur at home.[61] In general, blacks had to make a way for themselves, by themselves; they could not depend on the Republican party.[62] On the direct problem of lynching, Roosevelt appears to have been of a divided perspective on the issue. One scholar notes: "Roosevelt, like many whites of his day, had mixed feelings about lynchings. At times he could interpret it as a rough form of popular justice, an inevitable corrective to the failings of the formal criminal justice system."[63] On the other hand, Lewis L. Gould found that while Roosevelt felt "the gravest alarm over the growth of lynching in this country, he warned black Americans that they must see that black criminals were legally punished so that lynching would not be necessary."[64] Thus, Roosevelt's position did not help to create a public policy against lynching and the problem only increased in the years ahead.

Booker T. Washington remained the major black leader in the United States during this period. He did speak out against lynching, but with a soft voice, given his philosophy of trying to work with the white South. Washington's task was a difficult one: to speak out against an injustice that greatly impacted his people, while always remembering to protect the interests of Tuskegee Institute.[65]

The major black intellectual to emerge from this period, W. E. B. Du Bois, was also forced to face the challenge that the lynching crisis placed on black Americans. Since Du Bois worked at Atlanta University, in Georgia, he had firsthand experience on the problem of American racism and the issue of lynching, including violence and race riots in Atlanta and the South. In fact, Du Bois would go on to play a major role in the efforts of Americans to end lynching in the coming decades of the twentieth century.[66]

American Jews, who suffered greatly in the Untied States due to anti–Semitism, also had an interest in the American problem of lynching.[67] As a minority group, Jews were aware of the significant number of lynching victims in the country, and to issues of general discrimination against many Americans, including Jews.[68] Furthermore, blacks could depend on some degree of seriousness on black concerns, and especially the problem of lynching, in the Yiddish press. One study notes, "For the most part, the Yiddish newspapers represented Black people as victims of racist oppression, focusing on the history of American slavery and racial violence."[69] In 1909, a small number of American Jews were supportive in helping blacks establish the National Association for the Advancement of Colored People.[70] This organization became one of the major African-American organizations active in the campaign to end lynching in this country. Therefore such American Jewish aid helped to make a difference in the long struggle to end lynching and to bring other much needed reforms to American life.

Clearly, by 1900–1909, African-Americans in Mississippi and the South were faced with a system of profound "psychic sources of racism," which were radically intractable and bound to exist for many years, even decades into the twentieth century.[71] The central problem lay in the fact that, as Joel R. Williamson observes, "in the 1890s [and after] in the South, a black man was lynched about every third day. Lynchings were not secret. On the contrary, they were very public. They were widely advertised in advance and widely reported. Often, thousands attended as railroad companies ran special trains into the vicinity."[72] Indeed, blacks in Mississippi were faced with a special challenge since their state was the leading lynching state in the country and, as Philip S. Foner has noted: "While legal emancipation had been made a fact in the United States, lynchings, peonage, and persecution of all kinds had reduced the Negro to a state of semislavery."[73] Thus, as the issues of black political, social and economic rights were curtailed in Mississippi and the South, blacks also had to contend with fear and the psychological consequences of living in a radically racist society.[74] Scholars have long noted that the opening decade of the twentieth century was also a time of tremendous growth in racist literature, of all kinds, on blacks and other minorities in American life. This body of work had major political, social and economic consequences for blacks and other groups, and was a dagger in the heart of improved race relations in America.[75]

In essence, during the years 1900–1909, the lynching crisis continued unabated in Mississippi and at least 152 citizens of the state were lynched. Surely justice was not served in

Mississippi. In fact, just the opposite took place—an unjust system continued, with dire consequences for blacks and other victims of lynch mobs. It was a time, as Lawrence M. Friedman describes it, when "the Southern lynch mobs were the most savage and the least excusable of all the self-help groups. Their law and order was naked racism, no more. Their real complaint against the law was that the courts were too careful and too slow; that some guilty prisoners went free; and that the lesson for the rest of the blacks was not sharp enough."[76]

Perhaps Paul Laurence Dunbar best captures the spiritual and physical dilemma facing black Mississippians in the early years of the twentieth century in his poem, "Lead Gently, Lord," written in 1895:

> Lead gently, Lord, and slow,
> For oh, my steps are weak,
> And ever as I go,
> Some soothing silence speak;
> That I may turn my face
> Through doubt's obscurity
> Toward thine abiding-place,
> E'en tho' I cannot see.
> For lo, the way is dark;
> Through mist and cloud I grope,
> Save for that fitful spark,
> The little flame of hope.
> Lead gently, Lord, and slow,
> For fear that I may fall;
> I know not where to go
> Unless I hear thy call
> My fainting soul doth yearn
> For thy green hills afar;
> So let thy mercy burn—
> My greater, guiding star![77]

6

The Era of World War I, 1910–1919

Mississippi entered the new decade of 1910–1919 with an increase in its population base, from 1,551,270 in 1900 to 1,797,114 in 1910. Blacks composed 56.2 percent of Mississippi's population in 1910, a gain of 11.2 percent from 1900. In 1910 the state contained 786,111 whites, 1,253 Choctaws (Native Americans), and several hundred Chinese Americans. The rural component consisted of 88.5 percent, while the urban sectors of the state represented only 11.5 percent (or 207,311) of the people.[1] Mississippi only had 29 urban locations in 1910.[2]

Economic matters were harsh for black Mississippians in the period 1910–1919. In general, according to Colin A. Palmer: "In 1910, 90 percent of rural blacks were either sharecroppers, tenants, or contract laborers. Wracked by poverty and disease, men and women had a life expectancy of thirty-three years."[3] Against this general background, of course, stood the Jim Crow system and its continuing impact as expressed in the segregationist policies of Mississippi and the South. By the decade of the 1910s, every aspect of economic, political and social life in Mississippi and the South was covered by the Jim Crow doctrine. In economic matters this also meant that "in the South it remained difficult for Negroes to find occupations outside agriculture and personal service. Most forms of wage labor were preempted by white workers, and the southern trade unions were mostly hostile to the Negroes."[4]

And, in some jobs, blacks were given no peace, even at work. One author notes, "The displacement of black labor was sometimes achieved by 'dramatic processes.' In Mississippi, for example, 'seven blacks were murdered, seven wounded, and one flogged because they held jobs as firemen on a division of the Illinois Central Railroad.'"[5] Under such extreme conditions, a small but growing black middle class continued to function during this decade in Mississippi. As in the past, it was largely composed of doctors, lawyers, teachers, ministers, and owners of small businesses. The segregated market in Mississippi meant that this group, for the most part, served black Mississippians. All-black towns, such as Mound Bayou, were service centers for some of this group, as were the 20 or so largest towns in Mississippi.[6]

Leaders among the black middle class in Mississippi during 1910–1919 included Charles Banks, a banker at Mound Bayou, who established the Mississippi Negro Business League; Louis Kossuth Arwood, of Jackson, a lawyer and businessperson who organized the Southern Bank of Mississippi and the Union Guaranty and Insurance Company, and served as chief executive officer of each (Atwood owned personal property valued at $65,000); and Mrs. R. S. Lewis of Greenville, who established a charity hospital in her native city to aid African-Americans.[7] These individuals and thousands of others kept a light burning in the quest for the advancement of the African-American in Mississippi during a period of continued hardship.

Due to extreme conditions, many blacks sought to escape the burdens of "the Mississippi way of life," and migrated either to other Southern states with less violent climates and better economic opportunities, or entirely away from the South by moving to the North or West. Stewart E. Tolnay and E. M. Beck note the conditions for this major migration from such states as Mississippi in the period 1910–1919: "The forces contributing to the northward migration of blacks during the early part of the twentieth century are relatively familiar. Northern industries, faced with the loss of immigrant workers because of World War I and subsequent restrictive legislation, 'pulled' blacks from the South by paying attractive wages. Concurrently, social and economic conditions in the South were pushing blacks out. Blacks were locked into the bottom stratum of the southern plantation system of agricultural production."[8]

Mississippi lost 130,000 blacks between the years 1910 and 1920, while in the entire South for the decade, 454,000 blacks left the region.[9] Often Mississippi blacks wrote to northern black newspapers, such as the *Chicago Defender*, for relief. Their letters to the editors of papers outside of the state are another indication of the hazardous conditions facing black Mississippians in the First World War years.[10] White Mississippians, in general, did not wish to see an important labor and working force leave the state. But there were mixed white responses to black migration.[11] Pressure and violence was sometimes used by Southern whites in an attempt to stop black migration from Mississippi. Historian Neil R. McMillen notes that "many communities adopted antienticement ordinances, and labor agents generally received rough treatment from the law. In Greenville, police entered northbound trains, dragging off departing workers and ordering other blacks not to board. In Hattiesburg and Jackson departing blacks were arrested."[12]

Yet, in spite of the ability of some blacks to leave the state, many others were trapped on the farms and plantations of Mississippi. In fact, by 1910 the number of black farmers in Mississippi totaled 164,488. By 1920 this number would decline to 161,001.[13] As late as 1900, 59 percent of the cotton cultivated in Mississippi was produced by blacks; the other 41 percent was produced by whites.[14] A central theme from the past defined the lives of black and white sharecroppers in Mississippi: poverty and hard times.[15] This economic condition was a major key in understanding life in Mississippi for the 1910s.[16]

Black Mississippi women were faced with all of the hardship issues of the day, but also had to endure political inequality (no right to vote or hold office), difficulties because of gender discrimination, and the ageless problems growing out of their race (racism). As on the national scene, black women in Mississippi were very active between 1910 and 1919 in continuing to organize themselves on the local and state levels. This work included Mississippi chapters of the National Association of Colored Women, which by 1909 had created units in twenty states.[17] Such efforts were essential in advancing the black family, the black church, the community's concerns about youth, and the educational needs of blacks during the decade under study.

Social relations in Mississippi were defined, almost in stone, by the Age of Segregation and its twin, the Jim Crow system.[18] Social relations in Mississippi and the South—and much of the nation for that matter—were centered around white supremacy, and separate but unequal social opportunities for black Americans. The end result of social segregation was a public policy, by law and custom, which greatly impacted upon the daily lives of black Mississippians. For example, they could not use public conveniences such as hotels, restaurants, libraries and swimming pools; and on public transportation systems, they were generally segregated, or forced to occupy the back sections of certain trains.[19] The system was turned against them and their human rights.

So blacks continued to turn inward, in an effort to develop their own small businesses, social outlets, and other interests.[20] Yet they still faced special challenges and none were more severe than education. For one thing they were up against some white Mississippi politicians such as James K. Vardaman who even questioned the need for black education and determined that state tax dollars should not be used to fund black schools.[21] This was the state of affairs in Mississippi in spite of the fact that 259,438 Mississippians, or 35.6 percent of the student population in the state, were illiterate in 1910. Blacks in Mississippi were a majority of the state's population, but during this period public funds went to support 31 four-year high schools for white students only.[22] A small number of black students could attend the high school division at black-public-supported Alcorn College, or at other private black schools in the state for an additional cost to their families.[23] A report on black education for this period tells a sorrowful tale:

> Mississippi—The Negro population of this State in 1910 was 1,009,487; the number of secondary pupils was 934; the Baptists form about 68 percent of the total church membership and the Methodists about 30 per cent. Tougaloo College and Rust College are the only institutions with facilities to offer work of junior college grade. The enrollment of these schools above the elementary grades is 237 of whom 28 are in college classes. Of those reporting home address, 34 are from the places in which the schools are located, 154 are from other parts of the State, and 30 from other states.[24]

Nationally, according to W. E. B. Du Bois, "In 1910, not more than 5,000 Negroes were in college."[25] Such problems as these were the educational handicaps facing the African American people in the 1910s.

And yet, as elsewhere in the black world, black Mississippians struggled onward. For faith they turned to African American churches and black preachers. Here was a world, observes C. Eric Lincoln, where "their organizational and political skills were in that context second only to their spiritual gifts in importance. The fledgling black churches they led had no secure financial base and no managerial talent except that developed under the leadership of the black preachers whose life experience was most often limited to the plantation routine. But they did have spirit, and they did have staying power."[26]

For medical services between 1910 and 1920, black Mississippians could turn to 66 African American physicians.[27] Black Mississippi doctors were organized through the Mississippi Medical and Surgical Association, active in the state since 1900.[28] Of course Mississippi's system of segregation placed black doctors and their patients at a disadvantage; drawbacks included not being able to practice in white hospitals, an inability to join local county medical societies and no chance to continue advanced training.[29] Nevertheless, black doctors in Mississippi were a first line of defense against disease and health problems facing black people in this decade.[30]

For communicating with each other and the outside world, black Mississippians produced 51 commercial newspapers between 1900 and 1919, along with 21 fraternal organs, fifteen religious newspapers and ten educational journals.[31] Like all black institutions in Mississippi, these organs had to safeguard their voices by always being observant of the mores of Jim Crow. Nonetheless they offered their communities an outlet to the world, and generally a perspective of uplift and hope for a better tomorrow. However, they existed during a period when even the federal government took a special interest in their operations. For example, during World War I, black newspapers were closely watched for their attitudes toward the war, the role of the United States in the conflict, and the patriotism of black Americans for the allied powers.[32]

Black lawyers were another element among black Mississippians who played an interesting role in the life of the community during the 1910s. From a high of 26 black lawyers in the state in 1890, there were only 14 active by 1920.[33] Many had migrated away from Mississippi, since legal conditions for black lawyers were harsh in the state, and they had a difficult time making a living as a lawyer under the Jim Crow system.[34] But some stayed on in Mississippi and helped to make a difference in the struggles of their communities.

Indeed, this decade was an extreme period in black life, both in Mississippi and the nation. Perhaps historian Benjamin Quarles best captures the social scene of the era: "To blacks the opening two decades of the 1900s seemed to have brought a rise in the level of white hostility. Jim Crow seemed more securely enthroned than ever, with residential segregation more widespread, and with the Supreme Court in 1908 upholding a Kentucky law which forbade interracial schools. The early years of the Woodrow Wilson presidency, beginning in 1913, witnessed the establishment of the color line in various departments of the federal government."[35] Thus, everywhere that black Mississippians looked in 1910–1919, they found a world of oppression against black interests. Their special circumstances demanded that they face the future with determination and strength, and indeed, they would need all of their courage and more to face the coming events of the Age of Lynching in Mississippi.

The political fortunes of black Mississippians were crippled by Mississippi's Jim Crow system in the years 1910–1919. Pete Daniel observes what this process meant:

> The Mississippi legislature led the way in writing blacks out of power; it embodied the radical spirit. Small farmers of the hills and herders and lumbermen of the piney woods united against conservative Delta planters, who had maintained political control by manipulating the convention system. In 1902, Mississippi replaced this elite-dominated system with a primary. Blacks could not belong to the Democratic Party, nor could whites who failed to meet registration requirements. Yet whites who could register had a voice in the election of officials which had been denied them under the convention system, and this meant that politicians had to canvas voters in earnest. Since the plantation-dominated Delta counties had proportionately fewer whites, their ability to offer candidates for statewide and federal offices was lessened. The primary brought candidates face to face with voters and often with each other. Rural folk flocked to the county seats for the spectacle.[36]

The key task for white Mississippians remained: prevent blacks from voting. Indeed, as Arthur S. Link and William B. Catton note, during this era "the social and political status of blacks worsened by and large."[37] But poor whites also suffered a loss of political status in Mississippi and the South. Gabriel Kolko points out that "by educational property qualifications and grandfather clauses the blacks and poor whites were removed from politics. Mississippi disfranchised 70 percent of its electorate by 1892."[38]

Throughout Mississippi and the South, "A system of 'white primaries' excluded blacks from voting in Democratic primaries and conventions, which in practice denied them any influence in the South."[39]

Such political pressures forced blacks to organize, on local, state and national levels. One major effort resulted in the creation in 1909–1910 of the NAACP. The bi-racial group in New York City developed into an activist organization designed to protect the political, economic, and social oppression of blacks and other groups in American society.[40] In Mississippi the first chapter of the NAACP was created in 1917 at Vicksburg.[41] This branch grew slowly during its early years, but over time would come to play a major role in the struggle for advancing African-American civil rights in the state.

The political rights of black women remained a concern during this period. As a group black women had no legal right to vote in any U.S. election. But, like white women, blacks also struggled to advance women's suffrage during this period.[42] During the years 1910–1919, politics in Mississippi remained largely the business of white men.

Black Mississippians took a special interest in the major international event of the decade, World War I (1914–1919). The United States entered the war in 1917, and blacks played a major role in the struggle in spite of the segregation which they faced in the U.S. armed forces. As Neil R. McMillen points out, black Mississippians "contributed disproportionately to the state's conscript quotas—supplying 52 percent of Mississippi's draft registrants and 56 percent of its inductees" while nationally some 367,410 blacks served the country.[43] The war had a tremendous impact on black thinking. It signaled to many blacks that if they could fight abroad for the Four Freedoms of Europeans, then their own oppression at home must be addressed by society. This radical new spirit took hold of black America. The situation was a very volatile one and, as Paul Johnson notes: "The end of World War One, in which blacks had fought in large numbers, often with courage and distinction, and sustained heavy losses, drew attention to the fact that the Fourteenth and Fifteenth Amendments (1868–1870), constitutionally designed to give blacks, or at any rate black males, legal equality, had not succeeded in doing so though an entire generation had passed since their adoption. In the South blacks had actually lost ground, as a result both of unlawful activities by the white majority and of legal decisions."[44]

In essence, what black Mississippians and blacks nationally found after World War I was a return to the same old business of Jim Crow and segregation in the South. Little had changed in white thinking since the war.[45] The turning point came in 1919, as thousands of black soldiers returned to the United States from Europe. Many blacks suffered beatings and even death at the hands of some whites in the nation, but especially in the South.[46] Gail Buckley notes the violence of the national white response to blacks: "Seventy-eight blacks were lynched in 1919; ten were veterans, several of whom were lynched in uniform. By the end of the year, there had been race riots in twenty-eight cities, North and South."[47] Meanwhile in Mississippi, according to Neil R. McMillen, "violence" remained the watchword for the treatment of blacks.[48]

Black Mississippians found that little change took place in their lives, for the period 1910–1919, in terms of Mississippi's criminal justice system and its response to black people in the state. Like all aspects of life in Mississippi, justice was the concern of white Mississippians, and the first order of business during this decade was for whites to make sure that blacks understood this point. No institution in the state served to bring this realization home quicker to blacks than Parchman Prison, the state penitentiary, established in 1904.[49] By 1913, Mississippi's total prison inmate population consisted of 156 whites and 1,708 blacks.[50] Such numbers reflected the fact that Mississippi justice was established to keep blacks in their place. Overall, according to David M. Oshinsky, "blacks comprised about 90 percent of the prison population" at Parchman in the early 1900s.[51] Added to the situation at Parchman was the problem of peonage, which was especially a concern in the Mississippi Delta counties, and the turpentine areas of southern Mississippi. Pete Daniel describes this world as one in which "peons existed at the core of concentric circles of oppression, their entire world circumscribed by exploiters. Defrauded of their wages and deprived of mobility either by threats that they could not legally move until their debts were paid or by actual force, they lived in the vortex of peonage."[52] Thus, whether in court, prison, or trapped in peonage, black Mississippians understood that Mississippi justice did not have their security or interests in mind, as the state's criminal justice system continued its white supremacy mode during the 1910s.

Scholars have noted the tremendous impact of lynching in the United States between the 1880s and the 1910s. The totals given vary according to the writer in question. But all point out the large numbers of Americans who were killed during this forty-year period. The following data is illustrative of the range of the problem.

1. *The South Atlantic Quarterly* (July 1919)
   1889–1918   3,224 lynchings
                            [390 or 12.1% in the North and West]
                            [2,834 or 87.9% in the South]

2. *Teacher's Resource Manual* (1992)
   1889–1918   3,010 lynchings
                            [2,604 in the former slave states]
                            [1 in New England states—Maine]
                            [160 in the Western states]
                            [246 in other states]

3. *American Eras* (1997)
   1882–1903   2,552 lynchings in 15 Southern states
                            [1,985 blacks]
                            [567 whites]

4. NAACP (1919)
   1889–1918   3,224 lynchings
                            [2,522 blacks]
                            [702 whites][53]

Scholars Lee Sigelman and Susan Welch have observed that from the late nineteenth century to the decade following 1910 there was, in fact, a decline in lynching in this country, but still the great burdens of the crisis continued from decade to decade. However, it should be noted: "During the 1890s, about 100 lynchings took place annually, declining to about 80 in the 1900s and between 55 and 60 in the 1910s."[54] The tone of the era is captured by Manning Marable: "Violence against African-Americans was endemic to the Jim Crow segregated South. Between 1884 and 1917 more than 3,600 African-Americans were lynched across the South."[55]

This national situation was reflected worst of all in Mississippi, which had the highest totals for lynching victims from the 1880s to the 1910s: the problem was historic, and deep in the consciousness (or lack thereof) of white Mississippians and many other whites in American life. Michael R. Belknap points out, "The essence of the problem was that in the South whites could maim and kill deviant or assertive blacks, with impunity because their race controlled the criminal justice system."[56] Yet the tragedy of the period continued, and in Mississippi the range of lynching victims for 1910 to 1919 reached 107, including at least 91 blacks, 2 whites, and 14 unknown victims by race, but, most likely these latter victims were also black Americans (see Table 6.1). Nationally during the decade, 681 people were lynched. Five hundred sixty-three were black lynch victims, 53 were whites and 65 were unknown by race.[57] Three years stand out for high national lynching totals during the 1910s: the years 1910, with 90 victims, 1915 with 96 cases, and 1919 with 83 casualties. These high numbers

TABLE 6.1: LYNCHING VICTIMS, 1910–1919

YEAR	National				Mississippi			
	Total	Black	White	Unknown	Total	Black	White	Unknown
1910	90	67	9	14	5	5		
1911	71	60	7	4	5	5		
1912	64	61	2	1	11	8		3
1913	48	47	1	0	18	17		1
1914	54	50	4	0	21	19		2
1915	96	56	13	27	15	7	1	7
1916	58	50	4	4	3	3		
1917	50	36	2	12	2	1		
1918	67	60	4	3	7	7		
1919	83	76	7	0	20	19	1	
TOTALS	681	563	53	65	107	91	2	14

TABLE 6.2: BLACK LYNCHING VICTIMS BY COUNTY IN MISSISSIPPI, 1910–1919

County	Number of Victims	County	Number of Victims	County	Number of Victims
Adams	1	Jones	1	Pike	1
Attala	2	Kemper	3	Quitman	3
Bolivar	4	Lafayette	1	Simpson	1
Chickasaw	2	Lauderdale	2	Stone	1
Clarke	4	Leflore	1	Sunflower	5
Clay	5	Lowndes	2	Tate	2
Coahoma	3	Marion	5	Tishomingo	1
Copiah	2	Marshall	2	Tunica	3
Desoto	5	Monroe	3	Warren	4
Hinds	2	Newton	1	Washington	4
Holmes	11	Noxubee	3	Winston	5
Humphreys	2	Oktibbeha	3	Yazoo	1
Issaquena	1	Panola	2	TOTAL	107
Jefferson	2	Pearl River	1		

TABLE 6.3: BLACK WOMEN LYNCHING VICTIMS IN MISSISSIPPI, 1910–1919

Year	Name	Place	Cause
1914	Jennie Collins	Bolivar County	Alleged to have aided the escape of an accused murderer
1914	Mrs. Jane Sullivan	Byhalial, Marshall County	Arson (Nov. 24, 1914)
1915	Mrs. Cordella Stevenson	Columbus, Lowndes Co.	Alleged arson (Dec. 10, 1915)
1918	Alma House	Clarke County	Murder
1918	Maggie House	Shubuta, Clarke County	Suspected of murder

TABLE 6.4: WHITE MISSISSIPPI LYNCHING VICTIMS BY COUNTY AND YEAR, 1910–1919

Name	County	Date	Cause
Jack Hughes	Marion	1915	Murder
Charles Lanceskes	Warren	1919	Unknown

can be associated with the Great Migration and the tensions associated with World War I. In Mississippi the worst years were 1913 with 18 victims, 1914 with 21 cases, and 1919 with 20 casualties. Mississippi's impact with lynching cases is similar to the national scope during this period, and is especially highlighted with the brutal year of 1919, a year after the end of the war.

Lynching events took place in at least forty of Mississippi's counties between 1910 and 1919. This number represented half of Mississippi's 82 counties in the early twentieth century. From Tables 6.2 (page 65) and 6.6 it is clear that seventeen counties contained the largest number of known lynching victims for the decade. The Delta region leads the list with eight counties and twenty-eight victims, followed by East Mississippi with seven counties and twenty-six cases, and South Mississippi with two counties and nine victims. East Mississippi, with a smaller black population than the Delta region, has almost as many lynching cases as does the more populous Delta. Perhaps the greater economic difficulties of whites in East Mississippi led to significant attacks against blacks as scapegoats for the hardships of the period.[58]

Black men were the dominant victims of lynch mobs during this decade, but at least five black women were also lynched, generally on an allegation of murder or arson (see Table 6.3). Three of the black women victims were lynched in Eastern Mississippi in Clarke and Lowndes counties, one in the Delta, Bolivar County, and the last in North Mississippi in Marshall County. As Table 6.4 notes, only two white males appear to have been lynched in Mississippi during the decade, both in South Mississippi, one in Marion County and the second in Warren County.

TABLE 6.5: MISSISSIPPI LYNCHING VICTIMS, RANGE AND PERCENTAGE OF OFFENSES ALLEGED, 1910–1919

Offense	Number	Percentage
Murder	53	54.0%
Unknown	21	21.0%
Rape/attempted rape	10	10.0%
Insulting or annoying a white woman	4	4.0%
Arson	3	3.0%
Poisoning well water	2	2.0%
Writing an insulting note	2	2.0%
Bit off man's chin	1	1.0%
Desperado	1	1.0%
Entered a woman's room	1	1.0%
Theft	1	1.0%
TOTAL	99	

TABLE 6.6: MISSISSIPPI COUNTIES WITH LARGEST NUMBER OF LYNCHING VICTIMS, 1910–1919

County	Number of Victims	County	Number of Victims	County	Number of Victims
Holmes	11	Bolivar	4	Monroe	3
Clay	5	Clarke	4	Noxubee	3
Desoto	5	Warren	4	Oktibbeha	3
Marion	5	Washington	4	Quitman	3
Sunflower	5	Coahoma	3	Tunica	3
Winston	5	Kemper	3		

A large percentage (54 percent) of the total number of Mississippi's lynch victims between 1910–1919 were accused of murder (53 victims). Ten victims (10 percent) were charged with rape during this period. Other causes that appear two or more times include: insulting or annoying a white man (4 cases or 4 percent), arson (3 victims or 3 percent), poisoning well water (2 cases or 2 percent), and writing an insulting note (2 cases or 2 percent). Thus, as Ida B. Wells-Barnett noted in the 1890s, rape was generally not the main reason for a Mississippi lynching.[59]

The data review is uneven on the months of lynchings for this decade. The months they occurred is unknown in over 55 percent of Mississippi lynchings (see Table 6.7). The

TABLE 6.7: MISSISSIPPI LYNCHINGS BY MONTH
AND SECTION OF STATE, 1910–1919

Month	Events	Percentage
January	3	3.0%
February	6	6.0%
March	1	1.0%
April	2	2.0%
May	4	4.0%
June	9	9.0%
July	3	3.0%
August	0	0.0%
September	4	4.0%
October	6	6.0%
November	5	5.0%
December	2	2.0%
Unknown	54	55.0%
TOTAL	99	

summer month of June has nine lynchings and fits the national pattern of most lynchings occurring in the warmer weather.[60]

The period of the 1910s remained a brutal era for lynching in Mississippi and the South. James S. Hirsch notes the nature of this crisis from the 1890s to beyond the decade under study in this chapter. He writes: "By the 1890s ... disenfranchisement and segregation prevailed, and the next forty years saw brutal battles between the blacks who resisted the new social order and the whites who used escalating violence to enforce it. Lynchings were the preferred instrument to crack down on 'uppity' Negroes, particularly those accused of raping white women. This unholy trinity of race, rape and the rope set off many confrontations in the South, [and] defined an era of oppression."[61] Certainly, hundreds died during the height of the crisis. Just how many may never be known. Paul Johnson observes that in the South, "this system of political exclusion was reinforced by terror. From 1882 to 1903 a total of 1,985 blacks were killed by Southern lynch mobs, most being hanged, some burned alive. And for a variety of offenses, real or imaginary."

Then there was the Ku Klux Klan.... Blacks went in fear of it even when they were not directly threatened by its custom of whipping, torturing, or even murdering its enemies.[62] In Mississippi and the South, as the Klan was reborn in 1915, this racist organization now "accepted only native-born, protestant whites and stressed anti-black, anti-Semitic, and anti-foreign attitudes with equal fervor."[63] Such conditions reflected a harsh environment for blacks in Mississippi. In 1919 the NAACP conducted an investigation of "Darkest Mississippi." The report tells a harrowing story on conditions in the state.

Dean William Pickens has said that it takes courage for a Negro to live in Mississippi. This is strictly true, especially of the Delta and of those parts of Louisiana and Arkansas adjacent to the Delta. The Northerner's first thought upon entering this territory for the first time is that he has gone from civilization to a frontier. It is not only because so many citizens carry guns—and use them—or because political thought is fifty years behind the rest of the world, or because archaic ideas of gentility and "manners" take the place of wide-awake intelligence which one expects of Americans[,] that this part of the South resembles a frontier.[64]

Five case studies of the lynching events in Mississippi for the period 1910–1919 are filled with the tragedy and terror of this lynching era.

Case Study One: 1914
Leland, Miss., February 24—Sam Petty, a Negro, accused of having killed a deputy sheriff, Charles W. Kirkland, was shot by a mob of 300 men tonight and his body burned.

Petty, wanted on a trivial charge, killed Kirkland with a shotgun when the officer entered a cabin late to-day in which the negro had taken refuge. Petty was captured by a posse, bound and placed in an oil-soaked dry-goods box and the match applied. A moment later the man, his clothing aflame, broke from his fastenings and started to run, but before he could gain headway was shot dead.

The body was put back in the box, fresh inflammables were piled about it, and within half an hour it was burned to ashes.[65]

Case Study Two: 1915
"Mississippi Mob Lynches a Negro"
Vicksburg, Miss., Jan. 20—Edward Johnson, a young negro, was taken from a deputy sheriff by a mob within the Vicksburg city limits today and lynched. He had been arrested and charged with stealing cattle.[66]

Case Study Three: 1916
Mrs. Cordelia Stevenson, whose son was accused of burning a white man's barn, was taken from her home, near Columbus, Miss., and hanged by a mob.[67]

Case Study Four: 1918
Lloyd Clay, a 22 year-old local black man in Vicksburg, Mississippi was arrested on a charge of attempted rape of a young white woman, Mattie Hudson. Historian J. William Harris describes what happened to him on May 14.

"The city's sheriff hustled Clay on to jail, hoping for a quick identification by Mattie Hudson, the alleged victim. Then the city could order a quick trial and conviction and hope to avoid a mob scene. The sheriff was no doubt disappointed when Hudson not once but twice failed to identify Clay in a line-up.

"If Lloyd Clay began to breathe more easily, his relief did not last long. Too many people in Vicksburg were wrought up, and hundreds of whites, convinced of Clay's guilt, gathered before the jail, determined to seize him and administer their own brand of justice. By the evening of May 14, the crowd had swelled to perhaps a thousand, but many of its members were drunk. Shortly before 8:00 p.m., they stormed the jail and seized Clay. Some of the men in the crowd dragged their victim out to the street while others went for Mattie Hudson. Clay strongly denied his guilt. Though at first 'loathe to identify him,' Hudson finally told the crowd 'that he was the guilty one.' In terror, Clay cried out, 'I'm the man. Give me a pistol and I'll blow my brains out.' Such a relatively painless death, however, would not satisfy the mob. They stripped Clay, poured oil over his body, put a rope around him, and hanged him from a tree at the side of the street. As the rope pulled taut, 'the sight of the nude body rising above the crowd increased the excitement.' A fire set below his feet lapped at his legs. Without a cry, he 'lifted his arms' and 'placed his palms together in an attitude of prayer.' Finally, many in the crowd began to fire their guns at him, and 'even women were seen to shoot revolvers.' In the wild firing, a white bystander was fatally struck with a bullet. The flesh of Lloyd Clay continued to burn—described in gory detail in local newspapers—after he was dead. Eventually, the body was cut down, and the crowd, in a 'hubbub of gloating,' rushed in to seize souvenirs."[68]

Case Study Five: 1918
"The Shubuta Lynchings"

On Friday night, December 20, four Negroes—Andrew Clark, age 15; Major Clark, age 20; Maggie Howze, age 20; and Alma Howze, age 16, were taken from the little jail at Shubuta, Mississippi, and lynched on a bridge which spans the Chickaswha River near the town. They were suspected of having murdered a Dr. E. L. Johnston, whom the papers stated was "a wealthy retired dentist." These were the meager facts as given in the press dispatches. The real facts in the case are as follows:

"Instead of being an old man Dr. Johnston was thirty-five years of age, a failure at his profession and living at the time of the lynchings on his father's farm where he had with him Maggie Howze whom he had seduced and who was about to bear him a child. On the same farm where Maggie's sister Alma, also a victim of Johnston, and two colored boys, Major and Andrew Clark who were working out a debt of their father's to the Johnstons. Major Clark began going with Maggie and they planned to marry. Dr. Johnston, hearing of this quarreled violently with Major Clark telling him to leave his woman alone. Matters were at this point when the doctor was killed early one morning near his barn.

"It is common gossip about Shubuta that the murder was committed by a white man who had his grudge against Johnston and who felt he could safely kill the dentist and have the blame fall on the Negro. At any rate, after subjecting the boy to extreme torture, a confession was secured from Major that he had committed the murder. At this preparations for the lynching began.

"Major and Andrew Clark, Maggie and Alma Howze had all been arrested. After Major's 'confession' they were taken to Shubuta for trial and placed in a little jail there. The mob secured the keys of the jail from the deputy sheriff in charge of the place without trouble, took out the prisoners, and drove them to the place chosen for their execution, a little covered bridge over the Chickaswhay River. Four ropes were produced and four ends were tied to a girder on the under side of the bridge, while the other four ends were made into nooses and fastened securely around the necks of the four Negroes, who were standing on the bridge. Up to the last moment the Negroes protested their innocence and begged the mob not to lynch them. Just as they were about to be killed, Maggie Howze screamed and fought, crying out, 'I ain't guilty of killing the doctor and you oughtn't to kill me.' In order to silence her cries one of the members of the mob seized a monkey wrench and struck her in the mouth with it, knocking her teeth out. She was also hit across the head with the same instrument, cutting a long gash. The four Negroes, when the ropes had been securely fastened about their necks, were taken bodily by the mob and thrown over the side of the bridge. The younger girl and the two boys were killed instantly. Maggie Howze, however, who was a strong and vigorous young woman, twice caught herself on the side of the bridge, thus necessitating her being thrown over the bridge three times. The third time this was done, she died. In the town the next day, members of the mob told laughingly of how hard it had been to kill 'that big black Jersey woman.'

"The older girl of twenty was to have become a mother in four months, while the younger was to have given birth to a child in two weeks. This sixteen-year-old prospective mother was killed on Friday night and at the time of her burial on Sunday afternoon her unborn baby had not died—one could detect its movements within her womb.

"A press dispatch from Shubuta the day after the lynching took place reads as follows: 'The theory is advanced that the lynchers acted because of the fact that the next term of the court was not due to be convened until next March. It is hinted that the idea of the county being forced to care for and feed four self-confessed assassins of a leading citizen might have aroused the passion of the mob.'"[69]

As historian Neil R. McMillen suggests, the years 1910–1919 occur in what he calls the second major "sustained period of peak mob activity in Jim Crow Mississippi ... with the uneasy years during and immediately following World War I," 1918–1922.[70] As the five case studies demonstrate, the violence was ugly, the terror unparalleled, men and women were killed, the very young and older adults, it did not matter, especially if one was black and accused of a crime by white Mississippians. White supremacy and racism combined in a deadly game to checkmate African-American rights in Mississippi. Yet this was also a period of black activity against lynching, and a struggle to advance black rights, which took place in Mississippi and throughout the nation.

Black communities in Mississippi were in a crisis mode of operation in the era 1910–1919. It was a period of one crisis after another, and especially by the intense demands brought on by World War I, in 1917–1919. Among the major urban centers for blacks during this period was Jackson, the state capital. Mike Alexander points out the significance of Jackson: "The Jackson Business Directory for 1913–14 '(colored)' lists 11 attorneys, four physicians, three dentists, two jewelers, two loan companies and a bank, as well as two hospitals for blacks and a large number of retail and service businesses. They included funeral homes, meat markets, bakeries, flower shops, furniture stores, tailors, restaurants and theaters.... People who grew up in the Parish Street district [a black section of Jackson] in the 1910s and 1920s talk fondly of a culture where respect for self and others was the rule. At school, discipline was strict and excellence was demanded. And children had role models to look up to in every walk of life."[71]

Such black communities as Jackson, Natchez, Vicksburg, Greenville, Meridian, Gulfport, and others, and the majority of the black population in the rural areas of Mississippi made a courageous stand, against great odds, in the 1910s, to advance the African-American people in their Mississippi communities. Indeed, the work of black professions such as teachers, lawyers, doctors, and others cannot be underestimated in assessing the response of blacks to conditions in Mississippi during the 1910s. *The Crisis* noted in 1919 that Principal William H. Holtzclaw, President of the Twelfth Annual Utica Negro Farmers' Conference, held at Utica Institute (Miss.), spoke for many when he said: "We are proud of our soldiers and their exploits, both white and black. We are proud of the record they made. I would call to the attention of the Negro soldier that his record in the present war is greatly appreciated by both whites and blacks throughout the country. Now I would appeal to him most earnestly not to besmirch his record, to come back home, lay aside his uniform, take up his old occupation or a new one, and show to the world that as in war he is a soldier, so in peace he is a citizen."[72]

Yet black soldiers, as all blacks in Mississippi society, faced hardships before leaving or returning to Mississippi. All had to take the long view of their struggle for justice in Mississippi and the South. A Hattiesburg case is revealing of the general difficulties of blacks during this period in Mississippi history. Karla F. C. Holloway observes, "Just before World War I, in Hattiesburg, Mississippi's black township, Piney Woods, Malachi Collins and E. W. Hall opened the county's first black funeral home. The event so aggravated Hattiesburg's white undertaker, who had had the embalming business of Piney Woods blacks, that he passed out handbills in the black community with the warning 'Don't patronize these niggers, we can give you better service.' Intimidation and threats followed, but 'Hall and Collins Funeral Home weathered the hostility and survived for many years.'"[73]

This incident suggests the tone of the period, and what blacks in the state were up against. Nevertheless, the black struggle continued onward. Dewey W. Grantham observes the service record of black organizations during this time: "A subtle alteration was discernible in the bearing and outlook of many black southerners, who had begun to demonstrate a new assertiveness and independence. In the postwar period evidence of the 'New Negro' could be found even in Mississippi, with the appearance of the state's first NAACP branch, the revival of the state Federation of Women's Clubs, and the efforts of race uplift groups such as the Committee of One Hundred. The riots of 1919, the new militancy among blacks, and the hostile reaction of many whites galvanized southern progressives into action."[74]

Certainly black Mississippians supported the NAACP. In 1918, *The Crisis* listed the Vicksburg branch as having 27 members. By 1919 this number had increased to 55.[75] Five black Mississippians (of 265 delegates) attended the tenth anniversary meeting of the NAACP in Cleveland, Ohio, in June 1919.[76] And by 1918, 522 Mississippians were subscribers to *The Crisis* which, at this point in its history, had a national circulation of 75,187 copies.[77] Such support helped to advance the efforts of the major national black organization, to promote the fight against lynching in Mississippi and the South. It was an eloquent contribution to a major issue impacting the black community.[78]

Members of the black press in Mississippi also kept the faith during the 1910s in getting the voice of black Mississippians out to the world. Editors and publishers of the period include John J. Morant, of a monthly organ *Black Man* at Vicksburg; E. B. Topp of the *New Light*, a Baptist Publication at Jackson; and individuals at sixty-four other papers in the state during 1910–1919.[79] This group had a very difficult job in covering all aspects of the news, given the white Mississippi surveillance of the black community in the 1910s. But they continued to do their jobs and to carry on in spite of the odds and psychological terror they faced during this era.[80]

Yet the pressures and the terror were so great that many blacks could only respond to lynching by leaving the state of Mississippi. In 1900–1910, 30,900 blacks departed Mississippi for other states; and between 1910 and 1920, another 129,600 voted with their bodies to migrate from Mississippi.[81] Eric Foner suggests that black Mississippians viewed leaving the state "in apocalyptic terms of a Second Emancipation ... of Cross[ing] over Jordan or leaving the realm of pharaoh for the Promised Land. One group of emigrants from Mississippi stopped when their train crossed the Ohio River to sing 'I am bound for the land of Canaan.'"[82] Many black Mississippians believed that migration was the best solution to their problems, if in the final analysis they could successfully escape from the state and find employment and other opportunities elsewhere. As noted earlier, many wrote to Northern black newspapers such as the *Chicago Defender* for support.[83] Others turned to the *Pittsburgh Courier*.[84] And then there was the issue of black self-defense against lynching in Mississippi. One case seems to note this phenomenon in Mississippi during this decade: "In June 1910, Jim Brady questioned his sharecropping account with his landlord. Whites flogged Brady for his insolence. A short time later a mob sought to lynch him. Brady and a group of black friends defended themselves in a shoot-out that left three blacks and one white killed."[85] Such incidents did not occur daily in Mississippi, but the fact that they took place at all is another indication of strengths which the black community, as individuals and as groups, brought to bear on their life circumstances and struggle for survival and advancement in the American Siberia of the 1910s.

By 1910–1919 racism and white supremacy were ingrained into the very fabric of white Mississippi society. Neale's *Monthly Magazine*, in 1913, seemed to capture this state of "race orthodoxy" in Mississippi and the South, when the organ published the "racial creed" of the South.[86] Such perspectives meant that many white Mississippians were either in agreement with the prevailing lynching psychology of the state or remained silent on such a controversial subject. But courage sometimes came to the forefront, even among white Mississippians, and anti-lynching actions or statements were evident during this decade. For example, one scholar notes that in late 1917 "even white Mississippians had formed a group, the Mississippi Welfare League, that opposed lynching."[87] But the fact remained that the vast majority of white Mississippians were not in this anti-lynching mode. Dwyn M. Mounger notes that this point of view extended from Reconstruction to World War I: "During the period from 1876 to 1918 many public officials and private citizens expressed open approval of lynching, although there was more opposition to the practice than in the Reconstruction era. Local and state government leaders often were indifferent to mob killings."[88]

Certainly major Mississippi politicians such as James Kimble Vardaman and Theodore G. Bilbo (governor of Mississippi, 1916–1920) were proactive in the lynching cause in Mississippi. One scholar notes that Vardaman "advocated" lynching, especially "in the case of Negro men who were believed to have raped white women—so long as the mobs lynched their victims as quickly and simply as possible."[89] Theodore G. Bilbo was "one of the most outspoken demagogues and race baiters in the South's history."[90] Such extremism continued to aid the pro-lynching elements in Mississippi during this historical period.

On the national scene, black Americans waged a renewed campaign to bring public and governmental attention and policy to bear on the lynching crisis facing the country. In the broad scheme of things, the *Crisis* viewed the national situation of blacks as calling for action in seven key areas:

1. Disfranchisement of educated Negroes in the South.
2. The "Jim Crow" car system by which we are compelled to pay first-class fares for third-class accommodations, and usually denial of Pullman car accommodations.
3. The neglect of Negro education, including inadequate school facilities and lack of adequate attention to high schools and colleges.
4. The double standard of justice in the courts, and especially lynch law.
5. The denial of industrial opportunity and the double standard of wages.
6. The lack of protection for colored women, girls and children.
7. The neglect of sanitation and public health measures, physical and moral, particularly in Negro residential sections.[91]

Indeed, the issues were many and complex, as in the long black past of the African-American experience in America. Yet, certainly central in black considerations was the lynching issue. George M. Fredrickson notes that Joel Williamson views this historical era as one in which "the white South, between 1889 and 1915, succumbed to a racial panic or hysteria that revolutionized popular attitudes towards blacks."[92] How to deal nationally with this perplexing problem remained a challenge for blacks, and in many ways as an unappreciated topic in the white consciousness of the land, in spite of many press items and lectures on the issue during these years.

This national state of affairs was reflected in the two United States presidents of this decade: William Howard Taft (Republican) 1909–1913 and Woodrow Wilson (Democrat) 1913–1921. While both men may have had a personal dislike for lynching, their national policies as president did not address the brutal nature of or a solution to this problem in American life.[93]

In reality, the loudest voices nationally in the 1910s in the struggle against lynching came from black individuals and organizations. At the head of this list must be placed the NAACP,[94] organized in 1909–1919, which took an early leadership role with lynching as one of its major program goals for reform in American society. One important fact for the period was that W. E. B. Du Bois served as the editor of *The Crisis* (first printed in November 1910), and the official organ of the group, and he headed the Research Bureau of the association as well. This meant that the NAACP had one of the major black thinkers and social scientists as a member during a critical period in the anti-lynching efforts of this country. Scholar Grace Elizabeth Hale points out the central role of the NAACP: "The NAACP stepped up its investigations of lynchings in the 1910s and published its important anti-lynching book, *Thirty Years of Lynching* [1919]."[95] The group was also a major contributor toward seeking an anti-lynching law from Congress (Dyer Anti-Lynching Act) during the 1910s.

Other support for anti-lynching efforts came from the National Urban League, created in 1911 at New York City. Eugene K. Jones (1885–1954) served as the executive secretary of this group beginning in 1917.[96] The National Urban League played a significant role in the advancement of the African-American community during this period.

The list of black intellectuals who were active in the anti-lynching struggle of the 1910s is vast. Included among major contributors were Bishop Henry M. Turner (1834–1915); Marcus Moziah Garvey (1887–1940), founder of the Universal Negro Improvement Association (in the U.S., in 1917); William Monroe Trotter, editor of the Boston Guardian; Ida B. Wells-Barnett, working from Chicago; John Edward Bruce, a New York City journalist; J. Max Barber, editor of the Atlanta, Georgia *Voice of the Negro*; John Mitchell, editor of the Richmond, Virginia *Planet*; Alice Dunbar-Nelson, a writer and teacher; Booker T. Washington (although his activities were often done in secret); Monroe Nathan Work, organizer of the Tuskegee Institute lynching reports; and James Weldon Johnson, a writer and NAACP leader, among thousands of others.[97]

The black press played a major role in advancing black opposition to lynching. This was true of the national black commercial press, some religious organs and black magazines.[98] Such support was crucial for the advancement of a black perspective and call for action on lynching. Other papers which pressed for vigorous action against lynching were the *Cleveland Gazette*; the *Pittsburgh Courier*, edited by Robert L. Vann; the *Messenger*, edited by A. Philip Randolph and Chandler Owen; and the Baltimore *Afro-American*, edited by J. H. Murphy.[99]

Black women and their organizations were also active in the 1910s in the anti-lynching crusade. A central group in this effort was the National Association of Colored Women, active since 1896.[100] In 1919, the NACW called on all women to support an effort to end lynching in this country. The document on lynching noted:

1. We deplore lynching for any crime whatever, no matter by whom committed.
2. We believe that any person who commits a crime should have punishment meted out to him, but not without thorough investigation and trial by the courts. We further believe that the present safety of the country depends upon a just and fair trial for all persons, white and colored alike.
3. Corrective measures
   a. We therefore urge such courage and foresight on the part of the officers of the law as will guarantee trials which will insure punishment of the guilty, and acquittal of the innocent.
   b. Further, we appeal to the white women
      i. To raise their voices in immediate protest when lynching or mob violence is threatened.

ii. To encourage every effort to detect and punish the leaders and participants in mobs and riots.
iii. To encourage the white pulpit and press in creating a sentiment among the law-abiding citizens and outspoken condemnation of these forms of lawlessness.[101]

The NACW also recommended that "white women include in their local community program a united effort to correct this evil [lynching] and to secure greater attention to worthy efforts of Negro citizens."[102]

Black women spoke out against lynching with a single determination to see an end to this crisis facing the black community. National leaders in this effort were Mary Church Terrell, Frances E. W. Harper, Anna Julia Cooper, Ida B. Wells-Barnett, Pauline Hopkins, Madam C. J. Walker, an entrepreneur, and hundreds of others.[103] These women made a tremendous difference in the positive movement of their communities through a very difficult historical period.

Nationally, white individuals and organizations were mixed in their views on lynching. An example of a major white newspaper in the South is the *Commercial Appeal* of Memphis, Tennessee. In the early twentieth century, according to Thomas Harrison Baker, "Instead of condemning lynching on principle, the *Commercial Appeal* at this time judged each occurrence according to the victim's crime—it was excusable to lynch a Negro rapist, but wrong to lynch a Negro who refused to be vaccinated."[104] Yet a southern group meeting in Durham, North Carolina in 1916, the University Commission on Southern Race Questions, made up of eleven college professors from eleven southern states, declared the following on lynching: "especially that the wrong done to the victims is nothing as compared with the injury done to the lynchers themselves, and to the community and society at large."[105] Also active during this period was the Commission on Interracial Cooperation: "Organized in Atlanta on April 9, 1919 by black and white Southerners fearing postwar violence, the commission brought community leaders of both races together to ease tensions.... Yet it was eager to curb lynchings."[106]

In Congress, the major anti-lynching effort came in 1918–1919 when Representative L. C. Dyer, a white man of St. Louis, Missouri, introduced an anti-lynching bill in the House of Representatives. Scan Dennis Cashman observes, "The Dyer bill proposed to eliminate lynching by making counties in which the offence occurred responsible. If they failed to protect citizens or prisoners from mob rule and a lynching took place, then the county would be fined."[107] The bill did not come up for a vote in Congress during the 1918–1919 session, but it was a beginning effort, and one that would continue into the 1920s.

Blacks and American Jews have had an interesting history of cooperation and understanding. Certainly the issue of lynching served to promote communication between them. Historian Nancy J. Weiss even argues that American Jews have been "long-distance runners of the civil rights movement," in that they have played a significant role in "the governance and financing of both the NAACP and the National Urban League." In the case of the NAACP, they helped shape the organization's legal efforts, a significant accomplishment of the association's early years.[108] Paul Battle and Robin D. G. Kelley also point out a generally positive perspective by many Jewish newspapers on the plight of blacks in America. They note, "For the most part, the Yiddish newspapers represented black people as victims of racist oppression, focusing on the history of American slavery and racial violence.... Given the parallels between pogroms Russian Jews experienced prior to fleeing to the United States and the lynching of Southern African Americans, stories of lynching remained a dominant theme in Yiddish articles about black life."[109]

Perhaps the most shocking event of the decade to impact on the Jewish community was the lynching in Georgia of a Jewish citizen; a tragedy which brought home to the Jewish community the terror of the lynching era. Deborah Dash Moore describes the details:

> Occasional moments of conflict did erupt between Blacks and Jews, vividly indicating their contrasting positions in southern society. The most traumatic moment for Jews came from events that unfolded in 1913. On Confederate Memorial Day a teenage white worker, May Phagan, stopped by an Atlanta pencil factory to pick up her pay envelope from the manager, Leo Frank, on her way to celebrate the holiday. She never made it to the parade. Early the next day, the night watchman found her body in the basement. Her brutal murder led to the arrest, trial, and conviction of Frank, the northern education Jewish superintendent who was an active member of Atlanta's Jewish community. Despite lack of evidence and Frank's obvious innocence, the case aroused enormous passions and unleashed such vitriolic anti–Semitism in Georgia and throughout the South, that when the governor commuted his death sentence, Frank was taken out of prison, brought back to Mary Phagan's home town of Marietta, and lynched. Frank's lynching in 1915, the only lynching of a Jew in America, stimulated the establishment of the second Ku Klux Klan.[110]

This event was a watershed in Black-Jewish relations. It served to indicate the depths of Southern hatred, racism and anti–Semitism, and the need for both groups to work together to end this terror in the land.

During the long decade 1910–1919, at least 107 Mississippians were killed by lynching in the state. This figure compares to 152 who were lynched in the state between 1900 and 1919. The total by 1919 represented a decline in lynching, but not a reduction in the psychological torture of the era. There was also no decline in the intensity of the Jim Crow system, and blacks in Mississippi continued to suffer politically (loss of the right to vote and to hold public office), economically (burdened with tenant and sharecropping on the farm and discrimination in other areas of life), and socially (forced to deal with a segregationist world which displaced blacks from social contact with whites and left them with unequal public services). Added to this state of affairs in the 1910s was the continued terror and fear associated with the violence of lynchings, and the everyday intimidation which many whites compelled blacks to suffer in Mississippi. This was indeed a violent era—and Mississippi blacks could take little solace from the fact that at the end of the 1910s, both Georgia and Texas were in keen competition to take Mississippi's "place" as the leading lynching state in the United States. W. Eugene Hollon notes this intriguing state of affairs:

> The Southern states claimed the largest number of victims, 2834, while the North had 219 and the West 156. Georgia led the states with 386 lynchings, followed closely by Mississippi with 373 and Texas with 335 for the thirty-eight year period. However, after 1918 Texas assumed the lead, and it averaged more than five mob lynchings per year throughout the next decade. Of the fifty-five people lynched in Texas between 1918 and 1927, most were Negroes or Mexicans. In eleven cases, the victims were burned alive, in three instances their bodies were burned after death, while two individuals were killed by public beatings. The others were hanged publicly.[111]

And when black Mississippians looked at other states, the horror of lynching remained. This was true of Oklahoma and Missouri, or even Delaware and Pennsylvania, all of which experienced lynching events during this era. Historian Jimmie Lewis Franklin notes that in Oklahoma, "During the period of the greatest number of lynchings, between 1910 and 1918, the percentage of blacks in the state's population registered a slight decline."[112] Scholar Dominic J. Capeci, Jr., observes that in Missouri: "There were 85 total lynchings between 1889 and

1942: 58 black and 27 white."[113] Although both Delaware and Pennsylvania are not generally known as lynching states, events did take place in each of them. Yohuru R. Williams points out, "Violence against blacks was a common feature of the social, economic, and political landscape in Delaware." And on June 22, 1903, the white citizens of Wilmington lynched a local black man, George White, accused of assaulting and raping a white woman, Helen S. Bishop.[114] The lynching of Zachariah Walker, an African-American male, by burning, at Coatesville, Pennsylvania, on August 13, 1911 was, according to Dennis B. Downey and Raymond M. Hyser, "the eighth and final recorded lynching in Pennsylvania."[115] These events and countless others in the nation were a constant reminder to the African-American people of their own plight in the United States, and of how severe the lynching crisis was in the life of the nation. Blacks could also observe that, although their community suffered the most from lynching attacks, other Americans, including whites, Native Americans, Chinese-Americans, and Mexican-Americans were also greatly impacted by this terror upon the land. As people looked to the past the lynching phenomenon was with them. And, as they tried to forge ahead to the future, this issue remained an unknown burden, yet, one which progressive people had to face and challenge, with calls for additional reforms in American life. Nevertheless, the issue would remain an active one for the 1920s.

7

The Jazz Age, 1920–1929

Mississippi entered the 1920s with a population of 1,790,618, of which 1,550, 497 lived in rural areas and 240,121 (13.4 percent) in urban places.[1] Blacks consisted of 56 percent of the state's population, and 88 percent of them made their living in agriculture.[2] Both blacks and whites continued to migrate away from Mississippi during this decade, and the state's population decreased by 101,600 people.[3]

Economic conditions remained harsh in Mississippi during the 1920s. One author describes the black condition as one whereby "African-Americans in the South were bound as fast to the land by debt, ignorance, and intimidation as they had been by slavery itself."[4] Cotton still played its major part in the lives of Mississippians. In fact, according to Paul Johnson, "In the year before the Civil War, 1860, the South produced 3,841,000 bales of cotton. In 1929 the figure was 14,828,000 bales—still about 65 percent of the total world production."[5] But for the majority of blacks this system still meant largely tenant and share-cropping farming—and poverty. In 1920 Mississippi had 272,101 farms; by 1930 this number stood at 312,663. During this time black farmers in Mississippi totaled 161,001 in 1920 and 182,578 in 1930.[6] The end results of extreme agricultural conditions increased the migration of Mississippians to other states. Many Mississippians suffered because of the overproduction of cotton during this period.[7]

Black professionals and a small middle class struggled to stay afloat in Mississippi during the 1920s. One black bank, the Delta Penny Savings Bank, remained in operation at Indianola to 1928.[8] By 1920 Mississippi had only 14 black lawyers, 66 physicians, 351 restaurant and saloon keepers, and 657 merchants and retailers.[9] Black businesses served the black world of Mississippi, still forced to endure the harsh system of segregation in the state. During the 1920s the black press changed little in terms of general circulation, distribution, cost, background of editors, and so forth. In addition to other concerns, black journalists in Mississippi faced a disturbing decline in the number of black papers. Only thirty-one major black press organs appeared in the 1920s, down from a total of sixty-six papers during the years 1910–1919.[10] Such economic conditions were depressed even more by a major Mississippi flood in 1927 and by the Stock Exchange Crash in 1929.[11] The resulting Great Depression had a tremendous impact on Mississippi, already the poorest state in the Union. The black Mississippi community suffered greatly during this economic crisis. For one thing, the income level per person in Mississippi in 1929 was only $273.[12]

The economic crisis of the 1920s also extended into the realm of social issues impacting black Mississippians.[13] Social relations with whites were still defined by Jim Crow and segregation. I. A. Newby notes that "anti-Negro attitudes" were widespread during this period.[14] Langston Hughes reminds us of the direct, day-to-day consequences of Southern and Mississippi racism when he comments in his essay "Old Man River" on the fate which befell blacks impacted by the 1927 flood.[15]

This state of inequality was also felt in black education in Mississippi during the 1920s. Blacks in the state suffered on a number of negative social indicators of state support for black education. The school term averaged only 130 days for black Mississippi students in 1928–29 while white students spent at least 141 days in school. Tenants, who represented 87.6 percent of all Mississippi students, only attended school for 74 days by 1930. Mississippi contributed $5.94 for blacks and $31.33 for whites, per capita annual expenditure, for the education of Mississippi's schoolchildren in 1929–30. Finally, the average monthly salary of Mississippi's public school teachers in 1928–29 was very low with black teachers receiving on average $53.85, while white teachers were awarded $129.71.[16] Such appalling conditions were reflective of Jim Crow's attitudes toward the education of black children.

During the 1920s, black higher education in Mississippi was represented by Alcorn University at Lorman, the Mount Herman Seminary near Clinton, Mississippi Industrial College at Holly Springs, Natchez College at Natchez, Harris Junior College at Meridian, Okolona College at Okolona, Rust College at Holly Springs, Mary Holmes Seminary at West Point, Prentiss Institute at Prentiss, Piney Woods School in Rankin County, Saints Junior College at Lexington, Utica Normal and Industrial Institute at Utica, Campbell College at Jackson, Tougaloo College at Tougaloo, West Point Ministerial Institute and College at West Point, Jackson State College at Jackson, and Southern Christian Institute at Edwards. Special schools active during this period included an institute for the deaf and dumb at Jackson and a mental institution at Ellisville.[17] The latter two institutions were, of course, segregated. All of these institutions were impacted by Mississippi's system of segregation, but they often proved to be the only institutions where blacks could receive training beyond an elementary education.

Health care concerns of black Mississippians were pronounced during the 1920s. First, since 1892 when Mississippi "passed a law ... that required white and colored races to be kept in separate hospitals," blacks were faced with a segregated medical world and unequal health care facilities in the state.[18] The state even attempted to regulate whom they could associate with and marry. According to Henry Allen Bullock, "In a desperate attempt to prevent the races from mixing their blood, each Southern state enacted rigid laws against personal association and intermarriage.... Mississippi not only prohibited such marriages but also provided for a $500 fine to be imposed upon anyone found guilty of printing, publishing, or circulating printed or written matter urging or suggesting social equality or intermarriage between whites and Negroes."[19] What were the consequences of such policies? David M. Kennedy suggests that many blacks of this period were subjected to an early death because of racism, infant mortality rates for blacks were nearly double those for whites in 1930 (10 percent and 6 percent respectively) and that blacks had an average life expectancy fifteen years shorter than whites (forty-five years compared with sixty).[20] In essence, although blacks could seek out the services of white physicians in Mississippi, many had to depend on the 66 active black physicians in the state during the 1920s. These doctors were overworked, underpaid, and forced to endure the cruel nature of Mississippi's segregationist health system.[21] Of course many black physicians began to leave Mississippi with the Great Migration.[22]

Black Mississippians turned to their cultural institutions for relief from the social oppression of the decade. It was, indeed, a decade full of "renaissances," including the Harlem Renaissance, a national outpouring of black creative talent in all of the arts, the social sciences and humanities.[23] But black Mississippians were especially influenced by black gospel, jazz and blues forms of music. Paul Johnson believes that "jazz and the blues were the most eclectic of all in their historical origins. They were a product of the one aspect of the melting-pot in which blacks participated fully—sound (and behind the sound, sentiment)."[24] Mississippi bluesman John Lee Hooker notes, "I know why the best blues artists come from Mississippi. Because it's the worst state. You have the blues all right if you're down in Mississippi."[25] It was an era of outstanding black musical personalities. Ralph Ellison notes this fact with a reference to Bessie Smith (1896–1937) when he writes in *Shadow and Act*: "Bessie Smith might have been a 'blues queen' to the society at large, but within the tighter Negro community where the blues were part of a total way of life, and a major expression of an attitude toward life, she was a priestess, a celebrant who affirmed the values of the group and man's ability to deal with chaos."[26]

Black Mississippians also produced a crop of new writers in the 1920s. Most important was Richard Wright, born in 1908 near Natchez, who began to write short stories in the 1920s.[27] He would come to play a dominant role in African-American letters in the 1930s and 1940s, and more will be said about him later in this book. Black Mississippians were influenced in their thinking during the 1920s by the New Negro Movement, especially from such cities as New York and Chicago. Blacks also read northern newspapers, including the *Chicago Defender* (which recommended that blacks migrate from the South), and the *Pittsburgh Courier*, among others, when they could secure them.[28] Such humble efforts as these in the 1920s forged a way for hundreds of black Mississippi musicians, poets, writers and artists to come in the years ahead.

The black church was also a significant institution during the 1920s. The church offered blacks solace and spiritual comfort from the daily burdens of segregation, lynching, racism, and oppression in Mississippi. Although Baptists and Methodists were the major denominations among black Mississippians, the Holiness Movement also developed a large following in the state by the 1920s.[29] Religion was important to Mississippians. But according to Sally G. McMillen, Christian love and brother-sisterhood could not and did not do enough to put into practice what white Christianity preached. Historian Neil McMillen observes that Sunday schools were very important in Southern life, but many individuals did not leave them with a strong sense of tolerance of others; as is indicated by the many religious persons who joined the ranks of the Ku Klux Klan and other white supremacy groups.[30] Thus, in every area of life in Mississippi, the 1920s were also a very low point in race relations. Blacks and whites lived in two different worlds, yet both existed in the same country. It was a paradoxical state of affairs, and no area of black life was more extreme, as defined by the Jim Crow system of the period, than black political development in Mississippi during the 1920s.

John B. Skates views the period of the 1920s in Mississippi as one of decline: "The 1920s were largely a period of stagnation in Mississippi history. The tenant-sharecropping system of agriculture grew, and Jim Crow laws were strengthened. Total population for the first time in history actually declined slightly. At the mercy, as always, of the vagaries of the cotton market, Mississippians did not share in the prosperous roaring Twenties. Mississippi was not yet in the mainstream of American life."[31]

Politically, Mississippi remained a solid Democratic state for white voters. Five white Mississippians served as Democratic governors of the state during the decade. They were Theodore G. Bilbo (1916–1920), Lee M. Russell (1920–1924), Henry L. Whitfield (1924–1927),

Dennis Murphree (1927–1928), and Bilbo again (1928–1932).[32] Jesse O. McKee notes the low status of the political system in Mississippi during this period: "Politicians were able to produce few solutions for the state's problems. 'Businessmen governors' pursued policies friendly to big business, improved the educational system, and developed the industrial sector of the economy."[33]

And black voters? As late as 1900 there were only 15,000 registered black voters in Mississippi, out of at least 197,936 black males of voting age in the state.[34] The Jim Crow system in Mississippi continued to discourage black voters by forcing them to pay a poll tax and to meet other special requirements for voting in the state. This sad state of black political life in Mississippi lasted for decades. This factor is noted by James W. Loewen and Charles Sallis: "During these years, Mississippians lived under the constitution adopted in 1890. Jim Crow signs kept the races separate. Very few black people were allowed to vote, public facilities were not provided equally to both races."[35]

After decades of struggle, American women finally won the right to vote on August 26, 1920, when Congress enacted the 19th Amendment to the U.S. Constitution.[36] Legally this now meant that black women throughout this country could vote along with black men. However, it would take another fifty years of struggle for black people and other Americans to safely secure the vote for black people.

The consequences of Mississippi's political system in the 1920s meant that the majority population in the state—black people—did not have a political voice to foster their economic, social, and political development. During this era, blacks were in a staging area, holding on to their lives and institutions and looking ahead to the future where they hoped that Mississippi, the South, and the nation might be forced to change and reform the systematic oppression and discrimination of African Americans in this country.

Mississippi's criminal justice system remained a closed system during the 1920s. Blacks who had to face the system, for any reason, were at the mercy of whites who controlled every facet of justice. The state and the South, in general, remained a violent region. Dewey W. Grantham observes this: "The southern reputation for violence reflected a regional pattern of behavior that stood in sharp contrast to the rest of the nation."[37]

Evidence of Southern discrimination against blacks in the criminal justice system was the high rate of black convictions in the courts. Jerone G. Miller's study notes this racial bias:

In its 1918 report "Negro Population: 1790–1915," the Bureau of the Census noted that while blacks made

Dr. Sidney D. Redmond was a leading African American physician, attorney-at-law, and Republican politician in Mississippi between 1910 and 1948. He was born on October 11, 1871, in Holmes County, Mississippi. He graduated from Rust College in Holly Springs, Mississippi, in 1893, and later received a medical degree from the Illinois Medical College at Chicago. He was admitted to the Mississippi bar in 1903, and he received a law degree in 1915 from the Illinois College of Law in Chicago. Redmond was a major influence on the early career of black Mississippi journalist Percy Greene, founder of the *Jackson Advocate*, Mississippi's leading black newspaper, founded in 1938 in the capital city. Redmond died on February 11, 1948 (COURTESY OF THE *JACKSON ADVOCATE*).

up about 11% of the general population they constituted about one-fifth (21.9%) of the inmates in the prisons, penitentiaries, jails, reform schools, and workhouses of the states. They represented 56% of those held for "grave homicide" and about half of those held for "lesser homicide" and contributed slightly less than one-third of the commitments for robbery, burglary, and larceny. On the other hand, only about 15% of those held for drunkenness, disorderly conduct, or vagrancy were black.[38]

Yet, blacks in general also faced another pressing problem during the decade: "In the years 1920–1932 substantially more than half of all African Americans killed by whites were killed by police officers."[39] This indicated the grave dangers which blacks faced on having any contact whatsoever with the American criminal justice system, but especially with white male police officers.

Parchman Penitentiary remained the major state prison for Mississippi during the 1920s. The institution first opened in 1904 under the leadership of Governor James Kimble Vardaman. The prison became another outlet for white Mississippi's control of the African-American community, and as an expression of the Jim Crow system's "place" for blacks in Mississippi society. This central observation is noted by David M. Oshinsky, who says in his study that "blacks comprised about 90 percent of the prison population" at Parchman in the early 1900s.[40] Life at the 20,000 acre prison was harsh. Central to the deprivations of the prison was a rigid system of segregation, the use of a trustee system (prisoners as guards of other inmates), an emphasis on cotton production by the prisoners, and thus a "profit" from their labor for the state, and the use of violent methods of punishment to maintain control of inmates, most noted in the use of Black Annie, "a leather strap, three feet long and six inches wide" to impose fear in the prison population.[41] Mississippi was also a leader in the development of the convict leasing system which exploited the labor of prisoners at Parchman for many decades. While black men were the main category of the Parchman prison population, black women were also present. Their numbers for the 1920s, however, were never more than five percent of the state's prison population at Parchman. The women's camp at Parchman opened in 1915 with 26 inmates, all African-American. By 1925 there were 48 black women in the prison.[42] The racism of the system was also intense. Robert Perkinson's review of David M. Oshinsky's *"Worse than Slavery"* makes this issue very clear: "This treatment of black women reflected the white maintenance of a differential Southern gender system based on race. The informal and decentralized Southern criminal justice institutions often turned a blind eye to black prostitution confined to black communities and only rarely convicted a black man of raping a black woman."[43] Indeed, Mississippi's criminal justice system was a mirror's reflection of the larger society and its negative attitudes toward black Mississippians.

The crime of lynching was the ultimate outcome of Jim Crow and racism in Mississippi in the 1920s. The causes of lynching during the 1920s remain as much a part of the state's history as ever. Yet, as Martin Gilbert notes, there was a "revival" of the terrorist Ku Klux Klan, beginning in 1915 and extending into the 1920s. Gilbert notes that by 1921, "In the American South there had been a revival of activity by the Ku Klux Klan, with fifty-nine black Americans being lynched, five of them burnt to death, and five of them burnt after they had been killed. There were also mutilations, branding with acid, floggings, tarring-and-feathering and kidnappings."[44] Membership figures climbed during this period for the Klan. David Chalmers observes, "During its peak years in the early twenties, members were streaming in and out in such numbers that the Klan itself probably never knew its own size. At one time or another in the 1920s, perhaps at least one out of every ten white, native-born, Protestant adult males belonged to the Invisible Empire."[45] For black Mississippians this especially meant a strong climate of fear—and greater possibilities of lynchings. Like other states, Mississippi had many Klansmen, estimated in 1925 at 93,040.[46]

Thus, the reasons given for Mississippi lynchings during this decade were as varied as in previous decades. According to Stewart E. Tolnay and E. M. Beck: "[The] justifications represent a broad variety of criminal and noncriminal transgressions against the white community, ranging from rapes, murders, and assaults to insulting a white man, trying to vote, and being obnoxious."[47] Racial violence thus remained a cornerstone of life in Mississippi during the 1920s and another reason for black migration from the state, and, yet again, paradoxically another cause of lynching in Mississippi—to force blacks to stay in the state.[48] Yet, of course, the economics of lynching always remained a factor in Mississippi. One study notes this variable: "It happened in Mississippi, where a white man who owed a black farmer $1,200 led a mob against the black man, running him and his family off their farm forever and erasing the debt in the process."[49]

National data reveal at least 315 lynching victims in the United States during the 1920s (see Table 7.1). The opening years of the decade were most severe in terms of lynching events, with 61 victims in 1920, 64 in 1921, 57 in 1922, and 33 in 1923. Blacks composed 64 of Mississippi's lynching victims during this period and two whites were also lynched.[50] Mississippi's 66 lynching victims were distributed among 36 known counties in the state, with the locations of five events unknown. Four counties held the largest number of lynch victims: Forrest (3), Pike (3), Rankin (3), and Yazoo (4) (see Tables 7.2 and 7.6). Geographically the lynching victims were distributed in the following regions: 7 counties each in the Delta and North Mississippi, 6 in the Eastern region, 4 in Central Mississippi, and one county on the Gulf coast, with South Mississippi containing 9 counties. Lynchings were thus distributed in all parts of the state during the 1920s, but the region with the fewest victims was the Gulf Coast.[51]

TABLE 7.1: LYNCHING VICTIMS, 1920–1929

Year	National			Mississippi		
	Total	Black	White	Total	Black	White
1920	61	53	8	6	6	0
1921	64	59	5	17	16	1
1922	57	51	6	8	8	0
1923	33	29	4	13	13	0
1924	16	16	0	3	3	0
1925	17	17	0	6	6	0
1926	30	23	7	2	1	1
1927	16	16	0	5	5	0
1928	11	10	1	5	5	0
1929	10	7	3	1	1	0
TOTALS	315	281	34	66	64	2

TABLE 7.2: LYNCHING VICTIMS BY COUNTY, 1920–1929

County	Number	County	Number	County	Number
Alcorn	2	Lauderdale	2	Quitman	2
Benton	1	Leflore	2	Ronkin	3
Clarke	2	Lincoln	1	Sharkey	1
Coahoma	1	Lincoln	1	Sunflower	2
Copiah	1	Lowndes	1	Tunica	2
Desoto	1	Madison	1	Union	1
Forrest	3	Monroe	1	Walthall	2
Greene	1	Noxubee	2	Winston	2
Grenada	1	Panola	2	Yalobusha	2
Harrison	1	Pearl River	2	Yazoo	4
Holmes	2	Perry	1	Unknown	5
Kemper	1	Pike	3		
Lamar	1	Pontotoc	1	TOTALS	64

TABLE 7.3: BLACK WOMEN LYNCHING VICTIMS, 1920–1929

Year	Name	Place	Cause(s)
4 April 1921	Rachel Moore	Rankin County	Mother-in-law of man lynched (race prejudice)
1923	Unknown	Holmes County	Race prejudice

TABLE 7.4: WHITE MALE LYNCHING VICTIMS, 1920–1929

Year	Name	Place	Cause(s)
1921	Casey E. Jones (male)	Forrest County	murder
1926	Harold Johnson	Pearl River County	murder

The vast majority of lynching victims in the 1920s were black males, but Table 7.3 notes that two women, one each in 1921 and 1923, were lynched for "race prejudice," in Rankin and Holmes Counties in central Mississippi. Two white males were also lynched during this period in Southern Mississippi, one in Forrest County and the other in Pearl River County. Both were accused of committing murder.

A majority of Mississippi lynching victims were accused of committing murder—26 victims at 41 percent, followed by rape and attempted rape with 14 cases or 22 percent. Seven victims were charged with assault (11 percent) and 6 with insulting a white woman (9 percent). Another five victims were charged with other offenses, and the "crimes" of six victims are unknown (see Table 7.5).[52]

TABLE 7.5: MISSISSIPPI LYNCHING VICTIMS, RANGE AND PERCENTAGE OF OFFENSES ALLEGED, 1920–1929

Offense	Number	Percentage
Murder	26	41%
Unknown	6	9%
Rape, attempted rape	14	22%
Assault	7	11%
Insulting or annoying a white woman	6	9%
Race Prejudice	2	3%
Fight with white man	1	2%
Failure to leave the vicinity	1	2%
Failure to quit railroad brakeman's job	1	2%
Total	64	

TABLE 7.6: MISSISSIPPI COUNTIES WITH LARGEST NUMBER OF LYNCHING VICTIMS, 1920–1929

County	Number
Forrest	4
Pike	3
Rankin	3
Yazoo	4

Many of the months when Mississippi lynching victims died are unknown. Data is only available on eleven victims, and these are spread out over eight months. The warmer months of the year were the leading periods for lynching events in Mississippi.[53]

Blacks in Mississippi and the South were faced with one lynching every nine days in the 1920s.[54] Such events in Mississippi remained extreme examples of torture and madness. Five case studies from the 1920s are explored to reflect this fact.

Case Study One: 1923
"Mob Takes Negro From Deputy On Train, Hang Him"
Hattiesburg, Mississippi, January 3.

Ben Webster, a negro, was taken from an eastbound passenger train on the Alabama and Vicksburg railroad at Lawrence last night by a band of about twenty-five masked men, and his body was found this morning hanging from a bridge two miles from Waynesboro, Wayne County, twenty-five miles from Lawrence, according to reports reaching here today.... The men who took the negro from Deputy Sheriff Holston of Waynesboro had their faces covered ... he was lynched in an automobile. The negro is said to have killed

TABLE 7.7: MISSISSIPPI LYNCHINGS BY MONTH, 1920–1929

Month	Events	Percentage
January	1	2%
February	0	0%
March	2	3%
April	1	2%
May	0	0%
June	2	3%
July	0	0%
August	2	3%
September	1	2%
October	0	0%
November	1	2%
December	1	2%
Unknown	53	83%
TOTAL	64	

road contractor Alford at Waynesboro last November, and had been held in Jackson for safekeeping. He was being taken back to Waynesboro for trial. Alford, the man killed by the negro, was a resident of Hazelhurst, Miss.[55]

Case Study Two: 1925
"Negro Burnt at Stake—Union County Brute Pays Penalty for Committing Horrible Crime on White Girl"
New Albany, Sept. 21
    Since the lynching of J. P. Ivy, negro, for criminal assault on this young daughter of Bob Gaines, Sunday afternoon, this section has been comparatively quiet. Three negroes were arrested, on suspicion of being accomplices of Ivy, but were later freed when they convinced officers that they were innocent. Although it is said that a number of the members of the mob were recognized, no arrests had been made up to the present time.[56]

Case Study Three: 1928
"Shame to Mississippi"
    Five lynchings for 1928, not three as reported, blacken the name of Mississippi before the world. On December 26 Emmanuel McCallum, a Negro automobile mechanic, was lynched near Hattiesburg, Mississippi; on December 31, Charley Shepherd, Negro convict, was burned alive near the town of Parchman in the same State. Shepherd had murdered a prison guard and abducted his daughter; after three days of pursuit through the Delta, he gave himself up and voluntarily handed over his weapon to a white woman in return for her promise of protection from the mob—a promise which she vainly sought to keep. Shepherd thus presented no menace to officers of the law engaged in the legitimate

business of apprehending him as a murderer and confessed rapist; nothing stood in the way of his orderly and proper trial and punishment under the laws of the State—except complete disregard of the law by every State's officer connected with the case from Governor Bilbo down!

The night before the burning took place, the Governor passed through the town of Parchman; on his return he stopped off to view what remained of the corpse. He thus made himself a party to the lynching in the most revolting sense—that of bloodthirsty curiosity after the event. There is no record that he made his inspection as an indignant officer of the law, sworn to maintain order and decency in his State. There is, indeed, evidence to the contrary; for when Governor Bilbo was urged by citizens of his and other States to conduct an investigation into the gruesome affair, he announced: "I have neither the time nor the money to investigate 2,000 people," and let it go at that.

We respectfully suggest to Governor Bilbo that he need not investigate 2,000 people. He need only take steps to remove the sheriff of the county in which Shepherd was done to death, the Adjutant General of the Militia who declared that after he heard that the mob had the Negro, "he ordered his troops home as he was thirty miles from the scene and couldn't do anything anyway," and the prison superintendent who called for troops to find the Negro but not to protect him when he was found. We maintain that if the Governor were minded to act entirely within his rights and invoke the law in some manner as this, there would not be five lynchings in Mississippi in 1929. Other Southern States—notably Virginia, Georgia, and Tennessee—have by just such vigorous action removed lynching from the category of a pastime. There were no lynchings in those States last year.[57]

Case Study Four: Late 1920s
"Delta Lynching of a friend of Muddy Waters"
     One of Muddy's girlfriends had a friend from Stovall [in Coahoma County, six miles northwest of Clarksdale], who was promptly lynched after he allegedly flirted with a white woman. (Often this was the trumped-up charge for a lynching, when the real reason may have been "attitude," prosperousness, or a form of manhood interpreted as a threat to white womanhood.)[58]

These case studies from the 1920s are representative of the lynching crisis in Mississippi during the twenties. The general violence, terror, and heartache of the period are witnessed in these events.

Black Mississippians continued their struggle—against the odds—to oppose lynchings in the state during the 1920s. The challenge was a great one, a life and death task, a battle which had to be conducted on many levels, often in secret. Thousands of Mississippi blacks left the state between 1920 and 1929: one method of protest! Yet black organizations such as the NAACP, Garvey's UNIA in Mississippi, the Mississippi Federation of Colored Women's Clubs, the black press and the black church aided the anti-lynching efforts in the state. For most blacks during this harsh period, it was necessary to do little things in this struggle against great oppression, such as writing letters to newspapers; appealing for justice to Congress, religious groups, and local, state and national government officials; fighting to increase educational opportunities for black students; stressing black history (and the work of Carter G. Woodson's Association for the Study of Negro Life and History, Washington, D.C., active in the United States since 1915); and taking the long view, which the black struggle demanded, in order to fight for reforms and a change in society.[59] Perhaps one of the most shocking and striking events of black Mississippi protest against lynching took place in 1923 when "ten thousands blacks left Yazoo City, Mississippi ... following a lynching there."[60] The tragedy of Mississippi lynchings demanded a black response—and it came in a variety of forms and methods. One thing was sure for blacks: they had to face another hard decade ahead, in the 1930s, and many knew that the lynching crisis in the state, the South and the nation was far from over. Blacks had to keep the faith and look ahead and continue the struggle against lynching into another decade.

In general, white Mississippians during the 1920s supported the lynching status quo in the state. At the national level, in Congress, Mississippi's representatives, such as Senators John Sharp Williams and Pat Harrison, worked to defeat the Dyer Anti-Lynching Bill, first introduced in 1921.[61] Yet, Dwyn M. Mounger found more anti-lynching support coming from Mississippi's governors:

> Governors were more active in opposing lynching in Mississippi from 1919 to 1930 than congressmen. Governor Henry L. Whitfield in his inaugural message, January 1924, called its existence "a blow at law and order and a blot upon our national life." He asserted that all men were equal before the law, and he called upon local authorities "to use every means within their power to prevent lynchings, and thus eliminate a potent source of race friction and ill feelings."
>
> In 1925 Whitfield vigorously condemned the burning of a Negro for alleged rape at New Albany. He labeled the lynching "shocking to every sense of respect for law and Christianity." In the same statement he informed all peace officers in the state that as long as he was chief executive, "every possible help" would be extended to them in enforcing the law. At least twice during this term of office he implemented this policy by calling out the National Guard to prevent lynchings. Governor Dennis Murphree on five occasions used this means of thwarting mob killings. From all indications he was more active than any other Mississippi chief executive in ordering the National Guard to prevent prisoners from being lynched.
>
> There is no evidence, however, that Governor Theodore G. Bilbo took an active stand in opposing mob killings. When a Negro Association [NAACP] sent him a telegram to protest against a lynching which had occurred in the state, he responded with the words: "Go to hell."[62]

Some elements among white Mississippi religious groups were opposed to lynching. For example, as early as 1906, "The Southern Baptist convention declared that 'lynching blunts the public conscience, undermines the foundations on which society stands, and if unchecked will result in anarchy.' But the Baptists took pains to affirm that 'our condemnation is due with equal emphasis, and in many cases with even greater emphasis, against the horrible crimes which cause the lynchings.' ... In 1913 the convention also established a social service commission 'to deal with other such wrongs which curse society today, and call loudly for our help.'"[63] Nevertheless, it would take additional years of hard work by anti-lynching activists to help increase a mood in Mississippi for more whites to begin to see a need for reforms on the lynching issue.

For the 1920s then, the major anti-lynching efforts came from outside Mississippi and the South. The NAACP continued to play a very active role in the struggle against lynching. One scholar notes that the NAACP was active in anti-lynching efforts "most intensively in the years 1920 to 1922."[64] In essence, then:

> The NAACP relied on investigations of incidents and patterns of discrimination, circulated its findings and recommendations through press releases to white and Negro newspapers—and later through other communications media—held rallies and working conferences that focused on specific interracial problems, lobbied for corrective legislation in the federal and state legislatures, and litigated at all levels of the judicial system—but most especially before the Supreme Court of the United States. These tactics were designed to generate and mobilize public support, to move public officials to remedial action, and to lay the bases for additional reforms over time.[65]

During the 1920s, major NAACP figures in the anti-lynching crusade were W. E. B. Du Bois and Jessie Fauset, editors of *The Crisis*; James Weldon Johnson, executive secretary; Mary White Ovington, chairwoman; Joel Spingarn and his brother Arthur Spingarn; Walter White, publicist; Roy Wilkins, journalist; and lawyers William Hastie, Charles Houston, and Thurgood Marshall, among others.[66] The NAACP invested tremendous resources and time in support of the Dyer Anti-Lynching Bill in Congress, but the bill never made it through both houses.[67]

Black intellectuals, writers, artists, journalists, editors, and publishers were also very dedicated to promoting anti-lynching efforts during the 1920s.[68] Black poets such as Langston Hughes, Claude McKay,[69] Countee Cullen, Arna Bontemps, Jean Toomer, and Georgia Douglas Johnson, among many others, wrote frequently on the lynching theme in their creative works.[70] This was also true of black playwrights, critics such as Alain LeRoy Locke and W. E. B. Du Bois, historians such as Carter G. Woodson, William Leo Hansberry (1894–1965), and Charles H. Wesley; journalists like Chandler Owen, A. Philip Randolph, Robert Vann (1879–1940), Ida B. Wells-Barnett, Carl Murphy, Charles S. Johnson, and so on.[71] This was also true of the National Association of Colored Women's Clubs, which endorsed anti-lynching legislation and a vigorous campaign to end lynching in the United States.[72]

One major poem of this period, Claude McKay's "The Lynching," is an example of the work of black poets from the 1920s on lynching. David R. Roediger notes that "The Lynching" (1922) "makes poetry of the role of terror in cementing white solidarity and in teaching racism to future generations."[73] This poem speaks across the generations on the problem of lynching in American life.[74]

Among white American groups which opposed lynchings in the 1920s were the American Federation of Teachers; the American Jewish Congress, and the Anti-Defamation League of B'nai B'rith.[75] Estelle B. Freeman observes that an early effort was made by the YWCA movement to improve race relations in this country: "The YWCA had begun to hold interracial conferences in 1915; in the 1920s its college branches confronted the organization's policy of segregated facilities."[76] All such efforts were helpful in promoting public discussion of lynchings in this nation.

A very mixed picture emerges of national white leaders and the lynching crisis of the 1920s. At the presidential level were the following figures: Warren G. Harding (Rep.), 1921–1923; Calvin Coolidge (Rep.), 1923–1929; and Herbert Hoover (Rep.), 1929–1933. Although President Harding "denounced lynching," his term in office did not bring about any major improvements in black life, and certainly not an end to lynching. One scholar observes that "his understanding of racial problems was superficial, and in dealing with them he lacked a sense of moral urgency or of strong political necessity."[77]

Like President Harding, President Calvin Coolidge could talk a good game, but action to safeguard blacks was another matter. Coolidge often expressed support for the protection of the civil rights of African-Americans, however, Robert Sobel suggests that "what concrete measures he initiated was another matter," especially on the lynching crisis facing the nation.[78]

President Herbert Hoover was largely silent on lynching and black rights at the beginning of his term in office. Richard B. Sherman found that President Hoover's

> handling of several other matters did little to bolster the declining reputation of the Republican party among black Americans. At the beginning of Hoover's presidency it became known that he intended to appoint a commission to study the problem of the widespread disrespect for law in America. The difficulties over prohibition prompted the original idea for such a commission, but its work did not have to be limited to this subject.

The NAACP tried unsuccessfully to have a Negro appointed to the commission and to have an investigation into the violation of the rights of Negroes put on its agenda. The government, however, showed no interest in requiring the commission to look into such problems as lynching and mob violence, peonage, segregation, or disfranchisement.[79]

There was a small movement in Congress to enact a federal anti-lynching law in the 1920s. David L. Porter notes that Representative L. C. Dyer of Missouri introduced a bill that made lynching a national crime subject to federal prosecution and penalty. The House in January 1929 easily adopted the Dyer Bill, 220 to 119.[80] In the Senate, however, Southerners filibustered and killed the bill.

The lynching crisis remained a major issue of concern for black Mississippians in the 1920s. They could look back to the last twenty years and realize that from a high of 107 lynching victims in Mississippi between 1910 and 1919, the figures had dropped to 66 for the years 1920–1929. A reduction, yes, but in the 1920s, 64 of the 66 Mississippi lynching victims were African-Americans. This problem produced a great psychological burden as well as physical safety concerns for black Mississippians. As in the last fifty years, many protested their status in Mississippi by seeking opportunities elsewhere. Others tried to escape the farms and plantations of the state and headed toward Southern cities. All blacks in Mississippi had to fight a daily battle for survival—against the Jim Crow system. They lived in a harsh world, but were given some encouragement by the strengths of black families, the black church, the national black press, black music and the renewed interest in black history, culture, Africa and the works of black intellectuals on black people. They could also pull strength and enlightenment from the historical struggles of blacks in Mississippi, to overcome the centuries of slavery, discrimination, Jim Crowism, and oppression, which had impacted them over time. Thus, as another decade ended, they could look ahead to more years of struggle. But, as they had learned from Marcus Garvey, they had to continue to seek "a reborn feeling of collective pride and a new awareness of individual work" with hope, determination and faith as the struggle against lynching in Mississippi and the nation would continue in the 1930s.[81]

8

The Great Depression, 1930–1939

Mississippi opened the 1930s with a total population of 2,183,796, of which 1,106,327 were white and 1,077,469 were blacks. Blacks had been the majority population in Mississippi from 1840 into the 1930s. Whites became the majority in 1940 for the first time since the 1830s.[1] Mississippi was still largely a rural state. By 1940 its urban citizens represented only 19.8 percent of the state's population, or 432,882 people. Mississippi had only 48 urban locations in 1940.[2] Migration from Mississippi to other states was still a topic of great concern to both black and white Mississippians. During the previous decade, 90,300 blacks left the state.[3] James R. Grossman quotes a black Mississippian to explain the continued migration out of Mississippi: "Just a few months ago they hung Widow Baggage's husband from Hirshbery bridge because he talked back to a white man. He was a prosperous Farmer owning about 80 acres. They killed another man because he dared to sell his cotton 'off the place.' These things have got us sore. Before the North opened up with work all we could do was to move from one plantation to another in hope of finding something better."[4]

Blacks faced hardships whether in Mississippi or other states. Yet a major shift was beginning to form in black life, a move from a rural to an urban experience for most blacks.[5] Nevertheless, the tremendous new crisis in America's economic life brought on by the Great Depression in 1929 through the 1930s was devastating for Mississippi. Pete Daniel describes the complex set of circumstances in the state: "The conditions in Mississippi were typical of other Southern states. In 1932, the state was bankrupt, and when Governor Theodore Bilbo left office in 1932 it owed $14 million and had barely a thousand dollars in the treasury. Since depression struck in 1929, the number of jobs in manufacturing fell from 52,000 to 28,000, and unemployment in the state's larger cities rose above ten percent."[6]

Black Mississippians, who were among the poorest of the poor, of course, faced the greatest crisis. One author notes that even when it came to relief, blacks received less: "only nine percent" of blacks "were receiving aid in 1933 as compared to 14 percent of the whites."[7] The only thing open for many blacks was to move on from place to place. Richard Wormser relates this issue to American trains: "By 1930, 50 percent of southern blacks were already unemployed; having little or no money, they either starved or lived by their own wits. For those who chose the latter, traveling as a 'hobo' was a way of finding work and consequently some food."[8] On top of all these problems lay a central issue facing Mississippi: the state was defined by Charles Angoff and H. L. Mencken in 1931 as "the worst American state," when a comparison was made of the 48 states of the union at that time, in terms of wealth, education and public order, and only South Carolina had a worse health record than Mississippi. Overall, the author's average rank placed Mississippi at the bottom of the American states.[9] The study was not a shock to black Mississippians, since they lived in the state and existed under the terrible conditions of life there.

The social conditions of blacks in Mississippi remained static in the 1930s, and a continuing problem for the black community was based, as one study notes, on "black subordination and exclusion from the major institutions of society."[10] This was a world of continued segregation.[11] Thus, racism was widespread in Mississippi and strongly supported by whites in the state.[12] Furthermore, this system had a daily impact on the psychological and physical realities for black people in the state (not to mention its negative consequences for whites!). James T. Patterson makes this observation: "Daily humiliations continue to remind black people of their third-class status."[13] Perhaps a story related by Ray Sprigle can best sum up the social situation facing black Mississippians during the Age of Jim Crow and lynching. Dr. Hugh Morris Gloster, then a professor of English at Hampton Institute, Virginia, suffered an almost life-threatening incident abroad a train traveling through Mississippi, on his way from Birmingham, Alabama, to Memphis, Tennessee. Dr. Gloster sought relief for black riders who were standing in their section of the train, because several whites took seats in the black section and refused to move. For his troubles, Dr. Gloster was later arrested. The degree of racism which he, a professional black, suffered was great. But at least he got out of Mississippi with his life.[14]

One institution in which black Mississippians tried to advance was the school. In spite of great hardships since Reconstruction, black Mississippians had displayed a great love for learning and support for education, just the opposite of what many white Mississippians wanted for them.[15] Yet conditions in Mississippi for black education remained very harsh. For example, during the school year in 1939–40 the value of school property per African-American pupil in Mississippi was only $14 (compared to $186 in Maryland). Mississippi spent $52.01 on the educational expenses of each white student, while giving $7.36 per black pupil (this meant that whites in the state exceed black expenses by 606.6 percent!).[16] Black Mississippians received their first public high school in 1932, when the Rosenwald Fund made a grant to aid the establishment of an agricultural high school in the Mississippi Delta.[17] The intensive interest of black Mississippians in education is revealed in their increasing literacy rates in the state, most notable between 1890 and 1930. In 1890 the black literacy rate in Mississippi was only 32.2 percent, but by 1930 it had increased to 76.8 percent, (an increase of 95.9 percent).[18] This was a tremendous achievement for black people in Mississippi.

Other black institutions and groups were also hard pressed in the continuing struggle for survival in Mississippi during the 1930s. The experiences of two key black middle-class groups are interesting for this period: lawyers and doctors. At the end of the 1930s there were only three black lawyers still active in Mississippi, and 55 black physicians.[19] Jackson, Mississippi, seems to have been the center of the activities of black lawyers in the 1930s, with all of them located on or near North Parish Street, the historic black business district in the capital city. This list probably included S. D. Redmond (also a physician), P.O. Cooper, and W. L. McLoan.[20] A study by sociologist Charles S. Johnson found that in 1932, "of the 1,247 Negro lawyers in the United States 61.5 percent are in 16 northern and mid-western states, where only 20 percent of the Negro population resides, but where the level of incomes is higher than in the South. There is a variance between the median salaries of the lawyers by sections; in the South Atlantic States $2,218.75 and in the Middle Atlantic States $2,700.00."[21] Of course the figures would have been much lower for Mississippi. This helps to explain, along with Mississippi's other intensive problems, why so many black Mississippi lawyers migrated from the state in the 1930s. In fact, in 1920 there were 14 black lawyers in the state, but, as noted above, this number reached the low point of three at the end of the 1930s.

There was also a decline of black physicians in Mississippi in the period 1920–1939. However, the totals who migrated out of Mississippi were much less for black doctors than for black lawyers. In 1920, Mississippi contained 66 black physicians, but only 55 by the end of the 1930s, a reduction of 11 physicians.[22] Black physicians were concentrated in Mississippi cities: R. A. Gordan at Alcorn; Walter A. Zuber at Corinth; James L. Randall and L. R. Young at Hattiesburg; J. H. Howard at Holly Springs; C. B. Christian, R. L. Johnson, S. L. Martin, and S. D Redmond in Jackson; R. B. Mathews and D. W. Sherrod at Meridian; W. H. Bromfield and S. P. Lee at Mound Bayou; T. B. Coleman, A. W. Dumas, R. W. Harrison, and J. C. Mazique in Natchez; C. H. Wheeler at Okolona; J. P. Sherrod at Port Gibson; and J. W. Holmes and Thomas L. Zuber at West Point; among others.[23] Incomes were generally much higher for black doctors than for black lawyers in the 1930s. One study notes: "In comparison with the incomes of physicians generally in the United States that of the Negro physician is smaller by approximately $1,000.00. The majority of the Negro physicians' salaries fall within the range of $1,000 to $5,000. Only 16.2 percent of the Negro physicians' annual incomes exceed $5,000, as compared with 35.9 percent of all physicians."[24]

But black doctors in such states as Mississippi were also greatly impacted by the general poverty and low incomes of their patients, who were largely sharecroppers. This fact is observed in a study that notes:

> The unmet health needs of large sectors of the population constitute one of the most serious problems in the United States today. In general, average family expenditures for all medical services, medicines, and health and accident insurance appear to be rather small, particularly in view of the fact that public-health provisions for free or semifree services meet but a small part of the need and are still nonexistent in many rural areas. In the Georgia and Mississippi counties sampled, expenditures for medical care averaged only $12 and $18 for Negro sharecroppers and farm operators, respectively, and $20 and $51 for white sharecroppers and farm operators.[25]

Thus, both black doctors and lawyers were at a disadvantage in practicing in Mississippi. They generally worked against the odds to stay in the state and to serve their communities.[26]

This plight also befell black journalists, editors and publishers in Mississippi during the 1930s. A study on the black press in Mississippi during this period reveals: "Between 1930 and 1939, only thirty-three black publications existed in Mississippi, including fifteen commercial, six religious, two fraternal, and ten educational journals. These figures compare to sixty-six papers produced in the period 1910–19 and forty-six in the 1890s. Jackson remained the leading center for black journals, with seven, followed by Mount Bayou with three and Vicksburg with two."[27]

Black business developments were hard hit by the Great Depression in Mississippi but continued to serve a largely black world. Strikingly, there is an increase in black businesses in the state in the 1930s, in spite of the Great Depression. For example, in 1920 there were 351 African-American restaurant and saloon keepers in Mississippi. By 1940 this number had increased to 573. Likewise, in 1920 there were 657 black merchants and retailers in the state, and by 1940, 699.[28] Perhaps the Mississippi situation is a reflection of the intensive racism of the period, when more blacks had to turn to their own communities for aid and comfort.

Black musical developments were extensive during the 1930s. There was a tremendous expansion of music by black Mississippi artists, especially in the form of the blues, jazz, and gospel.[29] Race records, as they were called during this period, and black performances were highly attended in the country, and radio introduced many of these artists to a national audience. Many of them were also active in performing at Mississippi juke-joints and other locations. One of the giants in the field, Bessie Smith, recorded "Nobody Knows You When You're Down and Out" in 1933. One study notes her fate: "After the [car] accident she was taken to a black hospital in Clarksdale, Mississippi, where she died from massive injuries she had suffered."[30] But along with Gertrude "Ma" Rainey, Billie Holiday, and countless thousands of other black artists, they helped to lift the spirits of black Americans during a bleak period in the nation's history.[31]

Finally, the black church remained an important institution in the African-American community in Mississippi during the decade. As Chalmers Archer reminds contemporaries: "Growing up black in rural Mississippi—memories of a family, heritage of place," were all centered on the traditions of the black church and the key place which this institution played in black lives.[32] While most black Mississippians were Baptists and Methodists, other important church membership for blacks were in the Roman Catholic Church, the Presbyterian Church, the Congregational Church, and especially the Pentecostal, or the Church of God in Christ, and others. By the 1930s many blacks became interested in the Islamic faith.[33] One scholar notes the importance of the black church: "As the result of the social forces to which the Negro population was subjected, a separate Negro world had been created in America; and the Negro church was partly the product of this segregated society with a distinctive life of its own."[34] During the Great Depression the black church in Mississippi was of special importance because of its key role in promoting African-American spirituality, aiding the common efforts of the black community for relief from the daily oppression of white Mississippians, and promoting the long-term struggle of blacks for greater social, political and economic advancement in American society.[35]

The rapidly moving events of the 1930s did not have an important impact on the political situation of blacks in Mississippi. State and local governments were still run by and for white men, although a few white Mississippi women were able to enter political life after securing the vote in 1920. Two examples of white Mississippi women in this role were Belle Kearney (1863–1939), "the first woman in the South to be elected a state senator," and Nellie Nugent Somerville (1863–1952), "elected to the Mississippi House of Representatives," both in the 1920s.[36] Both women suffrage leaders were conservatives in Mississippi, especially when it came to black rights. Many other white leaders in Mississippi were more reactionary, including Theodore G. Bilbo, governor of Mississippi in 1928–32, known for his racism against blacks and especially of the dangers "of an educated Negro," and Pat Harrison, also a Mississippi senator during the 1930s and a supporter of the status-quo (white supremacy) in Mississippi.[37]

According to John Skates, the 1930s were very difficult years for Mississippi in every area of the state's existence. He notes: "If the 1920s were a decade of stagnation, Mississippians in the period from 1930 to 1940 suffered an economic disaster. Cotton prices dipped toward 5c per pound, and by 1932 one Mississippi farm in every ten was going under the auctioneer's hammer. By the middle of that decade more than one-half of all Mississippi farmers were tenants or sharecroppers."[38]

Black Mississippians longed for more political rights and advancement of their interests in the 1930s, but the situation remained detestable. Very few blacks were allowed to vote in Mississippi. The voting system was guaranteed to block black political advancement.[39] Thus, during the 1930s, black Mississippians lived in a segregated world, where their economic, social and political lives were circumvented by the age of Jim Crow. One court case during the decade seems to denote the predicament of blacks in Mississippi. As Richard C. Cortner has written, this case

> arose out of the bigotry and the terror engendered by lynch-mob injustice in the American South, a system that allowed coerced confessions to be used in the conviction of those accused of crime. In the spring of 1934, a white planter was discovered in his home in Kemper County, Mississippi, dying of wounds that had been inflicted by a brutal beating. Amid reports that lynch mobs were organizing, three black sharecroppers—Ed Brown, Henry Shields, and Arthur (Yank) Ellington—were arrested for the murder, tortured until they confessed to the crime, and hastily indicted, tried, convicted, and sentenced to death by hanging. Only one week separated the discovery of the murder and the death sentences imposed on the three black defendants.
>
> Since Brown, Shields, and Ellington were penniless, under ordinary circumstances the story of their case would have ended with their hanging by Mississippi authorities, but one of their court-appointed trial lawyers—John A. Clark—was convinced of their innocence and resolved to appeal the trio's case. Clark lost the appeal in the Mississippi Supreme Court, however, and the pressure and ostracism to which he was subjected because of his involvement in the case led to his physical and mental collapse. An ex-governor of Mississippi, Earl Leroy Brewer, was then persuaded to enter the case, and with the support of the National Association for the Advancement of Colored People, the Commission on Interracial Cooperation, and white Mississippi moderates and liberals, Brewer succeeded in appealing the Kemper trio's case to the United States Supreme Court.
>
> The result was the Supreme Court's landmark decision in Brown v. Mississippi during February of 1936 in which the Court reversed the convictions of Brown, Shields, and Ellington, and for the first time held that the used of coerced confessions as evidence in a state criminal trial violated the Constitution's guarantee of due process of law. While the states had broad latitude to regulate criminal procedure, Chief Justice Charles Evans Hughes declared for a unanimous Court, they could not adopt "trial by ordeal. The rack and the torture chamber may not be substituted for the witness stand." In the Brown case, the Court therefore applied the Constitution to police interrogations of criminal suspects and took the first step down the path of constitutional development that led to the controversial Miranda decision thirty years later.[40]

Mississippi's criminal justice system remained a closed system against the black community during the years 1930–1939. In fact, an era of Jim Crow segregation statutes continued to define life for black Mississippians in the Magnolia State.[41] Katheryn K. Russell denotes what this situation meant for many blacks in Mississippi: "Blackness itself was a crime. The codes permitted Blacks to be punished for a wide range of social actions. They could be punished for walking down the street if they did not move out of the way quickly enough to accommodate White passersby, for talking to friends on a street corner, for Parchman Penitentiary, in Sunflower County, Mississippi, remained the key state prison in the 1930s."[42] African-Americans knew the place very well. David L. Cohn, a native son of Mississippi, notes the significance of crime and violence in the state: "Negro and white prisoners, male and female, are completely separated in the prison, although they live under the same conditions and receive the same kind of treatment. Its ever-increasing population now consists of nearly 2,200 Negroes and 500 whites." The cardinal characteristic of crimes in

Parchman penitentiary, created in 1904 as the central state penitentiary, became well-known nationally and internationally for its mistreatment of prisoners, especially African-Americans. Covering more that 21,000 acres, the institution not only housed convicts, but has served the Delta region of Mississippi as a major producer of cotton. This scene from the 1930s shows the presence of black women prisoners (COURTESY OF MISSISSIPPI DEPARTMENT OF ARCHIVES AND HISTORY).

the Delta is that they are crimes of violence. As of March 1935, 787 Delta prisoners in the state penitentiary were serving terms for the following crimes:

Assault and battery with intent to kill	46
Grand larceny	69
Burglary and larceny	70
Burglary	149
Robbery	19
Forgery	8
Arson	3
Attempt to rape	4
Rape	1
Violating age of consent	1
Obtaining property under false pretense	3
Attempt to commit robbery	2
Aiding jail breaks	3
Robbery with firearms	2
Highway robbery	5
Possessing stolen goods	1
Distilling	1
Counterfeiting	2
Uttering forgery	92
Murder	304

The Delta is, to begin with, an armed camp. It is common knowledge that almost every person, white or black, carries arms on his person or has them at home. The poorest white and the poorest Negro have usually one or more rifles or shotguns because hunting is the common sport of the country. Both frequently have pistols in addition.[43]

These general conditions, when mixed with Mississippi's racist traditions and history, made for a voluminous state of affairs. This was especially true in terms of Mississippi's capital offenses policy. People could be executed for at least sixteen crimes, including: "Murder of a peace officer or correctional officer; murder while under a life sentence; murder by bomb or explosive; contract murder; murder committed during specific felonies (rape, burglary, kidnapping, arson, robbery, sexual battery, unnatural intercourse with a child, nonconsensual unnatural intercourse); murder of an elected official; rape of a child under fourteen years old by a person eighteen years or older; aircraft piracy."[44]

David M. Oshinsky's study observes the historic patterns of this problem for Mississippi:

For several hundred convicted felons, capital punishment became the fatal alternative to Parchman Farm. As expected, the process was deeply rooted in race. According to a comprehensive report of legal executions in Mississippi, blacks accounted for 87 percent of the 433 people put to death there since the Civil War, a figure slightly above the Southern average of 80 percent. The report listed the crimes for which blacks had been executed (331 males and 4 females for murder, 33 males for rape, 8 males for armed robbery), as well as the race of their victims (41 percent of the murders, 85 percent of the rapes, and all of the armed robberies were committed against whites). Not surprisingly, black-on-white crime—a marginal phenomenon in comparison to black-on-black crime—accounted for more than half of the legal executions in Mississippi.

Of the sixty-one whites put to death in this period, all were convicted murderers, and all but one had killed another white (or whites). What this meant, among other things, was that every single person executed for rape and armed robbery in Mississippi was a Negro

TABLE 8.1: LYNCHING VICTIMS, 1930–1939

	National			Mississippi		
Year	Total	Black	White	Total	Black	White
1930	31	20	1	8	8	0
1931	13	12	1	8	8	0
1932	8	6	2	4	2	2
1933	28	24	4	6	6	0
1934	15	15	0	7	7	0
1935	20	18	2	10	10	0
1936	8	8	0	1	1	0
1937	8	8	0	3	3	0
1938	6	6	0	4	4	0
1939	3	2	1	1	1	0
Total	130	119	11	52	50	2

TABLE 8.2: LYNCHING VICTIMS BY COUNTY, 1930–1939

County	Number	County	Number	County	Number
Benton	2	LeFlore	2	Sunflower	1
Bolivar	3	Lowndes	9	Warren	2
Calhoun	2	Madison	3	Winston	3
Desoto	1	Marshall	1		
Hinds	2	Montgomery	2	Unknown	5
Jones	2	Pearl River	2		
Kemper	2	Rankin	1	TOTAL	50
Lafayette	1	Sharkey	1		
Lawrence	1	Stone	2		

and that only one white person had ever been executed for an interracial crime. His name was Mel Cheatham.

In the summer of 1889, Cheatham was tried and convicted for the murder of James Tillman, a plantation worker known to whites as a "good" "reliable" "inoffensive," "churchgoing" Negro. Cheatham had ambushed Tillman on a lonely road, killed him with a shotgun blast, and dumped his body into the Yalobusha River, near Grenada, Mississippi, where it was found caught on a log. "There was no mystery to the murder," wrote a local historian. "Everyone in the little community knew who had killed [the Negro] and why." Tillman had just told a grand jury about the notorious gambling den that Cheatham ran behind his general store, and he was set to testify again. In

TABLE 8.3: BLACK WOMEN LYNCHING VICTIMS, 1930–1939

Year	Name	Place	Cause
7/5/30	Viola Dial	Unknown	accident?
9/10/30	Holly White	Scooba, Kemper County	Robbery of tourists

TABLE 8.4: WHITE MALE LYNCHING VICTIMS, 1930–1939

Year	Name	Place	Cause
1932	Unknown	Pearl River County	Unknown
1932	Unknown	Pearl River County	Unknown

this particular case, the black man spoke for law and order, so his death could not easily be ignored.

The jury took less than an hour to decide. Cheatham went to the gallows on March 19, 1890. He walked briskly, made a short prayer, said "Boys, good-bye," then firmly, "I am ready." Sheriff Jones cut the rope holding the trap with one clean stroke of a hatchet, and Mel J. Cheatham dropped into eternity, strangling slowly when the fall failed to break his neck.[45]

In addition to the harshness of the state's capital punishment system was the fact that its convict-leasing program was still in place during the 1930s and brought untold misery to thousands of Mississippians during this decade. According to Pete Daniel, peonage was a system in "the shadow of slavery," where it "remained invisible, improbable, but real. It lay hidden by the inability of most Americans to believe that peonage could exist, and by the willingness of those who knew to allow it."[46] Such horrible conditions remained for another generation to resolve in the future.

During the 1930s the causes of the violent problem of lynching in Mississippi were as varied as ever, in a historical perspective. The Ku Klux Klan continued to remain a threat. Many white Mississippians still proclaimed a defense of lynching to prevent black rapes of white women; others targeted blacks for violations of Southern race etiquette. Successful black farmers and holders of any wealth could become lynching victims. And, as in so many cases, countless blacks were lynched for assault and murder, especially of whites.[47]

Mississippi continued to experience a decline in lynchings during the 1930s. This was also true of the national lynching rates. Table 8.1 notes the national and state rates for this period. At least 130 individuals were lynched in the nation during the thirties, including 119 blacks and 11 whites.[48] In Mississippi a total of 52 lynching victims are noted for the 1930s, 50 blacks and 2 whites.[49] With such high numbers, Mississippi continued to be the leading lynching state in the country. Nationally, three years stand out for high lynching totals: 1933 with 28 victims, 1930 with 21 cases, and 1935 with 20 lynchings. The three highest years for Mississippi are 1935 with 10 cases, and 1930 and 1931 with 8 victims each. The early 1930s were indeed difficult years and represent the growing state and national crisis generated by the Great Depression.

Lynching victims in Mississippi, as noted in Tables 8.2 and 8.5 (page 100), were

TABLE 8.5: MISSISSIPPI COUNTIES WITH LARGEST NUMBERS OF LYNCHING EVENTS (3 OR MORE VICTIMS), 1930–1939

County	Number of Victims
Bolivar	3
Lowndes	9
Madison	3
Winston	3

TABLE 8.6: MISSISSIPPI LYNCHING VICTIMS, RANGE AND PERCENTAGE OF OFFENSES ALLEGED, 1930–1939

Offense	Number	Percentage
Murder	9	18%
Rape/attempted rape	7	14%
Disrespectful to white person	6	12%
Altercation with a white man	4	8%
Assault	2	4%
Robbery	3	6%
Wounding a white farmer	1	2%
Too prosperous	1	2%
Organizing sharecroppers	1	2%
Striking a white man and being too smart	1	2%
Work related	1	2%
Owed a balance of money	1	2%
Race prejudice	1	2%
Accident	1	2%
Resisting officer of the law	1	2%
Problem with the law	1	2%
Unknown	9	18%
Total	50	

distributed throughout the state, but lynchings are known to have taken place in at least 21 counties. The county sites of five lynching victims are unknown. Lynchings took place in five of the six geographical regions of the state. Only the Gulf Coast region, represented by the counties of Hancock, Harrison, and Jackson, did not record a lynching for the 1930s. East Mississippi had a total of 14 lynchings in three counties (Kemper 2, Lowndes 9, and

Winston 3), the highest totals for the decade. South Mississippi followed with nine lynchings in five counties (Jones 2, Lawrence 1, Pearl River 2, Stone 2 and Warren 2). The Delta and North Mississippi regions, each with seven lynching victims, were next. The four Delta counties included Bolivar 3, Leflore 2, Sharkey 1, and Sunflower 1. The five North Mississippi counties were Benton 2, Calhoun 2, Desoto 1, Lafayette 1, and Marshall 1. The distribution of lynching victims by region in Mississippi suggest that in the 1930s blacks were at risk for a lynching regardless of where they lived, except for the Gulf Coast. Lynching was certainly still a problem in the largely black populated area of the Delta or in South Mississippi. But even in regions with smaller black populations, such as East and North Mississippi, this crime against black people was a real possibility for many. This factor is also highlighted in Table 8.5, which notes that the four Mississippi counties with the highest totals for lynching victims during the decade are in three regions of the state: Bolivar County in the Delta (3 victims); Madison County in Central Mississippi (3 victims); and Lowndes (9 cases) and Winston (3 victims) counties in East Mississippi.

While black men remained the majority of lynching victims in Mississippi during the 1930s, Tables 8.3 and 8.4 indicate that at least two victims each were black women and white males.

Victims in the 1930s were lynched for at least 16 causes, as described in Table 8.6. A clear majority, 18 percent or nine cases, were lynched for murder. This was followed by rape or attempted rape at 14 percent or seven victims. Being disrespectful to a white person could be a serious problem for a black Mississippian, and six such cases, or 12 percent of the victims, are noted. Having an altercation with a white male for any reason could also be deadly for a black man in Mississippi, and at least four cases, or 8 percent, are noted. "Economic" crimes were also a problem for blacks. Being too prosperous (one person or 2 percent of the total) could get one lynched in Mississippi. Owing a balance payment or a debt could lead to lynching (one case at 2 percent of the total), and so on.

Mississippi lynchings generally could take place in any month of the year, as observed in Table 8.7 (page 102). Yet the summer months—note June with five known lynching victims, July with 12 and August also with five—are among the highest totals of lynching victims for the decade. This seasonal variation followed a rather Southern pattern for lynchings during the Age of Lynching.[50]

The terrible burden of the 50 known lynchings in Mississippi between 1930 and 1939 were a continuing statement on the inventory of hundreds of lynchings in the state, and thousands in the nation, since the Reconstruction period. James S. Hirsch notes the significance of this historic epoch:

> Between 1890 and 1930, 2,771 people were lynched, most of whom lived in the South, and were black, according to the Tuskegee Institute in Alabama. Lynchings had been used for decades in the West, but what distinguished these hangings was their blending of torture and public theater. If the victim was executed by fire, the ritual included the application of a red-hot poker to his eyes and genitals, the smell of burning flesh as the body roasted over flames, the sizzling of blood. If killed by hanging, the spectacle promised convulsive movements of the limbs. Thousands of white would watch these scenes, and the body might hang for days as a warning to other "impudent" blacks.[51]

For Mississippi, as well as nationally, the lynching phenomenon had witnessed a continuing decline since 1910. Mississippi's total lynching victims in 1910–19 were recorded at 107 (91 blacks, 2 whites, and 14 victims unknown by race). In the 1920s the totals were 66 (64 blacks and 2 whites). In the 1930s there were 50 lynching victims in the state (48 blacks and 2 whites). Thus a clear decline in total known lynchings had taken place in the state

TABLE 8.7: MISSISSIPPI LYNCHINGS BY MONTH, 1930–1939

Month	Number	Percentage
January	1	2%
February	0	0%
March	5	10%
April	4	8%
May	1	2%
June	5	10%
July	12	24%
August	5	10%
September	4	8%
October	0	0%
November	2	4%
December	0	0%
Unknown	11	22%
TOTAL	50	

since 1910. Yet the horror of the lynching event remained as powerful as ever and still gripped life in Mississippi and the South.[52]

A selection of five case studies from the fifty known Mississippi lynchings in the 1930s serve to demonstrate the continuing heartache suffered by so many.

Case Study One: 1933
"Mysterious Lynching in Mississippi"
Columbus, Miss., July 22

Mystery shrouds the lynching of a Negro which took place at the little town of Caledonia, 15 miles north of here.

First reports merely stated that a Negro had been lynched last Friday after he allegedly "insulted a white woman." Subsequent efforts by newsmen to secure details of the lynching met with outright denials that a lynching had taken place. Later it was admitted, however, that an unnamed Negro had been hanged. It was said that the Negro went to a farm house and made an improper proposal to a white girl.

The white girl sent him away with the understanding that he was to meet her later in a nearby cotton field. When he appeared at the designated time, he was met by a band of white men who were waiting for him.

The band seized him, hanged him, and riddled him with bullets and quietly dispersed.[53]

Case Study Two: 1933
Minter City, Leflore County, September 18

Richard Roscoe, Negro Farmer, was seized at his home by a mob and shot. His "bullet-filled body" was fastened to an automobile, dragged through town and then taken back and deposited in the yard. He was accused of "striking a white man in a fight and being too smart."[54]

Case Study Three: 1934
"Eyewitness Tells of Lynching"
Clarksdale, Miss., June 9

Despite the reluctance of witnesses to openly discuss the lynching of two Mississippi negroes that took place here yesterday, the local newspaper was able to secure the following eye-witness account of the affair from a man who nevertheless, refuses to give his name for fear of retaliation by townsmen:

"I saw them hang two Negroes last night. The Negroes screamed and prayed, but they died. Just before they died they called on the Lord to help them.

"'It won't do you no good to pray niggers, where you're goin',' someone in the crowd shouted to them. Some of the men wanted to cut them up. 'We better not waste too much time,' someone else said, ''cause the sheriff will be along any time.'

"It was getting pretty dark when we got to a bridge over a small creek near Lambert. 'Here is a good spot to get rid of them niggers,' a fellow in the car with them said.

"We all stopped. There must have been close to 200 men from around the neighborhood. The Negroes were thrown out of the car. Ropes were tied around their necks. They screamed louder. 'Cut out that crying you black So and So's,' someone shouted.

"One of the Negroes was hit in the ear. He fell down. 'Oh Lordy, save me,' he shouted. Someone kicked him. He got up swaying from side to side as if drunk.

"The crowd dragged the Negroes to the edge of the bridge. 'Push them off,' a voice cried. They were pushed. Swinging down you could hear their necks crack. It made me right sick for a minute.

"The bodies started swaying around, spinning back and forth. Around and around they spun, sort of like two black tops on a string. 'Shall we cut them down now?' someone asked. 'Hell, no,' another man said. 'Leave them up there for crow-bait.'

"For a while no one said anything. Everybody just stood still and watched them swing. Finally we started movin' away. I went home. I couldn't eat no supper. I saw them bodies swinging."[55]

Case Study Four (A): 1934
"Hernando Hanging"

Fortnight ago the Mississippi Senate passed a bill to permit Clyde Collins, outraged father, to hang three negroes convicted of attacking his daughter Mildred. Reason for the special privileges was that an appeal by him to a mob had saved the three attackers from lynching. Last week [March 1934] as the day for the hanging approached, Father Collins saw his chance of executing personal justice gradually fade. The Mississippi House buried the hanging bill in committee.

In Mississippi hangings are generally held at noon but to avoid a mob scene ten trucks loaded with guardsmen left Jackson before midnight to carry the three prisoners back to Hernando and to death. At 4:30 in the morning the three Negroes stood in the Hernando jail under garish electric lights, praying aloud while the gallows was made ready. Father Collins, a favored spectator, stood beside Sheriff Roscoe Lauderdale. In the hall below the trap through which the bodies would fall were about 150 Hernandoans who did not mind getting up early for such an occasion.

As the noose was put around the neck of the first Negro, Isaac Howard, he said: "Tell others of my kind never to attack none who don't belong to them. I believe in God." Then he began to sing "The Other Shore."

The sheriff sprang the trap. Isaac Howard plunged through the floor, his song ended. Said the sheriff: "That bastard won't bother you any more." Said Father Collins, "Hell no!"

In the hall below someone said: "That's Isaac Howard." The crowd laughed. Fifteen minutes later the doctor with his stethoscope pronounced Isaac Howard dead. Another spiritual began above, another body plunged through the trap. A dozen young girls who had been lazy about getting up came in a moment later. "Look how long his neck is," one exclaimed. "That's because it's broken," explained an officer.

The girls giggled. The doctor ordered silence so that he could listen for heart beats with his stethoscope. Fourteen minutes later he was still hearing them. "Aw, hell," someone yelled, "knock him on the head with a hammer." An officer patted his six shooter: "I know a faster way than that."

Thus the spectacle went on for over an hour until all three were hanged and dead. Father Collins standing beside the sheriff smiled through it all. Since Hernando Negroes did not want the bodies buried in their cemetery, the guardsmen, followed by the crowd, took the corpses in their trucks to the poor farm where a hole 7 ft. square had been dug.

"Throw 'em in," shouted the crowd. Sheriff Lauderdale warned them: "I'm still in charge, and I'm going to see they are buried right."

While the dirt was shoveled in some members of the crowd chanted, "I'm Headin' for the Last Round Up, I'll Be Glad When You're Dead, You Rascal, You, Bye, Bye, Blackbirds." Finally Hernando went home to breakfast.[56]

Case Study Four (B): 1935

It is probably easier to get lynched in Mississippi than in any other state. The ideal American is supposedly the man who works with his hands and thus prospers, takes loving care of his family, building honestly for their future; he can lend a helping hand to his fellowman in passing, so much more to his and his community's credit. Not so in Mississippi. Take these two cases of March, 1935.

In Lawrence County the body of R. J. Tyronne, a prosperous Negro farmer, was found shot to pieces in the woods near his home on the night of the twenty-sixth, where he had been lynched by a mob of white Mississippians about four days previously. Tyronne was said to have been too prosperous for his white neighbors.

Four days later, at Hernando, the body of the Reverend T. A. Allen, of Marks, a Negro, was found weighted down with a chain in the Coldwater River. His only crime had been the effort to organize the sharecroppers of his neighborhood.[57]

Case Study Four (C): 1935
1 Negro Slain, Another Beaten in Stone County
Wiggins, June 23

One Negro was lynched and another was spirited into the woods and whipped during 24 hours of mob rule by citizens which ended today in Wiggins.

R. D. McGee, 25 year old Negro, was lynched and riddled with bullets about 9 a.m. today for an attack yesterday upon the 11 year old daughter of a white dairy farmer and another unidentified Negro was whipped and released by a crowd of white men because of an insult to a white woman.

Stone County was in a state of high excitement until the lynch mob of about 300 men dispersed and then Stone County settled down into normalcy and Sheriff J. A. Simpton and the coroner had the body of the negro cut down and started an investigation.

Physicians said the white girl was not criminally attacked, but that she was choked into unconsciousness by the negro as he seized her at a pasture gate near her home and struck her over the head with a shovel handle.

The girl's father said that after his daughter had been knocked unconscious her attacker dragged her into a field and left her there for dead.

When she was found, physicians said, her eyes were bloodshot, and small blood vessels were ruptured in her throat, her face was bruised. The child was still confined to bed today under medical treatment.

Immediately after the attack a citizens posse was formed and started a search for the

Negro. Last night about eleven o'clock, McGee was taken from his bed by members of the posse and was secreted in the woods away from officers until today when he was carried before the girl and identified by his clothing.

The mob then carried the Negro across town into a side road leading to the graveyard where witnesses said he admitted attacking the girl and said that his only reason was "I must have been crazy."

McGee was hung by a rope to an oak tree beside the narrow road and his body was riddled with bullets. Then the mob members cut down his body and hung it to another tree beside the main highway where the coroner and peace officers met and held their formal inquest. The verdict was that the Negro "came to his death at the hands of unknown parties." No arrests have been announced.[58]

Case Study Five (A): 1937
Duck Hill, Mississippi, April 13

Two Negroes accused of the murder of a country merchant on December 30, 1936, were snatched by twelve men from the Sheriff and two deputies as they were being returned to jail. "Boot Jack" MacDaniels and Roosevelt Townes, the victims, were hurried to the scene of their crime, stripped to the waist, and chained to trees. A member of the mob brought out a gasoline blow-torch. The torch flames were sprayed on the Negroes' bared breasts and they were ordered to confess. MacDaniels was the first to feel the searing blow-torch and readily confessed that he had robbed the merchant after Townes had killed him. He was then riddled with bullets. Townes, the Associated Press reported, died under the torture of the blow-torch. Both men in their confessions implicated another man, who was later captured and brought to the carnival. The third man admitted he had originally been a party to the conspiracy but insisted he had withdrawn before the crime. He was severely beaten and ordered to leave the state. The lynch mob, assisted by the hundred spectators, piled brush high about the victims and burned their bodies. Governor White was reported "outraged," but even at that there were no arrests, no indictments, and no convictions.[59]

Case Study Five (B): 1938
Rolling Fork, Sharkey County, July 6

Tom McGehee, Negro blacksmith, was killed in gun battle with a posse of about seventy-five men after the murder of a white planter for whom he worked. Later a mob seized the body, poured gasoline over it, set it on fire, tied it to an automobile, and hauled it down to Rolling Fork.[60]

These examples from the 1930s illustrate the continued nature and horror of Mississippi lynchings during the period. The events helped to galvanize opposition to lynching on the state, regional, national, and international levels. Black poets were especially moved to capture in their verse the nature of lynching as a problem. An excellent poet who emerged in the 1920s and wrote during this period in this regard is Langston Hughes. His 1938 poem "Lynching Song" was one of many written during his long career to note the sorrow and anger of the lynching problem.[61]

Black Mississippians continued to be challenged and disturbed by the lynching crisis in the state during the thirties.[62] Black Mississippi organizations and leaders did what they could, under the restrictions imposed by the Jim Crow system, to garner support for the anti-lynching movement in Mississippi. However, as historian Neil R. McMillen observes, there were "feasible limits" to actual black protest in Mississippi during the 1930s. He writes:

With the notable exception of the 1904 streetcar boycotts ... the half century after 1890 witnessed no direct-action campaigns. Black spokesmen frequently demonstrated for better jobs, better schools, and full citizenship rights. But neither massive street demonstrations against economic and educational discrimination nor voter registration campaigns

designed to arouse the disfranchised black underclass were within the realm of possibilities.... Avoiding direct confrontations they could not hope to win, black leaders of the
period from the turn of the century through the interwar years ... occasionally sought
redress in court and more typically petitioned public carriers and the state legislature for
more equitable transportation facilities.[63]

Nevertheless, working quietly, such Mississippi groups as the NAACP, the Federation of Colored Women's Clubs, the Committee of One Hundred, and in such cities as Greenville,
the General Colored Committee with Levye Chappie as a central leader, among other
groups, stressed the wrongs done to the race by lynching, as well as the harm done to white
citizens, and, of course, the negative world opinion created for Mississippi by lynchings in
the state.[64]

A group of black Mississippi writers also emerged in the 1930s with a powerful voice
against the injustices which faced blacks in Mississippi, the South and the nation. At the
top of this list appears the name of Richard Wright (1908–1960), the most important black
writer of the 1930s and 1940s. His short stories from the 1930s which covered the theme of
lynching included such works as "Big Boy Leaves Home."[65] Wright also wrote poetry and
essays during the 1930s, and he would produce other important books, including novels,
in the 1940s and 1950s. Of course he had to leave Mississippi in order to write. Another
notable black writer from the thirties was George Washington Lee (1894–1976), born in
Indianola, Mississippi, and educated at Alcorn College. In the 1930s he produced two important books, *Beale Street: Where the Blues Began* (1934), a history; and *River George* (1937), a
novel. Although not directly on the theme of lynching, Lee's works nonetheless demonstrated
a skill "with promoting pride in black business."[66] Lee, like Wright, had to leave Mississippi
in order for his creative spirit to develop. He lived in Memphis, Tennessee.

In addition to the above two writers, six black poets were also active in Mississippi during the 1930s. One study observes:

> One of the most widely published black poets connected with Mississippi during the 1930s
> was Jonathan Henderson Brooks (1904–1945). Brooks was born near Lexington, Missis-
> sippi ... his work appeared in *Opportunity*, and also in the Crisis, as well as several antholo-
> gies.... Thomas D. Pawley (1917–) is best known for his works in drama; however, during
> the 1930s he also published poetry. Four other poets who also wrote during this period
> were Effie T. Battle, Eudora V. Marshall Savage, Anselm J. Finch (1902–1969), and Joseph
> Clinton Brown (1908–1998).[67]

Such writers helped to foster a growing recognition of black poetic talents in Mississippi,
and to express that talent to the world's peoples on the black condition in Mississippi, the
South and the nation.

The thirty-three active black publications in Mississippi during this period were another
source of news and inspiration to the black community. They received especially hard censorship from Mississippi's Jim Crow system, but, in spite of the intensive oppression, these
organs were a black voice to the wider world, and they certainly gave blacks encouragement to fight on for a future day of freedom, even in Mississippi.[68] Even an attempt by
the *Pittsburgh Courier* in 1935 to increase its circulation base in Mississippi can be viewed
as a significant avenue of black protest against the status-quo in the state. For one thing,
white Mississippians hated the idea that a black northern newspaper might circulate among
blacks in the state. At the top of the white hate list were such organs as the *Chicago Defender*
and the *Pittsburgh Courier*, two of the leading black newspapers in America. For many years
both newspapers had sharply criticized conditions in Mississippi and the South, and had

encouraged blacks to migrate out of the South to the North.[69] The fact that some black Mississippians would even consider buying such papers and receive them in the mail took courage.

The black church of the 1930s in Mississippi was also an institution of encouragement to blacks. The church served as a central focus of black spiritual needs, and would, over time, serve to advance black economic, social and political rights.

Black college students were active during this era in stressing a need for reforms, both on their campuses and in the wider society. For example, as late as 1929, "Seven hundred students at Mississippi's Alcorn A. & M. College staged a short strike ... when their president suspended two students for 'unbecoming conduct.'"[70] Students at Tougaloo College probably began their movement toward becoming champions of civil rights in Mississippi during this period.[71]

The Great Depression greatly impacted the migration of blacks from Mississippi and the South to the North; 400,000 blacks left the region during the decade.[72] Such movement must be considered a continuing protest on the part of black Mississippians against lynching and other ills. Black Mississippians also continued during the 1930s to move to Mississippi urban areas. This is reflected in the fact that in 1930, 39.5 percent of blacks lived in Mississippi cities, where by 1940, this percentage increased to 41.1 of the total black population in the state.[73] Thus black Mississippians continued to "vote with their feet" on leaving Mississippi outright, or escaping from rural areas, whenever they could do so.

During the 1930s, white citizens of Mississippi appear to have been supporters of the lynching. Neil R. McMillen notes, "In the last analysis, then, lynching was deemed necessary because black Mississippians could not otherwise be trained to subordination, because they rejected the ideology of a white man's country. Black aspirations could be checked, in the end, only through violent measures."[74]

Mississippi government generally was silent on lynchings, but, as McMillen also observes: "Although Governor Bilbo used the National Guard in 1919 to hunt down a black fugitive but not to stop his lynching, every other governor from Henry L. Whitfield (1924 to 1927) to Paul B. Johnson (1940–1943) used state troops to protect a black suspect from a mob."[75] This process saved a few victims but did not end lynchings.

The state's major politicians, such as Senator Theodore Bilbo and Senator Pat Harrison, strongly supported the status quo in Mississippi. Bilbo remained known as one of the leading negative forces in the country on black affairs. He opposed any measure that would uplift blacks, and was very active in blocking an anti-lynching measure in Congress. Active in the Ku Klux Klan, he also advocated "a $1 billion Congressional appropriation in 1939 to deport all blacks to Africa."[76]

Mississippi's criminal justice system also presents a mixed picture on the problem of lynching in Mississippi. Many sheriffs in the state were not protective of black prisoners in their charge during this decade.[77] Poor whites in Mississippi were also generally opposed to black rights and in favor of lynching as a tool to control the black community. They also viewed blacks as an economic competition factor in the state.[78]

A number of white Mississippi women were active in the creation of the Association of Southern Women for the Prevention of Lynching in 1930. In fact, twelve white Mississippi women were at the organizing meeting of this group. White leaders active in the Mississippi group of the ASWPL were Mrs. J. Morgan Stevens, Jackson, Superintendent, Department of Christian Social Relations, Mississippi Conference, Methodist Episcopal Church, South; Mrs. Ernest Moore, Clarksdale, President, Women's Missionary Society, North Mississippi Conference, and Mrs. Bessie C. Alford, McComb, Superintendent,

Christian Social Relations for the Methodist Women's Missionary Conference. One scholar notes that Alford was effective in 1930 in building the ASWPL in Mississippi and "with the assistance of other key women obtained over five hundred signatures of white women (including students) who pledged themselves to the principles of the original resolution."[79]

By November 20, 1931, there were 560 Mississippi pledges for anti-lynching efforts in the state, including 19 ministers, with work in 44 of 82 counties. By 1935, the Mississippi Council was active in 81 counties and 260 towns, and contained 3,563 women, 371 men, and three peace officers (2 sheriffs and 1 other officer).[80]

Outside of Mississippi a tremendous range of public discussion and opinion centered on lynching in Mississippi and the South and the related problems associated with the Jim Crow system in the region. The NAACP continued to play a significant role in the anti-lynching movement from its base in New York City. At the top of its agenda was an effort to secure passage of an anti-lynching bill in Congress, a campaign underway since 1919, when Congressman L. C. Dyer of St. Louis, Missouri, had first introduced the measure.[81] Although the Dyer anti-lynching bill passed in the House of Representatives in 1922 and again in 1937, Southerners filibustered the bill to death in the Senate.[82]

The *Crisis*, the official organ of the NAACP, also continued to promote an anti-lynching theme during the 1930s. W. E. B. Du Bois served as editor of the publication between 1910 and 1934, a period of distinguished editorship for twenty-three and a half years.[83] Roy Wilkins (1901–1981) was the second editor of the *Crisis*, and he was very active between 1934 and 1939 in waging a strong public battle against lynching and other areas of discrimination against black Americans.[84] In fact, hundreds of news items, articles, and editorials appeared in the *Crisis* across the 1930s on lynchings and other economic, political, social and cultural issues of the day.[85] Working with Du Bois and Wilkins were other NAACP leaders who also played a major role in the organization's anti-lynching efforts, including James Weldon Johnson (1871–1938), field secretary 1916–1920, executive secretary 1920–1929, vice president and board member 1931–1938; Walter Francis White (1893–1955), assistant secretary 1918–1931 and executive director 1932–1955, author of nine books including a major study on lynching, *Rope and Faggot: A Biography of Judge Lynching* (1929); J. E. Spingarn (1875–1939), president 1930–1939; and many others.[86] In essence, according to B. Joyce Ross, besides the anti-lynching bill in Congress, the NAACP's anti-lynching efforts focused on "investigations, education of the public through the widest possible publicity, attempts to enlist the aid of influential Southerners, and the bestowing of accolades upon the few Southern officials who dared oppose the lynch mob."[87] In this work the association was a leading player during the decade.

A central white Southern women's group which emerged during the decade to protest lynching was the Association of Southern Women for the Prevention of Lynching.[88] This anti-lynching movement in the South signaled a new willingness among some Southern whites to be outspoken and willing to take risks on an institution—lynching—that was dear to the hearts of many white Southerners and especially white men in the South. Thus the involvement of Southern white women who opposed their men on the lynching issue is quite significant. June Melby Benowitz notes the historical importance of the ASWPL:

> Founded in Atlanta in 1930 by Jessie Daniel Ames (1883–1972), the Association of Southern Women for the Prevention of Lynching (ASWPL) was an association of white women who worked through church organizations to protest the lynching of African-American men. These women pledged that their association would do everything in its power "to create a new public opinion in the South which will not condone for any reason whatever acts of mobs or lynchers" (ASWPL Bulletin No. 4, p. 2). In the 1930s an increasing num-

ber of southern women were taking a stand against lynching. As they became more educated, sophisticated, and independent, many came to realize that what they had once considered male chivalry was in many ways a means of controlling and repressing women. They now understood that lynching which was often based on false charges of rape, was not only immoral but was an extension of male domination. Although many of the women had not previously participated in political activities, their hatred of lynching inspired them to publicly deny the truth of the idea that black men were lynched because they had raped white women.

With much of its initial backing coming from the Methodist Church, the anti-lynching movement grew until the women of the ASWPL numbered in the thousands. In 1934, the Southern Methodist Woman's Missionary Council voiced unanimous support for a federal law that would outlaw lynching. Probably referring to the ASWPL, in 1935 the editors of *Woman's Home Companion* announced that seventeen thousand women had organized in eight southern states and were "actively working to stamp out lynching and the perverted sentiment that inspires it" [*Woman's Home Companion*, August 1935].[89]

The lasting importance of the ASWPL is revealed in Estelle B. Freeman's observation that: "the group collected forty thousand signatures from southern white women [who] pledged to stop lynching in their localities."[90]

Outside of the South the anti-lynching movement also received the support of liberal white women's groups, including "the Women's Trade Union League, the Women's Joint Congressional Committee (which was the major women's lobbying group in Washington), and the YWCA, which in the 1940s fully integrated and adopted the goals of racial equality and civil rights for minorities."[91]

On the national stage during the thirties stood Eleanor Roosevelt, the wife of President Franklin D. Roosevelt. She was an outspoken and an outstanding defender of democracy, anti-lynching advocate, and promoter of humanitarian causes.[92] Eleanor Roosevelt left a lasting legacy of support for good causes to the American people.

A number of other white groups supported the anti-lynching crusade of the 1930s. The list includes: (1) American Jewish groups, including many English-language Jewish publications, and such groups as the American Jewish Congress; the Anti-Defamation League of B'nai B'rith; and the National Council of Jewish Women, which "added an anti-lynching plank to its platform in 1935."[93] (2) The American Federation of Teachers, which during the 1930s sought to create "a greater awareness of the inequities, increasing their efforts at organizing black teachers, and demonstrating to their black members that the federation would hold true to its own pronouncements about democracy and equality."[94] (3) The Southern Conference Movement, founded in Birmingham, Alabama, in 1938, stressed a need for "equal opportunities without the handicap of racial bias perpetuated by segregation."[95] (4) The Commission on Interracial Cooperation, founded in 1919 at Atlanta, Georgia, was active in opposing lynching and "published a major study condemning the practice."[96] (5) Socialist and communist parties, which "gave top priority to the organization of America's most exploited workers, including black sharecroppers in the South and Hispanic and Filipino agricultural laborers in the West. Especially after 1935 they did so with the announced goal of making America live up to its cherished political principles of equality, democracy, and the elimination of all prejudice."[97] According to historian Rayford W. Logan, however, few blacks were willing or able to join the U.S. Communist Party. In fact, by 1934 "only some 2,500 Negroes were members of the American Communist Party out of a total of about 24,000."[98]

Two presidents served the American peoples in the 1930s. Republican Herbert Hoover, 31st president, was in office from 1929 to 1933. Democrat Franklin D. Roosevelt was in office during the remainder of the 1930s. President Hoover was generally silent on lynching but did make a statement in 1930 which "had condemned lynching as 'undermining the very essence of justice and democracy,' although his statement had been reported in the press, it had gone almost unnoticed."[99] Hoover did not support the anti-lynching bill in Congress. Overall he was a disappointment to blacks and the Great Depression began under his administration.

Franklin D. Roosevelt was a much more complicated case. His "New Deal" seemed to offer some blacks some degree of hope and justice at last and with the 1932 national elections, blacks had moved from the Republican Party to the Democratic Party. But the Democratic Party had a large showing in the South and this made civil rights for blacks and an anti-lynching bill in Congress a no-win situation as Roosevelt and his advisors understood the problem. Thus, Franklin D. Roosevelt "refused to endorse an anti-lynching law because he was afraid of losing Southern support. From 1933 to 1935 lynch mobs murdered sixty-three blacks while Southern sheriffs and deputies looked the other way. The House passed [a measure in] 1937 that would have made lynching illegal. [The] measure expired in the Senate, however, because of forceful and consolidated opposition from southern Democrats. Roosevelt, realizing the bill's divisive potential, resigned himself to its defeat and never took a public stand."[100] Therefore presidential leadership was not effective in the 1930s in promoting a vigorous program to end lynching in Mississippi and this nation.

Between 1933 and 1938, several attempts were made in Congress to introduce an anti-lynching bill before the nation, but in each case the end result was failure, as with the Dyer Bill of 1922. One study notes, "In June 1934 Senators Edward C. Costigan of Colorado and Robert F. Wagner of New York introduced a new anti-lynching measure. In most respects similar to the earlier Dyer proposal, the Costigan-Wagner bill narrowed the definition of a mob from five to three persons, added a penalty of a five to twenty-five-year prison sentence for a state or local official participating in a lynching, and provided compensation for the victim's family ranging from two thousand to ten thousand dollars."[101]

By 1938, Mississippi politician Theodore G. ("The Man") Bilbo felt compelled to attack the Costigan-Wagner bill as an object that would "open the floodgates of hell in the South, and ignite a firestorm of looting, rape, and lynching."[102] In the end efforts at reform of the problem of lynching came down to a defeat in both the House of Representatives and the Senate due to Southern filibusters on the various bills presented to Congress.[103]

At least several hundred black American writers were active during the late stages of the Harlem Renaissance to 1935 and for the remainder of the decade.[104] The lynching phenomenon in America was of major concern and interest to black intellectuals, creative writers and artists, musicians, social scientists, fraternal groups, black journalists and black women's organizations. The theme of lynching appears widely in the work of black writers during the decade. This is certainly a theme that is reflected in much of the poetry, novels, plays, essays and non-fiction works of the period. The major black poets of the decade were James Weldon Johnson (1871–1938), Claude McKay (1890–1948), Jean Toomer (1894–1967), Sterling A. Brown (1901–1989), Countee Cullen (1903–1946), Langston Hughes (1902–1967), Georgia Douglas Johnson (1886–1966), Anne Spencer (1882–1975), and Arna Bontemps (1902–1973), among others. These writers produced some of the most moving creative poems in the early parts of the last century, including such masterworks as Claude McKay's "If We Must Die" and "Harlem Shadows" (1922), Jean Toomer's *Cane* (1923), Countee Cullen's *Color* (1925), *The Black Christ* (1929) and *The Media and Some Other Poems* (1935); Langston Hughes' *The Ways of White Folks* (1934); Sterling Brown's *Southern Road* (1932); and Georgia Douglas Johnson's *Bronze* (1922), which highlight the black condition in America.[105] Major critics and editors of the era who continued supporting the Harlem Renaissance and black arts in general were Alain L. Locke (1885–1954), editor of *The New Negro* (1925); Charles S. Johnson, editor of the Urban League's magazine, *Opportunity*; and W. E. B. Du Bois and Roy Wilkins, editors of the *Crisis*.[106] These individuals were key players in promoting black writers and in keeping the anti-lynching message before the public.

Among major black novelists of the period who championed the theme of anti-lynching were Jessie Fauset, *There is Confusion* (1924); Walter White, *The Fire in the Flint* (1924) and the non-fiction work *Rope and Faggot* (1929); Arna Bontemps, *God Sends Sunday* (1931); and Zora Neale Hurston, *Jonah's Gourd Vine* (1934), *Their Eyes Were Watching God* (1937), and *Mules and Men* (1935) on black folklore.[107]

Black playwrights were also active in producing creative works in the 1930s on the lynching theme. Georgia Douglas Johnson penned three anti-lynching works and "more than two dozen anti-lynch plays written mostly by women have survived."[108] Thus, black writers of the 1930s were an inspiration to the anti-lynching movement in America, and their creative works from the period continue to radiate a message of hope, understanding and enlightenment on the historical problems of lynching and discrimination in the life of the nation. Kenneth Patchen's poem "Nice Day for a Lynching" is reflective of this contribution.[109]

Black social scientists—including historians, sociologists, librarians, economists, philosophers, educators, higher education administrators, and others—were also active in the anti-lynching movement and as interpreters of the meaning and impact of the lynching crisis in America. Historians on the list from the thirties include Carter G. Woodson, founder and head of the Association for the Study of Negro Life and History (1915); publisher of the *Journal of Negro History* (1916), *The Negro History Bulletin* (1937), and the publishing arm of the Association, the *Associated Publishers* (1921); and author of sixteen books, many with a historical focus, such as *The Negro in Our History* (1922), *Negro Makers of History* (1928) and *Story of the Negro Retold* (1935). In 1926 he organized an annual celebration of black life and culture into Negro History Week to be held each year during the month of February. Because of his immense contributions, Woodson has become known as the Father of Black History.[110] William Leo Hansberry (1894–1965), a major scholar on Africa at Howard University during the 1930s, has been recognized as "the first American Negro to devote his life exclusively to the study of Africa and its ancient civilizations. Forty years before the idea gained wide acceptance his research led him to the conclusion that Africa's past constituted a unique and highly developed cultural heritage."[111] William E. B. Du Bois, author of *Black Reconstruction in America, 1860–1880*, was the leading black scholar in America during the 1930s.[112] Charles Harris Wesley (1891–1987), head of the history department at Howard University in 1921–1942, authored *Negro Labor in the United States, 1850–1925: A Study in American Economic History* (1927) and was editor of *Negro History Bulletin* in 1967–1973.[113] Rayford Whittingham Logan (1897–1982), head of the department of history at Atlanta (Ga.) University 1933–38 and professor at Howard University 1938–1939, authored many articles in the 1930s in such organs as the *Journal of Negro History*, *Journal of Negro Education*, *Negro History Bulletin*, *Crisis*, *Opportunity*, *Southern Workman*, *Current History*, *Nation*, *New Republic* and others.[114]

Other important social scientists of this period made important scholarly contributions to the overall goals of the anti-lynching movement and toward advancing the rights of all Americans. One was E. Franklin Frazier (1894–1962), a sociologist at Fisk University, Nashville, Tennessee 1931–1934, head of the department of sociology and director of the social work program at Howard University 1935–1943, and author of the essay "The Pathology of Race Prejudice" (1927) and books *The Negro Family in Chicago* (1932) and *The Negro*

Family in the United States (1939).[115] Eugene Kinckle Jones (1884–1954) was an educator and leader in the National Urban League (Executive Secretary 1917–1941) and key founder, with Charles S. Johnson, of *Opportunity*, the league's official organ.[116] St. Clair Drake, an anthropologist (1911–1990), did important field work in the South and studies at the University of Chicago in the 1930s.[117] Ralph Bunche (1904–1971), political scientist and diplomat, was the first African American to receive the Nobel Peace Prize (1950) for his efforts in promoting peace in the Middle East. He served as Undersecretary General of the United Nations from 1955 to 1971.[118] Abram Lincoln Harris, Jr., was a key economist who worked at Howard University from 1927 to 1945 and at the University of Chicago from 1946 to 1963. He was a major force in noting black economic and labor interests in the world.[119] Ida B. Wells-Barnett, the legendary anti-lynching crusader, died on March 26, 1931. In her final years she penned her autobiography which was edited by her daughter, Alfreda M. Duster, in 1970. Wells-Barnett remains the leading advocate in the anti-lynching movement from the late nineteenth century to the early 1930s.[120]

Black musicians were a special component during the 1930s in black life and their creative works helped to advance the anti-lynching message to the world. A central personality in this orbit was Billie Holiday (1915–1959) who made "Strange Fruit," an anti-lynching ballad, world famous. Angela Y. Davis observes:

> This song, which Billie Holiday called her "personal protest" against racism, radically transformed her status in American popular culture. She previously had been acknowledged by her contemporaries on the jazz scene as a brilliant and innovative musician, but her performance of "Strange Fruit" firmly established her as a pivotal figure in a new tendency in black musical culture that directly addressed issues of racial injustice. Though she was only twenty-four years old when she recorded this song in 1939 and integrated it into her repertoire, she had already been striving for some time to reach a mass audience and thus to achieve recognition beyond the circles of musicians and jazz cognoscenti who so unanimously praised her work.[121]

Lewis Allan's song "Strange Fruit" has been recorded by many singers.[122] It endures today as a witness against the lynching crisis and as "a potent song of protest."[123]

Other major artists made exceptional contributions to the anti-lynching effort. Paul Robeson (1898–1976), singer, actor and great humanitarian, was noted especially for his work for the "promotion of racial equality."[124] Edward K. "Duke" Ellington (1899–1974) must also be noted during this period. He was a giant in American jazz in both performing and composing the music.[125] Ellington's music and words gave black people and all lovers of music an uplifting message and encouragement in the struggles of life. Finally, out of the thousands of black musicians of this period, one more name must be mentioned: Marion Anderson (1902–1993), an opera singer. Her moment came in 1939. Donald Henahan gives the background: "The Daughters of the American Revolution had prevented an already celebrated contralto named Marion Anderson from appearing at the Constitution Hall in Washington because she was black. The D.A.R. ladies insisted that local custom would have been violated by such a dark presence. After all, Washington was a Southern City. That, apparently, was that."

Not quite: Eleanor Roosevelt, the president's well-born wife, immediately resigned from the organization and other prominent citizens weighed in with expressions of dismay and outrage. A group of comparatively enlightened Washingtonians led by Harold L. Ickes, the Secretary of the Interior, invited her to sing from the steps of the Lincoln Memorial, which she did on April 9, 1939, for a throng estimated at 75,000 people. That landmark day established Miss Anderson as an early symbol for black advancement, not only in the arts but throughout American society.[126] Her courage and dedication stand as a hallmark among the contributions of black musicians during the decade of the 1930s.

Many of the organizations of black women continued to support the anti-lynching efforts of the 1930s. A central figure in the orbit of black women's activities was Mary McLeod Bethune (1875–1955), a leading educator, president of Bethune-Cookman College in Daytona Beach, Florida, and an able administrator of the largest black women's group in the country, the National Council of Negro Women, formed by Bethune in December 1935.[127] A major goal of Bethune and other black women during this period was to bring an end to lynching in the nation. Malu Halasa notes this emphasis when she writes:

> As the leader of the National Council of Negro Women and a member of the Commission on Interracial Cooperation, an organization formed in 1919 to improve race relations in the south, Bethune was determined to put a stop to the alarming number of lynchings that victimized blacks. Lynchings were usually practiced by white vigilantes who wanted to maintain racial supremacy by terrorizing blacks into remaining in subservient roles. Most of these acts of mob violence took place in the South, where whites were unwilling to accept the rising status of blacks in American society.
>
> Bethune told Will W. Alexander, the president of the Commission on Interracial Cooperation, she planned to enlist the aid of white women in the South to stop the increasing tide of racial violence. A white Methodist minister and leading crusader against racism, Alexander was familiar with Bethune's ways of persuasion.[128]

Another goal of Bethune and other black women leaders in the 1930s was to secure passage of a federal anti-lynching bill long supported by the NAACP.[129] Bethune's influence was also felt in Washington, D.C. In 1936 she was appointed director of the National Youth Administration's Division of Negro Affairs, and "she traveled over 40,000 miles through twenty-one states in an average year to supervise programs for black youth."[130] In this position she became known as a member of Franklin D. Roosevelt's "Black Cabinet," a group of black federal government officials appointed by the president and who reported to him on minority affairs.[131]

Black press publishers, editors, and reporters were also very active in the 1930s in advancing the anti-lynching message to the nation and to the world, especially in northern and western states. There were at least 211 active black newspapers in the United States—with a total circulation of reporting papers at 1,206,787—that served 2,803,756 black families in 1930.[132] Many of the giants of the U.S. black press during the decade were forceful on the lynching issue in the pages of their papers. Among them were Carl Murphy (1889–1967) publisher of the *Baltimore Afro-American* from 1922 to 1961; Robert Abbott (1868–1940), who published the *Chicago Defender*, a very important black paper that, by 1929, had a circulation of 250,000; Robert L. Vann (1879–1940), editor, treasurer, and legal counsel to the *Pittsburgh Courier*, 1910–1940, a paper which reached a circulation of 150,000 by 1936; and George S. Schuyler (1895–1977), a leading commentator and reporter for the *Pittsburgh Courier* and *The Messenger* in the 1920 and 1930s who also served as managing editor of the latter journal. Ted Poston (1906–1974) was a leading reporter for the *Amsterdam News*. In 1931 this paper "mounted a campaign against lynching and Ted [Poston] penned a series 'Judge Lynch Presides' relating to the practice's atrocities." Williams A. Scott II (1902–1934) was founder in 1928 of the *Atlanta World*, which in 1932 became the *Atlanta Daily World*. With support from his brother, Cornelius A. Scott (1908–), the *Atlanta Daily World* became the first daily newspaper published by blacks in the United States. The paper placed an emphasis on "calling for an end to racism and police brutality." Mrs. Chris J. Perry, Sr., and her two daughters were publishers of the *Philadelphia Tribune* from 1921 into the Great

Depression years; P. Bernard Young (1884–1962) published the Norfolk (Va.) *Journal and Guide* from 1910 to 1962; Chester Arthur Franklin (1880–1955) was founder of the *Kansas City Call* in 1919; and Louis E. Martin (1912–1997) was publisher and editor of the (Detroit) *Michigan Chronicle* from 1936 to 1947.[133] The black press is a major institution in the U.S. and during the 1930s black journalists continued the never-ending struggle to get the black story out to the world and to advance the case against lynching in Mississippi, the South and the nation.

The Age of Lynching in Mississippi during the 1930s remained a brutal period, especially in the daily lives of black Mississippians, but there were many poor whites in the state as well. Nevertheless, the violence, fear and terror generated by lynching and discrimination continued throughout the decade. In fact, according to historian C. Vann Woodward, the Jim Crow system "reached its perfection in the 1930s."[134] The end result was a system which checkmated black political, social and economic rights, and which too often promoted the violent system of lynching and certainly an unjust criminal justice system when it came to defending and protecting the rights of African Americans. Even the life expectancy of blacks was at the bottom of the scale for this country. One scholar notes: "During the 1930s this statistic [life expectancy] rose from 63 to 67 years for white women, 60 to 62 for white men, 49 to 55 for black women, and 47 to 52 for black men.[135] On top of the general black condition in Mississippi and the nation stood the Great Depression, which had its most important impact during the 1930s. Joe R. Feagin observes the significance of this key problem: "During the Great Depression of the 1930s, unemployed whites frequently pushed black workers out of even menial jobs. Whites in Atlanta organized a 'Black Shirts' organization under the slogan of 'no jobs for niggers until every white man has a job.' By 1932 half of all black workers in cities were unemployed. Extreme hunger or starvation was often their lot. Less than one-fifth received relief aid from southern governments, and private charities sometimes refused to let unemployed blacks into soup lines."[136]

Such conditions make the fifty known cases of Mississippi's lynching victims during the 1930s just that more heartrending and almost impossible to fathom. Yet the reality of the period suggests that the violent deaths were very real indeed. Still most scholars view the decade as a period of declining lynchings in this nation. One observer suggests:

> By 1922, however, lynching was on the decline again, the annual total falling to seven in 1929. What seemed to be a dying phenomenon revived in 1930, probably resuscitated by economic competition between the races, made bitter by the Great Depression. Lynchings became briefly more common and more brutal. But after 1935 the number of blacks summarily executed each year dropped below ten and stayed there. A race firmly locked into a subordinate caste position did not need frequent violent reminders that its place was at the bottom of the southern social hierarchy.[137]

And so blacks who were citizens of Mississippi and the nation had to defend themselves with courage, faith in the future, a special skill at surviving under hostile conditions, and a willingness to seek support from all quarters in the never-ending struggle, it seemed in the 1930s, to end lynching, discrimination and racism against black Americans.[138]

9

The Era of World War II,
1940–1949

Mississippi entered the decade of the forties with a population of 2,183,796, of which 80.2 percent were rural and 19.8 percent were urban.[1] There were 1,106,327 whites and 1,077,469 other groups, mostly African-Americans, with smaller numbers of Native Americans, Chinese-Americans, and others in the state's population makeup.[2] Blacks continued to migrate from Mississippi in large numbers during the 1940s, with 326,000 or 30.2 percent departing by 1950. Meanwhile, between 1940 and 1950, 263,605 white Mississippians also migrated from the state.[3] Economically, Mississippi was still a depressed state. One study notes that "in 1940, Mississippi had an economy based on low-wage, subsistence or sharecropper agriculture and a system of racial segregation enforced often by violence. Per capita income in Mississippi was 36% of the national average in 1940."[4] In 1940 conditions were especially harsh for most farmers in Mississippi, who numbered 1,399,884 on 219,092 farms with an average acreage of 65.8. The percentage of black tenant farmers in Mississippi was 70 percent at the beginning of the forties.[5] To make matters worse, according to Gilbert C. Fite, "Planters in the Mississippi Delta were moving rapidly toward full mechanization of cotton growing by 1947 and 1948, partly because of a scarcity of labor, and also because of their desire to reduce production costs."[6] Table 9.1-A notes the heavy concentration of blacks in agriculture and service industries in Mississippi in 1940.[7] The data review suggests that black income levels remained low in Mississippi for the 1940s. In fact, one study notes that "in 1940, 60 percent of all employed black women were domestic servants."[8]

Among the black professional groups in Mississippi, there were 71 African-American physicians and 29 dentists in 1940.[9] In 1944 there were 1,063 black lawyers in the United States with two-thirds of them were located outside of the South. Mississippi had only two black lawyers that year, W. L. Moon, who practiced in Jackson, and Taylor G. Ewing in Vicksburg. According to J. Clay Smith, Jr., "By 1935 the number of black lawyers in Mississippi had been reduced to five. The exodus of black lawyers from Mississippi was due in large measure to the negative treatment they received in the courts. Judges ruled against them, the bar excluded them from its circles, and black people, observing this treatment, flocked to white lawyers out of necessity."[10] Thus at every turn in life during the 1940s, black Mississippians were faced with the direct consequences of institutional racism their daily

TABLE 9.1-A: BLACKS EMPLOYED IN MISSISSIPPI, 1940

Occupational Group	Male	Female
Professional, Technical and kindred workers	.8%	3.2%
Farmers and farm managers	52.6%	12.2%
Managers, official and proprietors	0.4%	0.5%
Clerical and kindred workers	0.1%	0.2%
Sales workers	0.2%	0.2%
Craftsmen, foremen, and kindred workers	2.2%	0.1%
Operatives and kindred workers	4.6%	2.2%
Private household workers	1.2%	37.7%
Other service workers	2.7%	5.5%
Farm laborers and farmers	23.0%	37.2%
Other laborers	2.7%	5.5%
Not reported	0.3%	0.5%
TOTAL	100.0%	100.0%

economics, lives, social relations, and lack of political participation at the local and state levels of government.[11]

Social relations in Mississippi continued to be defined by the Jim Crow system during the 1940s. World War II appears to have had a positive impact on the state in helping to break down its isolation, add to its industrialization and urbanization, transform many aspects of daily life for rural Mississippians, increase options for women and encourage black Mississippians to demand more of their rights.[12]

Yet Mississippi remained a segregationist state with all of its unequal treatment facilities for whites and blacks. Indeed, Mississippi native David L. Cohn observed that Mississippi "was marked by strange paradoxes and hopelessly irreconcilable contradictions. It possessed elaborate behavior codes written, unwritten, and unwritable."[13] The etiquette of race relations produced a strange world in Mississippi and the South, which "governed every social situation from hunting to casual meetings on the street."[14] This world was coded in Mississippi law and custom, and its restrictions on the black community were harsh and brutal.

Black education was segregated in Mississippi during the decade and still unequal when compared to white educational opportunities. For example, in 1944–45 there were 483,736 black school age children in the state, but only 270,615 were enrolled in school. Whites numbered 378,932 school age students and had 288,246 enrolled in school. The black average daily attendance during this period was 218,145, compared to 230,539 days for whites. Only 5 percent of black high school age children attended secondary school, compared to 20 percent of whites. Mississippi employed 16,000 teachers in 1944–45, but only 6,547 of these were African-American. At this late date, blacks only had 98 high schools with 444 black classroom teachers, compared to 557 white public high schools with 2,298 white high school teachers. Salaries for black and white teachers were low, but much lower for blacks than for whites. In the mid–1940s, black teachers at all levels averaged only $407.81, while their white counterparts received $1,018.01 per year.[15] It was a cruel and unequal world, but one where blacks took their meager resources and trained a generation.

These same harsh conditions were also evident at historically black Alcorn College and Jackson College, the largest state-supported black institutions of higher education during the 1940s. In 1945–46 Alcorn College employed 60 teachers and had an enrollment of 256 students (43 males and 213 females), while the high school division at Alcorn had 127 students. Jackson College employed 27 teachers during this period and had a college student enrollment of 237 (26 males and 211 females).[16]

During this same period white Mississippians had nine senior colleges (five of which were publicly supported). They were much larger institutions than either Alcorn College or Jackson College. The annual average salaries of whites was $2,700 at the University of Mississippi, $2,800 at Mississippi State, $2,300 at the University of Southern Mississippi, $2,080 at Mississippi State College for Women, and $2,400 at Delta State University. Faculty at Alcorn College and Jackson College received $1,600 and $1,661 respectively for a nine-month school term.[17]

Healthcare facilities were also primitive for blacks in the forties. As noted earlier, there were 71 black physicians to service a segregated black community of 1 million people. One scholar notes that as late as 1938, "there were in Mississippi 0.7 [hospital] beds per 1,000 Negroes as compared with 2.4 beds per 1,000 whites."[18] This was a crucial issue for black Mississippians since for many death could result without proper medical facilities and treatment. Although there was an increase in the average life expectancy of African-Americans by 1949, it was still less for blacks than for whites. By 1949 black men in the United States had a life expectancy of 58.6, compared to 65.9 for white males. Black women averaged 62.9 years, with white women at 71.5 years.[19]

The position of the black press in Mississippi during this period can be summarized in the following manner:

First, [the black press] considered World War II, the blacks' role in the war, the treatment of black soldiers, and the status of blacks in the postwar period. Second, the cold war conflict erupted between the United States and the Soviet Union, creating the "West" versus "East" paradigm. Third, race relations in Mississippi and the rest of the nation and the related problems of racism and segregation concerned Mississippi's blacks, as did the emigration of blacks from Mississippi and elsewhere in the South during the war years. The black press also pondered the economic, political and social status of blacks in Mississippi, as well as lynching and other violence against blacks. Next, blacks expressed interest in the goals and programs of black organizations, such as the NAACP, in Mississippi and in Richard Wright as a leading black writer and thinker of the era. Finally, black interest in the Democratic party increased, and with it concern about Strom Thurmond, Dixiecrat candidate in the 1948 presidential election, about lingering problems of the Great Depression, and about discrimination by New Deal relief agencies. Thirty-nine black journals were published during this period, a slight increase over the thirty-three papers published during the Great Depression of the 1930s.[20]

One major problem that plagued the black press, both in Mississippi and the nation, was the continued issue of censorship. This issue came to a head during World War II, with both state and federal government interest in what the black press said. The black press was in a difficult position, but fought to retain its independence while remaining critical of racism and discrimination at home, as the war with the Axis powers was carried forward abroad.[21]

The black church in Mississippi was very active in the 1940s in continuing to promote the spiritual life of the black community. Jessie Mosley notes that by 1944 there were "3,638 churches in all, with membership numbering 585,733, more or less. These figures show that a little more than half of the Negro population of Mississippi are church members."[22] Yet an unmistakable fact is that the black church played a central role in the lives of black Mississippians regardless of whether they were active. This development extends from the African background through slavery and Emancipation to the present period. The forties are a rich period in the continued growth of black culture in Mississippi and especially black music. Such artists as Arthur "Big Boy" Crudup and John Lee Hooker took the blues from the Mississippi Delta to the world stage.[23] With gospel music and rhythm and blues, Mississippians made a lasting impression on the music of American society.[24]

Politically, Mississippi was as strong as ever in the orbit of the Jim Crow system and the Age of Segregation.[25] But even in the South, Mississippi was considered a special place because of its extreme viewpoints. Racism was evident at every turn in the political life of Mississippi. Scholars believe that between 2,000 and 5,000 black Mississippians were registered to vote for the period 1940–1947.[26] In 1940 this represented about 0.5 percent of the potential black vote in the state, and only about 5.0 percent in 1947.[27]

In 1944 the Supreme Court outlawed the white primary. This helped to advance black political rights in Mississippi, in spite of the segregationist stand of the state. The real opportunity for blacks came in 1946 when the state would elect a new senator. White opposition to black voting was intense, and Senator Theodore Bilbo headed the anti-black effort. Blacks protested, and a special five person senatorial committee investigated the charges against Bilbo. Blacks told the committee that "private citizens and public officials had subjected them to discriminatory interrogation, intimidation, and physical violence ... that there is no evidence in the record connecting Senator Bilbo with an illegality or impropriety other than perhaps in certain cases departure from ordinarily accepted good taste as some view it"[28] Yet the violence did not end there.

Three examples from the 1940s are additional evidence of the difficulties which black Mississippi citizens had in attempting to vote or trying to promote the democratic rights of African-Americans in their native state. Patricia Sullivan notes a case from 1940: "That same year the Mississippi legislature enacted a law requiring that textbooks used in black schools exclude all references to voting, elections, civic responsibility and democracy. In a bold stroke, Rev. James Arthur Parsons, pastor of four black churches in Tupelo, Mississippi, declared his candidacy, with the support of the National Negro Congress, for John Rankin's seat in Congress in 1942. Parsons abandoned the race when whites in Tupelo demonstrated 'forcibly' that they did not approve 'of the idea of a Negro running for Congress.'"[29] Two cases from 1946 and 1948 are especially noteworthy. First, David R. Goldfield observes: "Though the electoral process was more open to blacks than at any time since the Reconstruction era, outside of cities and especially in the Deep South exercising the suffrage was dangerous. In 1946, black army veteran Etoy Fletcher was publicly whipped in Brandon, Mississippi, for attempting to register."[30] Secondly, Langston Hughes notes that in 1948 "in Mississippi, the Reverend William Bender, instructor at Tougaloo College and president of a branch of the NAACP, was kept from the polls by three whites, one of whom brandished a pistol. Walter White stated: 'Either the Negro must attain full citizenship status with all the rights and obligations thereby involved, even in the most remote sections of Mississippi, or the democratic process for all America will be made meaningless.'"[31]

Thus, Mississippi's segregationist system remained in force throughout the 1940s. Mississippi was still represented by men such as Senator Theodore Bilbo until his death on August 21, 1947, of "cancer of the mouth." Pat Harrison was followed later by James O. Eastland and John C. Stennis.[32] John Egerton notes that "in the House, John Rankin of Mississippi celebrated twenty-five years on the job with a pledge to hold fast against any hint of creeping equality for those unfortunate enough to stand outside the protective tent of white Anglo-Saxon Protestantism."[33] Such men were gatekeepers of Mississippi's segregationist system, and blacks had to wage a long struggle in Mississippi to overcome such opposition.

Mississippi's criminal justice system remained racist to the core during the 1940s.[34] In essence there was little change in the treatment of blacks from the previous decade. Most scholars argue, however, that World War II at least opened Mississippi for more of the world to see because of the military bases located in the state. This created other problems for blacks since African-American soldiers from throughout the nation were sent to Mississippi for training. They, of course, received a Jim Crow welcome. Many protested the conditions under which they were forced to live, and many suffered the consequences. Nationally, 1,154,000 blacks participated in the United States military during World War II. Of this number 85,000 were from Mississippi.[35] Case after case emerges in Mississippi during the war of racism and discrimination against black soldiers. The black soldiers sought relief through the Army Command, the NAACP and the black press. Phillip McGuire gives several examples of this abuse. "In Centerville, Mississippi, a sheriff kills a Negro soldier. At

The lynching phenomenon was widespread throughout the South, as witnessed by this Kentucky triple lynching in the early twentieth century. In fact, at least 191 confirmed lynching victims were killed in Kentucky, while Mississippi has the highest number for any state, at 538 confirmed victims. Mississippi has had more double and triple lynchings than any other state since Reconstruction (COURTESY OF MISSISSIPPI DEPARTMENT OF ARCHIVES AND HISTORY).

Table 9.1-B: Mississippi Lynching Victims, 1940–1949

Name	Date	County
1. "Texas Red"	2/3/40	Claiborne
2. Edward S. Cook	1940	Tallahatchie
3. Charlie Long	10/12/42	Quitman
4. Ernest Green	10/12/42	Quitman
5. Howard Wash	10/17/42	Jones
6. Unknown	May 1943	Itawamba
7. Unknown	1943	Forrest
8. Unknown	1943	Forrest
9. Rev. Isaac Simmons	3/26/44	Amite
10. Unknown	1944	Unknown
11. Leon McAtee	7/24/46	Holmes, whipped to death near Lexington
12. Versie Johnson	8/1/47	Prentiss
13. Malachi Wright	7/9/49	Chickasaw
14. Etoy Fletcher	6/6/46	Holmes, near Lexington
15. Negro Farmer	7/28/46	Forrest

Camp Shelby, Mississippi, two Negro soldiers lie in a hospital, wounded in an affair with highway patrolmen."[36] Such conditions did little to endear black people to Mississippi's system of justice.

Parchman Prison remained the central state penitentiary for Mississippi during the 1940s.[37] And black Americans remained in their historical position as most of the prisoners. Blacks were also the largest group put to death (capital punishment) by the state of Mississippi.[38] Thus, as lynchings began to decline in the South in the 1930s and 1940s, a new phenomenon began to take shape, an increase in the number of legal killings of blacks by the state, in place of mob lynchings.[39]

In the long past the causes of lynchings in Mississippi and the nation have been varied, covering economic, political, and social boundaries. Scholar Arnold Rose gives a good summary statement on this historical problem:

> The psychopathology of the lynching mob has been discussed intensively in recent years. Poverty and economic fear have been stressed as background factors. It is generally held that the rise of lynchings during and immediately after the First World War had much to do with the increased mobility of and competition from Negroes during this period. There is a substantial correlation from year to year between low cotton prices and a high number of lynchings. Economic fear is mixed with social fear: a feeling that the Negro is "getting out of his place" and that the white man's social status is being threatened and is in need of defense.[40]

TABLE 9.2: LYNCHING VICTIMS, 1940–1949

	U.S.			Mississippi		
Year	Total	Black	White	Total	Black	White
1940	5	4	1	2	2	0
1941	4	4	0	0	0	0
1942	6	6	0	3	3	0
1943	3	3	0	3	3	0
1944	2	2	0	2	2	0
1945	1	1	0	0	0	0
1946	6	6	0	3	3	0
1947	1	1	0	1	1	0
1948	2	1	1	0	0	0
1949	3	3	0	1	1	0
TOTAL	33	31	2	15	15	0

TABLE 9.3: LYNCHING VICTIMS BY MISSISSIPPI COUNTY, 1940–1949

County	Number of Victims	County	Number of Victims	County	Number of Victims
Amite	1	Itawamba	1	Tallahatchie	1
Chickasaw	1	Jones	1	Unknown	1
Claiborne	1	Quitman	2		
Forrest	3	Rankin	1	TOTALS	15
Holmes	1	Simpson	1		

The World War II years and after brought a period of reduced lynchings in Mississippi and the South. Table 9.1-B reveals an official records count of fifteen lynchings in the state. When compared to Table 9.2 it is clear that the decline in lynching was a national event during the decade. However, on the national level and in Mississippi, the vast majority of the lynching victims were African-American males: 31 of 33 national victims and all 15 victims in Mississippi.[41] In Mississippi, as evidenced by Table 9.3, lynchings took place in at least eleven counties with a concentration of events in South Mississippi (five counties, seven cases), two counties in the Delta (three victims), two counties in North Mississippi (two victims) and two counties in Central Mississippi with two lynchings. An official lynching did not take place in East Mississippi or the Gulf Coast area. (The location of one lynching event remains unknown for this period.) This distribution of lynching data suggests that most parts of Mississippi, especially where there was a large black population, were at risk

TABLE 9.4: DISTRIBUTION OF LYNCHING VICTIMS
BY COUNTY IN REGIONS OF MISSISSIPPI

Delta	North	East	Central	South	Gulf Coast
Quitman	Chickasaw	None	Holmes	Amite	None
Tallahatchie	Itawamba		Rankin	Claiborne	
				Forrest	
				Jones	
				Simpson	

for lynching as can be seen especially in South Mississippi, Central Mississippi, and the Delta regions (see Table 9.4). The known data for this period is too small to suggest any major patterns with regard to the range and percentage of offenses alleged against lynch victims (Table 9.5). It is clear, however, that alleged crimes against white males remained a problem for blacks in the 1940s (murder, being disrespectful to a white man, robbery and problems with a local sheriff). Yet three victims were alleged to have completed rape, a historical pattern which is often alleged of lynching victims. Table 9.6 also suggests that the data is incomplete on the months when lynching events took place in Mississippi during the 1940s. Yet it is observable from the data that at least 60 percent of the lynching events took place during the warmer months of the year, another historical pattern. All the known lynching victims in Mississippi for the decade appear to have been African-American men. There is no documentation of the lynching of a black woman for the decade, nor of a white male.

The official fifteen lynching events in Mississippi for the forties weave a tale of shocking sadness, like all of the other lynching cases which came before this decade. Fear and terror were present at each of these events and the black community had to endure another decade of pain and sorrow. Five lynching cases are selected from the decade to note the range of the lynching problem for Mississippi during the forties.

Case Study One: February 3, 1940
"Texas Red"
Lynched by mob which trailed him for 34 days, at Port Gibson, Mississippi, on February 3. Suspected of having shot a deputy sheriff. Man hunt assumed such proportions the governor sent troops "who never quite caught up with the lynchers."[42]

Case Study Two: October 11, 1941
Double Hanging of Charlie Lang and Ernest Green
Quitman, Mississippi
The boys were in the habit of playing with the [white] girl at various times and they played under the bridge. This day they were running and jumping when the girl ran out from under the bridge and the boys behind her. A passing motorist saw them ... the boys were taken from the Quitman jail, where they had been held on charges of attempted assault of a white girl, and hanged by a mob from a river bridge in a woods section on October 11. It was the seventh reported lynching in the Shubuta locality in recent years.... The boys were mutilated in the following fashion. Their reproductive organs were cut off. Pieces of flesh had been jerked away from their bodies with pliers and one boy had a

TABLE 9.5: MISSISSIPPI LYNCHING VICTIMS, RANGE AND PERCENTAGE OF OFFENSES ALLEGED, 1940–1949

Offense	Number	Percentage
Murder	2	13%
Rape/attempted rape	3	20%
Disrespectful to white person	2	13%
Robbery	1	7%
Tried to hold his 220 acre farm	1	7%
Problem with local sheriff	2	13%
Unknown	4	27%
TOTAL	15	

TABLE 9.6: MISSISSIPPI LYNCHINGS BY MONTH, 1940–1949

Month	Number	Percentage
January	0	0%
February	1	7%
March	1	7%
April	0	0%
May	1	7%
June	1	7%
July	3	20%
August	1	7%
September	0	0%
October	3	20%
November	0	0%
December	0	0%
Unknown	4	27%
TOTAL	15	

screwdriver rammed down his throat so that it protruded from his neck. After the lynching was over, people came to their home and told them that they were through with them and that they could have what was left. The parents ignored this and the two authorities had to take them down and bury them. I understand that arrests were made but the suspects were turned out free again.[43]

Case Study Three: March 26, 1944
Amite County, Mississippi
Reverent Isaac Simmons
Liberty, Mississippi

In Amite County, Mississippi in 1944, local whites coveted the 295-acre debt-free farm of black preacher Isaac Simmons. Rumor had it that oil reserves lay beneath Simmons' land, and white speculators tried to lay claim to the property. When Reverend Simmons hired an attorney to help him protect his property, six white vigilantes attacked the sixty-six-year-old preacher and his son, Eldridge. They forced the son to watch as they killed the elder Simmons with three shots in the back; then they beat Eldridge, ordering him to vacate the land in ten days. When Simmons' friends and family came to claim the body, they found that all of the preacher's teeth had been knocked out with a club, his arm broken, and his tongue cut out. "They kept telling me that my father and I were 'smart niggers' for going to see a lawyer," Eldridge Simmons later recalled.[44]

Case Study Four: July 24, 1946
Near Lexington, Mississippi
Leon McAtee

Floating face down in the sluggish waters of a bayou, the body of a small, 35-year-old Negro was found one day near Lexington, Miss. His name was Leon McAtee, and he had not died by drowning. The evidence was that his body had been thrown into the water from a car. He had been working on the farm of Jeff Dodd. Questioned, the thin-faced, 57-year-old farmer had a lot to say about McAtee. Two days before a saddle had disappeared from Dodd's barn. He never thought twice. He knew McAtee had done time in the state penitentiary for stealing. He took him right into town and turned him over to the sheriff.

Still pretty mad, he'd got to talking with some of the boys. A hill-country farm like his took a lot of hard working for the $76 he put out for that saddle. A couple of boys pricked up their ears. Stole a saddle, huh? Done time? They had had saddles stolen too. How about getting that nigger out of jail and asking him a few questions?

Last week Jeff Dodd and his son, Jeff Dodd, Jr., Dixie Roberts of Greenwood and his nephew, James Roberts, and Spencer Ellis faced a Holmes County jury. Sure, they had whipped Leon a little. Dodd explained: During the questioning McAtee "made a break at me and I hit him." He said the other four "hit him a few licks, I think, but I was excited I don't know." The defendants testified that after the whipping, the last they saw of McAtee he was able to hump a fence and keep running.

But pretty, young Hazel Brannon, crusading editor of Lexington's weekly newspaper, *The Advertiser*, was not satisfied. She waylaid McAtee's widow, Henrietta, on her way out of the courtroom. Henrietta had been told not to talk to anyone about the case. But Miss Brannon got a story: "Henrietta McAtee, the Negro's wife, testified that she saw McAtee that afternoon with the five defendants. She said his limbs were bruised, his eyes 'poppish,' and that his hands were bound with rope. Later, she said, she saw Ellis's pickup truck go by with McAtee doubled up in the back."

The all-white jury took only ten minutes to return a verdict: not guilty. As for Hazel Brannon, the judge cited her for contempt of court. And the case ended on this ironic note: McAtee's 16-year-old stepson confessed that it was he, not McAtee, who had stolen the saddle.[45]

Case Study Five: August 1947
Prentiss, Mississippi

The body of Versie Johnson, 35, ripped by bullets, was left at the scene of his murder near Prentiss on or about August 1. Johnson was shot dead by police for the alleged rape of a white expectant mother, according to the three patrolmen responsible for his custody. In a statement by Sheriff G. O. Berry the prisoner was fired on when he suddenly attacked one of the three patrolmen responsible for his custody. A statement released by the sheriffs clerk indicated that a lynch mob had begun to gather round the jail soon after the prisoner was arrested, and that previous to the slaying members of the mob had given Sheriff Berry an ultimatum to get Johnson's confession by 8 o'clock that evening. Johnson protested his innocence. He reportedly attempted to grab the gun of one of the officers.

Sheriff Berry, State Highway Patrolman J. S. Puckett, and a patrolman named Kapkins were subsequently tried "merely as a formality necessary to clear their names."[46]

These cases demonstrate the outrages of the era of lynching at this late date. They reveal the continued horror of the situation in Mississippi, and the brutal nature of the events and the deep psychological and physical wounds which they imparted upon the black community in Mississippi.[47]

Black Mississippians faced hundreds of incidents against their physical and psychological safety in the 1940s.[48] A random selection of nine special cases of violence against blacks, some short of death, are noted below.

Incident 1: August 1943
Winona, Mississippi
Turner E. Brown was badly beaten at a bus station by white fellow-passengers and the baggage attendant to whom he had allegedly replied "yes" instead of "yes, Sir."[49]

Incident 2: September 1943
Clarksdale, Mississippi
Romeo Parker, a Negro farm worker, active in the Southern Tenant Farmers' Union, has been arrested and is being held on $2,000 bail on a charge of impersonating a federal officer. According to Union officials, Parker's impersonation consisted in wearing government issue woolen shirt and trousers (World War I vintage) without insignia. (Such clothing are sold in "Army and Navy Stores" throughout the South and are worn frequently by lower-income rural folk.) Parker had been previously arrested in Ruleville, Mississippi and had been told by the arresting officers to get out of Mississippi because they didn't "have that sort of thing" (union organization) in the Delta.[50]

Incident 3: October 1943
Meridian, Mississippi
Donald Castle, Lauderdale County sawmill operator, has been convicted of "willfully, unlawfully, knowingly, and feloniously" abducting and holding Rossy Wyse (a Negro in Peonage). Castle was charged with holding Wyse prisoner by the simple expedient of shackling him to a bed with a long chain around his neck.[51]

Incident 4: April 1944
Oxford, Mississippi
Sheriff Wm. J. Papst, Jailor Wm. L. Cole, James McCrary, Jr., J. E. McCrary, and J. F. Goolsby, all of Lowndes County, Miss., have been indicted by a Federal Grand Jury on charges of conspiring to deprive persons of civil rights. It is charged that in one month, June 26 to July 29, 1943, the defendants used the "third degree" on six Negro prisoners in attempts to obtain confessions.[52]

Incident 5: June 1944
Jackson, Mississippi
Declaring that they had heard that Negroes were planning to hold a committee to lay plans "to get even with the white folks," police are said to have raided several places in Jackson's residential district looking for "Negro leaders." No arrests are reported as having been made by the squads who are alleged to have carried sawed-off shot guns and tommy guns. The raid was apparently one of intimidation, perhaps in response to the scare edito-

rials that have been appearing in Major Fred Sullins' *Jackson Daily News*. The only meeting of any consequence being held by Negroes on the night in question was sponsored by the far-from-radical Negro Chamber of Commerce.[53]

Incident 6: August 1944
Camp Van Dorn, Mississippi

A Negro private was reprimanded and beaten by a white MP (at the instruction of a white sergeant) for some defect in his military apparel. Frightened, the Negro fled and was shot down and killed by the local sheriff, who arrived at the scene.

Three Negro soldiers omitted saying "Sir" to the white attendant when requesting cigarettes at the Post Exchange. A fight ensued. The next night a Negro soldier was killed by a white cab driver.

Soon after this incident, a Negro soldier was killed and another severely injured in an outbreak. The rumor spread that the outbreak was caused by an attempt on the part of the Negro soldiers to raid an ammunition dump.[54]

Incident 7: February 1945
Port Gibson, Mississippi

Upon pleading guilty to the fatal shooting of a Negro soldier who was on furlough after twenty-six months overseas, Byron McClure, white Claiborne county farmer, has been sentenced to life imprisonment. The shooting is said to have grown out of an argument during a crap game (dice to the uninitiated), one of the few occasions on which Negro and white persons of the same sex in Mississippi indulge together.[55]

Incident 8: April 1945
Jackson, Mississippi

Two Jackson policemen who described themselves as having a hankering to "beat up some niggers" picked up four Negro men in business establishments along Parish Street, took them out of town and beat them sadistically. Returning to town the men, including a discharged and disabled sailor, were released. (The Guardians of the Peace took one of them to the hospital!) Neither of the men were arrested. All of the victims are regularly employed except for the veteran who is not physically able to work.[56]

Incident 9: Timeline, Early 20th Century
Alcorn College, Mississippi

Noted writer Chester Himes (1909–1984) grew up in Mississippi. His family offended their white neighbors in rural Mississippi at the end of World War I by becoming the first owners of the first private automobile in their county. The sight of a black family riding around in such a modern, expensive, and noisy vehicle (loud enough to frighten their neighbors' mule teams) outraged white farmers to such a degree that they got Himes' father fired from his job at Alcorn A. & M. and then forced the family to leave the state.[57]

These nine cases are illustrative of the hazardous conditions facing blacks who lived in Mississippi as the United States fought in the 1940s to advance the "Four Freedoms." It was a lonely journey.[58]

The black community in Mississippi attempted to wage a campaign in the 1940s against the abuse of the group by white Mississippians, with a focus on the lynching crisis. Some elements among the black press in the state tried to lift the voice of this institution to note the wrongs of lynching and discrimination by whites against blacks. An interesting person and paper in this regard was Percy Greene (1908–1977), publisher and editor of the *Jackson Advocate*, which was created in Jackson in 1938–1939.[59] Greene developed one of the best black weekly newspapers in modern Mississippi. Although he was viewed largely as a radical black in the 1940s, he was identified as a radical black conservative in later decades. Yet

Greene had displayed courage in bringing controversial issues before his readers in the *Advocate*. In 1942 he spoke out against the deaths by lynching of the two fourteen-year-old black boys at Shubuta, Mississippi. Greene told his readers:

> Added to the effects of an already overburdening number of incidents of oppression and suppression occurring almost daily, the Shubuta lynching, at such a time as this, when Negroes are sending their sons to the armed forces of the nation to fight and die for the principles of Christian Democratic Civilization ... might well have resulted in a complete breakdown of Negro spirit and morale in Mississippi.
>
> Indeed, the Shubuta lynchings would seem to all but justify the growing fears being widely felt among Negroes throughout Mississippi, that the spirit of the Dred Scott Decision, as expressed by Justice Taney—that a Negro had no rights that a white man was bound to respect—was about to prevail in the state....
>
> It was ... heartening and reassuring to the Negroes of Mississippi when Governor Johnson publicly expressed his condemnation of the lynchings, asserted that he would do everything that it was his duty as Governor to do to see that the guilty parties were apprehended and punished, and that such acts were spots upon the good name of Mississippi and condemned by the better class of its people.[60]

Many other black papers of the period, such as the *Delta* (Greenville) *Leader*, edited by Rev. Harrison H. Humes (1902–1958), and Jackson's *Mississippi Enterprise*, published by Willie J. Miller, largely remained silent on the lynching crisis in Mississippi. The topic was just too controversial for some black editors to undertake in their newspapers.[61]

The state branches of the NAACP in Mississippi were also active in trying to foster change in the state and draw public attention to the lynching problem *in Mississippi*. However, the state branches of the NAACP were under tremendous pressure and opposition by many white Mississippians. This "opposition" had an impact on the growth and development of NAACP branches in the state. In fact, as late as 1944 there were only six branches organized in Mississippi with a total membership of 129.[62] John Dittmer observes that under the pressures of the period, little could be accomplished: "National officials visited the state during the Depression years, but aside from legal advice and assistance in several court cases, the organization's work in Mississippi consisted mainly of limited solicitation of membership."[63] One fact of the period stands out: it took courage for black Mississippians to join this organization during the 1940s, and their efforts must be counted as a form of protest against lynchings and racism.

A moderate and middle-class political group, the Mississippi Progressive Voters' League, was active in the 1940s. This group encouraged black citizenship rights, including voting, in Mississippi. By 1947 the group had 5,000 members and was headquartered at Jackson with major branches in Clarksdale (the Delta region) and Hattiesburg (South Mississippi). The group's president was T. B. Wilson. John Dittmer notes that the group had an "easier time attracting church and lodge support and recruiting members than did local NAACP branches, which drew bitter opposition from whites."[64]

Two early black Mississippi leaders emerged in the 1940s, Medgar Wiley Evers (1925–1963) and his brother, Charles Evers (1922-). Both worked to advance the NAACP in Mississippi. They were born in Decatur, Newton County, and attended Alcorn College. Both served in the United States armed forces during World War II.[65] They decided in 1946 to try and register to vote, a courageous act in the difficult 1940s. According to Charles Evers, "Decatur had nine hundred whites registered to vote, but not one Negro. Even the president of Alcorn [J. R. Otis] told Medgar and me not to register. Boy that stung. But in 1946, as Alcorn students, Medgar and I decided to go to the Newton County Courthouse to register to vote."[66] Such a decision, even to try to register and then to vote, required determination in Mississippi in the World War II era. Any public stand against Jim Crow must be recognized as a symbol of black protest, and thus a challenge against the mistreatment of black Mississippians by the whites of the state and, of course, as opposition to the lynching of black citizens.

Several black Mississippi writers were active in the 1940s and helped to bring attention to the plight of blacks there. Certainly at least three names come to the forefront for the period: Richard Wright (1908–1960), Margaret Walker (1915–1998) and George Washington Lee (1894–1976). Each made outstanding contributions to American letters and culture in the 1940s. Richard Wright is considered by many critics to be the dominant African-American writer of his generation in the 1930s and 1940s. In fact, Blyden Jackson (1910–2000) calls this period the "Age of Wright."[67] He wrote poetry, short stories, essays and novels which reflected deeply upon his home state of Mississippi and the black experience in such works as *Uncle Tom's Children* (1938), *Native Son* (1940) and *Black Boy* (1945), among other works.[68] Margaret Walker migrated to Mississippi in 1949 to teach in the English department at Jackson State College. She brought with her a world-wide recognition for her poetry collection *For My People* (1942). She was the most famous black writer teaching in Mississippi in 1949.[69] George Washington Lee continued his efforts as a writer in the forties producing a collection of short stories, *Beale Street Sundown* (1942).[70] Wright, Walker and Lee were able to demonstrate the power of the black experience and through their collective creative works to foster public attention on the historical importance of the black experience and of a continuing need for Americans to be made aware of this history, to challenge the status quo, and to seek a redress of the damages caused to the black community by the problem of lynching in Mississippi and the nation.

Two other black institutions in Mississippi during the 1940s were also concerned about black uplift and decreasing the opposition which blacks faced: the black church and fraternal organizations. The city of Jackson, Mississippi, is illustrative of these concerns. In 1945 there were 58 black churches in the capital city and at least a dozen fraternal and social organizations, including the eight traditional black fraternities and sororities and members of the mason orders, such as the Most Worshipful Stringer Grand Lodge, Free and Accepted Masons, and Prince Hall Affiliate of the State of Mississippi.[71] Such institutions generally worked quietly and often in the background to help foster change and reforms in society. Indeed, this is the overall historical contrast that comes forth from such groups as the historically black Mississippi Baptist State Convention headed by the Rev. Dr. A. A. Cosey (?–1944).[72] In a positive manner the black women members of Alpha Chi Sigma Chapter of Delta Sigma Theta Sorority, Inc. (the Jackson Alumna Chapter after college), have been active in Jackson since 1941. Aurelia Young, a former music professor at Jackson State College, was the chapter's first president. This group of college women "pledged itself to serious endeavors and community service, demonstrating a vital concern for social welfare, academic excellence, and cultural enrichment."[73] Such efforts helped to propel the black experience in Mississippi.

In general the white press of Mississippi remained very pro-segregationist in the 1940s. This attitude toward lynching is reflected in the Jackson *Daily News*: "If any sympathy is to be expressed, let it be in behalf of that poor, old woman, living alone in a hill top home, who underwent an experience far worse than death.... It is not likely that the mob made a mistake.... Every Negro in the South, even though he be a half-wit, well knows that rape means rope."[74]

By the 1940s Mississippi's white politicians began to take a variety of approaches to the lynching problem in the state. Some governors such as Paul B. Johnson (1940–1943) could state publicly an opposition to lynching and make pledges to prosecute lynchers. Governor Fielding L. Wright (1946–1952) appears to have been more of a traditionalist with a desire to protect "southern institutions and traditions."[75] At the extreme end of Mississippi politicians for the 1940s stood Theodore Bilbo, a figure who was, according to Wilson Jeremiah Moses, "a white supremacist and former Governor of Mississippi, elected to the U.S. Senate in 1934 (and again in 1940 and 1946). He denounced the anti-lynching bill and advocated the deportation of all Negroes to Africa. He later admitted membership in the Ku Klux Klan. His Negro repatriation bill was even more racist than nineteenth-century colonization."[76] On the other end of the spectrum was Frank E. Smith, a white Mississippi moderate and veteran who won a Delta seat in the House of Representatives in 1950.[77]

In 1942 a federal grand jury brought an indictment for the lynching of Howard Wash (age 45), a black, against deputy sheriff Luther Holder of Laurel, Jones County, Mississippi, and four leaders of the lynch mob including Williams Oscar Johnson, Nathaniel Shorts, Allen Welborn Pryor, and Barney Jones. This was the first such trial held in Mississippi in forty years. None of the men were found guilty of the crime of lynching.[78]

Moderate whites in Mississippi were active in the Mississippi Council on Interracial Cooperation in the early 1940s, including the officers: Rt. Rev. Theodore D. Bratton, chairman; Rt. Rev. William Mercer Green, first vice-chairman; Mrs. M. M. Hubert, second vice-chairman; Mrs. Frank S. Sutton, secretary, all of Jackson; and R. P. Neblett, Jr., treasurer, of Brookhaven. Major goals of the council were to secure state support and funding for a training school for black delinquents in Mississippi and to improve race relations in the state.[79]

Many of these same leaders were also active in the Mississippi Council of the Association of Southern Women for the Prevention of Lynching. By July 1940, the group had distributed and received anti-lynching pledges from among 5,893 women, 551 men, and 160 public safety officers in 356 locations in Mississippi.[80] One author notes that "The ASWPL became the most effective organization created to stop lynching. Men found it difficult to argue for lynching against the women whom they claimed to be protecting."[81]

Other support for anti-lynching efforts among white Mississippians came from community groups, religious groups and women's organizations, including the Race Relations Committee of the Southern Crusaders, J. H. McMillan, chairman, Jonestown; Episcopal Women's Auxiliary, Diocese of Mississippi; Federation of Women's Clubs; Methodist Woman's Society for Christian Service, North Mississippi Conference; Methodist Church, North Mississippi Conference; Methodist Young People's Conference, North Mississippi Conference; Parent-Teacher Association; Temple Sisterhoods, Mississippi Federation; and Women's Christian Temperance Union.[82] These groups helped to bring additional public awareness on the severe problem which lynching represented to life in Mississippi and the South.

Several white Mississippi authors were significant for the forties, especially in their creative efforts to explore the southern distinctiveness of life and culture in the state, including the historic nature of lynching. Major writers in this group certainly include Stark Young (1881–1963), William Alexander Percy (1885–1942), Tennessee Williams (1911–1983), William Faulkner (1897–1962), Eudora Welty (1909–2001), and Walker Percy (1916–1991).[83]

White Mississippians thus presented a mixed lot when it came to the lynching phenomenon in the 1940s. Yet the evidence does suggest that at long last some were beginning to see the light, and to understand that an end to lynching was a goal to which many Mississippians, indeed, many Americans, should seek in the years ahead.

On the national level black Americans continued a valiant effort in the 1940s to wage a campaign against lynching. As ever, the NAACP stood on guard in this undertaking and, as Nan Elizabeth Woodruff suggests, placed an emphasis on using "the traditional liberal tactics of political lobbying, federal intervention, and public education to destroy the social evils" of lynching in the South.[84] By 1940 this work was carried forward with the cooperation of 355 branches and 50,556 NAACP members, and in 1946 1,073 branches with 450,000 members.[85] During this period, major leaders of the association included Walter Francis White, executive secretary; Roy Wilkins, assistant executive secretary (1931–1949) and editor of the *Crisis* (1939–1949); and Thurgood Marshall (1908–1993), legal advisor.[86] The NAACP still fought for Congressional passage of an anti-lynching bill. No act became law in the 1940s, however.[87]

Second to none were the 250 African American newspapers and magazines of the 1940s which courageously fought the lynching problem in this country.[88] Major black newspapers of this era included the Chicago *Defender*, the *Pittsburgh Courier*, the *New York Amsterdam News*, the *Detroit* (Michigan) *Chronicle*, and the *Norfolk* (Virginia) *Journal and Guide*. Among major magazines most active in the 1940s were the *Crisis*, the official organ of the NAACP; *Opportunity*, official organ of the National Urban League; *Ebony Magazine* and *Negro Digest*, publications of Johnson Publishing Company of Chicago; and *Our World*, active in New York from 1946.[89] These organs sought to use the black press as one major medium by which the black community could wage a tireless struggle to overcome racism, discrimination and lynching in American life.[90]

On the lynching of two black youths at Shubuta, Mississippi, on October 11, 1942, the Chicago *Defender* editorialized:

> This Quitman (Shubuta) lynching provides the most impressive argument for an immediate passage of an anti-lynching measure. If our Representatives in the Congress have any sense of moral righteousness and political responsibility, they will not long delay remedial legislation for curbing the inexcusable barbarities committed against oppressed and defenseless citizens.
>
> One thing is certain[,] that is America cannot move forward toward national unity by stepping upon the charred bodies of her black citizens.[91]

In Pittsburgh, the *Courier* noted:

> The colored people of this country expect the Federal Government to take prompt action against the lynchers of those two 14-year-old colored children in Mississippi.
>
> Lynching is certainly an interference with the war effort and endangers national unity, and the Department of Justice has ample power to deal with it on that ground.
>
> We are sick and tired of seeing powerful Government officials cringe before the spectre of State's Rights and wail their helplessness when some Negro is beaten or murdered by a mob, and then turn right around and ignore State's Rights under the pressure of fighting a war....
>
> Colored soldiers, sailors, and merchant seamen serving at the ends of the earth will not be gratified to hear that two colored children were murdered for an "attempted" crime and that their Government hid inactively behind the myth of State's Rights.
>
> We are sure the Government would not tolerate any nest of spies and traitors in Meridian, Mississippi, so we cannot see why it should tolerate lynchers. If it legally canot [sic] bring these fiends to trial, it can at least establish their identity and challenge the local courts to act.[92]

This anti-lynching tone appeared often in the black press during the 1940s.[93] It served to keep public attention on an ageless problem, and to encourage the black community to keep up the fight and continue the struggle to help make American democracy a living reality for all people on these shores, so that one day justice would live, as the Chicago *Defender* pledged in the issue of September 26, 1942:

> We, the Negro people of America, pledge allegiance to the United Nations, and to the principles for which they are fighting. Democracy, international amity, and the right of every person to work so that he may live with dignity and enjoy a standard compatible with human decency are the basic requirements for world harmony and lasting peace....
>
> We pledge ourselves to fight segregation, discrimination, and all forms of racial bigotry and Hitlerism which impede our war effort, and give aid and comfort to the enemy.
>
> We pledge ourselves to respect the rights of all mankind.
>
> We dedicate our lives and our energies to the holy crusade against barbarism in which our nation is now engaged; so that our children, as well as our neighbors' children, may enjoy the full richness of a world in which freedom of speech, freedom of religion, freedom from want, and freedom from fear are their common earthly heritage.[94]

National black women's organizations were also a force in the 1940s to encourage an end to lynchings in the United States. A central effort was promoted by the National Council of Negro Women, a unity movement among black women's clubs organized in 1935 with strong support from Mary McLeod Bethune (1875–1955), who served for fourteen years as president of the group.[95] To this effort must be added the National Association of Colored Women's Clubs active in the United States since 1896 and headed in the 1940s by Jennie Booth Moton (1937–1941), Ada Belle Dement (1941–1945), Christine Smith (1945–1948), and Ella Philips Stewart (1948–1952).[96] Black college women groups were also responsive to the lynching crisis, and such organizations as Alpha Kappa Alpha Sorority, Delta Sigma Theta Sorority, Zeta Phi Beta, and others used their publications and organizational skills to bring public attention to the impact of lynching on American society.[97]

Among national black leaders who were exceptional in their demands for black freedom and for an end to American lynchings in the 1940s were Paul Robeson (1898–1976), W. E. B. Du Bois (1868–1963), William L. Patterson (1890–1980), Elijah Muhammad (1897–1975), Father Divine (1879–1965), and Ralph Bunche (1904–1971). As a group these men represented the full stage of African-American consciousness in the 1940s: from the radical left to the conservative center and beyond. But, as black leaders and thinkers of this period, they were champions of black human rights. Paul Robeson, internationally famous for his works in the arts, was deeply committed to seeing an end to lynching in the United States. According to one study, in September 1946 he joined "in sponsoring [a] Crusade Against Lynching, representing [a] coalition of some 50 organizations. As delegate to Washington, [Robeson] asks President Harry F. Truman to issue 'formal public statement' that would make clear his views on lynching, and urges him to establish a 'definite legislature and educational program to end the disgrace of mob violence.' Addresses mass meeting and speaks on radio against lynching."[98]

W. E. B. Du Bois was an elder black statesman in the 1940s, but was still the best known active scholar and intellectual among African-Americans. Eric Foner notes that in the 1940s, Du Bois moved more to the left and "sharply criticized the Truman Administration's cold war policies, supported the candidacy of Henry Wallace in 1948, [and] joined Paul Robeson at the Council on African Affairs...."[99] The correspondence of Du Bois makes clear his stand against lynching. He told Walter White in a memorandum of September 13, 1946, that "I have been fighting lynching for forty years, and I have a right to let the world know that I am still fighting. I therefore gladly endorsed the Robeson Movement [Crusade Against Lynching] which asked for my cooperation...."[100]

Activist William L. Patterson (1890–1980) was a force behind U.S. blacks' attempts to bring their situation before the attention of the United Nations in a document entitled "We Charge Genocide." Patterson became the national executive secretary of the Civil Rights Congress, formed in 1946 from a merger of the International Labor Defense and the National Federation for Constitutional Liberties.[101] "We Charge Genocide" was presented to the United Nations by Patterson and Paul Robeson, with strong backing from W. E. B. Du Bois. The document sought to put in historical terms the opposition and human rights violations that blacks had suffered in the United States, including the ageless problem of lynching.[102]

Two radically different religious figures were significant for the 1940s, Elijah Muhammad and Father Divine. Muhammad was the key leader at the Nation of Islam in the 1940s, but he was opposed to serving in the U.S. military during World War II, and was jailed from 1942 to1946 because of his refusal to obey the Selective Service Act.[103] In general, according to scholar C. Eric Lincoln, Muhammad "prefers to dissociate this movement from violent activity of any kind. His followers are forbidden to carry weapons, and they are cautioned not to carry any instrument that might conceivably be considered even a potential weapon, should they be searched by an overzealous police officer.... [But, he also taught his followers] to defend themselves and each other if they are assaulted."[104] Muhammad's philosophy meant, of course, that blacks had to organize themselves and fight to prevent lynchings in America.

Father Divine (George Baker, Jr.) organized the Peace Mission movement, a religious group active in Harlem, New York, in the 1930s and later relocated to Philadelphia, Pennsylvania, in 1942. Mina A. Vaughn observes that Father Divine's theology "centered on ideas of self-help, positive thought, and a promise of a brighter future."[105] He was a fervent opponent of lynching, and encouraged the development of "petition campaigns, marches, and other activities in which Peace Mission members engaged."[106] He was a strong supporter of the need for a federal anti-lynching law, "so that we will go on record as a nation refusing to endorse lynching, or murder, without due process of law, which is not according to the Constitution...."[107] Not everyone appreciated Father Divine's outspoken support for anti-lynching efforts in the 1940s. One study suggests that "The Peace Mission's activism on behalf of anti-lynching legislation is unquestionable, but its influence is much more suspect. The fact that Father Divine endorsed a bill imparted to it added controversy—the last thing sponsors of anti-lynching legislation wanted. There resulted the curious situation of supporters going to great lengths to ignore Divine's persistent aid, while opponents amply compensated by declaring him a prime mover in the struggle for passage."[108]

Yet the fact stands that Father Divine opposed lynching and helped to foster black protest "by providing an outlet for black proletarians to express their resentments against lynching and racism in constructive political ways: as petitioners, marchers and Washington lobbyists. If the techniques they and other civil rights workers employed were too often unpolished and unheeded, they were still gathering force for campaigns and triumphs to come."[109]

Finally, Ralph J. Bunche (1904–1971) represents an international perspective among black thinkers of the 1930s and 1940s on the era of lynching and the black condition during this period. Famous for his work with the United Nations and for receiving the Nobel Peace Prize (1950), Bunche offered a political analysis of the black condition in this country.[110] Therefore, Bunche's focus on class and economic considerations placed the lynching problem within this framework, and "he maintained that the black struggle was interwoven with the total fabric of American life, and any solution to it had to include a 'comprehension of the history and the political, economic and social forces at work' in America."[111]

Such leaders as Paul Robeson, W. E. B. Du Bois, William L. Patterson, Elijah Muhammad, Father Divine, and Ralph Bunche are representative of the thousands of black spokespersons who actively campaigned to advance black rights in the 1940s, and to force the nation to deal with the continuing lynching crisis, then still a national problem.

A number of other black intellectuals were also very active and noted for their work in the 1940s in advancing the black cause, including helping the nation come to grips with the lynching issue. This group includes Edward Franklin Frazier (1894–1962), sociologist; Charles Hamilton Houston (1895–1950), a major black lawyer of the period; the union leader and organizer A. Phillip Randolph; the writers Langston Hughes (1902–1967), Countee Cullen (1903–1946), Jessie Fauset (1827–1961), Zora Neale Hurston (1891–1960), May Miller (1899–1995), and Ralph Ellison (1914–1994); the scholars anthropologist St. Clair Drake (1911–1990); historian Rayford W. Logan (1897–1982), Morehouse College president Benjamin E. Mays (1894–1984), historian Benjamin Quarles (1904–1996), and musician Roland Hayes (1887–1977). Collectively these individuals used their talents to forge a greater public awareness of discrimination in American life, and especially to draw public attention to lynching and its associated evils in our nation during the forties. Their body of work stands as a living testimony to the courage, vision, and outlook of black intellectuals during the hardships of the era of World War II.

On the national scene, in Washington D.C., the campaign against lynching continued. In the office of president during the 1940s were Franklin D. Roosevelt, until his death on April 12, 1945, followed by Harry S. Truman, who served the last years of Roosevelt's term and then won his own election in 1948.[112] While Roosevelt may have personally been opposed to lynching he was fearful of losing southern support for the New Deal programs in Congress. For this reason he never forcibly tried to push anti-lynching efforts in either the executive or legislative branches of government. Hedda Garza captures the tone of the Roosevelt era very well when she writes:

> An ongoing united campaign against lynching was also put into high gear with the NAACP playing a leading role. Violence against blacks had increased alarmingly as angry unemployed southern whites took their hostility out on blacks. Anti-lynching legislation was regularly blocked in Congress by southern congressmen's filibusters. Pressed to take action against the barbarism, President Franklin Delano Roosevelt publicly condemned lynching but refused to intervene. He was, after all, dependent on the support of southern legislators in the forthcoming [1940 and 1944 elections].[113]

Harry S. Truman also appears to have been personally opposed to lynchings, but like Roosevelt he felt tied down by the realities of southern white political power in the 1940s. He could not publicly show his displeasure with racism, but as one historian points out, "Although his own ancestors were Confederates, Truman said, 'My very stomach turned over when I learned that Negro soldiers, just back from overseas, were being dumped out of Army trucks in Mississippi and beaten.... I shall fight to end evils like this.'"[114] Yet, he needed Southern political support for the Democratic party, and for his own election in 1948.[115] However, late in the 1940s Truman "called for state and federal action against lynching and the poll tax, an end to inequality in education, employment, the whole caste system based on race or color."[116] Nevertheless, as in the long past, by "1949 Truman's legislation on ... lynching, the poll tax, and civil rights ran into conflict with a coalition of southern Democrats and Republicans."[117] Thus very little national action was able to move through Congress on new civil rights laws in the 1940s. And an anti-lynching law was never adopted by Congress during the decade.[118]

In general, organized white religion, especially in the South, continued its adherence to the Southern way of life.[119] This stance did not help the anti-lynching efforts underway in the country. Progressive elements among some national white religious bodies did oppose lynching in the nation. But it remained for most protest to come from black churches in this country.[120]

In the South, certainly the Association of Southern Women for the Prevention of Lynching continued to play an active role in anti-lynching efforts. J. Egerton notes the importance of this group:

> By the beginning of the forties, the ASWPL held the signatures of more than forty thousand Southerners—mostly white women—who were openly committed to the abolition of lynching. They took some credit for the fact that this once-flagrant and near epidemic atrocity was diminishing (from an average of thirty a year in the 1920s to about six a year in the last half of the thirties), and that community sanction of it had been destroyed. Ames and her organization had shunned the very idea of help from Washington—even lobbying against a federal anti-lynching statute—and now, she proudly asserted, the South had almost eliminated this stain on its soul, and the ASWPL could soon bow out with its mission accomplished.[121]

A group of Southern white liberals should also be listed among those Americans who were opposed to lynchings in the 1940s. This list includes Lillian Smith (1897–1966), especially noted for her book *Killers of the Dream* (1949); Katharine Du Pre Lumpkin, Ralph McGill, Hodding Carter (1907–1972), Virginius Dabney, and Jonathan Daniels.[122] Such figures had their work cut out for them in the 1940s, for they lived in a region where, according to Lillian Smith, "[whites] found it easier to cultivate hate than love."[123]

The impact of lynchings in Mississippi for the years 1940 to 1949 are predisposed by the fact that the state continued to have a regional, national, and even international position as one of the most difficult places on earth for black people. William Stuart Nelson observed this relationship very closely:

> The totalitarian political mind of the South is accompanied by an explicit fascism with regard to the Negro. Although Negroes constitute one-third of the southern population, politically they are practically powerless. It would be difficult to find anywhere in the civilized world a more completely fascist state as regards the political treatment of Negroes than exists at this very hour in Mississippi. Likewise it would be difficult to find a political unit which has produced such puerility, demagoguery, and sinisterness in political matters. Recent Supreme Court decisions will alter this situation in time but it will be by no consent of the majority of southerners and the decisions may have come too late. Even now every resource is being employed to circumvent them. Expressed unblushingly is the determination to keep the Democratic party "an exclusively white party," whatever the cost.[124]

Against this backdrop comes the known lynching totals for the 1940s. Of the 33 cases nationally, 15 (or almost half) were in Mississippi. So, in spite of a general reduction in national totals for lynchings during the 1940s, Mississippi still stands out in a very negative way with the largest number of lynching victims in the United States.[125] In a decade when millions died in World War II, lynching was still an issue in the United States. Even the world renowned scientist Albert Einstein (1879–1955) noted for the world in 1947 that security against lynching is "one of the most urgent tasks of our generation."[126] Such was the case then, and such was the case to follow in the 1950s. Even public opinion during this era seems to have agreed with Einstein. According to public opinion polls in 1937 and 1940 a majority of Americans were against lynchings in this nation. The data review follows.[127]

TABLE 9.7: PUBLIC OPINION ON THE LYNCHING CRISIS, 1937 AND 1940

1. (US Jan. 5, 1937) Should Congress enact a law which would make lynching a federal crime?

Percentage by Geographic Section

	YES	NO
New England	75	25
Middle Atlantic	72	25
East Central	77	23
West Central	70	30
South	65	35
Mountain	65	35
Pacific Coast	59	41

Results by Special Groups

	YES	NO
Women	75	25
Young Persons	77	23
Reliefers	72	28
Farmers	69	31
Small Towns	75	25
Urban	70	30

2. (Oct. 28 '37) Should Congress pass a law which would make lynching a federal crime?

Percentage by Geographic Section

	YES	NO
New England	75	25
Middle Atlantic	46	21
East Central	77	23
West Central	57	43
South	57	43
Mountain	75	25
Pacific Coast	65	35

A clear majority of Americans were in support of a national anti-lynching law (70–72 percent). But Congress would not pass such an act in the 1930s or 1940s. Fifty-nine percent of the people in a poll of November 19, 1937, supported the federal government's right to punish a peace officer if he or she was negligent in protecting a prisoner from a lynch mob. Later polls also demonstrate a support by the public for anti-lynching efforts in this country. This was certainly an improvement over the earlier decades of the twentieth century.

Thus, as the 1940s came to an end, there was a decline in lynching in the United States, but people were still dying at the hands of mobs in this country. Why did lynchings continue? Robert L. Zangrando suggests that the reasons were many and included "the search for quick solutions, an enthusiasm for force as an instrument of public conduct, a strong sense of conformity to local or regional mores, a determination to impose majority rule upon a vulnerable minority, and support for a mechanism of control in a biracial environment."[128] Indeed, the problem would remain in-force for at least another decade, or longer; and, Americans would have to struggle to advance justice and equality for all the country's citizens into a new generation.

10

Changes in a New Era,
1950–1959

Black Mississippians entered a very conservative period—the 1950s—with hopes of a better future and prayers for the end of the lynching crisis which had plagued the state since the Reconstruction era. Now, for the first time in many generations, blacks found themselves in a minority position as the second largest population group in Mississippi. In fact, by 1950 the total black population in Mississippi was 986,707 compared to 1,188,429 whites and a very small number among other groups such as Native Americans and Chinese Americans, giving the state a total population of 2,178,914.[1] A majority of Mississippians were still concentrated in rural areas, with 76.5 percent of blacks in rural areas, and 68.5 percent (or 814,312) whites also in the country. Only 23.3 percent of blacks (232,842 people) and 31.5 percent (374,320) whites lived in urban centers.[2] Migration remained a major theme for both blacks and whites in Mississippi. Between 1950 and 1960, 323,000 blacks migrated from the state along with 338,966 whites.[3] Certainly such a large volume of migration had great consequences for such a poor state as Mississippi, including a brain drain and loss of laborers. A recent study notes the economic position of Mississippi during this decade:

> Mississippi still suffered from economic depression. The number of farm jobs declined during the decade as a result of the introduction of new machinery. This loss had a tremendous impact on blacks as more of them left the farm for the city. The problem for blacks and many poor whites was Mississippi's dubious distinction of having the lowest per capita income and median family income ($1,198 in 1950) in the United States; in 1950, 300,000 Mississippians worked on farms. By 1960, this figure shrank to 142,000. In 1960, only 2,123 families in the state had a yearly income of $25,000 or more. In such a climate, Ross Barnett, gubernatorial candidate in 1959, proclaimed, "The Negro is different because God made him different to punish him. His forehead slants back; his nose is different, his lips are different, and his color is sure different.... We will not drink from the cup of genocide." The psychological and physical terror spread during the 1950s had a major impact on all aspects of black existence. Of all Mississippi's institutions, white terror had perhaps its greatest impact on the black press.[4]

In general, the economic situation in the 1950s meant that black Mississippians lived in a system where the economic institutions were:

1. White ownership of enterprise
2. Employment
   Hiring practices
   a. employers can impose high educational standards
   b. application of subtle criteria by employers (e.g., speech and deportment)
   c. limited recruitment channels
   d. concentration of blacks in marginal or declining firms
   Promotional Systems
   a. occupational ceilings
   b. specific job classifications
   c. specific production units
   d. restriction to low-paying job classifications
3. Labor union participation
   a. restrictive apprenticeship programs
   b. membership in unskilled positions
4. Consumer exploitation
   Disparity in black-white economic power.[5]

The segregationist system of Mississippi kept blacks in an economic bondage. It would take the community years to overcome this condition.[6] Scholar John Dittmer notes the economic crisis facing black Mississippians during this period: "In postwar Mississippi most blacks were still working at jobs associated with slavery. Nearly two-thirds of the black male labor force engaged in some form of agriculture-related activity; more than 80 percent of these men were sharecroppers or day laborers on white-owned plantations. Few blacks held jobs in factories, and most of these were in the lowest-paying janitorial positions. For black women the designated place was still the white woman's kitchen. Of the 58,000 black women employed in non-agricultural jobs in 1950, two-thirds worked as domestics."[7] Thus, the economic situation in this state needed to be reformed and changed to benefit the citizens of Mississippi.

Social and race relations remained "separate" and unequal in 1950s Mississippi. Jim Crow continued in-place. What did segregation during this decade really mean for blacks? James W. Loewen and Charles Sallis note the impact: "In 1954 black and white children in Mississippi still attended separate schools. Most public places were 'white only.' Black people could not eat in a restaurant or sleep in a motel that served whites. Laws kept blacks out of some city parks and almost all swimming pools. Blacks were not allowed to use places like the main branch of the Jackson Public Library. Public transportation was also segregated. Blacks still had to sit in the back of buses, use separate cars on trains, sit in waiting rooms marked 'colored,' and use 'colored' restrooms. In small towns where there was only one library, pool, or park, black people simply had to do without."[8]

Life in the Magnolia State was a harsh reality and travail for black Mississippians, but they survived against the odds to press on for another new day. One traveler, John Gunther, was perplexed by this region:

Everywhere I went in the South I asked why it was so dry, legally speaking, and I got a considerable variety of answers. One was that Southerners fear outbursts of drunkenness by Negroes. Surely what this means is that they also fear outbursts of drunkenness by themselves.... The South contains a great number of profoundly schizoid people; the whole region is a land of paranoia, full of the mentally sick; most Southerners feel a deep necessity to hate something, if necessary even themselves. Their hatred (I fear) of alcohol is partly a reflection of bad conscience: the South feels that liquor will release its own most dangerous inhibitions. The Negro problem is inextricable involved; so is the sexual problem. A Southern will, perhaps without expressing it consciously or concretely, work out an equation something like the following: "We are not going to give up the Negro; therefore we must give up something else. We will not give up fundamentalism, sex, white supremacy or slavery; so we give up rationality instead."[9]

In the midst of such attitudes, a small black middle and professional class attempted to stay active in Mississippi during the bleak 1950s. By 1951, only two black lawyers were active in the state. Yet no black law school applicant had been allowed in Mississippi between 1941 and 1951 to pass the Mississippi bar examination.[10] Finally, two blacks were allowed to enter the legal system of Mississippi in September 1951 when Jack Harvey Young (1908–1976) of Jackson, a student of Sidney Redmond, and Lawrence C. Jones, Jr., son of the president and founder of Piney Woods Country Life School, and a graduate of New York University Law School, passed the state bar examination.[11] The dozens of active black lawyers from the past had either died or migrated from Mississippi to other more promising states. Scholar Neil R. McMillen suggests that as late as 1940 there were only 55 black physicians (fifty men and five women) practicing in Mississippi.[12] They were concentrated in Mississippi's central cities. Yet there existed in Mississippi a medical crisis for the black community. McMillen states: "Yet in a state with but one black doctor for roughly every 210,000 black people— the worst such ratio in the U.S.—medicine was perceived by both races as a white profession."[13] Black physicians had to continue to deal with a racist system which impacted every aspect of their work in the state, and sickness and lack of medical care continued to prevail in Mississippi among African-Americans.

Black students and teachers at all levels in Mississippi continued to suffer in a segregated world. John Dittmer notes the despair which blacks faced over educational policies in Mississippi: "Even the most ardent segregationist would admit that under the principle of 'separate but equal,' black children in Mississippi had been denied educational opportunity. As late as 1950, 70 percent of blacks twenty-five years of age and older had less than a seventh-grade education. Only 10,250, or 2.3 percent had completed high school. During that year the state spent $122.93 per pupil for the education of whites and $32.55 for blacks.... Where city and county governments refused to appropriate funds, blacks had to provide their own school buildings while paying taxes to support white schools."[14] At the black college level, conditions were also depressing. In all of the states institutions of higher education for blacks, there were only 3,131 students.[15] This list includes Alcorn College, Jackson State College, Mississippi Valley State College (established in 1946), publicly supported colleges; and the private black colleges, Tougaloo and Rust. Black public institutions also suffered discriminatory funding procedures and their structures, curricula and salary scales were much less than that of the historically white institutions: University of Mississippi, Delta State University, Mississippi State University, University of Mississippi for Women, and the University of Southern Mississippi.[16]

A real test for Mississippi came on May 17, 1954, with the Supreme Court's decision in *Brown vs. Board of Education*, in which "laws supporting school segregation were struck down. Subsequent rulings by the court said integration was to proceed with 'all deliberate speed.'"[17] White Mississippi responded with a live or die mentality toward the court's decision. According to James W. Loewen and Charles Sallis: "Fred Sullens, editor of the Jackson Daily News, wrote that 'human blood may stain Southern soil in many places because of this decision, but the dark red stains of the blood will be on the marble steps of the U.S. Supreme Court building.' Governor Hugh White argued more calmly: 'We shall resist ... by every legal means at our command. I want to say that there is no intention to "defy" the Supreme Court; we are simply exercising the same legal rights to resist the most unfortunate decision that the NAACP exercised.'"[18]

At long last the state's white leadership felt a need to "improve" black schools. Jesse O. McKee observes the outcome: "Governor White and the legislature prepared for that situation by planning to improve black schools. They proposed to raise salaries of black teachers to the same level as those of white teachers and to build black schools to match white schools. White called one hundred of the state's black leaders to Jackson to ask for their support of his separate-but-equal plan. The black leaders rejected his 'voluntary' segregation. Governor White was shocked. Like many white Mississippians, he had convinced himself that black people really did accept segregation. Negotiations ended with white leaders supporting segregation and black leaders demanding integration."[19] Yet this small opening gave blacks in Mississippi hope and faith that at long last, perhaps change was possible—even in Mississippi.

Politically, however, the black community seemed as checkmated as ever. The total number of blacks registered to vote told the story. Scholars have estimated that Mississippi in 1952 had 17,000 registered black voters, but in the elections of 1951 only 5,600 had been able to vote in the state. By 1954 there were 22,104 black registrations, however, Governor J. P. Coleman "told Congress [that] only 8000 of them had paid their poll tax."[20] Such conditions were evidence that most of the estimated black voting potential of 500,000 in Mississippi was not represented in state elections.

Three key black leaders emerged in the 1950s in Mississippi, all associated with the development of the NAACP in the state: Medgar Evers (1925–1963), Aaron Henry (1922–1998), and Amzie Moore (1911–1982). Evers was state field secretary of the Mississippi NAACP (1954–1963) and operated from Jackson. His work during the 1950s included organizing NAACP branches in the state, spreading the word through the state on the goals of the association, and, according to John Dittmer, "investigating racially motivated homicides" in Mississippi.[21] Henry, from Clarksdale, Mississippi, was especially influential in helping the NAACP grow in the Delta region of the state. In fact, he first joined the NAACP in 1939 when in high school. In 1953 he organized the Coahoma County branch of the association.[22] Henry was also a pharmacist and drugstore owner in Clarksdale. Moore, like Henry, was a key NAACP leader who emerged from the Delta, from his base at Cleveland, Bolivar County, where he operated a service station.[23] Collectively the three leaders represented a turning point in the 1950s for black political protest and organizing in Mississippi.

Opposite the NAACP stood the Progressive Voters League which had been active in Mississippi since 1946 under President T. B. Wilson. James W. Loewen and Charles Sallis note that this group had "successfully registered black citizens in some parts of the state, [but] their progress was halted by Bilbo's 1946 campaign."[24] This group received some support from black newspapers in Mississippi such as Percy Greene's *Jackson Advocate* and Willie J. Miller's *Mississippi Enterprise*, also published at Jackson.[25] Thus the era of the 1950s was a decade of challenges for black Mississippians in their struggles to advance the group economically, socially and politically. Yet change was in the wind, but the ageless problem of lynching was never far off the horizon. Nor were black daily problems in dealing with Mississippi's criminal justice system, a system completely tied to the Jim Crow tradition of discrimination and oppression of black Mississippians.

The administration of justice in Mississippi during the 1950s remained the business of the white community. Blacks were still on the outside looking in. James T. Patterson states it well when he notes that "Southern blacks who escaped the violence, only to be brought to trial for alleged offenses, faced all-white judges and juries and had virtually no possibility of justice."[26]

Capital punishment also remained a special concern of blacks in Mississippi. With a decline in lynchings, many people believed that state legal executions of blacks increased as a new form of social control.[27] In fact, one study observes that during this period "the majority of the executions took place in the Southern states, with the state of Mississippi leading with the most executions."[28] Added to this problem was the issue of police brutality in Mississippi. This form of white violence reached epidemic proportions in the 1950s, and especially as black protest campaigns increased in the state.[29] Then the state's number of black murder victims increased; some were killed by white policemen, others by unknown parties. John Dittmer notes, "Between 1956 and 1959 at least ten black men were killed by whites, none of whom was convicted."[30] Because of the special nature of the ten deaths, they are being added to the lynching totals for Mississippi during the 1950s. One example of police misconduct is illustrated here to note the terror of the period by police units in Mississippi: In April 1962, "army corporal Roman Duckworth, who was in Taylorsville to visit his ailing wife, refused to move to the back of a Trailways bus. In an altercation that followed, a city policeman shot and killed the unarmed serviceman. No charges were filed, and the murder of Corporal Duckworth received little media attention."[31]

Statewide, Parchman Penitentiary remained the central state prison during the fifties. Most of the prisoners were black. Reform efforts were slow in coming to Parchman. Mississippi passed its first prison parole laws in 1944. The state's system of legal executions underwent some changes during World War II. From 1940 to 1955 the state used a portable electric chair which traveled from county to county to execute 56 black males, 16 white males, and one black woman. In 1955 executions were performed at Parchman in a gas chamber.[32] In the 1950s Parchman remained "this nation's most brutal and oppressive penal institution."[33] Mississippi justice, or the lack thereof for blacks, remained a central concern of the black community as events unfolded during this decade.

As Stewart E. Tolnay and E. M. Beck have demonstrated, the causes of lynchings in Mississippi and other states vary from decade to decade, but some central issues seem to maintain themselves from period to period. Certainly by the 1950s, alleged crimes against white males remains a focus, as does murder and the issue of rape of white women. But blacks could still be lynched for very simple alleged transgressions against white people, such as perceived lack of black respect for a white man or woman, or failure to say "yes, sir," or simply for being considered an unpopular black man.[34] Yet, as in the Reconstruction years, some blacks could suffer a lynching due to their activism in black politics or civil rights.

The American people entered the decade of the 1950s with an assumption that the Age of Lynching was over and was now an event of the past. In fact, the news in a 1952 report from Tuskegee Institute, Alabama, "indicates that, for the first time in its 71 years of tabulation, no lynchings have occurred in the United States" for the prior year.[35] But, as Table 10.1 (page 142) indicates, there were at least seven officially recognized lynchings nationwide in this country during the decade, and six are listed for Mississippi![36] For half the decade, in the years 1952, 1953, 1954, 1956 and 1958, no lynchings took place. This decline in lynchings represented a tribute to the work of thousands of anti-lynching activists since the nineteenth century, including Ida B. Wells-Barnett, Frederick Douglass, Jesse Ames, W. E. B. Du Bois, Mary McLeod Bethune, and so many others who faithfully carried this struggle forward across so many decades. The year of 1955, however, was an especially difficult one; four black men were lynched in Mississippi. In terms of black consciousness, this brought back all of the terror and sorrow of the past associated with the lynching phenomenon (see Table 10.2, page 142).

The six officially recognized lynching victims of the state for the decade, all black men, were murdered in six counties: three in the Delta Region (Humphreys, Leflore, and Talla-

TABLE 10.1: LYNCHING VICTIMS, 1950–1959

	United States		Mississippi	
Year	Blacks	Whites	Blacks	Whites
1950	1	1	0	0
1951	1	0	1	0
1952	0	0	0	0
1953	0	0	0	0
1954	0	0	0	0
1955	3	0	4	0
1956	0	0	0	0
1957	1	1	0	0
1958	0	0	0	0
1959	1	0	1	0
TOTALS	7	2	6	0

TABLE 10.2: MISSISSIPPI LYNCHING VICTIMS, 1950–1959

Name	Location	Date	Causes
Willie McGee	Laurel, Jones Co.	1951	"Legal" execution by the State of Mississippi for alleged rape
Rev. George W. Lee	Belzoi, Humphries Co.	7 May 55	NAACP organizer and voter registration worker
Lamar Smith	Brookhaven, Lincoln Co.	1955	Organizer and for "messing around" in voter registration work.
Emmett Louis Till	Money, LeFlore Co.	28 Aug. 55	Wolf-whistled at a white woman
Clinton Melton	Glendora, Tallahatchie Co.	Dec. 55	Argument with a white man at a gas station
Mack Charles Parker	Popularville, Pearl River Co.	25 April 59	Rape

hatchie) and three in South Mississippi (Jones, Lincoln, and Pearl River) (See Tables 10.3 and 10.4). These counties continued to have a large black population during the 1950s.

    As in the past, black men were lynched in Mississippi for a variety of causes (see Table 10.5). The six official victims of the fifties were lynched for rape (2), for voter registration activities—a threat to white males (2), for disrespecting a white woman (1) and for a dispute with a white male (1). The justifications for lynchings follow the general historical patterns

TABLE 10.3: MISSISSIPPI LYNCHING VICTIMS BY COUNTY, 1950–1959

County	Number of Victims	County	Number of Victims
Humphreys	1	LeFlore	1
Jones	1	Pearl River	1
Lincoln	1	Tallahatchie	1

TABLE 10.4: GEOGRAPHIC DISTRIBUTION OF MISSISSIPPI LYNCHING VICTIMS BY REGION, 1950–1959

Delta	No.	South	No.	North	East	Central	Gulf Coast
Humphreys	1	Jones	1	none	none	none	none
LeFlore	1	Lincoln	1				
Tallahatchie	1	Pearl River	1				

TABLE 10.5: RANGE OF CAUSES OF MISSISSIPPI LYNCHINGS, 1950–1959

Cause	Number	Percentage
Rape	2	33%
Voter registration work	2	33%
Disrespect to a white woman	1	17%
Disrespect to a white man	1	17%
TOTAL	6	

from previous decades. Table 10.6 (page 144) proclaims, as does the lynching data from the past, that lynchers generally preferred to conduct a lynching event during the warm months of the year. This pattern is noted for the official victims of the decade when one was killed in April, two each in May and August, and one during the winter month of December.

Students who research the 1950s in Mississippi are faced with a difficult task—that of coming to a clear understanding of the violent deaths of another ten black men in the state. These victims are not generally placed under the category of lynching victims, but perhaps they should be. Of the ten men, seven of their names are known. A mystery surrounds the group of ten. Generally we do not know who killed them, or why. Table 10.7 (page 144) lists the men and the little information that is available about each case.[37] Their cases clearly

TABLE 10.6: TIME OF YEAR OF MISSISSIPPI LYNCHING EVENTS, 1950–1959

Month	Number	Percentage
January	0	0%
February	0	0%
March	0	0%
April	1	17%
May	2	33%
June	0	0%
July	0	0%
August	2	33%
September	0	0%
October	0	0%
November	0	0%
December	1	17%
TOTAL	6	

TABLE 10.7: TEN SPECIAL CASES OF BLACK MEN KILLED IN MISSISSIPPI, 1950s

Name	Location	Date	Causes
Edward Duckworth	?	1956	En route to ailing wife
Milton Russell	Belzoi, Humphreys Co.	1956	?
Charles Brown	Near Yazoo City, Yazoo Co.	1957	?
Woodrow Wilson Daniels	?	1958	?
George Love	?	1958	?
Jonas Causey	Clarksdale, Coahoma Co.	1959	?
Luther Jackson	Philadelphia, Neshoba Co.	1959	Killed by local policeman
Three unknown black men	?	1950s	?

represent the dangers of living in Mississippi for black men in the 1950s, for random violence as well as organized violence was a factor in the lives of black Mississippians. Then, too, being in police custody could be life-threatening for a black person. Scholar John Dittmer captures the essence of the last case of the ten men, Luther Jackson: "October 1959, Philadelphia, Mississippi—Hatti Thomas and Luther Jackson, a friend from out of town, were sitting in a parked car when a patrol car drove up and a policeman ordered the two to get out. According to Thomas the officer then pushed Jackson around the car, out of sight, and shot him twice. By the time Hattie Thomas reached him, Luther Jackson lay dead in a ditch. The Philadelphia police officer's name was Lawrence Rainey."[38]

If the ten cases noted above are added to the six official lynching victims for Mississippi during the 1950s, then the state has a total of sixteen lynching victims for the decade— more than twice the national total of nine. Five of these case studies, Willie McGee (1951), the Reverend George W. Lee (1955), Lamar Smith (1955), Emmett Louis Till (1955), and Mack Charles Parker (1959), are examined. These lynching cases are representative of the terror and continued brutal nature of the Jim Crow and segregationist systems of Mississippi.

Case Study One
Willie McGee (1923–1951) Laurel, Jones County, Mississippi May ?, 1951

The courts were especially cruel in cases involving sex crimes allegedly committed by black men against white women. On the morning of November 3, 1945, a Laurel housewife named Wilmetta Hawkins reported to the police that she had been raped by a Negro. Thirty-two-year-old Willie McGee, married and the father of four children, was arrested and charged with the crime. His trial lasted less than a day. The Laurel jury deliberated only a few minutes before finding him guilty; the judge sentenced McGee to die in the electric chair. This was to be the first of three trials. The Mississippi Supreme Court threw out the first verdict by ruling that McGee should have had a change of venue, overturned the second on grounds that blacks had been systematically excluded from the juries, and then upheld the third conviction. The case dragged on for over five years. After the first trial McGee turned his defense over to the Civil Rights Congress; his chief counsel was a young New York attorney named Bella Abzug. The Communist party took an interest in the McGee case and transformed it into a cause célèbre. Rallies and protests took place around the world. Governor Fielding Wright received thousands of letters including petitions signed by such notables as Josephine Baker, Jean-Paul Sartre, and Albert Einstein.

McGee's lawyers had originally argued that the penalty was unfair because no white man had ever received a death sentence for rape, but in their final appeal the Civil Rights Congress attorneys exploded a bombshell: McGee and his wife Rosalee presented sworn statements that the alleged victim had been having an affair with McGee for a number of years before she claimed to have been raped. Although this new evidence smacked of desperation, the revelation did not come as a shock to a number of Laurel citizens who had long suspected such a relationship. The Mississippi Supreme Court rejected the new evidence as a "revolting insinuation and plainly not supported." The U.S. Supreme Court refused to review the case. Both Governor Wright and President Harry S. Truman denied appeals for clemency. Late in the evening of May 7, 1951, a crowd of some 700 whites gathered outside the Laurel courtroom where the state's portable electric chair was now in place. At 12:07 a.m. they led out a loud, piercing rebel yell when word came that Willie McGee was dead.[39]

McGee's case, although officially a legal execution by the State of Mississippi, serves to remind us that in this late period of the Age of Lynching in Mississippi, just what an impact the large number of "legal" state executions had on the black community. This was terror practiced by the state, in general, the state as a violent lynching mob. Writer Walter Lowenfels captures the impact of state murder very well in his poem "Shoes That Walked for Willie McGee."[40]

Case Study Two
The Reverend George W. Lee (?–1955)
Belzoni, Humphreys County, Mississippi
May 7, 1955

The Reverend George W. Lee, a local black Baptist minister was an activist in Belzoni, Mississippi. One study notes that Lee, along with strong support from Gus Courts and sixty-two other local blacks: organized, early in 1954, a Belzoni branch of the National Association for the Advancement of Colored People (NAACP), and forwarded their application for a charter to New York. The backlash came quickly in the form of a white Citizens' Council. Its avowed purpose, according to Council Secretary C. L. Puckett, a Belzoni tax consultant, was to fight three evils: "the NAACP—because it's a Community Organization; the Communists; and the Supreme Court." George Lee and Gus Courts led the list of ninety-five Negroes who finally managed to achieve voter status. They believed that they were numbers one and two on a widely circulated reprisal list.[41]

For his voter registration work, Rev. Lee was killed on May 7, 1955, "by shotgun blasts from a passing car. Lee was the first black to register to vote in Humphreys County, and he had urged others also to register. No charges were brought in this case, and the sheriff reportedly stated that lead pellets in Lee's jaw and neck could have come from fillings in his teeth."[42] This case strengthened the resolve of local, state and national blacks and their organizations to struggle onward in the fight for civil and human rights.

Case Study Three
Lamar Smith (1892–1955)
Brookhaven, Lincoln County, Mississippi
August 13, 1955

In the broad daylight of Saturday afternoon, August 13, Lamar Smith was shot dead in front of the courthouse at Brookhaven, Miss. He had been active in getting voters out for the primary election August 2 and was working on the runoff primary scheduled for August 23.

Brookhaven is the home town of Circuit Judge Tom Brady who has been active in the formation of White Citizens Councils and who has made speeches in and out of Mississippi advocating the impeachment of the United States Supreme Court.

A grand jury on September 21, 1955, failed to return an indictment against the three men arrested in connection with the Smith murder.

The District Attorney is reported in a United Press dispatch as accusing the Sheriff of refusing to make an immediate arrest "although he knew everything I know" about the slaying. In another dispatch the District Attorney is quoted as saying: "The Sheriff told me he saw Noah Smith (one of the accused men) leave the scene of the killing with blood all over him. It was his duty to take that man into custody regardless of who he was, but he did not do it."[43]

Case Study Four
Emmett Louis Till (July 25, 1941–August 28, 1955)
Money, Mississippi
August 28, 1955

Emmett Louis Till, the only child of Mamie and Louis Till, was born July 25, 1941.

At the age of five, Emmett was stricken with polio from which he recovered except for a serious speech defect. Many visits to doctors, clinics and speech therapists failed to cure his stuttering. Illinois Research Hospital finally advised that he would "probably outgrow the problem."

Emmett was raised in Argo, Illinois, and attended school there until 1951. In Chicago, he attended the McCosh School until 1955, the year of his death.

Emmett was a humanitarian. Senior citizens were his main concern. They would depend upon him to run errands, shop, mow lawns, shovel snow, or whatever tasks they needed him to perform. At home, he voluntarily assumed responsibility for many household chores, including bill paying and laundry. He said: "Mom, if you can earn the money, I can take care of the house." This he did until his death.

Emmett attended the Argo Temple Church of God in Christ. In Argo he would stay with his great-grandmother, Nancy Jane Carthan. She depended upon him to do her shopping and mopping and other errands outside the home.

He was the chosen leader among his friends in Argo and Chicago. Emmett was known as the "mediator." He could move in and settle disputes and his judgment was acceptable. Parents depended upon his ability to steer the other young people in the right direction.

Emmett was killed on Sunday, August 28, 1955, in Money, Mississippi [for allegedly whistling at a white woman or talking back to her]. His confessed killers were J. W. Milam and Roy Bryant, plus others unknown. The jury's verdict was: Not Guilty. To this date, no one has been punished for Emmett's death or for his kidnapping.[44]

The Till case was a central event of the 1950s, and according to scholar Clenora Hudson-Weems, his death helped to "galvanize" the civil rights movement in this country. Furthermore, the Till case was a catalyst for the explosion, given the timing of the events, the swelling tension (such as the critical voter registration drives throughout the South and particularly in Mississippi), and the social rage and political upheaval (such as resistance to poll taxes and testing requirements at city, county, and state levels). The Till case exemplified one of the most dynamic forces of its time.[45]

James A. Emanuel's poem "Emmett Till" is one of many written by American poets to capture the impact, the historical reference, and the meaning of the Till lynching.

Emmett Till
I hear a whistling
Through the water.
Little Emmett
Won't be still.
He keeps floating
Round the darkness,
Edging through
The silent chill.
Tell me, please,
That bedtime story
Of the fairy
River Boy
Who swims forever,
Deep in treasures,
Necklaced in
A coral toy.[46]

Case Study Five
Mack Charles Parker (1936–1959)
Poplarville, Mississippi
Pearl River County
April 24, 1959

On Feb. 23, 1959, Mack Charles Parker, a 23-year-old black man from Poplarville, allegedly raped a white woman whose car had stalled alongside a road in rural Pearl River County.

While June Walkers' husband was walking to the nearest town for help, Mack Charles Parker reportedly committed a crime that cost him his life at the hands of a lynch mob on Friday, April 24, three days before his scheduled trial.

For at least two weeks prior to April 24, area citizens planned and conspired to carry out the lynching. The group included a Baptist preacher and a candidate for sheriff in the fall campaigns. They persuaded the jailer to give them access to the courthouse keys.

On that Friday, the mob stormed the jail, forcibly removed and beat Parker, drove him to a bridge over the Pearl River, shot him twice with a pistol, weighed his body with chains and threw it over the bridge into the river.

The FBI launched an immediate investigation that lasted over four weeks and involved at least 60 agents. The county was the focus of immense national press and congressional attention. But on May 25, the Justice Department announced that it had no firm evidence of a federal crime. The FBI was able to reconstruct the lynching and identify the members of the mob, but it could not obtain a single signed statement from any citizen in the county to implicate any participant in the lynching.

The press then wanted to know if state officials would bring murder charges. At the regular Pearl River County grand jury term in November, the district attorney and presiding judge ignored the FBI report, and the grand jury brought no indictments against any of the mob members.

As a result of the national outrage, the Justice Department reversed itself and convened a federal grand jury in Biloxi to consider new charges. Through the crafty rulings of Sen. James Eastland, appointed federal judge presiding over the case, this grand jury was unable also to bring any indictments....

The lynching was not carried out to avenge a specific crime—the constitutional protections were not thwarted to protect Southern women—but to preserve the "Southern way of life." Lynching was a "form of terrorism" against blacks used to enforce segregation and the economic and political power of whites over blacks.

Ironically, the lynching was partly necessary, in the minds of the mob members, as a result of a federal court decision that had overturned an earlier murder conviction against a black man in Vaiden [Miss.] because the jury was all-white. There were no black registered voters in Pearl River County in 1959 (even though the county was 25 percent black) and thus no blacks were eligible to serve on a jury....

The white South had crippled its own court system by rendering it incompetent to try black criminals. The only alternative in many white minds was lynch law. Lynch mobs, by 1959 at least, resulted from whites being ensnared by their own prejudice. Committed to seeing blacks punished for their offenses, whites now felt punishment was up to them rather than the legal system. They had already lynched the legal system.

And finally, the lynch mob was incensed that Mack Charles Parker's mother had retained a black attorney. The very thought of a black man asking questions of a white rape victim in a public courtroom was too much for the collective stomach of the mob....

The political implications [of the event included] the American Legion's [opposition] to the lynching because it turned out to be a wonderful piece of propaganda for the Soviets to employ during this period of the Cold War. The only people who argued against the lynching were Jimmy and June Walters. As a result, they became the butt of constant jokes and harassment.

And other Southern elected officials spoke out against the lynching because they feared it would give the Northern members of Congress more ammunition in their drive to pass tougher civil rights laws.

The lynching of Mack Charles Parker was also one of the main issues in the 1959 gubernatorial campaign between Ross Barnett and Carroll Gartin. The chief cause of Gartin's loss ... was his close tie to the incumbent governor, J. P. Coleman, whose "moderate brand of racism" during the investigation of the lynch mob could not withstand the fever pitch of Barnett.

Coleman supported the FBI during the investigation and encouraged state officials to pursue indictments in the Pearl River grand jury. Even though Coleman continued to campaign against civil rights legislation in Congress, his position on the lynching earned him the enmity of many Mississippians and damaged Gartin's campaign.

As a closing irony, however, his vocal support of the FBI helped his national image to the extent that the Eisenhower administration offered him a position on the newly created

U.S. Civil Rights Commission. Coleman declined the offer because he had been elected to the Legislature from Choctaw County.[47]

Outrage over the Parker lynching was widespread, and yet, as in the long past, the killers went free. Poet Keith E. Baird's poem "Poplarville II" notes the irony and complexity of the Parker case for 1959.[48]

Black Mississippians faced the 1950s and their responses to lynchings in a variety of ways, but the temper of the times brought a more sustained notice from blacks. Active at the NAACP in Mississippi were such leaders as Medgar Evers, who began organizational work for the association in the summer of 1952; Dr. A. H. McCoy of Jackson, who served as State NAACP president; and Aaron Henry, a key local leader from Clarksdale, Mississippi.[49] One study notes that by the end of 1953, "The NAACP had twenty-one branches in Mississippi, with 1,600 members—in large part due to Evers' efforts."[50] In addition to its anti-lynching efforts, the NAACP also fought to advance black voting rights and investigate police brutality against blacks in Mississippi.[51] The association remained the major civil rights organization working in Mississippi to advance black rights in the 1950s.

A second activist organization was created in 1951 by Dr. T. R. M. Howard, of the all-black town of Mound Bayou, and founder of the Magnolia Mutual Insurance Company, which employed Medgar Evers in the early 1950s.[52] The new group was named the Regional Council of Negro Leadership. John Dittmer notes that for six years, Dr. Howard "became the state's most charismatic advocate of black rights. Howard was a native of Kentucky who moved to Mound Bayou in the early 1940s as chief surgeon at the Knights and Daughters of Tabor hospital [for African-Americans]."[53] The group was active in twenty-nine Mississippi counties and had 500 members.[54] The group fought police brutality, supported voter registration drives for black voters and worked for advancement of black civil rights in Mississippi.[55]

Blacks in rural areas of Mississippi were most active during the 1950s in religious organizations. A 1953 study of 631 rural blacks in Lee, Choctaw, Forrest and Bolivar counties found that 543 individuals or 71 percent were active in churches.[56] This factor points out the historical importance of the black church in the black experience. Even in the oppressive back woods of Mississippi, the black religious experience helped blacks to face their ordeals under Jim Crow and the Age of Lynching and Segregation. The church provided a spiritual home for blacks and aided their long-term goals of greater freedoms in Mississippi.

Still, for thousands of Mississippi blacks during the 1950s, the greatest protest that they could individually and collectively wage against lynching, racism and segregation in Mississippi was to migrate from the state. And so they did, to Chicago, Detroit, St. Louis, and Milwaukee, among many other cities and states.[57]

The black press in Mississippi was another major institutional resource in the 1950s available to the black community in the never-ending campaign to advance black rights in the state and this nation. But by 1954 there were only five major black newspapers active in Mississippi: the *Delta Leader* (Greenville); the *New Albany Community Citizen*, and three organs at Jackson, the *Jackson Advocate*, the *Mississippi Enterprise*, and the *Jackson Eagle Eye*.[58] The first four papers were conservative to moderate in their political outlook, and as they operated under the "eyes and ears" of the Jim Crow system they were generally careful in their public statements, especially on the editorial pages. They generally referred to the issue of lynchings by carrying news items from other newspapers on this topic or printing items as they came to them from the wire services.[59] All were in opposition to lynchings in Mississippi and the South. The difficulty they faced was how to state this opposition without having the wrath of white segregationists in Mississippi come down on them and their press operations in the state. Yet, in spite of such hardships they helped to keep the voice of black Mississippians before the local, state, national, and world communities in the 1950s. The *Jackson Eagle Eye* was an underground and radical publication. The organ was edited by Arrington W. High (1910–1988). One study observes that the "*Eagle Eye* aimed solely to express a personal message against segregation ... seeing itself as 'America's Greatest Newspaper Bombarding Segregation and Discrimination.'"[60]

Black women leaders and their organizations remained committed to advancing the rights of black women in Mississippi, while promoting the general equality of the total black community. Violence and lynching remained action items on the agendas of the Negro State Federation of Women's Clubs under the leadership of such presidents as Ruby Stutts Lyells and others.[61] Also active were the traditional black sororities and the black women's organizations under the Masonic orders.

Like the black press in Mississippi during this period, the black teachers of the state faced harsh treatment at the hands of Jim Crow if their organization, the Mississippi Association of Teachers in Colored Schools, publicly exposed lynching and segregation. Leaders and members of this group generally had to work quietly in the background for reforms and changes in Mississippi.[62] A single black woman teacher sought, however, to reform the system. John Dittmer notes the impact of her case:

> In the spring of 1948 Gladys Noel Bates, a black science teacher at the Smith Robinson School in Jackson, filed suit in U.S. District Court charging that the local school board had denied her and all other black teachers and administrators salaries equal to those paid to white teachers with similar education and experience. A graduate of Tougaloo College, Bates had also done graduate work at the University of West Virginia. Her father, A. J. Noel, was a Jackson NAACP leader and NAACP Legal Defense Fund attorneys, Constance Baker Motley and Robert Carter represented her. The case dragged on for nearly three years. The Jackson school board had immediately fired Bates and her husband, also a teacher, and then argued in court that the case was moot since the plaintiff was no longer employed in the system. At that point R. Jess Brown, a teacher at Lanier High School, entered the case as an intervening plaintiff. (Brown, too, lost his job and went on to a career as an attorney.) Bates and Brown lost the case on a technicality. Taking his cue from a similar case in Georgia, Judge Sidney Mize ruled that the plaintiffs had not exhausted their administrative remedies before filing suit. In a significant footnote, Mize wrote that had he been forced to hand down a decision, he would have sided with the plaintiffs, as the weight of evidence was on their side.[63]

Black Mississippi writers and artists continued their untiring efforts to interpret the black condition in Mississippi and America, and to aid the anti-lynching efforts in this state and others. Richard Wright remained a strong voice for black advancement from his base in Paris, France, and wrote several major works during this the last decade of his life, including *The Outsider* (1953), *Black Power* (1954), *Savage Holiday* (1954), *The Color Curtain: A Report on the Bandung Conference* (1956), *Pagan Spain* (1956), *White Man, Listen!* (1957) and *The Long Dream* (1958).[64] Margaret Walker remained the major literary voice at Jackson State College in the 1950s; she hosted a literary festival on October 19–25, 1952, in honor of the 75th founding of Jackson State. The list of writers who attended this event included Owen Dodson (1914–1983), Arna Bontemps (1902–1973), Gwendolyn Brooks (1917–2000), Sterling Brown (1901–1989), J. Saunders Redding (1906–1988), Melvin Tolson (1898–1966), Robert Heyden (1913–1980), Era Bell Thompson (1906–1986), and a local talent, Ruth R. Dease (1912–1991). One scholar of the period notes, "Perhaps Walker's greatest contribution for the decade came in her willingness to teach three or four courses per academic semester. In this regard she was truly a cultural worker since she came into contact with so many students of the years."[65] Certainly Walker's masterpiece, the poem "For My People," gave encouragement and enlightenment to many Americans who sought a brighter future for all the citizens of this country.[66]

Hundreds of black Mississippi musicians continued to spread the unique cultural contributions of the blues, gospel, rhythm and blues, and other forms of music to the world during the 1950s. This impressive list includes: Muddy Waters [McKinley Morganfield] (1915–1983), B. B. King (1925–), the Staple Singers, W. C. Handy (1873–1958) (who was greatly inspired by black Mississippi music), Williams Grant Still (1895–1978), "Mississippi" John Hurt (1893–1966), and Sam Cooke (1935–1964), among so many others.[67] Such artists as those noted above were able to use their music to express universal themes of freedom, equality and justice.[68]

From the governor's office (Fielding L. Wright, 1946–1952; Hugh L. White, 1952–1956, and James P. Coleman, 1956–1960) to the legislature and the criminal justice system, state government in Mississippi remained dedicated to the cause of states' rights, or the Southern tradition, as defined by the Jim Crow and segregationist systems of the state and region.[69] Many white men in power in Mississippi were "militant segregationists" and promoters of white supremacy.[70] Most were violently upset over the Supreme Court's Brown decision of May 17, 1954, which called for an end to segregated education. Under Governor James P. Coleman the state took an extreme action to deal with this situation and the civil rights movement in general. According to James Dickerson:

> Early in 1956, Coleman sent a bill to the Mississippi Legislature that would create a super secret spy agency designed to protect the state against the encroaching power of the federal government. The new agency he proposed would be named the Mississippi State Sovereignty Commission. The bill was clearly a product of the gathering that had taken place in Memphis the previous December. Under the provisions set forth in the bill, the Commission would be empowered to "perform any and all acts and things deemed necessary and proper to protect the sovereignty of the State of Mississippi, and her sister states, from encroachment" by the federal government. The Commission was given the authority to examine the records and documents of any citizen organization dealing with matters "about which the commission is authorized to conduct an investigation."
>
> The language of the bill was explicit: "The commission shall have the power and authority to require all persons, firms and corporations having such books, records, documents and other papers in their possession or under their control to produce same within this state at such time and place as the commission may designate, and to permit an inspection and examination thereof by the members of said commission or its authorized representatives and employees.
>
> To enforce that authority, the Commission was provided with a broad-ranging subpoena power that included the authority to enforce obedience "by fine or imprisonment" at the discretion of the Commission. In addition, the Commission was authorized to receive contributions and donations from private groups or individuals. It was designed to operate independently of state government, when necessary, to utilize private funds to carry out covert operations."[71]

In time the files of the Sovereignty Commission would grow to contain information on 87,000 persons and 250 organizations.[72]

At the national level, Mississippi's two senators, James O. Eastland (chairman of the Senate Judiciary Committee in 1956) and John Stennis (a powerful figure in the Armed Forces Committee and chairman of the Senate Ethics Committee) carried the states' rights fight in Congress. In its final analysis this meant "keep blacks down!"[73]

The "massive resistance" to black rights, the civil rights movement, and anti-lynching efforts was expressed in Mississippi and the South by the creation of a new group on July 11, 1954, at Indianola, Mississippi.[74] Numan V. Bartley notes the significance of this white supremacy group, the Citizens' Council.

> Numerous segregationist groups sprang up throughout the South. An estimated fifty such organizations emerged in the years immediately following Brown v. Board of Education. With the rise of the Citizens' Councils, many, though by no means all, of these groups were absorbed into the mainstream of the resistance.
>
> By the end of 1955, the Council movement was the most vocal of all pressure groups in the South.... The Council also campaigned for passage of a suffrage restriction amendment to the state constitution, which was approved by heavy majorities in November, and then turned to support of the "last resort" school closing amendment, which was ratified by a comfortable majority in December. By the end of 1954, the Mississippi Association of Citizens' Councils claimed chapters in more than thirty counties, had participated in two winning political campaigns, and was dispatching organizers into neighboring states to spread the resistance.
>
> During 1955 and 1956 the association continued to expand, distending from the rural Mississippi River lowlands into the cities and hill country. The Jackson chapter, formed in early 1955, soon became the hub of state Council activity. Later in the year the association began publication of *The Citizens' Council*, a four-page monthly newspaper edited by William J. Simmons. As Council administrator, Simmons joined [Robert "Tut"] Patterson, [Tom] Brady, and a few others at the top of the Mississippi Councildom. Council membership increased rapidly, particularly after NAACP chapters in four Mississippi cities filed desegregation petitions during the summer of 1955. In August, 1955, the state association claimed 60,000 members; by the end of 1956 it claimed a membership of 85,000 with chapters in sixty-five of Mississippi's eighty-two counties. The Mississippi Association was, as Hodding Carter III described it, "the biggest, the most tightly organized, and the most powerful Citizens' Council of them all." Increasingly the Councils dominated the political life of Mississippi. After the inauguration of Ross R. Barnett, a longtime Council member, as governor in 1960, Leslie Dunbar could observe that "Mississippi is experimenting with a Soviet style government, with the Citizens Council paralleling the state machine in emulation of a successful Communist Party."[75]

With the Sovereignty Commission and the Citizens' Council in high gear during the late 1950s, conditions grew worse for blacks. They faced political, economic and social pressures by whites. Blacks such as T. R. M. Howard received death threats, and he was finally forced to leave Mississippi in 1955.[76] Others faced economic intimidation, such as Amzie Moore of Cleveland, when his local banker "called in Moore's $6,000 mortgage on his home and service station."[77] And, some blacks died "at the hands of persons unknown."[78]

The white press in Mississippi was an important medium to give expression to public policy issues in the state. One study notes:

> The vast majority of the white press remained pro-segregationist during the 1950s, led by the *Jackson Clarion-Ledger* and the *Jackson Daily News*. Other Jackson journals espousing this position included the *State Times*, an afternoon paper, and the *Citizens' Councils of America*. In the towns and rural areas, a variety of white dailies and weeklies followed the Example of the Jackson white press, and a policy of firm commitment to segregation and white supremacy held command in more than 90 percent of the white papers.
>
> Four white Mississippi editors of the 1950s constitute outstanding examples of the very best traditions in American journalism: Ira Harkey, co-publisher of the *Pascagoula Chronicle*, Hazel Brannon Smith (1914–1994), editor and publisher of the *Lexington*

Advertiser, Hodding Carter, Jr., editor of the Greenville *Delta Democrat-Times*; and P. D. East, editor and publisher of the *Petal Paper*, in Petal, located near Hattiesburg. As moderates, perhaps even radicals in Mississippi's frame of reference, they at least attempted to examine rationally the conditions of both whites and blacks in Mississippi and suggested that Mississippi needed change, growth, and development for its future. At the center of their arguments stood black men and women; life in Mississippi would never really improve until white Mississippians' view of black people had changed. As a group, these white editors suffered economic reprisals and social ostracism, but they withstood the bombardment of the segregationists and succeeded in keeping freedom of the press alive during a decade of doubt.[79]

A group of white Mississippi writers are also considered by critics as moderates for the period of the 1950s, and as individuals who by their body of work sought to suggest tolerance, respect for human rights, and, in general, a need to reform society in Mississippi, the South and the nation. Heading this list during the decade was William Faulkner (1897–1962), perhaps the most famous writer produced by Mississippi and winner of the Nobel Prize in Literature for 1950. Noel E. Polk and James R. Scafidel believe that "Faulkner obviously loved Mississippi, but he was not blind to its faults either, and he became an outspoken analyst of its racial and social problems, deploring all forms of intolerance and violence, advocating moderation and common sense, and believing that blacks and whites could solve their problems without outside interference, by drawing on a large reservoir of shared experiences."[80] Faulkner wrote many important works, including *The Sound and the Fury* (novel, 1929), *As I Lay Dying* (novel, 1930), *Sanctuary* (novel, 1931), *Absalom, Absalom!* (novel, 1936), *Go Down Moses* (novel, 1942), and *Requiem for a Nun* (novel, 1951), among many other works. Other white Mississippi writers of the 1950s who stand with Faulkner for their outstanding work and general humanitarian outlooks are Eudora Welty (1909–2001), Tennessee Williams (1911–1983) and Walker Percy (1916–1991), among others.[81]

The problem of lynching in Mississippi and the South still reverberated throughout American society in the 1950s. However, President Truman continued his watchful approach on lynchings in the early 1950s. Dwight D. Eisenhower (1890–1969), president 1953–1961, was too conservative to take forceful action against this problem. Philip Dray observes that Eisenhower "was uncomfortable with civil rights issues and had expressed sympathy for how desegregation had been forced on the South."[82] In Congress there were no successful efforts during the decade to push through an anti-lynching bill. Furthermore, no action was forthcoming from the Supreme Court on the subject. At the Federal Bureau of Investigation, J. Edgar Hoover was generally opposed to having his agency become entangled with lynching in Mississippi and the South. One historian reports on a March 1956 cabinet meeting at the White House:

"The South is in a state of explosive resentment over what they consider an unfair portrayal of their way of life, and what they consider intermeddling," Hoover warned his rapt audience. And for this he blamed the 1954 and 1956 U. S. Supreme Court desegregation decisions. Behind the tension over "mixed education," he cautioned, "stalks the specter of racial intermarriage." The NAACP and other civil rights groups were exacerbating the already tense situation by preaching "racial hatred," he claimed. Moreover, they had been targeted for infiltration by the Communist Party. (An initial finding that the NAACP was opposed to Communism did not keep the FBI from investigating the organization for another twenty-five years.) On the other hand, the White Citizens Councils which had recently sprung up throughout the South to oppose desegregation included among their members "bankers, lawyers, doctors, state legislators and industrialists ... some of the leading citizens of the South." It was clear with which group Hoover chose to take his stand.

As for the Ku Klux Klan, the FBI director airily dismissed it as "pretty much defunct." Accompanied as always with charts and graphs, Hoover used one of the latter to show that the number of lynchings was down; hence there was certainly no need for legislation giving the FBI formal responsibility for such cases.[83]

Thus, at the national level of the United States government there was no effective action taken on the problem of lynching in the 1950s.

Among the major black civil rights organizations of the 1950s, interest remained high on all aspects of violence, including lynchings, against blacks and other groups in American society. Four major black groups were active in the decade: the NAACP, with Roy Wilkins as executive secretary 1955–1964; the National Urban League, with T. Arnold Hill; the Congress of Racial Equality, under the leadership of James R. Robinson; and a new organization headed by Martin Luther King, Jr., the Southern Christian Leadership Conference, headquartered in Atlanta, Georgia. During the decade these groups agitated for social change and reforms in American society, including a special focus on bringing relief to black communities which suffered all forms of violence in their daily lives, from police brutality to lynching. The 1950s was a key decade for civil rights organizations. For instance, one study notes that by 1950, the NAACP had increased the number of chapters in the South to nearly one thousand.[84]

The national black press remained a strong supporter of anti-lynching efforts in the United States. As in the past, all of the major black newspapers and magazines of the decade covered the topic of violence and lynching in their press organs. Very active black press publications in this struggle included the *Chicago Defender*, the New York *Amsterdam News*, the *Pittsburgh Courier*, the *Michigan Chronicle*, the Atlanta *Daily World*, the *Crisis*, and *Negro Digest*, among others.[85]

Black American intellectuals were an active voice against violence and the crime of lynching during this period. Hundreds of black men and women—activists, scholars, artists, and writers—were responsive to the plight of blacks in the terror-filled 1950s. As a group they spoke out vigorously against injustice and oppression in their public statements, performances, lectures and speeches, interviews, articles, books, plays, poetry, art and music. The top personalities in this group for the 1950s should certainly include Elijah Muhammad, Malcolm X, Ralph Ellison, Mary McLeod Bethune (d. 1955), Rosa Parks, Ella Baker, Paul Robeson, John Hope Franklin, Thurgood Marshall, Carl Rowan, Walter Francis White (d. March 21, 1955), W. E. B. Du Bois, Ralph Bunche, James Baldwin, Rayford Logan, Edward Kennedy Ellington, Langston Hughes, Douglas Turner Ward, Benjamin E. Mays, Gwendolyn Brooks, Adam Clayton Powell, Jr., and so many others.[86]

Other national support for some movement toward civil rights for blacks and an end to violence and lynching came from such groups as the AFL-CIO, liberal politicians such as Senator Hubert H. Humphrey of Minnesota, an active anti-lynching personality, and radical New Left groups such as socialists and communists.[87]

After a century of lynchings in America, at long last public opinion had shifted on this subject. This was especially due to the tremendous efforts of anti-lynching activists in the NAACP, Ida B. Wells-Barnett, the work of black churches and club women, white women in religious groups, and the Association of Southern Women for the Prevention of Lynching.[88] World opinion had an impact, too, as did the progressive work of the United Nations. The Cold War between the Western and Eastern blocs also aided the international dimensions of this ageless problem. By the 1940s and 1950s, the United States was embarrassed by the lynching phenomenon at home and abroad, and this process helped to decrease lynchings in Mississippi and the South. More people in Mississippi and the South also became opposed to lynching on economic, social and moral grounds. This crime made Mississippi and the South appear underdeveloped, uneducated, and uncivilized in a world grown smaller by mass communication and the development of the Third World into a significant force to offer its judgment on violence in the American nation. However, a number of lynchers went underground in the 1950s in an attempt to hide their activities while maintaining a circle and climate of fear in Mississippi and the South.[89] Thus, a part of the problem in analyzing the 1950s comes about because some lynchings were hidden and kept quiet by mobs of lynchers. Certainly the civil rights movements of the 1950s proved a positive response for the black community on the issue of lynching. The movement highlighted violence in general as a key concern for the black community.

The 1950s witnessed a general reduction in the total number of lynchings. Nevertheless, the violence of the era had an important impact on blacks in Mississippi since it seems that mob actions against African-Americans, as well as police brutality, took place in the state at a high rate during the 1950s. The anti-black work of the Ku Klux Klan, the Citizens' Councils, and the Mississippi Sovereignty Commission also helped to increase terror and fear among blacks in Mississippi. Yet the positive work across over seventy-five years by anti-lynching foes had made lynching a very unattractive option for many whites in Mississippi and the South. A general new problem emerged in the 1950s when some white lynchers took their illegal activities underground. Yet, in spite of all the gains made in the anti-lynching struggle, as the 1950s came to an end, lynching was not quite over. The 1960s lay ahead and the intensity of the civil rights struggle would bring a renewed reaction of violence from whites against American citizens in Mississippi and the South.

The Freedom Struggle, 1960–1965

Black Mississippians entered the 1960s in a new mood to foster change and reforms in Mississippi society. Change was certainly needed, for poverty and oppression were still closely identified with Mississippi, and the black condition in the state was viewed world-wide as an extreme example of life in America for black people. As blacks entered the 1960s, one study found:

> The state's black population declined by 11 percent during this period, from 920,595 in 1960 to 815,770 in 1970. By 1970, blacks constituted 37 percent of the total population, a decrease of 5 percent from the 1960 figure of 42 percent. From 1865 to 1970, more than 700,000 black Mississippians emigrated. Seventy-one percent of Mississippi's black families had incomes of less than $5,000 in 1969, whereas 71 percent of white families had incomes higher than $5,000. By 1960, black Mississippians had a median of 6.0 years of education, while whites had a median of 11.0 years. The median black family income in 1969 was $3,865 for urban dwellers and $2,407 in rural areas, compared to $8,883 and $5,890 respectively for whites.[1]

By the early 1960s, according to historian James W. Silver, Mississippi remained encumbered in "The Closed Society."[2] It was a strange land, yet, like all places, it had its good and not so good points. Perhaps Etheridge Knight's (1931–1991) poem "A Poem for Myself (or Blues for a Mississippi Black Boy)" captures the complexity of this dual image of Mississippi and especially of black Mississippians.[3]

This contrast of Mississippi's condition, most notably for blacks, is well expressed by scholar Howard Zinn, who describes the state as existing in a nightmare: "Negroes were laborers, sharecroppers, farm laborers, maids, servants of various kinds. More than half of them lived in houses with no running water; for two-thirds of them there was no flush toilet, no bathtub or shower. They lived in tarpaper shacks and rickety wooden boxes sometimes resembling chicken coops. Most whites were also poor, though not as poor; Mississippi was a feudal land barony, in which a small number of whites controlled the political power and the wealth of the state, using a tiny part of this wealth to pay the salaries of thousands of petty local officials who kept the system as it was by force."[4] Mississippi's hardships for blacks during this period were reflected in the political circumstances facing them. One study observes that "few black citizens in Mississippi could vote or hold public office in the early sixties....

[By] 1960 only 6 percent of the voting age black population in Mississippi was registered to vote, and this figure increased to only 7 percent by 1964, or 29,000 voters. By this late date there were only six black elected officials in Mississippi. The state's poll tax and literacy tests were effective means, among other strategies employed, to keep blacks away from the voting booth."[5] Thus, as the civil rights movement gained strength and focus in the early 1960s, Mississippi appeared as one of the most difficult challenges facing the movement. The state's economic, social, and political institutions were all defined by Jim Crow and segregation, and they would take years to eradicate.

The big five among civil rights organizations: the NAACP, the Student Non-Violent Coordinating Committee (SNCC), the Congress of Racial Equality (CORE), the National Urban League, and the Southern Christian Leadership Conference (SCLC), were active in Mississippi during the 1960s. The greatest influence was held by the NAACP SCLC, and CORE. In 1961 the groups formed the Council of Federated Organizations (COFO) to coordinate their activities in Mississippi and to encourage and stress unity and cooperation among black Mississippians.[6] The ten major leaders to come out of the civil rights movement in Mississippi were (1) Medgar Evers, Mississippi NAACP field secretary, (2) Aaron Henry, state president of the NAACP and president of COFO, (3) Robert Moses, leader of SNCC in Mississippi and program director of COFO, (4) Dave Dennis, CORE's Mississippi field secretary and assistant director of COFO, (5) Tom Gaither, a leader in CORE, (6) Jimmy Travis, an SNCC organizer, (7) Amzie Moore, a Delta black leader from Cleveland, Mississippi, (8) James Meredith, who integrated the University of Mississippi in 1962, (9) Fanny Lou Hamer (1917–1977), an SNCC worker and major force in the Mississippi Freedom Democratic Party, and (10) Annie Devine, an organizer form Canton, Mississippi, and key figure in the Mississippi Freedom Democratic Party. There were, of course, hundreds of other activists.[7]

These historical figures and thousands of other citizens challenged the segregationist system of Mississippi, and helped to bring change and reforms to an oppressive state. But it was not an easy task. For one thing, civil rights activists were up against Mississippi's criminal justice system—dedicated to keeping the status-quo in place for another 1,000 years.

The freedom struggle in Mississippi consisted of a series of actions and programs between 1960 and 1965, including: (1) efforts to bring about desegregation, (2) the Freedom Rides campaign of 1961, to break the back of segregation in public transportation, (3) James Meredith's admission fight at the University of Mississippi, 1962, (4) voter registration campaigns to increase black voters in the state, (5) Freedom Summer 1964, to expand civil rights activities in Mississippi, and (6) the unsuccessful challenge by the Mississippi Freedom Democratic Party of the Mississippi Democratic delegation at the 1964 Democratic National Convention in Atlantic City, New Jersey.[8] The contributions of the movement were tremendous in helping to move Mississippi forward in the 1960s.

Nonetheless, Mississippi's criminal justice system was used to try to limit the effectiveness of the civil rights movement in the state. Violence and mistreatment of activists was the norm practiced by peace officers in Mississippi during the 1960s.[9] Parchman Prison remained a central state penal institution during the 1960s and was especially known for its cruelty toward blacks. Oppression in general took the form of beatings, overcrowding, poor food and sanitation conditions in prisons, and terror in cities, towns and rural areas, and on highways by policemen and others who often followed activists as they moved from place to place by car.[10] Some activists died in the struggle.

Most scholars note that very few lynchings were officially recorded in the United States in the early 1960s. Only one lynching is listed for 1961. Table 11.1 indicates that 15 cases are

Table 11.1: National and Mississippi Lynchings, 1960–1965

Year	United States		Mississippi	
	Blacks	Whites	Blacks	Whites
1960	0	0	0	0
1961	1	0	2	0
1962	0	0	1	1
1963	0	0	1	0
1964	0	0	7	2
1965	0	0	1	0
Totals	1	0	12	3

Table 11.2: Mississippi Lynchings, 1960–1965

Name	Location	Date	Causes
Herbert Lee (1912–1961; black male farmer)	Liberty, Amite Co.	9/25/1961	Confrontation at a Cotton gin. Lee was shot in the head and killed by E. H. Hurst, a white Mississippi state representative. Lee had been active in voter registration work in Amite County; a county which contained "3,560 negroes of voting age, but only one who was registered, and he had never voted" (Mendelsohn, 24). No convictions were brought in this case. Source: Michael R. Becknap, *Federal Law and Southern Order: Racial Violence and Constitutional Conflict in the Post-Brown South* (Athens, Ga.: The University of Georgia Press, 1987), 109. Jack Mendelsohn, The Martyrs, 21–40.
Eli Brumfeld	McComb, Pike Co.	Oct-61	Mistaken identity; believed to be an SNCC volunteer by policeman
Cpl. Loman Ducksworth, Jr. (black male)	Taylorsville, Smith Co.	9-Apr-62	"a military policeman shot (him) to death ... after refusing a police order to sit in the back of the bus. Source: "Remembering the Martyrs of the Movement," *Ebony*, February 1990: 60.
Paul Guihard (white male native of France)	Oxford, Lafayette Co.	9/30/1962	"a French news reporter shot in the back ... during race riots at the University of Mississippi." Source: "Remembering the Martyrs of the Movement," *Ebony*, February 1990: 60.

Name	Location	Date	Causes
Medgar Evers (black male)	Jackson, Hinds Co.	6/11/1963	Assassinated for his civil rights movement work. Shot outside his residence late at night by Byron de la Beckwith. Evers was the field secretary of the NAACP in Mississippi; his home was on a KKK hit list. (Beckwith was tried for murder twice, but each trial ended in hung juries by all white jurors. Finally, he was tried a third time in 1994 and a racially mixed jury found him guilty of murder and sentenced him to life imprisonment. Beckwith died in prison.) SOURCE: Maryann Vollers, *Ghosts of Mississippi: The Murder of Medgar Evers, the Trials of Byron De La Beckwith, and the Haunting of the New South* (Boston: Little, Brown and Co., 1995).
Louis Allen (black male farmer)	Liberty, Amite Co.	1/31/1964	Probably killed by nervous whites because of information that he knew about the killing of Herbert Lee. His death occurred when "two loads of Buck shot were fired into his face. The sheriff and the FBI investigated Louis Allen's murder, but no one was ever charged in the case." SOURCE: Ralph E. Luker, *Historical Dictionary of the Civil Rights Movement* (Lanham, Md., The Scarecrow Press, 1997), 154.
Henry H. Dee (black male)	Natchez, Adams Co.	5/2/1964	"a civil rights volunteer abducted, beaten and thrown into the Mississippi River ... by the Klan," p. 60.
James Chaney (1943–1964), a black male age 21, a native Mississippian on the Staff of CORE; Andrew Goodman (1943–1964), a white male age 20, a student from Queens College in N.Y.; Micheal Schwezner (1939–1964), a white male age 24, a social worker from N.Y. and a member of CORE.	Near Philadelphia, Neshob Co.	6/21/ 1964	Three Freedom Summer Civil Rights activists who were probably killed by the KKK because of their movement work in the state. Their bodies were discovered in an earthen dam 44 days after they were murdered. SOURCE: Athon G. Theoharis, with Tonny G. Poveda, Susan Rosenfeld, and Richard Gid Powers, eds., *The FBI: A Comprehensive Reference Guide* (Phoenix, Ariz.: The Oryx Press, 1999), 70–71. Jesse Kornbluth, "The 64 Civil Rights Murders: The Struggle Continues," the *New York Times Magazine*, July 23, 1989, Section 6, 16, 8, 46, 47, 48, 54, 60, 62, 63.
Black youth	Brandon, Rankin Co.	6/22/1964	Unidentified black youth killed in a hit-and-run accident. SOURCE: Doug McAdam, *Freedom Summer* (New York: Oxford University Press, 1988), 257.

Name	Location	Date	Causes
34-year-old black man	Doddsville, Sunflower Co.	6/27/1964	Black man with "history of mental illness" is killed by a highway patrolman. The case was ruled justifiable homicide in 17 hours. SOURCE: McAdams, *Freedom Summer* (New York: Oxford University Press, 1988), 259.
Local black man	Batesville, Panola Co.	6/28/1964	"Report local negro man beaten, missing." SOURCE: McAdams, *Freedom Summer* (New York: Oxford University Press, 1988), 259.
Charles Moore (black male)	Natchez, Adams Co.	7/11/1964	"A civil rights volunteer abducted, beaten and thrown into the Mississippi River near Natchez." "Half body found in Mississippi identified as Charles Moore, former Alcorn A&M student. Second half body found in river." (Moore was dismissed from Alcorn after a non-violent general grievance demonstration). SOURCE: McAdams, *Freedom Summer* (New York: Oxford University Press, 1988), 259. "Remembering the Martyrs of the Movement," *Ebony* (February 1990), 60.
Wharlest Jackson	Natchez, Adams Co.	2/18/1965	"An NAACP treasurer ... killed ... by a bomb after his promotion to a job once reserved for whites." SOURCE: "Remembering the Martyrs of the Movement," *Ebony* (February 1990), 60.

observed for 1960–65 in Mississippi, including 12 black males and 3 white men.[11] This period was at the height of the civil rights movement in Mississippi and the South, and violence against movement activists was a major problem.[12] Nineteen sixty-four was an especially harsh year with the death of seven blacks and two whites (see Table 11.2. pages 158–160). Lynching events for the period 1960–1965 took place in ten Mississippi counties, with Adams and Neshoba counties reporting three lynchings each, and with two in Amite County (see Table 11.3). Table 11.4 indicates that a majority of the lynching events took place in southern (six) and central and eastern (three each) counties, followed by the Delta region with two lynchings and one lynching in North Mississippi. No lynchings are noted for the Gulf Coast area. The vast majority of Mississippi lynchings were directed at civil rights movement activists, eight victims of 15 cases, followed by two victims who were killed by white policemen (see Table 11.5, page 162). As in the long past, most lynching events took place during the warm months of the year, with seven events noted for the month of June, one for May and July, and two for September (see Table 11.6, page 162). Lynchings for this period were rare during the colder months of the year.[13]

Mississippi represented a land of terror and brutal hardships for the civil rights movement during the early 1960s. In opposition to the movement stood the state government and various appendages to the status-quo system, such as the Ku Klux Klan, the Citizens'

TABLE 11.3: MISSISSIPPI LYNCHING VICTIMS BY COUNTY, 1960–1965

County	Number	Percentage
Adams	3	20%
Amite	2	13%
Hinds	1	7%
Lafayette	1	7%
Neshoba	3	20%
Panoca	1	7%
Pike	1	7%
Rankin	1	7%
Smith	1	7%
Sunflower	1	7%
Total	15	

TABLE 11.4: GEOGRAPHIC DISTRIBUTION OF MISSISSIPPI LYNCHING VICTIMS BY COUNTY, 1960–1965

Delta	North	East	Central	South	Gulf Coast
Sunflower 1	Lafayette 1	Neshoba 3	Smith 1	Amite 2	none
Panola 1			Hinds 1	Adams 3	
			Rankin 1	Pike 1	

Council and the Mississippi State Sovereignty Commission—all dedicated to keeping segregation and the Jim Crow system intact in Mississippi and the South. Certainly many whites in the state viewed violence as one method to achieve this goal. The end results of this policy included the beatings of thousands of American citizens, the disappearance of some, economic and social hardships and the deaths of others. Five murders between 1960 and 1965 highlight this issue. Even though lynching was now considered an item of the past, many of the events of the early 1960s indicate that the older patterns of the lynching phenomenon were still alive in Mississippi. One special case of the period deserves a note. The killing of Medgar Evers in 1963 is generally referred to as an assassination and not a lynching. However, due to the historical nature of the period, this study lists the event as a lynching because of the tremendous impact that Evers' death had on black Mississippians. In other words, this murder case had all of the significance of any lynching event since 1865 in terms of its range, emotions, and influence on black thinking and daily living in Mississippi. It is within this context that Evers is listed among the fifteen lynching victims of this period.[14]

Table 11.5: Range of Causes of Lynching Events in Mississippi, 1960–1965

Item	Number	Percentage
Civil Rights Activist	8	53%
Conflict with a white policeman	2	13%
Killed in a riot	1	7%
Feared by white males for information he held	1	7%
Hit-and-run car accident	1	7%
Mistaken identity	1	7%
Unknown	1	7%
Total	15	100%

Table 11.6: Time of Year of Mississippi Lynching Events, 1960–1965

Month	Number	Percentage
January	1	7%
February	1	7%
March	0	0%
April	1	7%
May	1	7%
June	7	47%
July	1	7%
August	0	0%
September	2	13%
October	1	7%
November	0	0%
December	0	0%
Total	15	

The five victims, as represented in three major lynching cases of the period, demonstrate the tremendous price which blacks and their allies paid in the civil rights struggle to overthrow segregation and the Jim Crow system in Mississippi and the South, and to advance the nation from its historic base of racism and discrimination against so many of its citizens. It is a story that still moves many people, yet remains mournful for others. The cases indicate the degree of sacrifice made by black Mississippians to the Freedom Movement.

Case Study 1
Herbert Lee (?–September 25, 1961)
Liberty, Amite County, Mississippi

Early in the morning of September 26, Herbert Lee had driven up to the cotton gin just outside Liberty with a truckload of cotton. E. H. Hurst, who was following directly behind in an empty truck owned by his son-in-law, Billy Jack Caston, stepped out, a huge man powerfully built. He strode up to Lee, who was sitting in the cab of his truck, and shouted at him, waving his arms. Suddenly, the witnesses told [Robert] Moses, Hurst pulled a revolver from his shirt. Lee told Hurst to put the gun away or he wouldn't talk to him, and Hurst slid the gun back under his shirt. As Lee, a small man five feet four inches compared to Hurst's more than six feet, climbed down from the cab of his truck on the side away from Hurst, Hurst ran around in front of the cab, took out his gun, pointed it at Lee and fired, the witnesses reported to Moses.

When Moses later related what he had been told to Howard Zinn, who summarized it in his book *SNCC: The New Abolitionists*, Moses lost control only as he said: "Lee's body lay on the ground that morning for two hours, uncovered, until they finally got a funeral home in McComb to take it in. No one in Liberty would touch it. They had a coroner's jury that very same afternoon. Hurst was acquitted. He never spent a moment in jail.... I remember reading very bitterly in the papers the next morning, a little item on the front page of the McComb Enterprise Journal said that a Negro had been shot as he was trying to attack E. H. Hurst. And that was it. Might have though he'd been a bum. There was no mention that Lee was a farmer, that he had a family, nine kids, beautiful kids, and that he had farmed all his life in Amite County."

Indeed, the coroner's jury found that Hurst was innocent of any crime, and "had committed an act of justifiable homicide."[15]

Case Study 2
Medgar Evers (1925–June 11, 1963)
Jackson, Hinds County, Mississippi

On Sunday, June 9, Evers spent the entire day with his family, something he seldom took time to do. On Tuesday, the 11th, John Kennedy gave the strongest civil rights speech of his administration and asked the nation's support for the civil rights legislation that he would be sending to Congress. Medgar was very pleased with the speech. There was a mass meeting that night, but it was not a good one. Attendance was poor and the spirit was weak. Evers got home after midnight. Police officers frequently followed him home, but apparently they did not do so that night. Myrlie [Evers] had let the children stay up to wait for him. They heard the car pull up and the door slam, and immediately after, they heard the gunshot. As he stepped out of his car, carrying a stack of "Jim Crow Must Go" t-shirts, he was hit by a shot from a high-powered rifle fired from a nearby vacant lot. Houston Wells, his next-door neighbor, heard the shot and Myrlie's scream. Looking out of his bedroom window, he saw the body lying there. He got his pistol, ran outside and fired a shot in the air to frighten the gunman away. Evers died shortly after he reached the hospital. He had his new poll-tax receipt in his pocket.[16]

Many white officials condemned the killing, after a fashion. Governor Ross Barnett said, "Apparently, it was a dastardly act." Apparently. The fingerprint on the rifle found in the vacant lot belonged to Byron de la Beckwith, a Greenwood fertilizer salesman, son of an Old Delta family, self-anointed defender of segregation and member of Greenwood Citizens' Council. It was proven that he had owned a rifle and a scope that matched the murder weapon. Two cab drivers testified that he had asked for Evers' address a few days before the shooting. Beckwith's attorney, Hardy Lott, past president of Greenwood's Citizens' Council, produced testimony from two Greenwood policemen who swore they saw Beckwith in Greenwood—ninety miles from Jackson—the evening of the slaying. Beckwith contended that his rifle had been stolen a few days before the killing. The trial reflected both the old Mississippi and the emerging one. On the one hand, the prosecutor, to Myrlie Evers' surprise, really tried for a conviction. On the other, Beckwith treated the trial as a royal joke. "The accused killer appeared to enjoy himself immensely. He rested his legs on another chair while he drank soda pop, scowled at Negro newsmen, and waved gaily to white friends. At one point, a bailiff had to escort him back to his place when he strode over to chat with members of the jury. With a courtly flourish he offered cigars to Prosecutor William L. Waller." The trial ended in a hung jury. When he got home to Greenwood, the town gave him a rousing parade. Subsequently, a second trial also ended in a hung jury and Beckwith was freed. However, in 1994, Beckwith was tried again, and convicted of murder.[17]

Case Study 3
James Chaney (1943–1964)
Andrew Goodman (1943–1964)
Michael Schwerner (1939–1964)
Near Philadelphia, Neshoba County, Mississippi
June 21, 1964

This case involved the disappearance of three civil rights workers near Philadelphia, Mississippi, on the night of June 21, 1964. These three men—Michael Schwerner and Andrew Goodman, both white and from New York, and James Chaney, black and from Meridian, Mississippi—had been arrested earlier that day by a Neshoba County deputy sheriff for speeding and had been jailed. Following their release from jail that night, around 10:00 p.m., they disappeared.

When it became apparent that local authorities were not seriously pursuing the case, Attorney General [Robert] Kennedy announced that the FBI would enter the case, initially regarding it as a kidnapping. Code-named miburn (for Mississippi burning, a reference to the church burning that the three civil rights workers had visited just prior to their arrest), the case became a high FBI priority. At that time, the FBI did not have a field office in Mississippi, so agents were brought in from other states to begin the search for the three missing civil rights activists. Eventually, 258 agents were involved in the massive investigation, interviewing over 1,000 Mississippians including 480 Klansmen.

The burned car of the three young men was found in a swamp, but not the bodies of the three activists. FBI agents ultimately broke open the case after paying an informant $30,000 to reveal the location of the bodies and to disclose the identities of those who had been involved in their murders. It was revealed that on the night of their disappearance, the three young men had been abducted from their car by 19 members of the Ku Klux Klan who shot and killed them. The informant, a Klan member who was also a participant in the crime, led agents to a dam construction project on the Ollen Burrage farm near Philadelphia, where the bodies of the three civil rights activists were recovered, having been buried under hundreds of tons of earth.

In the weeks following the discovery of the bodies of Schwerner, Goodman, and Chaney, state authorities failed to bring murder charges against any of the alleged coconspirators. Accordingly, FBI and Justice Department officials decided to proceed with federal civil rights charges and, on December 4, FBI agents arrested the 19 suspects, including Sheriff Lawrence Rainey and Deputy Sheriff Cecil Price. All 19 were indicted in January 1965, and after much legal wrangling, the trial was held in October 1967. An all-white jury found seven of the defendants guilty but acquitted Sheriff Rainey. The severest penalty went to Klan leader Sam Bowers, who received a 10-year sentence; in contrast, Deputy Sheriff Price was given a 3- to 10-year sentence.

The Philadelphia murders triggered a demand for a greater federal presence in Mississippi to control Klan violence. This had also been the recommendation of Allen Dulles,

MISSING CALL FBI

THE FBI IS SEEKING INFORMATION CONCERNING THE DISAPPEARANCE AT PHILADELPHIA, MISSISSIPPI, OF THESE THREE INDIVIDUALS ON JUNE 21, 1964. EXTENSIVE INVESTIGATION IS BEING CONDUCTED TO LOCATE GOODMAN, CHANEY, AND SCHWERNER, WHO ARE DESCRIBED AS FOLLOWS:

	ANDREW GOODMAN	JAMES EARL CHANEY	MICHAEL HENRY SCHWERNER

	ANDREW GOODMAN	JAMES EARL CHANEY	MICHAEL HENRY SCHWERNER
RACE:	White	Negro	White
SEX:	Male	Male	Male
DOB:	November 23, 1943	May 30, 1943	November 6, 1939
POB:	New York City	Meridian, Mississippi	New York City
AGE:	20 years	21 years	24 years
HEIGHT:	5'10"	5'7"	5'9" to 5'10"
WEIGHT:	150 pounds	135 to 140 pounds	170 to 180 pounds
HAIR:	Dark brown; wavy	Black	Brown
EYES:	Brown	Brown	Light blue
TEETH:		Good: none missing	
SCARS AND MARKS:		1 inch cut scar 2 inches above left ear.	Pock mark center of forehead, slight scar on bridge of nose, appendectomy scar, broken leg scar.

SHOULD YOU HAVE OR IN THE FUTURE RECEIVE ANY INFORMATION CONCERNING THE WHEREABOUTS OF THESE INDIVIDUALS, YOU ARE REQUESTED TO NOTIFY ME OR THE NEAREST OFFICE OF THE FBI. TELEPHONE NUMBER IS LISTED BELOW.

DIRECTOR
FEDERAL BUREAU OF INVESTIGATION
UNITED STATES DEPARTMENT OF JUSTICE
WASHINGTON, D. C. 20535
TELEPHONE NATIONAL 8-7117

June 29, 1964

who headed a fact-finding team sent by President Johnson to Mississippi in the midst of the search for the missing civil rights activists. Acting on this report, President Johnson ordered FBI Director Hoover to open an FBI field office in Jackson as soon as possible, stipulating that the director participate in the opening ceremonies. On July 10, 1964, the Jackson, Mississippi, field office was officially opened, with Hoover and his assistant, Clyde Tolson, presiding. A veteran agent, Roy K. Moore, was selected to head the Jackson office, where he served until his retirement in 1974.[18]

Black Mississippians responded to the fifteen lynchings of the early 1960s with a range of emotions and reactions. They turned out in droves for the funerals of major activists. For the funeral of Medgar Evers on June 15, 1963, they turned out in the thousands for the service at the Masonic Temple, and many followed the casket after the funeral, as Evers was returned to the Collis Funeral Home in Jackson. About 1,000 mourners also tried to march toward Capitol Street in downtown Jackson. The Jackson Police Department and other state law officers prevented this march.[19] Yet black Jacksonians had made their statement on the death of Evers. The civil rights movement in Mississippi went forward in his name and that of hundreds of other American citizens who had helped to prepare a way for the freedom struggles of the 1960s.

Mississippi's black writers, artists, and musicians were also active in responding to the lynching crisis and the issue of discrimination against blacks in Mississippi. Their body of work speaks eloquently on the contributions of these cultural workers in the black struggle. Table 11.7 denotes the range of black writers active in Mississippi in the second half of the twentieth century. Major voices in this group include Richard Wright, Margaret Walker Alexander, Lerone Bennett, Jr., Angela Jackson, Etheridge Knight, Thomas D. Pawley, III, Sterling D. Plumpp, Beau Richards, Jerry W. Ward, Jr., John A. Williams, Al Young, Endesha Ida Mae Holland, and Ahmos Zu-Bolton, among many others.[20]

Black Mississippi leaders such as Fannie Lou Hamer, Aaron Henry, Annie Devine, and Charles Evers, and civil rights organizations such as the NAACP, SNCC, CORE, the National Urban League, and SCLC continued the anti-segregationist fight throughout the 1960s. The deaths of so many blacks and the general violence of the period encouraged all of them to fight even harder for political, social, and economic change in Mississippi, the South, and the nation.[21]

The masses of black Mississippians responded to the crisis of violence in the state by registering to vote and becoming involved in the politics on the local, state, and national levels. Besides the major influence of the Freedom Movement and the violence which blacks suffered in the 1960s, black Mississippians were also encouraged by the Voting Rights Act of 1965. The number of registered black voters in Mississippi was only 28,500, or 6.7 percent of the black voting-age population, in 1964. By 1967 this number was 263,754, or 59.8 percent of black voting-age population. A tremendous growth in black political strength in the state was due largely to the actions of the Freedom Movement.[22] Over the next generation, or twenty-year period, black Mississippians were very successful in electing blacks to public office in the state—another tremendous achievement of the civil rights movement in Mississippi. The proof is in the numbers. For example, in 1964, only six blacks were elected to public office in Mississippi. By 1979 there were 210, and by 1980, 387 blacks were in elected office, one of the highest totals for black Americans in any state. And this figure included 17 blacks in the Mississippi Legislature and 27 black supervisors in the state.[23] This political struggle must be viewed as one of the major responses of black Mississippians to their historical circumstances, including the lynching crisis.[24]

Violence against blacks seems to have been the norm among many white Mississippians

TABLE 11.7: BLACK WRITERS IN MISSISSIPPI, 1940–2000

Name	L. name	Birthplace	Birthdate	Died
Margaret Walker	Alexander	Birmingham, AL	7/27/15	1998
Effie T.	Battle			
Lerone	Bennett	Clarksdale, MS	10/17/28	
Hermand	Bennett, Jr.			
Theodore "Ted"	Bozeman, Jr.	Jackson, MS	8/21/55	
Johnathan Henderson	Brooks	Lexington, MS	1904	1945
Isabella Marie	Browne	Jackson, MS	1917	
Charles K.	Chiplin	Vicksburg, MS	10/15/08	1998
Mary Wilkerson	Cleaves			
Willie	Cook	Russell County, AL	1/18/29	
Arthur R.	Crowell, Jr.	New York, NY	5/21/43	
Rhoyia Hope	Crozier	New Orleans, LA	12/17/35	
Ruth Roseman	Dease	Jackson, MS	11/9/12	1991
Doris A.	Derby	Bronx, NY		
L.C.	Drosey	Tribbette, MS	12/17/38	
Richard V.	Durham	Jackson, MS	1917	
John Albert	Ellis	Natchez, MS	10/5/56	
Anselm Joseph	Finch	Brandon, MS	6/9/02	
E. Yvonne	Foreman	Baton Rouge, LA	6/8/40	
E. C.	Foster	Canton, MS	1/4/39	
Clarence	Franklin	Jackson, MS	1932	
L.D.	Gallion			
Samuel	Girhan, Jr.	Pontotoc, MS	7/23/50	
Loyle	Hairston	Macon, MS	7/1/26	
Minnie L.	Harp	Greenville, MS	1/25/54	
Harrison	Harvard, Jr.	Vicksburg, MS	2/27/39	
Devonya	Havis	Jackson, MS		
Roland	Havis	Dumas, AZ	10/17/39	
M. Carl	Holman	Minter City, MS	1919	1988
John Authur	Horton	Goodman, MS	2/7/55	
Myrtle "Moss"	Humphrey	West Point, MS	1/13/34	

Name	L. name	Birthplace	Birthdate	Died
Dilla	Irwin		3/25/10	
Angela	Jackson	Greenville, MS	7/25/51	
Aurolyn Charise	Jacobs	Chicago, IL	5/15/57	
Jesse J.	Johnson	Hattiesburg, MS	5/15/14	
Nate	Johnson			
E. H.	Jones	Homes County, MS	7/8/25	
Helen H.	King	Clarksdale, MS	10/15/31	
Etheridge	Knight	Corinth, MS	4/19/31	1991
Henry J.	Kirksey	Tupelo, MS	1915	
Hillary K.	Knight	Natchez, MI		
Deborah D.	Lesure	Coldwater, MS	9/27/57	
George W.	Lee	Indianola, MS	1894	1976
Mollie	Lemons		1899	
Sinclair O.	Lewis	Greenville, MS	1930	
C. Liegh	McInnis			
Burns	Machobane	Southern Africa		
Pamela D.	Mack	Greenville, MS	9/24/60	
Isaiah	Madison	Hughes, AR	2/16/41	
Sheila E.	Malone	Holly Springs, MS		
Charles Victor	McTeer	Baltimore, MD	9/25/43	
Marion E. A.	Nicholes	New York, NY	7/19/44	
Thomas D.	Pawley III	Jackson, MS	8/5/17	
Sterling Dominic	Plumpp	Clinton, MS	1/30/40	
Helen H.	Pulliam	Buena Vista, MS	8/2/45	
Easley (Lyanju)	Quinn			
Beah	Richard	Vicksburg, MS		
Charlemae	Rollins	Yazoo City, MS	6/20/1897	2/3/79
Efo "Scott"	Rumah			
Virgia	Brocks-Shedd	Utica, MS	6/22/43	1992
Charles H.	Thompson	Jackson, MS	1906	
Julius E.	Thompson	Vicksburg, MS	7/15/46	
Bessye	Tobias-Turner			

Name	L. name	Birthplace	Birthdate	Died
Barbara	Townsend	LA	3/29/44	
Jonetta	Turner			
Melvin	Turner, Jr.	New Orleans, LA	8/7/48	
Alice	Walker	Eatonton, GA	2/9/44	
Jerry W.	Ward, Jr.	Washington, D.C.	7/31/43	
Barbara	Watkins	Atlanta, GA	7/31/40	
Tommy	Whitaker	Vicksburg, MS	1950	
Benjamin J.	Williams	Gulfport, MS	1947	
James Otis	Williams	Grenada, MS	1939	1997
John A.	Williams	Jackson, MS	1/5/25	
Richard	Wright	Natchez, MS	1908	1960
Degecha	X			
Alice	Young	Ocean Springs, MS	5/31/39	
Aurelia Norris	Young	Knottsville, KY	12/9/15	
Billie Jean	Young			
Ahmos	Zu-Bolton	Poplarville, MS	1935	2005

during the 1960s. Certainly, the state government was, in general, opposed to the civil rights movement and its goals of protest through freedom rides, demonstrations, boycotts, sit-ins and other forms of desegregation efforts in Mississippi and the South.[25] Lynching may now have seemed outdated for many whites in the state, but not the use of violence to help whites in their ageless struggle to keep blacks in their place, and to maintain the social system of white supremacy in Mississippi at all costs. Perhaps at this late date, however, many whites were embarrassed by the lynching issue, and thus more opposition could be expressed against this form of torment. Yet Mississippi still had major demagogues to deal with, as in the case of Governor Ross Barnett, in office from 1960 to 1964.[26] As Francis M. Wilhoit observes, Barnett became "a living symbol of bitter-end resistance to all forms of desegregation."[27] One idea was central to Barnett—white control and black inequality. Wilhoit also notes, "While governor he had a favorite saying that was indicative of his faith in white supremacy. 'The good Lord,' he liked to say, 'was the original segregationist. He put the Negro in Africa—separated him from all other races.'"[28] Such a perspective ruled in Mississippi during the 1960s.

Backing up the system and its general violent tendencies were the Ku Klux Klan, the Citizens' Councils, and the Mississippi State Sovereignty Commission. Violence and intimidation were an active part of the work of each group.[29]

Most of the white press in Mississippi during the 1960s occupied a strange position in the state. One study notes the following:

During this time, the white press fell into three groups. The first group consisted of extreme conservative papers, such as the *Clarion-Ledger* and the *Jackson Daily News*, both controlled by the Hederman Family of Jackson. This group also included the *Woman Constitutionalist*, a monthly tabloid published at Summit; the *Citizen*, a monthly that served as the official organ of the Citizens' Councils of America; and newspapers such as the *Natchez Democrat*, the *Hattiesburg American*, the *Fayette Chronicle*, the *Tunica Times-Democrat*, and the *Pike County Summit Sun*. In 1969, Pat Walters wrote that Mississippi papers like the *Clarion-Ledger* and the *Jackson Daily News* were "likely to be among the worst newspapers in the world." This statement holds true for much of the white Mississippi press of this period, because the papers were dishonest in their treatment of—or refusal to treat—blacks; were racist and prejudiced against minorities, non-Christian religious groups, and women; and were very weak in terms of journalist standards, ethics, fairness, and goodwill toward other human beings. But such papers represented the leading press voices in Mississippi, and as such they helped to support totally the system of segregation and oppression.

Moderate papers formed a second category of the white press—most notably, Hazel Brannon Smith's *Lexington Advertiser*, Hodding Carter, Jr.'s Greenville *Delta Democrat-Times*, and P. D. East's *Petal Paper*. Other constructive journals of the 1960s included the McComb *Enterprise-Journal*, edited by Oliver Emmerich (1896–1978), the *Tupelo Journal*, the Batesville *Panolian*, the Clarksdale *Press-Register*, and the Tylertown *Times*. As occurred earlier, segregationists often abused moderate editors, but most withstood the pressure and sought to offer guidance toward a better future through their papers.

Finally, several small, radical white organs constituted the third segment of the white press of this era, offering a progressive press voice. *Kudzu: Subterranean News from the Heart of Old Dixie*, established at Jackson in 1968, represents among the best-known of these papers. An eight- to twelve-page tabloid, *Kudzu* had "a moderate New Left point of view." In Mississippi, this represented a radical, even subversive, orientation. The paper sought the "cultural and political liberation of all people" as one of its major goals. For its efforts local authorities often harassed the paper. White students at historically white universities also published underground papers, like *Descant*, circulated during 1967–68 at the University of Mississippi.[30]

Other Mississippi moderates, as represented by some elements among religious groups in the state, white writers such as Walker Percy and Eudora Welty, and politicians like Frank E. Smith, were opposed to lynching and generally promoters of tolerance in Mississippi.[31]

Nationally, Presidents John F. Kennedy and his successor, Lyndon B. Johnson, were opposed to lynching. Johnson was also able to push through Congress a series of civil rights measures in the 1960s which aided the advancement of some blacks in American society.[32] Although Congress showed some sensitivity to black issues and concerns with the passage of the 1965 Voting Rights Act and other civil rights bills during this period, an anti-lynching bill was not one of them. At the FBI, Director J. Edgar Hoover ran a radically conservative investigating agency. According to one study: "The FBI was effectively at war with America's political dissidents [and] Hoover's agents also felt free to use [any] techniques against anyone else they believed presented a threat to the established order."[33] The problem of lynching was not a serious concern of the FBI.

Outside of Mississippi, black organizations and their leaders remained committed to promoting anti-lynching work, in spite of the drastic drop in official lynchings in this nation in the 1960s. As in the past, the NAACP covered this issue in its work, and the *Crisis* magazine noted the importance of continued protest to end lynching.[34] The killing of Medgar Evers was of major importance to the association in the early 1960s. Other national organizations—including the rest of the Big Five civil rights movement groups, the SCLC, CORE, SNCC, and the National Urban League—were active in noting the historical importance of

TABLE 11.8: HOW AFRICAN AMERICANS RANK THEIR LEADERS

Rank and File % Approve 1966	1963		*Leadership Group* % Approve 1966	1963
88	88	Martin Luther King, Jr.	87	95
71	79	James Meredith	35	81
66	80	Jackie Robinson	58	82
64	68	Roy Wilkins	62	92
56	60	Dick Gregory	65	80
54	X	Charles Evers	68	X
53	62	Ralph Bunche	49	87
48	64	Thurgood Marshall	81	94
47	X	James Farmer	70	X
44	51	Adam Clayton Powell	49	52
35	X	A. Philip Randolph	83	X
33	X	Whitney Young, Jr.	70	X
22	X	Bayard Rustin	53	X
19	X	Floyd McKissick	35	X
19	X	Stokely Carmichael	33	X
12	15	Elijah Muhammad	15	17

X—*not on 1963 list*

lynching as an issue that had greatly impacted the black community and as a contemporary issue of injustice and discrimination against black Americans.[35] A Newsweek poll using data from 1963 and 1966 describes how blacks ranked their male leaders in the 1960s. See Table 11.8.[36] Clearly Martin Luther King, Jr. (1929–1968), was the favorite black leader of the decade. Malcolm X (1925–1965) is mysteriously missing from this list. Perhaps his early death by assassination is a factor. Also of interest is the fact that two black Mississippians appear on the list: James Meredith, who received major credit by blacks for his struggle to desegregate the University of Mississippi in 1962, and Charles Evers, who became the NAACP's new field secretary in the state after the death of his brother, Medgar Evers.[37] In spite of the tremendous contributions of black women, none appears on this poll. Yet collectively, this group of black leaders were outspoken in demanding justice and civil and human rights for African Americans. Many also spoke out against the historic nature of lynching and its impact as a terrorist mechanism across many decades to bring fear and death into the lives of black Americans.[38]

Like the Harlem Renaissance of the 1920s and early 1930s, the Black Art Movement of the 1960s and early 1970s created a rich body of contributions in all fields of art. Especially active during the 1960s were black poets, dramatists, and musicians whose body of works explored all aspects of the black experience, including the historical dimensions of the lynching crisis.[39] Three poems which explore the lynching theme were written by Langston Hughes (1902–1967), "Mississippi," Primus St. John (1939–), "Lynching and Burning," and Sam Greenlee (1930–), "Lynch Parties."[40]

Each poet pulls from the historical consciousness of blacks on the terrible ordeal of lynching in the experiences of black people. These poetic expressions serve to capture the pain, the memories, and the essence of the impact of the lynching events of the past and present on the lives and struggles of contemporary blacks, as they struggle to overcome continued problems in their social, political, and economic conditions in the United States.[41]

Black playwrights were also active in the post–World War II era in capturing in drama the complexities of black life in America, with a special reference, in many cases, on the historic connections in the black experience, including the problems of slavery, racism, segregation, colonialism, and lynching. Among the major black dramatists of the forty-odd years since 1945 were Langston Hughes, "Don't You Want to Be Free?" (1938), "Shakespeare in Harlem" (1960), and "Tambourines to Glory" (1963); Ossie Davis, "Purlie Victorious" (1961); Adrienne Kennedy (1931–), "The Funny House of a Negro" (1962) and "A Rat's Mass" (1966); Amiri Baraka [LeRoi Jones] (1934–), "Dutchman" (1964), "The Toilet" and "The Slave" (1965); James Baldwin (1924–1987), "The Amen Corner" (1968) and "Blues for Mr. Charlie" (1963); John Oliver Killens (1916–1987) and Loften Mitchell (1919–), "Ballad of the Winter Soldiers" (1964); Alice Childress (1920–1994), "Trouble in Mind" (1955); Lorraine Hansberry (1930–1965), "A Raisin in the Sun" (1959) and "The Sign in Sidney Brustein's Window" (1964); Ed Bullins (1935–), "In the Wine Time" (1968); August Wilson (1945–), "Fences" (1985); Ntozake Shange [Paulette Williams] (1948–), "For Colored Girls Who Have Considered Suicide When the Rainbow is Enuf" (1976); Douglas Turner Ward (1930–), "Happy Ending" (1965) and "Day of Absence" (1965); Ronald Milner (1938–), "Who's God His Own" (1966); Charles Fuller (1939–), "A Soldier's Play" (1981); and Toni Morrison (1931–), "Dreaming Emmett" (1986), a play about the lynching of Emmett Till in 1955; and so many others.[42] Such powerful plays brought forth on the American stage the rich diversity and universal themes of freedom, justice and equality in the search for meaning in the human experiences of black Americans in the twentieth century.[43]

Black musicians were major voices in the black freedom struggles of the 1960s, and their body of work continues to inspire later generations not only in the United States, but around the world.[44] Freedom, especially from such overwhelming conditions such as lynching, are a major theme in black music from this era. One example is selected from the thousands of songs and compositions produced by black artists in the 1960s—Nina Simone's "Mississippi Goddam" (1964), which became one of the best known musical statements from the decade.[45]

Nina Simon's autobiography notes the importance of this song:

> But the Alabama church bombings and the murder of Medgar Evers stopped that argument and with "Mississippi Goddam" I realized there was no turning back. I went up to New York as planned and sang the song in public for the first time at the Village Gate. It brought the place down, and I got the same reaction wherever I sang it. We released it as a single and it sold well, except in the south, where we had trouble with distribution. The excuse was profanity—Goddam!—but the real reason was obvious enough. A dealer in South Carolina sent a whole crate of copies back to our office with each one snapped in half. I laughed, because it meant we were getting through. In some states the distributors

bleeped out the word "Goddam," changed the wording on the sleeve and released it under the title "Mississippi #**#!."[46]

Young white students and some white artists were among other groups which were key in the civil rights movement and in promoting anti-lynching work in the United States. White student volunteers, largely from Northern states, were a key component in the Mississippi Freedom Summer project of 1964, and an early active part of the work of SNCC. Of course two of these white volunteers died in Mississippi—Andrew Goodman and Michael H. Schwerner. The volunteers experienced the worse of Southern racism and violence. As one author notes, before the terror subsided four workers in all would be killed, and "80 more beaten, 1,000 arrested and 67 homes, churches and businesses would be bombed or burned."[47] But they helped bring much needed changes to Mississippi and the nation.[48]

The works of white artists such as Joan Baez (1941–), Leonard Bernstein (1918–1990), Bob Dylan (1941–), Jane Fonda (1937–), Allen Ginsberg (1926–1997), Peggy Lee (1920–2002), and Peter, Paul and Mary, among others, also helped to bring public attention to American social issues. Dylan was especially influential with such compositions as "A Hard Rain's A Gonna Fall" (1963), "Oxford Town" (1962), "It Ain't Me, Babe" (1964), and "The Times They Are A-Changin'" (1963), among many others.[49] Such works weave a rich travesty of American songs onto the social efforts for reforms of American society in the 1960s and beyond.

The impact of lynching in Mississippi between 1960 and 1965 must be viewed against the backdrop of the civil rights movement and the world-wide demands by black people for freedom from colonialism and the economic, social and political oppression which blacks had suffered for centuries at the hands of other races in Europe, the Americas and elsewhere. Mississippi represented a prime example of the harshness of the Southern Jim Crow system, and as such, the Freedom Movement of this era placed a major priority on trying to break the back of segregation and racism in this key deep South state. As Florence Halpern observes:

> There are still other reasons why the traditions and the behaviors of the southern black people have importance. One is the unique psychological significance that the south, and Mississippi in particular, has for both black and white people. For the black people everywhere, regardless of where they were born and where they now reside, the south is perceived as a kind of homeland, the place from whence their elders came and where many of their relatives still live. Miserable though it may be, it is the place to go to, to learn about one's origins, as the hero says in "My Sweet Charlie." Mississippi especially stands as a symbol of the worst horrors of American slavery and subsequent pseudo-freedom. Consequently, what happens in Mississippi has very special meaning and importance for the black people, wherever they are currently living. Similarly, for the white liberal and activist, the south, and again particularly Mississippi, represents all the prejudices and injustices against which he is fighting. Contrariwise, for the southern white man, especially the segregationist and die-hard racist, Mississippi stands as a monument to a treasured past and constitutes one of the last strongholds of the traditional southern way of life; and so for the southern white man too, the area has special importance.[50]

Lynching, of course, remained as one mechanism which some whites still attempted to use to control blacks, and to stress fear and white domination as twin themes in this historical process. For at least fifteen victims the past became the present in terms of contemporary lynching events in the early 1960s. But the matter did not end here, for modern scholars do not as yet have a clear count of the total numbers of blacks who just "disappeared" in the 1960s. Even when the most famous case of the 1960s is considered, the killing of the three Freedom Summer volunteers at Philadelphia, Mississippi, in 1964, questions remain. Alphonso Pinkney points this out in a study of the period: "The murder of three civil rights workers in Mississippi in the summer of 1964 was one of the most widely publicized events, but the disappearance of two young Negroes whose bodies were discovered during the search for these three had hardly been publicized at all. Certainly the number of events involving violation of civil rights could hardly be widely publicized if other news events are to receive any publicity at all, considering that they are so prevalent in the United States."[51]

And, against this special problem, one also has to contend with the general violent treatment of blacks in the system, and of Freedom Movement workers in particular, whenever they came up against any aspect of the criminal justice system in Mississippi, or some local whites in Mississippi communities.[52]

The impact of lynching and violence against blacks remains with the community decades after the events. This was brought home to blacks in the March 1965 issue of the *Crisis*, when a black Mississippian wrote to Roy Wilkins about people in his home state:

Mississippi: Then as NOW
    In a revealing letter to Executive Director Wilkins, Dr. David D. Foote, now a Chicago dentist, recalls the terror in his native Mississippi a half-century ago. Dr. Foote's letter follows: "Although 85, I am still practicing dentistry. I was exiled from Vicksburg, Mississippi, in 1918 by a committee known as the 'Vigilantes,' similar to the K.K.K. I am a life member of the NAACP and have been far more successful here than I would have been had I remained in Mississippi. I was born in Vicksburg, October 26, 1879, and lived there until 1918. No white man has ever been convicted in that state for the murder of a Negro."
    During the first World War, under the Administration of Woodrow Wilson, an appeal was made to various states for war funds, the purchasing of war stamps, etc. In order to raise the state's quota, Vicksburg held a mass meeting and called upon its Negro citizens to attend and help "make the world safe for Democracy." For the first time in its history, the Negroes were admitted on the main floor of the theater without discrimination. The speakers (all white) promised great changes would be made after the War.
    "Three Negroes, Dr. John Miller, a physician of Ann Arbor, Michigan, Dr. David Foote, a dentist of Howard University, and William P. Harrison, a pharmacist and owner of a rug store, formed a committee. Miller was made chairman. The 'Vigilantes' summoned Dr. Miller for a hearing. He spoke of the many injustices that prevailed at the time and asked that a change be made. 'Whom the gods would destroy they first made mad.' Dr. Miller was tarred and feathered by an unmasked mob, paraded around the town with a sign around his neck saying, 'I am disloyal.' He smiled and took the matter as a joke (this saved his life). One member of the mob ordered them to stop and Miller was given orders to leave town.
    "I was here in Chicago and received a telegram from my brother reading, 'Prepare to live in Chicago. You cannot live here any longer.' Dr. Harrison was in New Orleans, La., and received a similar message.
    "The Negro has caught hell in Mississippi ever since the Tilden-Hayes affair. The object is to keep him in fear. Fear is the weapon used in Mississippi. Mississippi is a closed society and injustices practiced against the Negro are just beginning to leak out.
    "I do not mean to bore you but since Miller and Harrison are dead, I am the lone wolf left to tell an unrelated story. Whether it will mean much in the infamous State of Mississippi, I am glad to see the civil rights bill passed, for I was 40 years ahead of my time."[53]

Yet, when the general public was polled on "The Bible and Segregation," the respondents were of a mixed opinion on this issue. Perhaps this poll helps to explain why segregation, lynching, and discrimination were so widespread in American life from the First to the Second Reconstructions in American history. A June 6, 1962, Gallup poll reveals the following.

The Bible and Segregation Interviewing Date 5/3–8/62
Do you believe that there is a basis in the Bible for segregation?
    About one-third of white Southerners feel that the Bible backs up their belief that "God just did not mean for the races to mix." Another third does not feel that the Bible offers such evidence. The remaining third feels they are unable to state from the evidence whether or not such a basis exists.
    Outside of the South, about one white person in eleven believes that this is so. Just over half state definitely that this is not so, while the remainder are undecided.
    About one Negro in ten in the South believes that the Bible does provide grounds for segregation.
    Outside the South, less than 1% of Negroes believes that a basis for segregation can be found in the Bible.
    A large proportion—about 40% when the views of everyone interviewed in the survey are considered—said they cannot point to any evidence in the Bible which supports or condemns the separation of races. Many of these persons frankly admitted that they don't know their Bible.[54]

    At this late (1965) date, a radical new spirit was at work among some black Americans. Certainly the horrors of the Age of Lynching for the period of one hundred years must be accorded as one factor. In recent decades newer leaders emerged among blacks, especially noteworthy was the life and career of Malcolm X (1925–1965), and the rising influence of Islam among some blacks.[55] This new mood among many African Americans indicated that some blacks were looking for other options besides Christianity, integration, and perhaps assimilation with white Americans. Indeed, the Nation of Islam under the leadership of Elijah Muhammad suggested such an approach since at least the 1930s.[56] This new school of thought even questioned the need for black Americans to vote in this nation. Poet Marvin X (1944–), a major force in the Black Arts Movement, raised this issue in his famous poem, "Did You Vote Nigger?"[57]

    Thus the new mood among some blacks indicated the historical deprivation which the black condition had suffered under the Age of Lynching in Mississippi and other states. This was the situation in spite of the tremendous work and challenge as put forward by the other major national black leader of this era, Martin Luther King, Jr.[58] One thing was certain as people surveyed the scene in the black community in America in 1965: the cries from the past were long and hard, the way forward was filled with bothersome and unknown questions and issues. Yet one fact stood out: at least 5,000 black Americans had been lynched in the United States between 1865 and 1965, and no one could give an accurate estimation of how many other blacks had simply disappeared across so many decades of black struggle in America.[59] The grimness of so many deaths was buried in the collective consciousness of African Americans. In essence, the black community had never really overcome its grief, or its grievance held against this country for so many mass murders, and the general theme of discrimination and racism across the decades. As things stood in 1965, these issues would have to be addressed by future generations of Americans, as each new decade would present the nation with challenges and concerns that must be addressed—that, indeed, begged to be addressed. For the past, as a historic memory and moment in the life experiences of the American people, remains a vibrant issue that will not go away.

Epilogue: Faith in Our Times,
1966–2002

Since the height of the civil rights movement in the mid–1960s, Mississippi has experienced tremendous changes. By 1990 its population base stood at 2,573,216, making it the 31st largest state in the United States.[1] By 2000 this number had increased to 2,844,658 with the ethnic division consisting of 61.4 percent white, 36.3 percent black and 3.3 percent others, including Asian-Americans, Native Americas and other groups.[2] Yet Mississippi still remains mired in poverty. One study notes that "one-fourth of all Mississippians and 62 percent of the state's black families lived below the poverty line during the early 1980s"[3] As late as 2002 Mississippi ranked fourth in the total number of children living in poverty.[4] The Delta region of Mississippi continues to help the state maintain its historic place as the poorest state in the Union.[5] In juxtaposition with these facts is the observation that by 1979 Mississippi held the 25th place in this country in the total number of millionaires in the state (4,557), most of whom made their wealth in the real estate market.[6]

At the end of the twentieth century Mississippi was still a key cotton producing state and "the leading cotton producer in the mid-south and fourth-largest in the United States behind Texas, California and Georgia."[7] Yet in recent decades farming overall has suffered a decline in Mississippi: "By 1974, the number of farms had been reduced to 53,620 and averaged 274 acres in size. In 1991, there were 38,000 farms averaging 337 acres. Mississippi had a total of 12,800,000 acres in farmland in 1991. As farms consolidated and became increasingly mechanized, many farm laborers left and looked for jobs elsewhere—particularly in the cities. Many counties in the Delta have lost between 5 and 20 percent of their population since 1970."[8]

Nevertheless, "Mississippi has made vast improvements, and there have been substantial gains in education and the attraction of out-of-state companies, especially light industry."[9] A large black middle class exists today in Mississippi, but some historical problems still linger to especially impact the lives of black Mississippians. For example, in 1973 only 28 African American physicians worked in Mississippi. By 1982 the total number of black physicians in the United States stood at 10,540.[10] Thus the economic and social aspects of health and medical care remain special burdens on the black community in Mississippi.

Since the civil rights movement, social and race relations have improved. Mississippi society is controlled by white males, as is general American society.[11] But the Age of Segregation as it existed in the 1890s to the 1960s is over. Yes, blacks and other groups in Mississippi still suffer from the historic consequences of segregation and racism, but a turn for the better has taken place in the state. Certainly the work of the civil rights organizations, religious groups, women's groups and national and international pressures have aided these positive developments in Mississippi. Yet many whites think, incorrectly, that blacks have reached parity in American life (politically, socially and economically) with whites.[12] Their error is observed most clearly in John Dittner's assessment of contemporary Mississippi. He writes:

> The Mississippi movement failed to bring about the social revolution envisioned by the militant activists. Whites continued to hold most of the positions of real political power and to dominate all aspects of economic life. In the early 1990s Mississippi still led the nation in poverty, infant mortality and illiteracy. Gains made by the black middle class were offset by the economic problems facing the majority of blacks who once again became Mississippi's forgotten people. According to Children's Defense Fund figures, more than half the state's black children, nearly 200,000, were living below the poverty line in 1990. Although black economic development agencies like Mississippi Action for Community Education (MACE) and the Delta Foundation worked to bring industry into black communities, black per capita income was less than half that of whites, and the state's per capita income remained the lowest in the nation.[13]

Nevertheless, the intensive Mississippi racism of earlier periods is now a thing of the past. Collectively this has given blacks in Mississippi a lift.[14]

Educational issues are of prime importance to Mississippians, and especially given the economic consequences of a poor education. Since the 1970s Mississippi has desegregated its schools, but many whites have abandoned the public school system for private white schools. Charles Bolton notes that "between 1966 and 1970 ... the number of private schools in the state rose from 121 to 236, and the number of students attending these schools tripled; much of this growth occurred in black-majority districts. Fewer whites fled from public schools in white-majority districts, not only because white fears of integrated schools were not as pronounced in places where they had numerical superiority, but also because whites in these areas generally had fewer resources to support a private system of education.[15]

While many whites left the Mississippi public school system voluntarily, many blacks were forced out. Charles Bolton observes:

> The loss of jobs or status by black teachers and administrators represented perhaps the most visible evidence that the wholesale integration of schools occurred on white terms.... Declining public-school enrollments meant that teaching staffs had to be reduced. In districts that became all-black, the number of black teachers actually increased as white teachers voluntarily abandoned the system, but in many other locales, black teachers lost their jobs as school integration became a reality. Some school officials used the opportunity to rid their districts of teachers who had supported the civil rights movement; others tried to weed out poorly qualified black teachers, even though state Department of Education officials such as assistant state superintendent W.S. Griffin admitted that the concern over the training of black teachers drew notice only once they started "teaching the white kids".... Overall, between 1970 and 1973, the number of white teachers in the state increased by almost nine percent, while the number of black teachers fell during the same period by almost twelve percent. The wholesale dismissal of black administrators was even more stunning.... In 1969–70, Mississippi had 168 black secondary school principals; that figure had declined to 19 by the 1970–71 school year.[16]

Overall, therefore, black educators suffered under the new system. The new reality also suggested that in terms of education, segregation in schools was still a factor of life for many black students. Lawrence H. Fuchs observes that:

> In Mississippi, African-American students constituted more than 85 percent of the population in 29 of 154 school districts, but only ten had black school superintendents. The pattern was changing in the late 1980s, partly because a large number of trained African Americans were becoming available for the jobs, and partly because of the increased black economic pressure, as in Indianola, Mississippi, where the school system was 93 percent black and where the African-American community forced the resignation of the white superintendent and the selection of a black through a boycott of the schools and of white merchants.[17]

In addition to addressing continuing challenges in education, Mississippi blacks have focused a tremendous amount of energy on the further development of their cultural institutions, which have a direct bearing on the daily lives of the people. African-American music is of major importance, as is the development of black museums such as Clarksdale's Delta Blues Museum, Jackson's Smith Roberson Museum, the Jacqueline House Museum in Vicksburg, and the mostly African Market Project of Southern Cross at Natchez under director Thelma Williams.[18] Such organizations seek to promote black cultural awareness, the preservation of black cultural artifacts and the long-term educational and cultural needs of African Americans in Mississippi and other states.

The social position of the black family and the special concerns of its three central components—black women, black men, and black children—has been a major theme in the life of black Mississippians since the 1960s, as is true of blacks nationally.[19] Yet the black family has been greatly impacted by urbanization in the twentieth century. Paul Johnson suggests the nature of the problem by the gloomy contemporary statistics on the American family:

> By 1991 only 38 percent of black women aged 15–44 were married, compared to 58 percent of white women. In 1960, 24 percent of black children were illegitimate, compared with 2 percent of white children. By 1991, the figures of illegitimate births were 68 percent of all births for blacks, 39 percent for Latinos, and 18 percent for non–Latino whites. At some point between 1960 and 1990, marriage, and having children within marriage, ceased to be the norm among blacks, while remaining the norm among whites (though a deteriorating one). By the end of 1994 it was 33 percent for the nation as a whole, 25 percent for whites, and 70 percent for blacks. In parts of Washington, capital of the richest nation in the world, it was as high as 90 percent.[20]

Such conditions remain a special challenge for black organizations such as the National Council of Negro Women, the National Urban League, black religious groups, and other black community agencies.[21]

The black church remains a central institution in the lives of black Mississippians. This is certainly a national story. One study notes that "black Americans are in many ways the most religious people in America. Some 82 percent of blacks (versus 67 percent of whites) are church members; 82 percent of blacks (versus 55 percent of whites) say that 'religion is very important in their life'; and 86 percent of blacks (versus 60 percent of whites) believe that religion 'can answer all or most of today's problems.'"[22] Thus, religion forms a core of black belief systems in Mississippi and the nation.[23]

A series of arson fires at black churches, especially in the South, in the mid-1990s, brought the destruction of many black religious buildings. In 1996 USA Today counted 64 (in 1995) fires at black churches and church buildings. Seven of these were in Mississippi.[24] Authorities blamed many of these incidents on white racists and traditional anti-black groups such as the Ku Klux Klan and radically conservative white youth individuals and groups.[25] Perhaps anti-black elements in the 1990s realized the historic importance of the black church to black people—and tried to destroy as many of these institutions as possible in order to wound the black community.[26] Yet this effort did not succeed. Blacks, with the support of other communities, rebuilt their churches.[27]

A new development has taken place in black religious life across the last thirty years, with the conversion of many African-Americans to Islam. This is true in Mississippi as in other states. Recent studies suggest that "some 40 percent of the estimated 5 million to 8 million new Muslims in the United States are African-American, making blacks the largest ethnic group of Muslims in America."[28] Thus in the new century, African Americans will be influenced, religiously speaking, by Christianity, Islam and the traditional African religions.

Health care issues are another special concern of black Mississippians who, because of the poverty in the state and the lack of healthcare resources, have greater healthcare problems. This generally means higher disease and death rates for blacks from such conditions as diabetes, cancer, heart disease, stroke, high blood pressure, and HIV/AIDS.[29] Paul Farmer observed the special impact of AIDS on black women: "In the United States, HIV has moved, almost unimpeded, through poor communities of color. By 1991, African Americans, who comprise approximately 12% of the U.S. population, accounted for 30% of all reported AIDS cases. During the eighties, the cumulative incidence of AIDS was more than 11 times higher for black women than for white women from 25 to 44; for Latinos in the age group, it is now the third leading cause of death."[30]

The life expectancy for blacks is much lower than for whites, but the lowest numbers are held by black men. Table 1 tells the story with striking clarity.[31]

TABLE 1: LIFE EXPECTANCY AT BIRTH IN THE UNITED STATES

	In 1969-1971	*In 1998*
Black men	60.0 years	67.6 years
White men	67.9 years	74.5 years
Black women	68.3 years	74.8 years
White women	75.5 years	80.0 years

Black males generally live seven years less than white males, and twelve years less than white women in the United States. Yet the worst situation for black males seems to be in Harlem, New York. Howard Zinn observes in recent study that "the life expectancy of a black man in Harlem, according to a United Nations report, was 46 years, less than that in Cambodia or the Sudan."[32] Such conditions seem to remind blacks in Mississippi and elsewhere of the special work which lies ahead for future generations of blacks and others.[33]

Political activity has also been a major interest of black Mississippians since the mid–1960s. As one study observes: "In Mississippi, for example, blacks are 36 percent of the population, but whereas only 6.7 percent registered in 1964, 70 percent registered in 1981."[34]

Such numbers greatly increased the political strength of blacks in Mississippi. After an intensive struggle from 1965 to 1979 to change Mississippi's legislature elections "from multimember districts to single-member districts, African American voters were able to move from four black elected legislators to 17 by 1980."[35] By 1988 the number of black Mississippi legislators stood at twenty-three. All were Democrats with the exception of Robert Clark (1919–) who ran as an independent. They served in a Mississippi Senate with 52 members (four black members in 1988), and a House of Representatives with 122 members (with 19 black members in 1988).[36] Their key impact has been to introduce "a number of bills ... to enhance the living conditions of the poor and undereducated in their districts."[37] Many black political activists feel that some white political figures in Mississippi are determined to maintain white control of political institutions at all costs.[38] This process indicates that a political struggle will continue in Mississippi during the twenty-first century.

On the national level, two black Mississippians won elections to represent the Second Congressional District of Mississippi in the House of Representatives. Michael Espy (D-Miss.) served in 1987–1992 and was President Clinton's Secretary of Agriculture 1993–1994. He was followed in office by Bennie Thompson (D-Miss.) in 1993 to the present; he serves on the Agriculture and Budget committees of the House.[39]

Such leaders serve in Mississippi and the nation's capital against the continuing economic problems of vast numbers of blacks. Writer and activist Tom Dent (1932–1998) described contemporary conditions as follows: "The ballot alone, devoid of economic strength, has proved to be of limited value. In fact a widening chasm is developing between the haves and have-nots even within the race ... as everyone testified to in every town I visited beginning in Greensboro, thereby eroding the Movement concept—or myth—of one Black community united by a common interest ... despite differences in education or income."[40]

Black Mississippians view the state's criminal justice system with a mixed set of opinions. For one thing, blacks report a higher rate of police threats, defined as situations where "blacks and Hispanics were twice as likely as whites to report that police used force or threatened to use force against them.... [Also] black drivers were more likely than whites to be stopped, searched, handcuffed or ticketed than whites."[41] Such conditions have increased black dissatisfaction levels with the American criminal justice system in Mississippi and other states. A recent study observes that:

> Nearly two-thirds of all blacks believe that racial equality will be achieved neither in their lifetime nor at any point in the history of the United States. These doubts about achieving racial equality are producing dramatic increases in support for independent politics. One half of blacks now support the formation of an independent political party, a doubling of such supporters since 1988. A majority of blacks now believe that blacks should belong exclusively to black organizations—a belief that obviously poses an enormous challenge for those who seek to build multiracial coalitions.
>
> The root of the problem is a corrosive dissatisfaction with American society as blacks experience it. Blacks continue to believe that They live in a country that is fundamentally racially unjust; 83 percent of blacks say that the legal system is not fair to blacks, 82 percent say the same about American society in general, and 74 percent say this about American corporations. An overwhelming 86 percent of blacks say that the American economic system is unfair to poor people. Significantly, large majorities see no prospect of an improving racial climate in the foreseeable future; indeed, a majority believe that the racial situation will get worse. This deep dissatisfaction and sense of exclusion challenge the ideal of an "American community." Over one half of blacks believe that blacks constitute a nation within a nation, not just another ethnic group.[42]

To make matters worse, a recent poll ranks Mississippi last in the United States in creating and maintaining a fair legal climate. Mississippi comes in last place on ten issues: (1) overall ranking, (2) overall treatment of tort and contract litigation, (3) punitive damages, (4) timeliness of summary judgment/dismissal, (5) discovery, (6) scientific and technical evidence, (7) judges' impartiality, (8) judges' competence, (9) juries' predictability, and (10) juries' fairness.[43]

Black Mississippians continue to be overrepresented in the prisons of Mississippi. In 1978 the state held 2,785 individuals as prisoners, and 1,860 or 66.9 percent of these were black Americans. Eight Mississippians were on the state's death row, with six of these, or 75 percent, also African-American.[44] Living conditions were especially difficult in the state's corrections system with jail overcrowding, poor food and poor health care facilities as such state institutions as Parchman Prison. The death of prisoners due to AIDS also developed as a problem in the 1990s.[45]

By the 1990s the problem of prisons became a major issue facing the African-American community in Mississippi and the nation. In fact, for the first time more than a million inmates were incarcerated in United States prisons in 1994.[46] Yet by 2002, Glen C. Loury notes, "We now have nearly 1.2 million African Americans under lock and key."[47] Added to these factors was a new problem of a growing suicide rate among young black males, in and out of prison. A study observes that: "Suicide by gun among 15- to 19-year-old black males rose to a peak of 13.9 per 100,000 in 1994 from 3.6 per 100,000 in 1979. The rate for 1997 ... was 8.4 per 100,000.[48]

The violent deaths of so many black males is a national problem. Robert Brent Toplins notes "African-Americans have been particularly affected by the crime wave of the last quarter-century. According to an epidemiologist who wrote a report for the federal government, in some areas in the United States 'it is now more likely for a black male between his fifteenth and twenty-fifth birthday to die from homicide than it was for a United States soldier to be killed on a tour of duty in Viet Nam.' Young black males in Harlem are less likely to survive to age 40 than young males in Bangladesh. Gun related homicides are the prevalent factor in these deaths."[49]

Conditions in the Mississippi and the national criminal justice systems are intensive areas of interest and concern to blacks and will most likely remain so for many decades into the future.[50]

Although most scholars officially close out the Age of Lynching with the 1940s and 1950s, lynching events continued to take place. This is clearly the case in Mississippi. Yet a decline in the causes given for lynching events seems to have taken place in later decades. Certainly for the period 1966–2002 conditions in Mississippi reflect the fact that hate crimes are a primary reason for lynchings. Contemporary lynchers also pull from the historic base of causes for lynchings of blacks, especially for economic competition with whites and interracial love affairs between black men and white women.[51] Leonard J. Moore notes the role of the Ku Klux Klan as an organization of hate in modern Mississippi and the nation: "During the era of the civil rights movement, a variety of Klan organizations surfaced with new found support and, like their predecessors of the Reconstruction Era, attacked and terrorized African Americans and racial reformers. As the twentieth century ended, isolated Klan groups, while generally discredited, continued to perpetuate an occasionally violent right-wing subculture."[52]

The range of violence against Mississippians of all races has been a major problem since the mid–1960s. Murder is still too common in Mississippi. In 1992, for example, 320 murder victims were recorded, making Mississippi rank among the highest in terms of its

TABLE E.2: MISSISSIPPI LYNCHINGS, 1966–2002

Name	Location	Date of Event	Background and Causes
Vernon F. Dahmer	Hattiesburg, Forrest Co.	Jan. 10, 1966	NAACP local leader, attacked for helping to register black voters; fire bombing of his home. Four Klansmen were convicted in his death.
Ben Chester White	Natchez, Adams Co.	June 12, 1966	A 65-year-old farmhand whose body was found in a creek near Natchez. Ernest Avants was charged in 2000 with White's murder. White was shot 12 times in the torso with an assault rifle and once in the head with a shotgun. Three alleged Ku Klux Klansmen—Ernest Avants, James Lloyd Jones and Claude Fuller—were accused of the killing. Avants was tried and acquitted in 1967; Jones' trial ended in a hung jury, and Fuller was never tried. The goal of the men was to lure Dr. Martin Luther King, Jr., to the area for assassination.
Wharlest Jackson	Natchez, Adams Co.	Feb. 27, 1967	NAACP leader in Natchez; killed by an explosion of his car.
Four black youths (males)	Picayune, Pearl River Co.	1976	Are killed in Picayune
James Calhoun	Sunflower Co.	1977	A 15-year old is killed by the Ku Klux Klan.
Black male	in Mississippi	1981	Is killed.
White male	in Mississippi	1981	Is killed.
Roy Washington	Holmes Co.	February 1981	His body "was found in Cypress Creek." He had been "badly beaten in the head and face," his hands bound behind him, and then shot in the head at point-blank range. The corpse was weighed down with a car jack and wrapped by barbed wire.
Unidentified black man	Cleveland, Bolivar Co.	1981?	"The tortured body of one unidentified black man was found floating down the river ... the man's sex organs had been hacked off and the coroner later reported finding his penis in his stomach."
Raynard Johnson (age 17)	Kokomo, Marion Co.	June 16, 2000	Found hanging from a pecan tree in the front yard of his home. Called a suicide by local and state authorities. He had dated two local white women. Two autopsies said he committed suicide. His parents, along with the Rev. Jesse Jackson, suspect foul play.

Name	Location	Date of Event	Background and Causes
			They say the boy showed no signs of despondency, met with a girlfriend hours before his body was found and looked forward to going to college.

SOURCES: *New York Times*, August 18, June 28, 2000, A-5; *Jackson Advocate*, July 6, 2000, 1, 8A; Evers, *For Us the Living*, 378; Thompson, *Black Life in Mississippi*, 71; Manning Marable, *Speaking Truth to Power: Essays on Race, Resistance, and Radicalism* (Boulder, Colo.: Westview Press, 1966), 29; *Columbia Missourian*, July 13, 2000, 7-A; *St. Louis Post-Dispatch*, July 13, 2000, 8-A; *USA Today*, June 30, 2000, 3-A.

murder rate. Only Louisiana (747), New York (2,397), California (3,921), and Texas (2,239) had higher rates.[53] And when general physical violence is added to this dimension, another kind of terror can greet a black community. One study notes this pattern in 1966:

> A mob of whites in Grenada, Mississippi, armed with axe handles, metal pipes and chains, attacks black students attempting to integrate two neighboring schools. The violence, which continues tomorrow, leads to accusations that local police officials allowed the beatings by refusing to intervene to protect the blacks. Tomorrow, news and cameramen in town to cover the unrest will also be attacked by local whites as they film the assaults. Grenada officials will be charged with willful neglect of their duty and 3 men will be arrested for conspiring against the civil rights of the blacks. On September 20, 300 local white citizens will publish a statement condemning mob violence.[54]

It is against this background that the issue and range of lynchings in Mississippi from 1966 to 2002 must be considered. Table 2 of the Epilogue notes that there are thirteen special cases of deaths in Mississippi which may be compared to the earlier definition and problem of lynching in the state. Table 3 below denotes that a concentration of eight late lynching events took place in Southern Mississippi in Adams, Forrest, Marion, and Pearl River counties, with one each in the Delta (Sunflower County) and Central Mississippi (Holmes County) regions. Twelve of the victims were black males, and one case was an unknown white male.[55] Black lynching victims were killed during this period for civil rights movement work and especially for voter education and registration efforts. Others were murdered, it seems, for dating or associating with white women. Still others appear to have been

TABLE E.3: DISTRIBUTION OF MISSISSIPPI LYNCHING VICTIMS, 1966–2002

County	Number of Victims	County	Number of Victims	County	Number of Victims
Adams	2	Pearl River	4	Unknown (White Male)	1
Forrest	1	Sunflower	1		
Holmes	1	Unknown (Black Male)	2		
Marion	1			TOTALS	13

the victims of hate crimes, committed by hate groups such as the Ku Klux Klan in Mississippi. These crimes have largely gone unsolved.[56]

In the 1980s and 1990s, Mississippians began to observe the mysterious deaths by hanging of many young men held in county jails or the state prison at Parchman,. Mississippi authorities generally attributed the deaths as suicides by the prisoners. However, black activists and journalists questioned this position. Table 4 denotes the range of this problem. Perhaps as many as 62 individuals have died under mysterious circumstances in Mississippi over the last twenty years, with a clear majority of these deaths having taken place in prison.[57] The cases seem to have taken place all over Mississippi. They also remain unsolved.

State executions, especially of black men, remain a special challenge facing blacks in Mississippi and other states. In 2000, Mississippi held 20,241 persons in prison. One study notes that "in the 25–29 age group, nearly 10 percent of black males are in prison."[58] Since 1930 Mississippi has executed 158 individuals, most of them African-Americans.[59] Thus the legal killing of blacks remains a black community concern in Mississippi. In fact, the high imprisonment rates and high executions of blacks served as a control device by whites to keep blacks in their places, and to further maintain the status-quo in Mississippi and other states.

Black Mississippians have remained steadfast in their attention to the economic, social and political issues which impact the community in Mississippi and the nation. They still live in one of the poorest states in the Union, and their life chances are still greatly impacted by the historical circumstances of their past in Mississippi. Yet because of the determination of blacks and their supporting allies across many decades, life has changed for the better, even in Mississippi. The intensive violence of the past is no longer a reality in spite of the continued brutal nature of many aspects of the criminal justice system in Mississippi. Journalist Paul Delaney notes this development:

> The South has made tremendous strides in race relations ... the fact that random lynchings of blacks have practically ceased qualifies as progress. Additionally, the South certainly has reached parity with the North and the rest of the country in race relations and treatment of its black citizens.... Indiscriminate violence by whites against blacks is no longer common in the South, although old fears and suspicions linger.... [Yet, although] the overt relations between the races have moderated in the South, there is still anger and hostility among blacks over their treatment by whites. While blacks are comforted by the changes that have taken place, there is wide belief that the root of the problem is the refusal of white Americans to acknowledge that we live in a racist society, and then do something about it.[60]

A summary of black anger, frustration, and inner-consciousness is reflected in the memories of black people in Mississippi and America. This is a central theme in the life-giving works of Mississippi's black musicians, writers, religious leaders, teachers, and activists. Blues artist B. B. King (1925–) is eloquent in his "memories" of a giant among black twentieth century Mississippi leaders, Medgar Evers. King writes in his autobiography:

> The men I respected most were doers, not talkers. My friend and fellow Mississippian Medgar Evers showed me more courage than a thousand pistol-wielding militants. I was closest to Medgar. He wasn't interested in proving his manhood. He recruited plantation workers into the NAACP. I knew these plantation owners lorded over their land like absolute dictators. They could do anything on their land that they wanted to; they could get away with murder. So to come on a plantation, to walk right into the lion's den and openly say, "Here I am, I'm an organizer. I'm here to change the way things have been

TABLE E.4: MYSTERIOUS DEATHS IN MISSISSIPPI, 1966–2002

Name	Location	Date of Event	Background and Causes
Unknown (12)	Mississippi	1981	"In May, 1981, the *Jackson Advocate* reported that in Mississippi alone there have been 12 murders 'in as many months which are suspected by blacks of being [racially motivated].'"
Lloyd Douglas Gray	Tallahatchie Co.	Jan. 11, 1981	A black male was "found hanging from a tree in Tallahatchie Co.," but the incident was ruled a suicide by coroner A. W. Hulett.
24 black men	Mississippi	1987–1993	"All had died by hanging while in police custody in various county jails." By 1994, it was reported that Mississippi had "more than 50 reported cases of jail hangings."
23 white men	Mississippi	1987–1993	These white prisoners were found hanged in Mississippi jails.
David Scott Campbell	Philadelphia, Neshoba Co.	Oct. 1990	Death in city jail by hanging called a suicide by local authorities. He had dated a white woman, Nikki Griffin. This case was called a lynching by the *Jackson Advocate*.
Cedric Walker	Sunflower Co.	Oct. 1992	Prisoner at Parchman State Prison, found "dead in his cell, a rope tied around his neck. Prison officials said he hung himself while sitting upright in his bed. His family believes he was murdered. Ruled a suicide.

Sources: Marable, *Speaking Truth to Power*, 29; *Jackson Advocate*, January 13, 1994, A-11, March 20, 1997, A-1, 4, 5-C; Alton Hornsby, Jr., and Deborah Gillen Straub, *African American Chronology, Vol. 2, 1973–1993* (New York: UXL/Gale Research, 1994), 343; James Johnson and Jamaine Dickens, "Mississippi Jail Hangings," *USA This Week* (March 1, 1994): 10.

done for hundreds of years" ... Man that took guts. I didn't have those kind of guts, but Medgar did. Medgar had more guts than anyone. Remember, he was doing this back in the fifties and early sixties. They called him an agitator, but I called him a hero. I worried for his safety. I feared for his life.

Medgar was assassinated in 1963 and Dr. King in 1968. Those murders crushed me. In memory of Medgar, I've gone to Indianola for the first week every June to plan a four-day music festival for free. Been doing it now for nearly thirty years. It helps heal some hurt. It helps to see thousands of little black and white kids playing together, to see the big crowds so happy to hear blues that feels good to everyone. I like when the children come running up and call me B. B. like they've known me forever. I like reminding them of the bravery of a man like Medgar.[61]

Others have explored the continuing impact of the lynching issue in Mississippi history. Two examples from the period are illustrative of this theme. Perhaps no lynching event has captured the historical memories of black people in Mississippi and perhaps the nation as did the death of Emmett Till in 1955. The importance of this case is suggested by Clenora Hudson-Weems and Cloyte Murdock Larsson, in their separate essays on the Till murder. Clenora Hudson-Weems believes that the Till case served as "the catalyst of the civil rights movement of the 1950s and 1960s."[62] Thus Emmett Till's life and death was a watershed event in African-American history. Cloyte Murdock Larsson re-visited the scene of the Till murder 30 years later in 1986. The Till case was one that she could "never forget no matter how hard one tries."[63] Poet Pauli Murray (1910–1985) reflected on the lynching of Mack C. Parker in 1959.[64]

Such expressions by black thinkers are a witness to the long-term impact of lynching and murder in Mississippi and the nation. This body of work also suggests that each generation of Mississippians and Americans must come to grips with the historical challenges of the past; for in order to understand the present and the possibilities of the future, it is necessary to understand, appreciate, and learn from the lessons of the past.[65]

The perspectives of white Mississippians on contemporary life and conditions in the state and nation are just as complex as are those of blacks. Yet many studies seem to indicate that white perceptions of change and progress for blacks is viewed in much greater degree than the views held by blacks themselves. Frederick M. Wirt points out that whites "see the racism and discrimination of the old South as bad and in need of overturning by the law. However, whites differ from blacks in their outlook because they believe that blacks have been granted too many civil rights and live now without much discrimination."[66] Yet behind white attitudes and some black progress lies the age-old issue of white supremacist groups such as the Ku Klux Klan in modern Mississippi and the South. Such groups remain in the background but are a reminder of the bad old days when segregation and the Jim Crow system were the powerful voices of control in the South. Such extremists remind more moderate citizens of the continued need for dialogue, tolerance, and good race relations efforts by all citizens in society. [67]

Historical memory remains a powerful source of strength and tension among many white Mississippians. No single issue in recent years has raised tempers as has the protest of blacks and liberals over the Confederate emblem that is a part of the state's flag. Matters came to a head in 2001 when the majority of citizens of the state voted on keeping or changing the state flag. David Firestone reported from Mississippi:

> Voters who favored the current design rejected the argument of many political and business leaders that it was retarding the state's economic progress, limiting outside investment and tourism by projecting a retrograde, backwater image. Many black lawmakers and community leaders have worked for decades to rid the state of a Civil War relic they consider to be a coded emblem of support for racism.[68]

The state flag issue demonstrates the range of tensions still evident in the state's population and indicates that more work must be performed in helping to create a more tolerant attitude among Mississippians for all of the people in the state.

Opposite the flag issue, the state has made progress in the struggle over the Sovereignty Commission papers. A report notes:

> Most of the records of the Mississippi State Sovereignty Commission were opened today in accordance with an order issued by U.S. District Court Judge William H. Barbour, Jr., on January13, 1998. Approximately 6% of the Sovereignty Commission records are still the subject of litigation and remain sealed.
>
> The Sovereignty Commission existed from March 29, 1956 until March 4, 1977, and the records contain information that the agency gathered, maintained and distributed about

the activities of certain people who may have been involved either directly or indirectly in the civil rights movement and related activities in Mississippi. In 1977, the Mississippi Legislature voted to disband the Commission, seal the records until the Year 2027, and deposit them at the Mississippi Department of Archives and History. On March 4, 1977, the Secretary of State transferred six filing cabinets and assorted boxes and folders of records to the Department. The records were sealed and placed in the vault where they remained during more than two decades of legal proceedings over their fate.[69]

The struggle and outcome over the Sovereignty Commission papers at least suggest that the state is being forced to deal with an unpleasant aspect of its history, when the rights of American citizens were violated in the name of the state of Mississippi to protect the Jim Crow system.

Mississippi remains a major concern of the national civil rights movement organizations and currently the NAACP, the National Urban League, the SCLC and the CORE are represented by branches in the state. For several generations the black struggle in Mississippi has been viewed as a national issue for blacks, and, given the extreme condition of blacks in Mississippi and their status as being on the front lines for black liberation and freedom in America, national groups have sought to aid and encourage black struggle in Mississippi.[70]

A leader in this effort has been the NAACP, which experienced an economic crisis in the mid–1990s. But under the leadership of President Kwisi Mfume and Chairman Julian Bond, the group regained its earlier strength and is active today. "With 2,200 chapters in 50 states and 4 foreign countries, [the NAACP] supports programs ranging from armed services and veteran affairs to education, health and labor, designed to protect and promote the rights of people of color. The Association has more than 500 thousand members nationwide."[71] The association has been outspoken on the issue of violence in America, and in recent decades has called for a death penalty moratorium in this country, especially since African-Americans are over-represented in the number of Americans who receive the death penalty in this nation's courts of justice.[72]

Black Mississippians have also been influenced by a number of national events from the 1980s and 1990s, including the following:

1. In 1986 the first national Martin Luther King, Jr., holiday is celebrated on January 20.
2. In 1988, Reverend Jesse Jackson receives 1,218 delegate votes at the Democratic National Convention.
3. In 1989, General Colin Powell is named chairman of the Joint Chiefs of Staff.
4. In 1989, L. Douglas Wilder becomes the first African-American governor of Virginia.
5. In 1992, Carol Moseley Braun becomes the first African-American woman elected to the United States Senate.
6. In 1993, Toni Morrison becomes the first African-American woman to win the Nobel Prize for Literature.
7. In 1995, the Million Man March goes to Washington, D.C., and African-American men re-dedicate themselves to both personal responsibility and rebuilding of their communities.[73]

These national events serve to remind the black community of the rich legacy and impact of the civil rights movement and the complex changes that this movement, with key support from black Mississippians, helped to bring about in the United States and helped to influence in other countries.[74]

Another major influence on black consciousness in Mississippi and the nation has come in recent decades from the collective works, thinking and influence of black intellectuals, writers, and activists. Perhaps no one in this group expresses the black memory as well as does Vernon E. Jordan, Jr., former director of the National Urban League and a major player in the civil rights movement and American politics. He notes the importance of Mississippi in black historical thinking and the key role of Medgar Evers in promoting black freedom. He writes:

> Mississippi occupied a place all its own in the modern civil rights struggle—as it has in the black consciousness from slavery until modern times. No place was harder or meaner. But because he was my friend and colleague, no death in that violent decade wounded me more deeply than Medgar's. For any black person in the South, and certainly any black man, danger was a constant companion—the threat of violence lurked behind even the most innocuous circumstances. Medgar's activities were the very opposite of innocuous to the white supremacists who ran his home state, and there he was—out in the open, exposed. He was, I believe, the most courageous man in the movement because he dared to stand tall in Mississippi.[75]

Other black intellectuals have focused on an international agenda for black Americans. Kwame Ture [Stokely Carmichael] (1941–1998), a leading Pan-Africanist, "became a globe-trotting exponent of the Al African Peoples Revolutionary Party, returning to American campuses to recruit. He maintained that continued progress for black Americans would be made only through 'mass political organization on a Pan-African scale.'"[76]

Black artists such as writer and director John Singleton (1968–) have used film to capture the black experience. In 1997 his film *Rosewood*, about the white destruction of a black Florida community in January 1928 appeared. This film places the burdens of lynching and anti-black violence in historical perspective.[77]

Many black intellectuals have fought hard in recent decades to challenge and protest continued American racism, especially as this problem has impacted on blacks and other people of color. Activists and scholars in this regard have included Frances I. Cress Welsing (1935–), Cornel West (1953–), Molefi K. Asante (1942–), Angela Davis (1944–), Rev. Jesse Jackson (1941–), and, from American prisons, certainly among many, stands Mumia Abu-Jamal (1954–).[78] These are only a few of black America's national voices who have spoken and written on all aspects of the black experience, from Mississippi and across the nation. They continue to make a difference in the national debate on racism and discrimination in American life.

The voices of younger blacks in Mississippi and other states have been especially influenced in recent decades by the range of issues raised by the artistic movement known as hip hop culture, or rap. According to writer Bakari Kitwana (1966–): "Hip Hop has staged a coup on American popular entertainment, [to] bring back youth culture into the national spotlight.... Young blacks born between 1965 and 1984 are the first African Americans to have grown up in post-segregation America. Their historical significance is tremendous.... [Yet they live in a society where] the integration their parents fought for has not been fully achieved. Although many blacks are doing better than ever, even more experience everyday America's unfulfilled promise of inclusion."[79] The question for this generation is—how will they use hip hop culture to advance the political, social, and economic interests and concerns of African-Americans in a new century?

A black American health issue of major prominence since the 1980s has been the AIDS crisis, which continues to impact large numbers of black men and women in the United States, but especially on the continent of Africa and in the Caribbean. In addition to medical personnel and activists who have fought to bring public attention and funds to this issue, black personalities such as Maya Angelou (1928–) and Coretta Scott King (1927–2006) have been significant voices in raising public consciousness on this health concern.[80]

Nationally the United States has had a series of mostly conservative Republican presidents from 1966 to 2002. This conservative list includes Richard M. Nixon (1913–1994), in office 1969–1974; Gerald R. Ford (1913–), in office after Nixon was forced to resign, 1974–1977; Ronald Reagan (1911–2004), chief executive 1981–1989; George Bush (1924–), in office 1989–1993; and George W. Bush (1946–), elected in 2000. The Democratic presidents during this era were L. B. Johnson (1908–1973), 1963–1969; Jimmy Carter (1924–), 1977–1981; and Bill Clinton (1946–), 1993–2001. The range of public policy issues from such a diverse group of politicians has been a mixed blessing for blacks in Mississippi and the nation. The most popular president for blacks in the last quarter century has been Bill Clinton. In 2001 he had a 93 percent approval rating by blacks, but only 6 percent among whites.[81]

Mississippi has had a tremendous impact upon contemporary life in the United States. The state ranks as one of the major agricultural areas of the nation and its literary contributions in music, literature and the fine arts are second to none. Yet the state's history has suffered a great burden due to the issue of violence among its citizens and the terror of lynching in its historic past. Indeed, Mississippi leads the nation in total lynchings.[82] Scholar Neil R. McMillen notes the significance of this factor when he writes that Mississippi ranked first in virtually every category—the most total lynchings, the most multiple lynchings, the most per capita, the most female victims, the most victims taken from police custody, the most lynchings without arrest or conviction of mob leaders, the most public support of vigilantism.[83] Thus Mississippi has served as an example of what a society has to overcome to increase justice, equality and opportunity for all of its citizens. The question remains—can this goal be achieved or at least attempted in Mississippi? If so, then perhaps it may also be possible on the national level. This possibility suggests the power of hope and faith in society's future in spite of continued issues in Mississippi and the nation, such as hate crimes, racism, violence among youth, overbearing prison conditions, and rampage attacks by killers on individuals and groups of people.[84]

In trying to understand the extremists in Mississippi—lynchers and segregationists, among others—we gain a greater awareness of discrimination against others in society, including religious bias against Jews or Muslims, sexual orientation crimes (especially against gay people), or the targeting of individuals or groups because of their ethnicity and national origin. Such issues of violence are daily reminders of this critical issue in American history.[85]

In the over 500-plus lynching cases in Mississippi between the Reconstruction era and modern Mississippi history stands the stark reality that it sometimes takes generations for people to express their grief about the past and then to overcome that experience and move on with their lives and the new challenges that face them in another time and place. The 1964 lynching of James Chaney, Mickey Schwerner and Andrew Goodman serves to indicate the collective grief of the history of lynching in Mississippi. Curt Gentry says of the lynchers behind this case: "Nineteen men were indicted, eight convicted, for conspiring to violate the civil rights of the three young men by kidnapping and shooting them. Everyone charged [belonged] to the KKK, including the informant, a law officer who had worked with the FBI on the case—and [had] known all along that the bodies had been dumped into a thirty-foot deep hole at a dam construction site and buried under hundreds of tons of dirt by a bulldozer."[87] Such events live long in the minds of some citizens. They should suggest to all of us, however, that such major crimes affect the masses of society in a very negative way—and society has to answer at some point for the evils committed, often in the name of the state, against some of society's reformers.

On the other hand, the challenges presented by historical memories offers Mississippians and all Americans an opportunity to seriously reflect upon our historical past as an ever increasing feature in our human consciousness, growth as individuals, citizens of the United States, and members of the world community. To aid this development, Americans have increased the number of museums that reflect on and teach about the black past in Mississippi and other states. Black Mississippians have at least ten museums that seek to preserve the African-American past in the state.[87] This development has also included an effort by official Mississippi to recognize the importance of the state's segregationist history. According to David R. Goldfield:

> Since 1985, the Mississippi state Historical Museum in Jackson has featured a permanent exhibit, "The Struggle for Equal Rights," the first such permanent display in the nation. It includes a fourteen-minute videotape of police dragging and clubbing demonstrations, and of white mobs taunting sit-in protestors in Jackson. Also included are the complicated voter-registration forms white registrars used for black applicants, posters advertising black protest meetings and Klan rallies, and a glass door panel from a Hattiesburg business on which "White Waiting Room" was neatly lettered, as well as a metal sign from a physician's office in Greenville designating the "Colored Entrance." Just a short time ago, these items were scarcely museum pieces—they represented an active way of life in Mississippi. The exhibit concludes with a quote from James Meredith: "I can love Mississippi because of the beauty of the countryside and the old traditions of family affection, and for such small things as flowers bursting in spring.... Why should a Negro be forced to leave such things? Because of fear? No. Not anymore."[88]

As Howell Raines has observed, "Portraits of Southern Lives Reveal a Record of Pain and Progress."[89] But remembering the past is a very important theme in human history.[90] Certainly the Emmett Till case of 1955 is still a shock to many, including his mother, Mrs. Mamie Mobley, who "still thinks about how her son was killed [47] years ago."[91] In 1991, Chicago renamed 71st Street in Till's honor. His mother told the public: "His untimely death was the call for freedom that was heard around the world. Emmett Till Road will be a symbol of hope and inspiration to the young and old that this world can be a better place if we try."[92]

Medgar Evers has also not been forgotten: "Jackson, Mississippi, holds an annual Medgar Evers Homecoming weekend, which in 1983 featured old adversary Ross Barnett participating in renaming a Jackson street in Evers' honor."[93] Even Mississippi's courts have answered the call for justice: "Sam Bowers, the Imperial Wizard of the Mississippi White Knights, recently convicted of ordering the death in 1966 of civil rights leader Vernon Dahmer, is said to have assured a fellow Klansman: 'No jury in the state of Mississippi is going to convict a white man for killing a black person.'"[94] In this case justice came late but won the day.

The need for reflecting on a collective memory of lynching and the traumatic experiences witnessed from this history was revealed in 2000 with a New York Historical Society photographic exhibit of American lynchings. The *New York Times* reported: "The victims are mainly black, mainly Southern. Some of the photographs are postcards and some are souvenirs that were printed by the dozens and hundreds by commercial photographers who had been at the scene. This exhibition, a chronicle of lynchings in this country between 1890 and 1930, is called 'Without Sanctuary: Lynching Photography in America.'"[95] In 2000, a book with the same title appeared and helped to bring more public attention to this historical problem.[96]

The problem of lynching in Mississippi and the nation remains an issue for this gen-

eration and for new generations to come. Each generation must seek to understand the political, economic, and social implications of this issue, and its impact on modern society—not
an easy challenge. This challenge comes at a time when David G. Myers suggests that we
face "the American paradox: spiritual hunger in an age of plenty."[97] Americans in the 21st
century must overcome the burdens of racism, discrimination against vast sections of our
population, a greater willingness to share our resources with others at home and abroad,
and a conscious decision to increase peaceful change in our own land and others'. Then
American spiritual life will catch up with our material existence. Like people in Mississippi,
Americans must overcome the victimization of blacks and Native Americans—the two groups
who have suffered most in American history. Our scholars must also make an extra effort
to explore all aspects of American history, including the various dimensions of lynching in
this country. Joel R. Williamson made this point very well in a recent essay:

> Professor [C. Vann] Woodward in *The Strange Career of Jim Crow* acknowledged that lynch-
> ing existed and let it go. Understandably. It hardly fit into a plea that southern tradition,
> truly understood, urged racial moderation. But further, none of his several dozen doctoral
> students wrote a book about lynching. Neither, for that matter, did one of my own two
> dozen students nor had anyone else even begun such a study before recent times. It is a
> remarkable, striking omission in the historiography. But it is a gruesome subject, awesome
> in emotional power, difficult to deal with within the accepted canons of the historian's
> profession. It is, at one level, a sort of American Auschwitz. Describing the behavior is
> lard labor; explaining it is virtually impossible.
>
> And yet this is the most striking behavior in race relations in the South in the turn-of-
> the-century years, the era with which *The Strange Career of Jim Crow* centrally deals.... One
> can no longer tell the story of race relations in the South without including lynching.[98]

The Age of Lynching in Mississippi and the nation also suggests that American society must consider addressing the historical problem of slavery and lynching—with reparations for blacks and other groups which have suffered the consequences of this tragic
situation in the American past. Such restitution may help to solve the extreme dimensions
of the racial situation in this country. A number of black spokespersons have spoken on
this issue. A major voice in this effort has been Randall Robinson (1946–), who recently
noted that:

> On January 5, 1993, Congressman John Conyers, a black Democrat from Detroit, intro-
> duced in Congress a bill to "acknowledge the fundamental injustice, cruelty, brutality, and
> inhumanity of slavery in the United States and the 13 American colonies between 1619 and
> 1865 and to establish a commission to examine the institution of slavery, subsequent de
> jure and de facto racial and economic discrimination against African Americans, and the
> impact of these forces on living African Americans, to make recommendations to Congress
> on appropriate remedies, and for other purposes."
>
> The bill, which did not ask for reparations for the descendants of slaves but merely a
> commission to study the effects of slavery, won from the 435-member U.S. House of Repre-
> sentatives only 28 cosponsors, 18 of whom were black.[99]

Such efforts continue to indicate the national interests of African-Americans in justice and
reconciliation—if only others will hear them.[100]

Yet much work remains to be undertaken in all aspects of the lynching phenomenon
in Mississippi and the nation. Black and white grief over violence and that of other groups
remains an issue in society, for an epitaph for the Age of Lynching has not yet been written. Neither have the needs of the lynching victims and their descendants been properly
recognized.[101] Indeed, we live at a time, as Bob Blauner reminds us in the title of his book,

that its *Still the Big News: Racial Oppression in America.*"[102] Lynching is certainly a part of this historical issue, and so is "white privilege," and continued black inequality.[103] The Age of Lynching in Mississippi, from 1865 to modern times, was a period of terror in our history. The lessons of that historical era still serve to guide human beings in the never-ending search for human freedom, equality and dignity in our own times, and for future generations as yet unborn.

Lord, I Can't Stay Here By Myself
—Traditional African-American Spiritual

Lord, I can't stay here by myself, by
Myself.

My mother has gone and left me here,
My father has gone and left me here,
I'm going to weep like a willow
And mourn like a dove,
O Lord, I cannot stay here by myself.

Yes, I am poor little motherless child,
Yes, I am a poor little child of God
In this world alone,
O Lord, I cannot stay here by myself.

I got my ticket at the low depot,
Low depot.
Yes, I got my ticket at the low depot,
Low depot.
Yes, I got my ticket at the low depot,
O Lord, I cannot stay here by myself.

Appendix: Chronology of Lynching in Mississippi, 1865–1965

1865
Emancipation year for African Americans in the United states.

1865–1866
The Black Codes are enacted in Mississippi and the South.

William L. Sharkey is governor of Mississippi in 1865.

What may have been Mississippi's first lynching takes place in Oktibbeha County, in Northeast Mississippi, in 1865.

1865–1869
Many blacks and a smaller number of white men are lynched throughout Mississippi.

1865–1868
Benjamin G. Humphreys serves as governor of Mississippi.

1868–1870
Adelbert Ames is governor of Mississippi.

1870
Hiram R. Revels, Blanche K. Bruce and John Roy Lynch emerge as three of the most important national black leaders in the United States during the Reconstruction period.

The Black population of Mississippi is 444,201; the white population is 382,896.

1870–1871
Hiram R. Revels is the first African-American to serve in the U.S. Senate; he is elected from Mississippi.

1870–1871
James L. Alcorn, governor of Mississippi.

1871–1874
Ridgley C. Powers, governor of Mississippi.

1874–1876
Adelbert Ames, governor of Mississippi.

1876–1882
James M. Stone, governor of Mississippi.

1879–1880
At least 10,000 blacks migrate from Mississippi and Louisiana to Kansas.

1870–1879
At least 769 persons are lynched in Mississippi during the 1870s.

1880
Blacks compose 650,291 of Mississippi's population; whites number 479,398.

During this year Mississippi's per capita income is $82.

1882–1890
Robert Lowry, governor of Mississippi.

1882–1889
277 Mississippians are lynched during these years (257 blacks and 20 whites).

The national figures for lynching victims stand at 534 black cases, and 669 whites.

1890
94.6 percent of Mississippi's citizens live in rural areas.

1890–1896
John M. Stone, governor of Mississippi.

1890s
Mississippi is a leader in the efforts of the South to enforce the Jim Crow system on the region.

1892
The first black-owned bank, the Lincoln Savings Bank, opens in Vicksburg, Mississippi, headed by Robert W. Ware and Henry C. Wallace.

1896–1900
Anselm J. McLaurin, governor of Mississippi.

1890–1899
There are 1,709 lynchings in the United States, including 1,175 blacks, 517 whites, and 17 Mexican-Americans and Native Americans.
Mississippi has at least 195 lynching victims in the 1890s.
Ida B. Wells-Barnett advocates a strong campaign against American lynching.

1900
The black population of Mississippi stands at 910,070; whites compose 641,200 of the state's population.
During this year 92.3 percent of the state's residents live in rural areas.
Mississippi has only 3,300 black voters by this late date.

1900–1909
There are 904 lynching victims nationwide during this decade; of which 797 are blacks, and 107 are white.
In Mississippi, 152 people are lynched during this period, including 141 blacks and 11 whites.

1900–1904
Andrew H. Longino, governor of Mississippi.

1904–1908
James Kimble Vardaman, governor of Mississippi.

1908–1912
Edward Favor Noel, governor of Mississippi.

1909
The NAACP is formed in New York City, and begins an active program to end United States lynchings.

1910
Black Mississippians compose 56.2 percent of the state's population.

1910–1920
130,000 blacks leave the state of Mississippi.

1912–1916
Earl Leroy Brewer, governor of Mississippi.

1913
There are 1,708 blacks in Mississippi's prison system, and only 156 whites.

1916–1920
Theodore Gilmore Bilbo, governor of Mississippi.

1910–1919
681 Americans are lynched during this decade, including 563 blacks, 53 whites, and 65 unknown by race.
In Mississippi, 107 people are lynched.

1882–1919
Over 3,200 Americans are lynched in the United States.

1919
"Red Summer" and 78 blacks are lynched in the United States.

1920
Mississippi has a total population of 1,790,618; of this number 56 percent are black.

1920–1929
There are at least 315 lynching victims in the United States.
Mississippi records 66 lynching victims during the 1920s, with 64 African-Americans and two whites.

1920–1924
Lee Maurice Russell, governor of Mississippi.

1921–1922, 1929
The Dyer Anti-Lynching Bill goes down in defeat in Congress.

1924–1927

Henry Lewis Whitfield, governor of Mississippi.

1925

There are estimated to be at least 93,000 Ku Klux Klansmen in Mississippi.

1927–1928

Dennis Murphree, governor of Mississippi.

1928–1932

Theodore Gilmore Bilbo, governor of Mississippi.

1927

Mississippi experiences a tremendous flooding of the Mississippi River.

1930

The total population of Mississippi is 2,183,796; 1,106,327 whites and 1,077,469 blacks.

1930–1939

There are 130 lynchings in the United States during this decade.

Fifty lynchings are reported for Mississippi in the 1930s; 48 are black and 2 are white.

1932–1936

Martin Sennett Conner, governor of Mississippi.

1936–1940

Hugh L. White, governor of Mississippi.

1910–1934

W. E. B. Du Bois serves as editor of the *Crisis*, the official organ of the NAACP, which places a major interest on the lynching problem in the United States.

1935

White Mississippi women are active in the state's branches of the Association of Southern Women for the Prevention of Lynching (created in 1930).

1940–1950

326,000 blacks migrate from Mississippi to other states.

1940

Only 55 black physicians (50 men and 5 women) practice medicine in Mississippi.

1940–1949

There are 33 lynching victims nationwide for the decade.

In Mississippi, 15 blacks are lynched for the decade.

1940s

The Age of Richard Wright in African-American literature.

1940–1943

Paul B. Johnson, governor of Mississippi.

1943–1944

Dennis Murphree, governor of Mississippi.

1944–1946

Thomas L. Bailey, governor of Mississippi.

1946–1952

Fielding L. Wright, governor of Mississippi.

1947

Senator Theodore Gilmore Bilbo dies due to "cancer of the mouth."

1950

The black population of Mississippi is 986,707, compared to 1,188,429 whites in the state.

1950–1959

There are at least seven lynchings in the United States; six of these are listed for Mississippi.

1951

Willie McGee (1923–1951) is lynched at Laurel, Mississippi.

1952–1956

Hugh L. White, governor of Mississippi.

1956–1960

James P. Coleman, governor of Mississippi.

1955

Major Mississippi lynchings take place during this year: Rev. George W. Lee at Belzoni; Lamar Smith at Brookhaven; and Emmett Louis Till at Money, Mississippi. The Till case is considered by scholars as a catalyst for the Civil Rights Movement.

1959

Mack Charles Parker is lynched at Popularville, Mississippi.

1960

The black population of Mississippi is
  920,595. By 1970, this would be reduced
  to 815,770.

1960–1965

The Big Five Civil Rights Movement
  organizations (NAACP, SNCC, CORE,
  the National Urban League, and SCLC)
  lead the Freedom Struggle in Mississippi.

1961

Herbert Lee is lynched at Liberty, Missouri.

1962

James Meredith attends the University of
  Mississippi.

1960–1964

Ross R. Barnett, governor of Mississippi.

1963

Medgar Evers is killed at Jackson, Mississippi.

1964–1968

Paul B. Johnson, governor of Mississippi.

1964

Freedom Summer in Mississippi is a major
  event in the history of the movement.
The Mississippi Freedom Democratic Party
  seeks to be seated at the 1964 Democratic
  National Convention at Atlanta City, New
  Jersey.

1960–1965

Only one lynching (in 1961) is noted in the
  nation for this period.
In Mississippi, 15 lynching cases are noted, 12
  black males and 3 white males.

1964

Nina Simone records "Mississippi Goddam," a
  key song of the movement.

1964

James Chaney (1943–1964), Andrew Goodman
  (1943–1964), and Michael Schwerner
  (1939–1964), are lynched near Philadelphia,
  Mississippi.

1965

Malcolm X (1925–1965) is assassinated in New
  York City.

Chapter Notes

Chapter 1

1. U.S. Census, 1860; Jesse O. McKee, ed., *Mississippi: A Portrait of an American State* (Montgomery, Ala.: Clairmont Press, 1995), 270.

2. U.S. Census, 1860.

3. John Blassingame, *The Slave Community: Plantation Life in the Antebellum South* (New York: Oxford University Press, 1979); Noralee Frankel, *Freedom's Women: Black Women and Families in Civil War Era Mississippi* (Bloomington: Indiana University Press, 1999), 112–117.

4. David G. Sansing, *Mississippi: Its People and Culture* (Minneapolis: T. S. Denison and Co., 1981), 190, 194.

5. James W. Loewen and Charles Sallis, eds., *Mississippi: Conflict and Change* (New York: Pantheon Books, 1974), 146; Vernon Lane Wharton, *The Negro in Mississippi, 1865–1890* (New York: Harper & Row, Publishers, 1965), 80–96.

6. Eric Foner, *Reconstruction: America's Unfinished Revolution, 1865–1877* (New York: Harper & Row, Publishers, 1998), 77–123.

7. Loewen and Sallis, *Mississippi: Conflict and Change*, 155; Allen W. Trelease, *White Terror: The Ku Klux Klan, Conspiracy and Southern Reconstruction* (Westport, Conn.: Greenwood Press, 1971), 88, 274–78, 287.

8. David M. Chalmers, *Hooded Americanism: The History of the Ku Klux Klan* (Chicago: Quadrangle Books, 1965), 10, 15–16, 66–69.

9. Julius E. Thompson, *The Black Press in Mississippi* (Gainesville: University Press of Florida, 1993), 3.

10. Eric Foner, *Freedom's Lawmakers: A Directory of Black Office Holders During Reconstruction* (New York: Oxford University Press, 1993), xiv.

11. Julius E. Thompson, *Black Life in Mississippi: Essays on Political, Social and Cultural Studies in a Deep South State* (Lanham, Md.: University Press of America, 2001), xxii.

12. Larry J. Griffin, "Why Was the South a Problem to America?" in Larry J. Griffin and Don H. Doyle, eds., *The South as an American Problem* (Athens: The University of Georgia Press, 1995), 118–119. Mississippi also refused to ratify the Thirteenth Amendment to the U. S. Constitution. See Eric L. McKitrick, *Andrew Johnson and Reconstruction* (Chicago: The University of Chicago Press, 1960), 169.

13. Loewen and Sallis, *Mississippi: Conflict and Change*, 146. Also see Robert W. Johannsen, ed., "The Mississippi Black Code: Governor Humphrey's Message, 1865." *Reconstruction, 1865–1877* (New York: The Free Press, 1970),

39–42; Francis Butler Simkins, *A History of the South* (New York: Alfred A. Knopf, 1961), 267.

14. Trelease, *White Terror*, xxii; William Peirce Randell, *The Ku Klux Klan: A Century of Infamy* (Philadelphia: Chilton Books, 1965), 101–102.

15. Darryl Paulson, "Lynching," in *Ready Reference, American Justice*, Volume II (Pasadena, Calif: Salem Press, 1996), 478.

16. *Ibid.*, 479.

17. *Ibid.*, 479; Wilma Mankiller, ed., *The Reader's Companion to U. S. Women's History* (Boston: Houghton Mifflin Co., 1998), 350–52; and *Encyclopedia International*, Volume 11 (New York: Grolier, 1971), 151.

18. Terence Finnegan, "Lynching and Political Power in Mississippi and South Carolina," in W. F. Brundage, ed., *Under Sentence of Death: Lynching in the South* (Chapel Hill: The University of North Carolina Press, 1997), 191–192.

19. W. Fitzhugh Brundage, "Lynching," in Ronald Gottesman and Richard Maxwell Brown, eds., *Violence in America: An Encyclopedia*, Volume 2 (New York: Charles Scribner's Sons, 1999), 301.

20. David M. Oshinsky, *"Worse Than Slavery": Parchman Farm and the Ordeal of Jim Crow Justice* (New York: The Free Press, 1996), 100–104; Trelease, *White Terror*, xvii, xliii, 88.

21. James W. Silver, *Mississippi: The Closed Society* (New York: Harcourt, Brace & World, 1963), 15, 85–86, 90; Herbert Shapiro, *White Violence and Black Response: From Reconstruction to Montgomery* (Amherst: The University of Massachusetts Press, 1988), 223–24, 253–54; Robert Fulton Holtzclaw, *Black Magnolias: A Brief History of the Afro-Mississippian, 1865–1980* (Shaker Heights, Ohio: The Keeble Press, 1984), 2; McKee, *Mississippi: A Portrait of an American State*, 111–114; Simkins, *A History of the South*, 388; Gayle Graham Yates, *Mississippi Mind: A Personal Cultural History of an American State* (Knoxville: The University of Tennessee Press, 1990), 56.

22. Neil R. McMillen, *Dark Journey: Black Mississippians in the Age of Jim Crow* (Urbana: University of Illinois Press, 1989), 228.

23. Wharton, *The Negro in Mississippi*, 224–225; McMillen, *Dark Journey*, 228; James W. Garner, *Reconstruction in Mississippi* (New York: The Macmillan Co., 1901; Reprinted, Gloucester, Mass.: Peter Smith, 1964), 339–340; Loewen and Sallis, *Mississippi: Conflict and Change*, 155, 162; Shapiro, *White Violence and Black Response*, 10; Oshinsky, *"Worse Than Slavery": Parchman Farm and the Ordeal of Jim Crow Justice*, 25–27; Philip Dray, *At the Hands of Persons Unknown: The*

Lynching of Black America (New York: Random House, 2002), 49.

24. Wharton, *The Negro in Mississippi*, 224–225.

25. McMillen, *Dark Journey*, 228.

26. Silver, *Mississippi: The Closed Society*, vii–xxix.

27. William J. Cooper, Jr. and Thomas E. Terrill, *The American South, A History*, Volume II (New York: The McGraw-Hill Co., 1996), 525.

28. McKee, *Mississippi: A Portrait of an American State*, 128.

Chapter 2

1. Buford Satcher, *Blacks in Mississippi Politics, 1865–1900* (Washington, D.C.: University Press of America, 1978), 209.

2. William C. Harris, "James Lynch: Black Leader in Southern Reconstruction," *The Historian* 34, No. 1 (November, 1971): 40–61.

3. Vernon Lane Wharton, *The Negro in Mississippi, 1865–1890* (New York: Harper & Row, Publishers, 1965), 163; Arnold H. Taylor, *Travail and Triumph, Black Life and Culture in the South Since the Civil War* (Westport, Conn.: Greenwood Press, 1976), 9, 13.

4. David G. Sansing, "Mississippi," in: *Dictionary of American History*, Vol. IV (New York: Charles Scribner's Sons, 1976), 369.

5. Esmond Wright, *The American Dream: From Reconstruction to Reagan* (Cambridge, Mass.: Blackwell, 1996), 50.

6. Noralee Frankel, *Freedom's Women: Black Women and Families in Civil War Era Mississippi* (Bloomington: Indiana University Press, 1999), 84–86, 170–173; Edward L. Ayers, *The Promise of the New South: Life After Reconstruction* (New York: Oxford University Press, 1992), 160–164.

7. Cleopatra D. Thompson, *The History of the Mississippi Teachers Association* (Washington, D.C.: NBA Teachers Rights and Mississippi Teachers Association, 1973), 164; Melerson Guy Dunham, *Centennial History of Alcorn A. & M. College* (Hattiesburg: University and College Press of Mississippi, 1971), 14–15; "The Size and Composition of Alcorn A. & M. College Alumni, 1871–1930," in Julius E. Thompson, *Black Life in Mississippi: Essays on Political, Social and Cultural Studies in a Deep South State* (Lanham, Md.: University Press of America, 2001), 75–89. On the importance of black schools, also see the work of Sarah Dickey and her school, the Mount Hermon Seminary, created in 1875 to educate young black women. Eleanor Flexnor, *Century of Struggle: The Woman's Right Movement in the United States* (Cambridge, Mass.: The Belknap Press of Harvard University Press, 1975), 130; James M. McPherson, "First Black Power Bid in U.S. Education," *University: A Princeton Quarterly*, No. 45 (Summer 1970): 3–6, 31–34.

8. Frank J. Scaturro, *The Supreme Court's Retreat from Reconstruction: A Distortion of Constitutional Jurisprudence* (Westport, Conn.: Greenwood Press, 2000), 12; James W. Loewen and Charles Sallis, eds., *Mississippi: Conflict and Change* (New York: Pantheon Books, 1974), 202; Eric Foner, *Freedom's Lawmakers: A Directory of Black Office Holders During Reconstruction* (New York: Oxford University Press, 1993), 29–30, 180–181.

9. Loewen and Sallis, *Mississippi: Conflict and Change* (New York: Pantheon Books, 1974), 202; Eric Foner, *Freedom's Lawmakers: A Directory of Black Officeholders During Reconstruction* (New York: Oxford University Press, 1993), 97, 146, 192, 225–226, 235; I.C. Mollison, "Negro Lawyers in Mississippi," *The Journal of Negro History* 15, No. 1 (January, 1930): 40.

10. Loren Schweninger, "Black Owned Businesses in the South, 1790–1880," in Donald G. Nieman, ed., *African Americans and Non-Agricultural Labor in the South, 1865–1990*, Vol. 4 (New York: Garland Publishing, 1994), 50–51.

11. Mauris Lee Porter Emeka, *Black Banks, Past and Present* (Kansas City, Mo.: Mauris L. P. Emeka, 1971), 81.

12. Kevern J. Verney, "Trespassers in the Land of Their Birth: Blacks and Landownership in South Carolina and Mississippi During the Civil War and Reconstruction, 1861–1877," in Donald G. Nieman, ed., *From Slavery to Sharecropping: White and Black Labor in the Rural South, 1865–1900* (New York: Garland Publishing, 1994), 74.

13. James T. Currie, "From Slavery to Freedom in Mississippi's Legal System," *The Journal of Negro History* 65, No. 2 (Spring 1980): 12.

14. W. Marvin Dulaney, *Black Police in America* (Bloomington: Indiana University Press, 1996), 13.

15. Christopher R. Adamson, "Punishment After Slavery: Southern State Penal Systems, 1865–1890," *Social Problems* 30, No. 5 (June 1983): 561.

16. Philip A. Klinkner and Rogers M. Smith, *The Unsteady March: The Rise and Decline of Racial Equality in America* (Chicago: The University of Chicago Press, 1999), 91.

17. Wharton, *The Negro in Mississippi*, 237; Adamson, "Punishment After Slavery," 562.

18. Adamson, "Punishment After Slavery," 562.

19. *Ibid.*, 565.

20. Celeste Michelle Condit and John Louis Lucaites, *Crafting Equality: America's Anglo-African World* (Chicago: University of Chicago Press, 1993), 10.

21. Stetson Kennedy, *After Appomattox: How the South Won the War* (Gainesville: University Press of Florida, 1995), 257. Also see Hans L. Trefousse, *The Radical Republicans: Lincoln's Vanguard For Racial Justice* (New York: Alfred A. Knopf, 1969), 432–435; William B. Hesseltine, "Reconstruction: Changing Revolutionary Tactics," in Allen F. Davis and Harold D. Woodman, eds., Conflict and Consensus in Modern American History (Lexington, Mass.: D.C. Heath & Co., 1980), 12–13.

22. Kennedy, *After Appomattox: How the South Won the War*, 239.

23. *Ibid.*, 242–43.

24. Dickson A. Mungazi, *The Journey to the Promised Land: The African American Struggle for Development Since the Civil War* (Westport, Conn.: Praeger, 2001), 47; Alexander Keyssar, *The Right to Vote: The Contested History of Democracy in the United States* (New York: Basic Books/Perseus Books Group, 2000), 105–107.

25. John Charles Willis, "On the New South Frontier: Life in the Yazoo-Mississippi Delta, 1865–1920" (Ph.D. diss., University of Virginia, 1991), 248–49.

26. Allen D. Grimshaw, "Lawlessness and Violence in America and Their Special Manifestations in Changing Negro-White Relationships," *The Journal of Negro History* 44, No. 1 (January 1959): 62.

27. Henry Lee Swint, *The Northern Teacher in the South, 1862–1870* (New York: Octagon Books, 1967), 122–131.

28. William C. Harris, *The Day of the Carpetbagger: Republican Reconstruction in Mississippi* (Baton Rouge: Louisiana State University Press, 1979), 606–607.

29. William Cohen, *At Freedom's Edge: Black Mobility and the Southern White Quest for Racial Control 1861–1915* (Baton Rouge: Louisiana State University Press, 1991), 301–302; James B. Runnion, "The Negro Exodus," *The Atlantic Monthly* 46, No. 262 (August 1879): 223.

30. Editors of Salem Press, *The Civil Rights Movement*, Vol. 2 (Pasadena, Calif: Salem Press, 2000), 579–580.

31. Robert Cruden, *The Negro in Reconstruction* (Englewood Cliffs, N.J.: Prentice-Hall, 1969), 92–95.

32. Grimshaw, "Lawlessness and Violence in America and Their Special Manifestations in Changing Negro-White Relationships," 23.

33. Robert Fulton Holtzclaw, *Black Magnolias: A Brief History of the Afro-Mississippians, 1865–1980* (Shaker Heights, Ohio: The Keeble Press, 1984), 30; Loewen and Sallis,

Mississippi: Conflict and Change, 162–163; Herbert Aptheker, "Mississippi Reconstruction and the Negro Leader, Charles Caldwell," in *To Be Free: Pioneering Studies in Afro-American History* (New York: International Publishers 1968), 163–187; James W. Garner, *Reconstruction in Mississippi* (Baton Rouge: Louisiana State University Press, 1968), 334; Holtzclaw, *Black Magnolias*, 30; Allen W. Trelease, *Reconstruction: The Great Experiment* (New York: Harper & Row, Publishers, 1971), 156–159, 181, 287; Richard Maxwell, *Brown Strain of Violence: Historical Studies of American Violence and Vigilantism* (New York: Oxford University Press, 1975), 323; John R. Steelman, "A Study of Mob Action in the South" (Ph.D. diss., Department of Sociology, The University of North Carolina, Chapel Hill, 1928), 88; David M. Oshinsky, *"Worse Than Slavery": Parchman Farm and the Ordeal of Jim Crow Justice* (New York: The Free Press, 1996), 28, 38–39; William Peirce Randell, *The Ku Klux Klan: A Century of Infamy* (Philadelphia: Chilton Books, 1965), 84, 102; Willis, "On the New South Frontier," 335; Michael and Judy Ann Newton, *The Ku Klux Klan: An Encyclopedia* (New York: Garland Publishers, 1991), 396; Robert Fulton Holtzclaw, "The Negro in the Reconstruction of Mississippi," (M.A. thesis, History Department, Howard University, June, 1936), 87, 91; Richard Hofsadter and Michael Wallace, eds., *American Violence: A Documentary History* (New York: Vintage Books, 1970), 223–229; "The Story of Charles Caldwell" (Bolton, Miss.: Bolton Bicentennial Project, 1975), 1–4.

34. W. E. Burghardt Du Bois, *Black Reconstruction in America* (New York: Russell and Russell, 1935), 449.

35. Wharton, *The Negro in Mississippi*, 225.

36. Keyssar, *The Right to Vote*, 105–106; Harris *The Day of the Carpetbagger*, 397–99, 707–708.

37. Scaturro, *The Supreme Court's Retreat for Reconstruction*, 12.

38. As quoted by Keyssar, *The Right to Vote*, 105.

39. James M. McPherson, *The Negro's Civil War* (New York: Vintage Books, 1965), EX.

40. Du Bois, *Black Reconstruction in America*, 433.

41. Charles Crowe, ed., *The Age of Civil War and Reconstruction, 1830-1900: A Book of Interpretive Essays* (Homewood, Ill.: The Dorsey Press, 1975), 353.

42. Holtzclaw, *Black Magnolias*, 206–207.

43. Eric Foner, *Freedom's Lawmakers: A Directory of Black Officeholders During Reconstruction* (New York: Oxford University Press, 1993), xiv–xv.

44. John Roy Lynch, *Reminiscences of an Active Life: An Autobiography of John Roy Lynch*, ed., John Hope Franklin (Chicago: The University of Chicago Press, 1970), ix–xxxix; Ann Jennette Sophie McFarlin, *Black Congressional Reconstruction Orators and Their Orations, 1869-1879* (Metuchen, N.J.: The Scarecrow Press, 1976), 7–32, 137–175, 281–306; William C. Harris, "Blanche K. Bruce of Mississippi: Conservative Assimilationist," and "John Roy Lynch: Republican Stalwart From Mississippi," in Howard N. Rabinowitz, ed., *Southern Black Leaders of the Reconstruction Era* (Urbana: University of Illinois Press, 1982), 3–58; Julius E. Thompson, *Hiram R. Revels, 1827-1901: A Biography* (New York: Arno Press, 1982), 1–50.

45. Julius E. Thompson, *The Black Press in Mississippi, 1865-1985* (Gainesville: The University Press of Florida, 1993), 4–5.

46. Du Bois, *Black Reconstruction in America*, 447. Also see David W. Wills, "Exodus Piety: African American Religion in an Age of Immigration," in Jonathan D. Sarna, ed., *Minority Faiths and the American Protestant Mainstream* (Urbana: University of Illinois Press, 1998), 139–140; Eric Foner, *America's Unfinished Revolution, 1863-1877* (New York: Harper and Row, Publishers, 1988), 88–96.

47. John R. Lynch, *The Facts of Reconstruction*, ed., William C. Harris (Indianapolis, Ind.: The Bobbs-Merrill Co., 1970), xlii.

48. Carter G. Woodson, *A Century of Negro Migration* (Washington, D.C.: The Association for the Study of Negro Life and History, 1918), 134–135.

49. Robert G. Athearn, *In Search of Canaan: Black Migration to Kansas, 1879-80* (Lawrence: The Regents Press of Kansas, 1978), 93.

50. Mary Frances Berry, *Black Resistance, White Law: A History of Constitutional Racism in America* (New York: Allen Lane/The Penguin Press, 1994), 98.

51. Lerone Bennett, Jr., *Before the Mayflower: A History of the Negro in America, 1619-1964* (Baltimore: Penguin Books, 1966), 193.

52. Foner, *Reconstruction: America's Unfinished Revolution*, 561.

53. Kennedy, *After Appomattox*, 239.

54. Allen W. Trelease, *White Terror: The Ku Klux Klan Conspiracy and Southern Reconstruction* (Westport, Conn.: Greenwood Press, 1971), 288.

55. Bennett, *Before the Mayflower*, 199.

56. Trelease, *Reconstruction: The Great Experiment*, 182.

57. Trelease, *Reconstruction: The Great Experiment*, 182.

58. Martha Hodes, *White Women, Black Men: Illicit Sex in the Nineteenth Century South* (New Haven, Conn.: Yale University Press, 1997), 148–161.

Chapter 3

1. Pete Daniel, "The Metamorphosis of Slavery, 1865–1900," in: Donald G. Nieman, ed., *From Slavery to Sharecropping: White Land to Black Labor in the Rural South, 1865-1900* (New York: Garland Publishing, 1994), 89.

2. Buford Satcher, *Blacks in Mississippi Politics, 1865-1900* (Washington, D.C.: University Press of America, 1978), 209.

3. Jonathan M. Wiener, "Class Structure and Economic Development in the American South, 1865–1955," in: Nieman, *From Slavery to Sharecropping*, 983.

4. James W. Loewen and Charles Sallis, eds., *Mississippi: Conflict and Change* (New York: Pantheon Books, 1974), 174.

5. Tom Ownby, *American Dreams in Mississippi: Consumers, Poverty and Culture, 1830-1998* (Chapel Hill: The University of North Carolina Press, 1999), 83.

6. Mary Frances Berry and John W. Blassingame, *Long Memory: The Black Experience in America* (New York: Oxford University Press, 1982), 200.

7. Arthur James, Jimmie James, Jr., and Robert E. James, *The Mississippi Black Bankers and Their Institutions* (Jackson, Miss.: By the Authors, 1996), xi, 3–7.

8. *Ibid.*, iii; also see Loren Schweninger, *Black Property Owners in the South, 1790-1915* (Urbana: University of Illinois Press, 1990), 295–298.

9. Irvin C. Mollison, "Negro Lawyers in Mississippi," *The Journal of Negro History* 15, No. 1 (January 1930): 40.

10. Julius E. Thompson, *The Black Press in Mississippi, 1865-1985* (Gainesville: University Press of Florida, 1993), 7. Also see Emma Lou Thornbrough, "American Negro Newspapers, 1880-1914," *Business History Review* 40, No. 4 (Winter 1966): 467–490.

11. Jesse O. McKee, *Mississippi: A Portrait of an American State* (Montgomery, Ala.: Clairmont Press, 1995), 128.

12. Zhang Juguo, *W. E. B. Du Bois: The Quest for the Abolition of the Color Line* (New York: Routledge, 2001), 17.

13. *Ibid.*, 18.

14. Shirley Wilson Logan, *"We are Coming": The Persuasive Discourse of Nineteenth-Century Black Women* (Carbondale, Ill.: Southern Illinois University Press, 1999), 1; Martha H. Patterson, "Recovering the Work of American Clubwomen," *American Quarterly* 51., No. 1 (March 1999): 221–227; Darlene Clark Hine and Kathleen Thompson, *A Shining Thread of Hope: The History of Black Women in America* (New York: Broadway Books, 1998), 5, 166, 177–83.

15. C. Vann Woodward describes the slow growth of

segregation in Mississippi in this way: "On May 21, 1879, the Negroes of Jackson, after a parade of their fire company, gave a picnic in Hamilton Park. On the night of May 29, 'the ladies of the [white] Episcopal Church' used Hamilton Park for a fete. After their picnic the Negroes went to Angelo's Hall for a dance. This same hall was used for white dances and parties, and was frequently the gathering place of Democratic conventions.... Throughout the state common cemeteries, usually in separate portions, held the graves of both whites and Negroes. Wharton points out, however, that as early as 1890 segregation had closed in and the Negroes were by that date excluded from saloons, restaurants, parks, public halls, and white cemeteries." C. Vann Woodard, *The Strange Career of Jim Crow* (New York: Oxford University Press, 1974), 42.

16. Edward L. Ayers, *The Promise of the New South: Life After Reconstruction* (New York: Oxford University Press, 1992), 144.

17. John Hope Franklin and Alfred A. Moss, Jr., *From Slavery to Freedom: A History of African Americans* (New York: McGraw-Hill, 1994), 279. Also see Janet Sharp Hermann, *The Pursuit of a Dream* (New York: Oxford University Press, 1981); David Bradley, "Black Utopias," *The New York Times Book Review* (July 19, 1981): 8, 12.

18. August Meier, *Negro Thought in America, 1880-1915: Racial Ideologies in the Age of Booker T. Washington* (Ann Arbor: The University of Michigan Press, 1966), 28.

19. Nell Irvin Painter, *Standing at Armageddon: The United States, 1877-1919* (New York: W. W Norton & Co., 1987), 164.

20. J. Morgan Kousser, *The Shaping of Southern Politics: Suffrage Restriction and the Establishment of the One-Party South, 1880-1910* (New Haven, Conn.: Yale University Press, 1974), 14.

21. Ayers, *The Promise of the New South*, 147.

22. Juguo, *W. E. B. Du Bois: The Quest for the Abolition of the Color Line*, 19.

23. David M. Oshinsky, *"Worse Than Slavery": Parchman Farm and the Ordeal of Jim Crow Justice* (New York: The Free Press, 1996), 46.

24. Ibid., 46–47.

25. W. Marvin Dulaney, *Black Politics in America* (Bloomington: Indiana University Press, 1996), 15.

26. Ibid., 1881.

27. Gilbert Osofsky, ed., *The Burden of Race: A Documentary History of Negro-White Relations in America* (New York: Harper & Row, Publishers, 1967), 376.

28. Christopher R. Adamson, "Punishment After Slavery: Southern State Penal Systems, 1865–1890," *Social Problems* 30, No. 5 (June 1983): 562.

29. Ibid., 567.

30. Robert Zangrando, *The NAACP Crusade Against Lynching* (Philadelphia: Temple University Press, 1980), 8.

31. Some scholars disagree with this assessment. See Stewart E. Tolnay, E. M. Beck, and James L. Massey, "Black Lynchings: The Power Threat Hypothesis Revisited," *Social Forces* 67 (1992): 605–23.

32. Martha Hodes, *White Women, Black Men: Illicit Sex in the Nineteenth-Century South* (New Haven, Conn.: Yale University Press, 1992), 176. Also see Walter White, *Rope and Faggot* (New York: Alfred A. Knopf, 1929), 251–252; Chalis Holton, "Sexual Fears of Racism," in *The Civil Rights Movement* Vol. 2 (Pasadena, Calif: Salem Press, 2000), 579–580; Robert Cruden, *The Negro in Reconstruction* (Englewood Cliffs, N.J.: Prentice-Hall, 1969), 92.

33. Hail Rederman, *Manliness and Civilization: A Cultural History of Gender and Race in the United States, 1880-1917* (Chicago: The University of Chicago Press, 1995), 47.

34. Francis Butler Simkins, *A History of the South* (New York: Alfred A. Knopf, 1961), 388.

35. Darryl Paulson, "Lynching," in: *Ready Reference American Justice* Vol. 2 (Pasadena, Calif: Salem Press, 1996), 478–479.

36. E. M. Beck and Stewart E. Tolnay, "The Killing Fields of the Deep South: The Market for Cotton and the Lynching of Blacks, 1882–1930," *American Sociological Review* 55 (August 1990): 526–539; Jay Corrine, Lin Huff-Corzine, and James C. Creech, "The Tenant Labor Market and Lynchings in the South: A Test of Split Labor Market Theory," 261–278.

37. Theophus H. Smith, *Conjuring Culture: Biblical Formations of Black America* (New York: Oxford University Press, 1994), 97.

38. Katheryn K. Russell, *The Color of Crime: Racial Hoaxes, White Fear, Black Protectionism, Police Harassment, and Other Macroaggressions* (New York: University Press, 1998), 20–21.

39. Thomas F. Gossett, *Race: The History of an Idea in America* (Dallas, Texas: Southern Methodist University Press, 1963), 269.

40. William F. Holmes, "The Leflore County Massacre and the Demise of the Colored Farmers' Alliance," *Phylon* 4, No. 3 (1973): 267–74; John R. Steelman, "A Study of Mob Action in the South," (Ph.D. diss., Department of Sociology, The University of North Carolina, Chapel Hill, 1928), 108, 170, 256; William C. Culberson, *Vigilantism: Political History of Private Power in America* (New York: Greenwood Press, 1990), 149; Richard Maxwell Brown, *Strain of Violence: Historical Studies of American Violence and Vigilantism* (New York: Oxford University Press, 1975), 324; N. Clifford Young, "A Case Study of the Tarboro Lynching," (M. A. Thesis, Department of Sociology, University of North Carolina, Chapel Hill, 1931), 16-B; "Lynchings in Mississippi, 1882–1959," (Jackson, Miss.: Mississippi Department of Archives and History, Subject File, no date), 146–150; Ida B. Wells-Barnett, *Thirty Years of Lynching in the United States, 1889-1918* (New York: NAACP, 1919; reprint, New York: Arno Press and the New York Times, 1969), 74–75; http://www.concentric; net/0/07 Eccharity/Mississippi-lynched.htm, p. 5; Ralph Ginzburg, *100 Years of Lynchings* (Baltimore, Md.: Black Classic Press, 1988), 94.

41. William Cohen, *At Freedom's Edge: Black Mobility and the Southern White Quest for Racial Control, 1861-1915* (Baton Rouge: Louisiana State University Press, 1991), 210.

42. Maurice S. Evans, *Black and White in the Southern States: A Study of the Race Problem in the United States, From a South African Point of View* (London: 27 Hongmans, Green and Co., 1915), 174.

43. Michael R. Belknap, *Federal Law and Southern Order: Racial Violence and Constitutional Conflict in the Post-Brown South* (Athens: The University of Georgia Press, 1987), 5.

44. Julius E. Thompson, "The Distribution of the Lynch Victims in Mississippi, 1865–1966," in *Black Life in Mississippi* (Lanham, Md.: University Press of America, 2001), 55, 60–62.

45. Ida B. Wells-Barnett, *A Red Record: Tabulated Statistics and Alleged Causes of Lynchings in the United States, 1892-1893-1894* (Chicago: Donohue and Henneberry, 1895), 10–11; and *Mob Rule in New Orleans* (Chicago: I. B. Wells-Barnett, 1892), 45.

46. L. Ray Gunn, "Lynching," in Jack Salzman, ed., *The African-American Experience* (New York: Macmillan Library Reference, 1998), 438.

47. Ibid., 438.

48. Cohen, *At Freedom's Edge*, 211.

49. Ibid., 295; David M. Sansing, *Mississippi: Its People and Culture* (Minneapolis: T. S. Denisant Co., 1981), 244; Robert G. Athearn, *In Search of Canaan: Black Migration to Kansas, 1879-80* (Lawrence: The Regrets Press of Kansas, 1978), 90–93.

50. Alexander Keyssar, *The Right to Vote: The Contested History of Democracy in the United States* (New York: Basic Books/Perseus Books Group, 2000), 106.

51. Cohen, *At Freedom's Edge: Black Mobility and the Southern Quest for Racial Control 1861-1915*, 210.

52. Neil R. McMillen, *Dark Journey: Black Mississippians*

in the Age of Jim Crow (Urbana: University of Illinois Press, 1989), 228.

53. Martin Dunn, *The Black Press (1827–1890): The Quest for National Identity* (New York: G. P. Putnam's Sons, 1971), 7, 23–25; William G. Jordan, *Black Newspapers and America's War for Democracy, 1914–1920* (Chapel Hill: The University of North Carolina Press, 2001), 16–17.

54. Louis R. Harlan, *Booker T. Washington: The Making of a Black Leader, 1856–1901* (New York: Oxford University Press, 1972), 262–63; David Levering Lewis, *W. E. B. Du Bois: Biography of a Race, 1868–1919* (New York: Henry Holt & Co., 1993), 67; Benjamin Brawley, *The Negro Genius* (New York: Dodd, Mead and Co., 1937), 51–58, 116–120, 190–202; Melba Joyce Boyd, *Discarded Legacy: Politics and Poetics in the Life of Frances E. W. Harper, 1825–1911* (Detroit: Wayne State University Press, 1994), 197–236; W. E. B. Du Bois, *Dusk of Dawn: An Essay Toward an Autobiography of a Race Concept* (New York: Harcourt, Brace and World, 1940), 29–30; Philip Dray, *At the Hands of Persons Unknown: The Lynching of Black America* (New York: Random House, 2002), 59; Donald L. Grant, *The Anti-Lynching Movement 1883–1932* (San Francisco, Calif: R and E Research Associates, 1975), 21.

55. Justus D. Doenecke, *The Presidencies of James A. Garfield and Chester A. Arthur* (Lawrence: The University Press of Kansas, 1981), 182–183.

56. W. Laird Clowes, *Black America: A Study of the Ex-slave and His Late Master* (Westport, Conn.: Negro Universities Press, 1970; London: Cassell & Co., Limited, 1891), 278–79, 288.

57. Grant, *The Anti-Lynching Movement: 1883–1932*, 20.

58. Stewart E. Tolnay and E. M. Beck, *A Festival of Violence: An Analysis of Southern Lynchings, 1882–1930* (Urbana: University of Illinois Press, 1992), 14–15, 259; Grant, *The Anti-Lynching Movement: 1883–1932*, 1.

59. Dray, *At the Hands of Persons Unknown: The Lynching of Black America*, 9, 49, 169, 213–14.

60. Grant, *The Anti-Lynching Movement: 1883–1932*, 78.

61. Kate Turtle, "Lynching," in Kwame Anthony Appiah and Henry Louis Gates, Jr., eds., *Africana: The Encyclopedia of the African and African-American Experience* (New York: Basic Civitas Books, 1999), 1210.

62. Robert L. Zangrando, *The NAACP Crusade Against Lynching, 1900–1950* (Philadelphia: Temple University Press, 1980), 6–7; Allen D. Grimshaw, *Racial Violence in the United States* (Chicago: Aldine Publishing Co., 1969), 58–59. These totals for lynching victims in the 1880s would be even higher, if we add the estimated number of lynching victims for 1880 at 37, and for 1881, at 43, giving a possible total number of lynching victims for 1880–1889 at 1,283.

63. Frenise A. Logan, *The Negro in North Carolina, 1876–1894* (Chapel Hill: The University of North Carolina Press, 1964), 186.

64. Robert Cook, *Sweet Land of Liberty?: The African-American Struggle for Civil Rights in the Twentieth Century* (New York: Longman, 1998), 27. On a related topic, blacks and whites in Mississippi prisons, which contained 1,163 of the latter, and 148 of the former in 1880, see E. Merton Coulter, *The South During Reconstruction, 1865–1877* (Baton Rouge: Louisiana State University Press, 1947), 381.

65. Brown, *Strain of Violence: Historical Studies of American Violence and Vigilantism*, 216.

66. James S. Olson, *The Ethnic Dimension in American History* (New York: St. Martin's Press, 1994), 90, quoting from W. W. Brown, *Narrative of William W. Brown, A Fugitive Slave* (Boston 1847), 51.

Chapter 4

1. Paul L. Dunbar, "We Wear the Mask," in *The Complete Poems of Paul Laurence Dunbar* (New York: Dodd, Mead & Co., 1913), 71.

2. John R. Skates, "Mississippi," in David C. Roller and Robert W. Twyman, eds., *The Encyclopedia of Southern History* (Baton Rouge, La.: Louisiana State University Press, 1979), 835; W. D. Weatherford, *Present Forces in Negro Progress* (New York: Association Press, 1912), 77; Buford Satcher, *Blacks in Mississippi Politics, 1865–1900* (Washington: University Press of America, 1978), 209. Also see James Loewen, *The Mississippi Chinese, Between Black and White* (Cambridge, Mass.: Harvard University Press, 1971); Samuel J. Wells and Roseanna Tubby, eds., *After Removal: The Choctaw in Mississippi* (Jackson, Miss.: University Press of Mississippi, 1986), 84–85; Steve Hallam, "The Indians: Very Few Traces of Mississippi's First Inhabitants Remain Today," *The Clarion-Ledger/Jackson Daily News*, July 22, 1984, 2F.

3. U. S. Census, 1890; John N. Burrus, "Urbanization in Mississippi, 1890–1970," in Richard A. McLemore, ed., *A History of Mississippi*, Volume II (Hattiesburg, Miss.: University and College Press of Mississippi, 1973), 347–348.

4. "Migration of the Negroes," in John David Smith, ed., *Emigration and Migration Proposals: Solutions to the Negro Problem*, Volume II (New York: Garland Publishing, 1993), 225–228; Carter G. Woodson, *The Negro in Our History* (Washington, D. C.: The Associated Publishers, 1947), 434–35.

5. Dewey W. Grantham, *Southern Progressivism: The Reconciliation of Progress and Tradition* (Knoxville: The University of Tennessee Press, 1983), 37.

6. Gilbert C. Fite, *Cotton Fields No More: Southern Agriculture, 1865–1980* (Lexington, Ky.: The University Press of Kentucky, 1984), 238.

7. Kelly Miller, *Race Adjustment, Essays of the Negro in America* (New York: The Neale Publishing Co., 1910), 107.

8. Manning Marable, "Booker T. Washington and the Political Economy of Black Accommodations," in Charles Eagles, ed., *Is There a Southern Political Tradition?* (Jackson, Miss.: University Press of Mississippi, 1996), 53–54.

9. Neil Fligstein, *Going North: Migration of Blacks and Whites From the South, 1900–1950* (New York: Academic Press, 1981), 37.

10. Edwin S. Redkey, *Black Exodus: Black Nationalist and Back-to-Africa Movements, 1890–1910* (New Haven, Conn.: Yale University Press, 1969), 7.

11. Edward L. Ayers, *Vengeance and Justice: Crime and Punishment in the 19th Century American South* (New York: Oxford University Press, 1984), 197.

12. Pete Daniel, *The Shadow of Slavery: Peonage in the South, 1901–1969* (New York: Oxford University Press, 1973), ix–xii.

13. James W. Loewen and Charles Sallis, eds., *Mississippi: Conflict and Change* (New York: Pantheon Books, 1974), 195.

14. Edward A. Johnson, *A School History of the Negro Race in America From 1619 to 1890* (Philadelphia, Pa.: Sherman and Co., 1893), 165.

15. D. W. Woodward, "Negro Progress in a Mississippi Town: Being a Study of Conditions in Jackson, Mississippi," in *Committee of Twelve, For the Advancement of the Interests of the Negro Race* (Cheyney, Pa.: The Biddle Press, 1908), 3.

16. Booker T. Washington, *The Story of the Negro: The Rise of the Race From Slavery*, Volume II (New York: The Outlook Co., 1909; reprint, New York: Doubleday, Doran and Co., 1940; reprint ed., Gloucester, Mass.: Peter Smith, 1969), 205.

17. Jessie Mosley, *The Negro in Mississippi History* (Jackson, Miss.: Helderman Bros., 1950), 94–95.

18. J. Clay Smith, Jr., *Emancipation: The Making of the Black Lawyer, 1844–1944* (Philadelphia, Pa.: University of Pennsylvania Press, 1993), 22.

19. *Ibid.*, 288–296.

20. James C. Duram, in a review of J. Clay Smith, Jr., *Emancipation: The Making of the Black Lawyer, 1844–1944*. *American Historical Review* 100, No. 5 (December 1995): 1691.

21. Arthur James, Jimmie James, Jr., and Robert E. James, *The Mississippi Black Bankers and Their Institutions* (Jackson,

Miss.: By the Authors, 1996), 13–20; *The Clarion Ledger*, February 10, 1991, G-1.

22. Julius E. Thompson, *The Black Press in Mississippi, 1865–1985* (Gainesville, Fla.: University Press of Florida, 1993), 8. Also see Pamela Newkirk, *Within the Veil: Black Journalists, White Media* (New York: New York University Press, 2000), 42; Armistead Scott Pride, "The Names of Negro Newspapers," *American Speech* 29, No. 2 (May 1954): 114–118.

23. Liz McMillen, "An Oral History of Jim Crow: Researchers Document the Lives of Black People in the Segregated South," *The Chronicle of Higher Education* 41., No. 49 (August 18, 1995): 6.

24. A review of Sven Lindqvist, *Exterminate All the Brutes: A Modern Odyssey into the Heart of Darkness. The Journal of Blacks in Higher Education*, Number 23 (Summer 1996): 114.

25. Stuart Grayson Noble, *Forty Years of the Public Schools in Mississippi: With Special Reference to the Education of the Negro* (New York: Teachers College, Columbia University, 1918), 74.

26. J. W. Gibson and W. H. Crogman, *Progress of a Race* (Miami, Fla.: Mnemosyne Publisher, 1902), 691; Zhang Juguo, *W. E. B. Du Bois: The Quest for the Abolition of the Color Line* (New York: Routledge, 2001), 18; Mary Helm, *The Upward Path: The Evolution of a Race* (New York: Eaton and Mains, 1909), 322.

27. Gibson and Crogman, *Progress of a Race*, 692–95.

28. Aubrey K. Lucas, *Developing the Human Capital of Mississippi* (New York: Newcomen Society of the United States, 1986), 54.

29. Robert L. Jenkins, "The Development of Black Higher Education in Mississippi (1865–1920)," *The Journal of Mississippi History* 45, No. 4 (November 1983): 276–280.

30. W. E. B. Du Bois, *The Negro Church* (Atlanta, Ga.: Atlanta University Press, 1903, Publication 8; reprint ed., New York: Octagon Books, 1968), 39.

31. Paul R. Griffin, *Seeds of Racism in the Soul of America* (Cleveland, Ohio: The Pilgrim Press, 1999), 41.

32. LeRoi Jones, *Blues People: Negro Music in White America* (New York: William Morrow and Co., 1963), 60–61; Waldo Martin, "The Making of Black America," in Luther S. Luedtke, ed., *Making America: The Society and Culture of the United States* (Chapel Hill, N.C.: The University of North Carolina Press, 1992), 341–354.

33. Rayford W. Logan, *The Betrayal of the Negro: From Rutherford B. Hayes to Woodrow Wilson* (New York: Da Capo Press, 1997), 1–20.

34. Hanes Walton, Jr., *Invisible Politics* (Albany, N.Y.: State University of New York Press, 1985), 53.

35. Moshe Y. Sachs, ed., *World Mark Encyclopedia of the States* (New York: World Mark Press and John Wiley and Sons, 1986), 302.

36. James P. Coleman, "The Mississippi Constitution of the 1890 and the Final Decade of the Nineteenth Century," in McLemore, *A History of Mississippi*, Volume II, 3. Neal R. Pierce notes that: "The 1890 Constitution, Sen. Theodore Bilbo could Boast half a century later, was a document 'that damn few white men and no niggers at all can explain.' But it was so successful in disenfranchising black people—legally and permanently—that the 'Mississippi Plan,' as it came to be known, was rapidly adopted by most of the other Southern states." See Neal R. Pierce, *The Deep South States of America: People, Politics, and Power in the Seven Deep South States* (New York: W. W. Norton & Co., 1974), 169. The editors of the Booker T. Washington Papers offer us a glimpse into the thinking of Isaiah Montgomery: "Montgomery was the only black delegate at the Mississippi constitutional convention in 1890. In [his speech to the delegates], Montgomery in a frankly accommodating manner advocated reduction of the black vote by literacy and property qualifications. This brought charges that he was a 'traitor,' a 'Judas.' As T. Thomas Fortune remarked, 'No flippant fool could have inflicted such a wound upon our cause as Mr. Montgomery

has done in this address.' (Quoted in Meier, *Negro Thought in America*, 38.) The historian Vernon L. Wharton found it 'hard to believe that Montgomery, regarded by whites and blacks alike as honorable and sincere, deliberately betrayed his race and his country merely to retain his seat in the convention, an empty honor at best.' Perhaps, like BTW in many of his compromises with southern whites, Montgomery hoped that race relations would be improved, in an era of unprecedented lynchings and other violence, by reducing the black vote to a total considerably below that of white voters, and thus ending the threat of black supremacy. Perhaps Montgomery thought that the better educated and more affluent blacks could reenter the political mainstream in a subsequent era of greater racial harmony. Yet Montgomery's reasoning for what seems a race betrayal remains a mystery." (Wharton, *Negro in Mississippi*, 211–12). See Louis Harlan, S. B. Kaufman, and R. W. Smock, eds., *The Booker T. Washington Papers, Volume 3, 1889–1895* (Urbana: University of Illinois Press, 1974), 85.

37. Grantham, *Southern Progressivism: The Reconciliation of Progress and Tradition*, 114; J. Morgan Koussar, *The Shaping of Southern Politics: Suffrage Restriction and the Establishment of the One-Party South, 1880–1910* (New Haven, Conn.: Yale University Press, 1974), 239; R. Grann Lloyd, *White Supremacy in the United States: An Analysis of Its Historical Background, with Especial Reference to the Poll Tax* (Washington, D.C.: Annals of American Research, 1952), 11; Edward L. Ayers, *The Promise of the New South: Life After Reconstruction* (New York: Oxford University Press, 1992), 148.

38. P. Thomas Stanford, *The Tragedy of the Negro in America* (Boston: By the Author, 1898), 201–202; William Alexander Mabry, "Disfranchisement of the Negro in Mississippi," *The Journal of Southern History* 4 (1938): 329; J. W. Schulte Nordholt, Translated by M. B. Van Wijngaarden, *The People That Walk in Darkness* (New York: Ballantine Books, 1956), 200; Philip A. Klinkner and Rogers M. Smith, *The Unsteady March: The Rise and Decline of Racial Equality in America* (Chicago: The University of Chicago Press, 1999), 104; Jesse O. McKee, ed., *Mississippi: A Portrait of an American State* (Montgomery, Ala.: Clairmont Press, 1995), 123. McKee notes that "more than 30,000 whites who were too poor to pay the poll tax were eliminated from the voting lists." *Ibid.*, 123.

39. Robert Fulton Holtzclaw, *Black Magnolias: A Brief History of the Afro-Mississippian, 1865–1980* (Shaker Heights, Ohio: The Keeble Press, 1984), 71.

40. *Ibid.*, 53; John Hope Franklin, "John Roy Lynch (1847–1939)," in Rayford W. Logan and Michael R. Winston, eds., *Dictionary of American Negro Biography* (New York: Arno Press, 1982), 60–75.

41. Janet Sharp Hermann, *The Pursuit of a Dream* (New York: Oxford University Press, 1981), 236–37; August Meier, *Negro Thought in America, 1880–1915* (Ann Arbor, Mich.: University of Michigan Press, 1966), 66. Readers should also remember that the 1880s and 1890s were a difficult period for black people in terms of the role of the Supreme Court, and its negative decisions which greatly impacted the black community in this nation. Gilbert Osofsky captures this factor very well: "From 1876 through 1898 the United States Supreme Court curtailed the human protections of the Fourteenth Amendment while it expanded the amendment's meaning in terms of property. The Court's rulings on the Reconstruction amendments helped sanctify individual acts of racial discrimination, permitted Negro segregation in public facilities, and allowed Negroes to be disfranchised. The Court was an active participant in the national movement to deny Negroes full equality. As Justice John Marshall Harlan predicted in his dissenting opinion in Plessy vs. Ferguson, 'the judgment this day rendered will, in time, prove to be quite as pernicious as the decision made by this tribunal in the Dred Scott case.'" See Gilbert Osofsky, ed., *The Burden of Race* (New York: Harper & Row, Pub-

lishers, 1967), 191–192. Also see Dickson A. Mungazi, *The Journey to the Promised Land: The African American Struggle for Development Since the Civil War* (Westport, Conn.: Praeger, 2001), 47; Nell Irvin Painter, *Standing at Armageddon: The United States, 1877-1919* (New York: W. W. Norton & Co., 1987), 8; Charles A. Lofgren, *The Plessy Case: A Legal-Historical Interpretation* (New York: Oxford University Press, 1987).

· 42. Edward N. Akin, *Mississippi: An Illustrated History* (Northridge, Calif.: Windsor Publications, 1987), 89.

43. Mary Frances Berry, "Repression of Blacks in the South, 1890-1945: Enforcing the System of Segregation," in Robert Haws, ed., *The Age of Segregation: Race Relations in the South, 1890-1945* (Jackson, Miss: University Press of Mississippi, 1978), 29.

44. W. Martin Dulaney, *Black Police in America* (Bloomington: Indiana University Press, 1996), 15.

45. Oshinsky, *"Worse Than Slavery": Parchman Farm and the Ordeal of Jim Crow Justice*, 95, 137.

46. Christopher R. Adamson, "Punishment After Slavery: Southern State Penal Systems, 1865-1890," *Social Problems* 30, No. 5 (June 1983): 566.

47. David R. Moton, Jr., "Southern Violence: An Analysis of Lynching in the South-Central Region of the United States From 1889 to 1918" (M. A. Thesis, Department of Sociology, Northern Illinois University, DeKalb, August 1986), 43.

48. Robert L. Zangrando, *The NAACP Crusade Against Lynching, 1900-1950* (Philadelphia, Pa.: Temple University Press, 1980), 8, 47; Jessie Parkhurst Guzman, *1952 Negro Year Book: A Review of Events Affecting Negro Life* (New York: Wm. H. Wise & Co., 1952), 278.

49. Walter White, *Rope and Faggot: A Biography of Judge Lynch* (New York: Alfred A. Knopf, 1929), 251–259; E. M. Beck and Stewart E. Tolnay, "The Killing Fields of the Deep South: The Market for Cotton and the Lynching of Blacks, 1882-1930," *American Sociological Review* 55 (August 1990): 526–539.

50. Ayers, *The Promise of the New South: Life After Reconstruction*, 153.

51. William C. Culberson, *Vigilantism: Political History of Private Power in America* (New York: Greenwood Press, 1990), 79; Michael R. Belknap, *Federal Law and Southern Order: Racial Violence and Constitutional Conflict in the Post-Brown South* (Athens, Ga.: The University of Georgia Press, 1987), 5.

52. NAACP, *Thirty Years of Lynching in the United States, 1889-1918* (New York: NAACP, April 1919), 75–77; Wells-Barnett, *On Lynchings*, 1892, 91–93.

53. N. Clifford Young, "A Case Study of the Tarboro Lynching" (M.A. Thesis, Department of Sociology, University of North Carolina at Chapel Hill, 1931), 3–5, 16.

54. Osofsky, *The Burden of Race: A Documentary History of Negro-White Relations in America*, 178–179.

55. Dana B. Brammer, "Mississippi," *Encyclopedia Americana*, Volume 19 (Danbury, Conn.: Grolier, 1981), 235.

56. Pierce, *The Deep South States of America*, 169–170.

57. *Thirty Years of Lynching in the United States, 1889-1918*, 75–77; Wells-Barnett, *On Lynchings*, 1892, 91–93.

58. Wells-Barnett reminds us of the problem of press truths and lynching. She noted in 1892 that: "In a county in Mississippi during the month of July the Associated Press dispatches sent out a report that the sheriffs eight year old daughter had been assaulted by a big, black, burly brute who had been promptly lynched. The facts which have since been investigated show that the girl was more than eighteen years old and that she was discovered by her father in this young man's room who was a servant on the place. But these facts the Associated Press has not given to the world, nor did the same agency acquaint the world with the fact that a Negro youth who was lynched in Tuscumbia, Ala., the same year on the same charge told the white girl who accused him before the mob, that he had met her in the woods often by appointment. *Ibid.*, 65. Also see Phillip Foner and Robert

James Branham, eds., *Lift Every Voice: African American Oratory, 1787-1900* (Tuscaloosa, Ala.: The University of Alabama Press, 1998), 756.

59. Parsons, Kansas, *Weekly Blade*, May 30, 1896; Roland E. Wolseley, *The Black Press, U.S.A.* (Ames, Iowa: Iowa State University Press, 1990), 39.

60. Stanford, *The Tragedy of the Negro in America*, 165.

61. Tolnay and Beck, *A Festival of Violence*, 41–44.

62. *Ibid.*, 47.

63. *Ibid.*, 32–34.

64. Deborah Gray White, *Too Heavy A Load: Black Women in Defense of Themselves, 1894-1994* (New York: W. W. Norton & Co., 1999), 26.

65. See Evelyn Brooks Higginbotham, *Righteous Discontent: The Women's Movement in the Black Baptist Church, 1880-1920* (Cambridge, Mass.: Harvard University Press, 1993), 4, 11, 172; Patrick H. Thompson, *The History of Negro Baptists in Mississippi* (Jackson, Miss.: The R. W. Bailey Printing Co., 1898), 519; Willard B. Gatewood, *Aristocrats of Color: The Black Elite, 1880-1920* (Bloomington, Ind.: Indiana University Press, 1990), 235–246. On a minority black Christian perspective see: Richard M. Tristano, "Holy Family Parish: The Genesis of an African-American Catholic Community in Natchez, Mississippi," *The Journal of Negro History* 73, No. 4 (Fall 1998): 258–283; Tommye Hague Rosenbaum, *A History of the Mississippi Federation of Women's Clubs, 1898-1998* (Jackson, Miss.: Mississippi Federation of Women's Clubs), 1998.

66. Higginbotham, *Righteous Discontent*, 11.

67. W. C. Handy, *Father of the Blues: An Autobiography* (New York: DaCapo Press, 1991), 1–25.

68. See David W. Wills, "Exodus Piety: African American Religion in an Age of Immigration," in Jonathan D. Sarna, ed., *Minority Faiths and the American Protestant Mainstream* (Urbana, Ill.: University of Illinois Press, 1998), 164–165; Gilbert Anthony Williams, *The Christian Recorder, Newspaper of the African Methodist Episcopal Church* (Jefferson, N.C.: McFarland & Co., 1996), 32–33, 39–40.

69. John Tomasi, "Justice," in Kermit L. Hall, ed., *The Oxford Companion to American Law* (New York: Oxford University Press, 2002), 461.

70. *Ibid.*, 461.

71. Peter Thompson, *Dictionary of American History, From 1763 to the Present* (New York: Facts On File, 2000), 257.

72. Thomas J. Moyer, "Extralegality," in Hall, *The Oxford Companion to American Law*, 288.

73. "Lynching," in Kwame Anthony Appiah and Henry Louis Gates, Jr., eds., *Africana: The Encyclopedia of the African and African-American Experience* (New York: Basic Civitas Books, 1999), 1210.

74. Bettina Aptheker, *Woman's Legacy: Essays on Race, Sex, and Class in American History* (Amherst, Mass.: The University of Massachusetts Press, 1982), 66–71; Linda O. McMurry, *To Keep the Waters Troubled: The Life of Ida B. Wells* (New York: Oxford University Press, 1999); Paula Giddings, *When and Where I Enter: The Impact of Black Women on Race and Sex in America* (New York: William Morrow & Co., 1984), 31. In the 1890s, Wells-Barnett also gave service as head of the Afro-American Council's Antilynching Bureau. See Joy James, *Transcending the Talented Tenth: Black Leaders and American Intellectuals* (New York: Routledge, 1997), 197. The career of Mary E. Church Terrell (1863–1954) is also noted during this period. Terrell, as a leader in the black women's club movement, also gave support to the antilynching crusade. See Ruth Leon W. Butler and A. Cheree Carlson, "Mary Eliza Church Terrell," in Richard W. Leeman, ed., *African-American Orators: A Bio-Critical Sourcebook* (Westport, Conn.: Greenwood Press, 1996), 318–331; Beverly W. Jones, "Mary Church Terrell and the National Association of Colored Women, 1896 to 1901," *The Journal of Negro History* 67, No. 1 (Spring 1982): 20–33; Paula Giddings, "Mary Church Terrell, Ida B. Wells, and the Crusade

204 NOTES—CHAPTER 5

Against Lynching," in Leon Fink, ed., *Major Problems in the Gilded Age and the Progressive Era: Documents and Essays* (Lexington, Mass.: D. C. Heath & Co., 1993), 249–260.

75. Harvey Wish, ed., *The Negro Since Emancipation* (Englewood Cliffs, N.J.: Prentice-Hall, 1964), 14, 22–29; Frederick Douglass, "Lynch Law in the South," *The North American Review* 155, No. 428 (1892): 17–24.

76. Waldo E. Martin, Jr., *The Mind of Frederick Douglass* (Chapel Hill, N.C.: The University of North Carolina Press, 1984), 281–84.

77. Lerone Bennett, Jr., *Before the Mayflower: A History of the Negro in America, 1619–1964* (Baltimore, Md.: Penguin Books, 1969), 276–277.

78. Lawrence M. Friedman, *A History of American Law* (New York: A Touchstone Book/Simon & Schuster, 1985), 352–53.

79. Dewey W. Grantham, *The South in Modern America: A Region at Odds* (New York: HarperCollins Publishers, 1994), 32.

80. William F. Holmes, *The White Chief: James Kimble Vardaman* (Baton Rouge, La.: Louisiana State University Press, 1970), 37; Ralph McGill, *The South and the Southerner* (Boston, Mass.: Little, Brown & Co., 1959), 119–120; Paul R. Coppock, "Bilbo's 31 Years at 'Prince of the Peckerwoods,'" *Commercial Appeal*, May 30, 1976.

81. Scott L. Malcomson, *One Drop of Blood: The American Misadventure of Race* (New York: Farrar Straus Giroux, 2000), 213.

82. On other national leaders of this period see: Alyn Brodsky, *Grover Cleveland: A Study in Character* (New York: St. Martin's Press, 2000), 450–53; Samuel Eliot Morison, *The Oxford History of the American People* (New York: Oxford University Press, 1965), 795; Lewis L. Gound, *The Presidency of William McKinley* (Lawrence, Kansas: The Regents Press of Kansas, 1980), 28–29.

83. Richard A. Couto, *Ain't Gonna Let Nobody Turn Me Round: The Pursuit of Racial Justice in the Rural South* (Philadelphia, Pa.: Temple University Press, 1991), 236–237.

Chapter 5

1. R. B. Kleazer, *Understanding Our Neighbors: An Educational Approach to America's Major Race Problem* (Atlanta, Ga.: Conference On Education and Race Problems, 1940), 13. One scholar observes that: "In 1900 there were more than 8.8 million black people in the United States, composing over 11 percent of the entire population. About 85 percent of the blacks resided in the eleven states that had made up the Southern Confederacy; another 8 percent lived in the four border states of Delaware, Maryland, Kentucky, and Missouri." See Oscar Theodore Barck, Jr., and Nelson Manfred Blake, *Since 1900: A History of the United States in Our Times* (New York: McMillan Publishing Co., 1974), 4.

2. Ronald Bailey, *Remembering Medgar Evers...For A New Generation* (Oxford, Miss.: The Civil Rights Documentation Project, 1988), 1–10. In 1900, thirty-five of Mississippi's seventy-five counties had a black majority population. See Jesse O. McKee, ed., *Mississippi: A Portrait of an American State* (Montgomery, Ala.: Clairmont Press, 1995), 271.

3. *Rowell's American Newspaper Directory* (New York: The Printers' Ink Publishing Co., 1905), 530.

4. David Tyack, *Nobody Knows: Black Americans in the Twentieth Century* (New York: The Macmillan Co., 1969), 18–19.

5. McKee, *Mississippi: A Portrait of An American State*, 132. Yet, according to Gilbert C. Fite, "By 1900 there were 707,364 black farmers in the South. Of these, 162,000 or about 23 percent, were owners or part owners. Most black farmers, even the owners, had very small farms, averaging only 52 acres in 1900. See Gilbert C. Fite, *Cotton Fields No*

More: *Southern Agriculture, 1865–1980* (Lexington, Ky.: The University Press of Kentucky, 1984), 20.

6. Joe Williams Trotter, Jr., *The African American Experience* (Boston: Houghton Mifflin Co., 2001), 300.

7. Leon F. Litwack, "Race Relations in the South From Reconstruction to the Civil Rights Movement," in: Harry J. Knopke, Robert J. Norrell, and Ronald W. Rogers, eds., *Opening Doors: Perspectives On Race Relations in Contemporary America* (Tuscaloosa, Ala.: The University of Alabama Press, 1991), 11. Also for this period see: Booker T. Washington, "A Cheerful Journey Through Mississippi," *World's Work* (February 1908): 11278–82; Theodore Hemmingway, "Booker T. Washington in Mississippi: October, 1908," *The Journal of Mississippi History*, 96, No. 1 (February 1984): 29–42.

8. Arthur James, Jimmie James, Jr., and Robert E. James, *The Mississippi Black Bankers and Their Institutions* (Jackson, Miss.: By the Authors, 1996), 8.

9. Washington, "A Cheerful Journey Through Mississippi," 11280.

10. Hemmingway, "Booker T. Washington in Mississippi: October, 1908," 31.

11. Peter Thompson, *Dictionary of American History: From 1763 to the Present* (New York: Facts On File, 2000).

12. Scott L. Malcomson, *One Drop of Blood: The American Misadventure of Race* (New York: Farrar Straus Giroux, 2000), 351.

13. David Levering Lewis, ed., *W.E.B. Du Bois: A Reader* (New York: Henry Holt and Co., 1995), 412. Also see David L. Smiley, "Quest for a Central Theme," in Paul D. Escott and David R. Goldfields, eds., *Major Problems in the History of the American South, Vol. II: The New South* (Lexington, Mass.: D. C. Heath & Co., 1990), 9–21.

14. "Mississippi Medical and Surgical Association Celebrates 100 Years," *Jackson Advocate*, May 3, 2001, 3-A.

15. *Delta* (Greenville) *Leader*, November 2, 1940, 1. On women during this period also see: Karin Klenke, *Women and Leadership: A Contextual Perspective* (New York: Springer Publishing Co., 1996), 46–49, 52–54.

16. Thomas E. Gossett, *Race: The History of an Idea in America* (New York: Schocken Books, 1965), 276–277.

17. *Ibid.*, 277.

18. Lewis, *W.E.B. Du Bois: A Reader*, 412. On the period also see: Arnold Cooper, "The Tuskegee Machine in Action: Booker T. Washington's Influence on Utica Institute, 1903–1915," *The Journal of Mississippi History* 58, No. 4 (November 1986): 283–295.

19. Arthur S. Link, *American Epoch: A History of the United States Since the 1890s* (New York: Alfred A. Knopf, 1955), 28.

20. C. Eric Lincoln, "The Black Heritage in Religion in the South," in: Charles Reagan Wilson, ed., *Religion in the South* (Jackson, Miss.: University Press of Mississippi, 1985), 53. Also see Gregory A. Willis, *Democratic Religion: Freedom, Authority and Church Discipline in the Baptist South, 1785–1900* (New York: Oxford University Press, 1997), 68–70.

21. Pete Daniel, *Standing at the Crossroads: Southern Life Since 1900* (New York: Hill and Wang, 1986), 29.

22. *Ibid.*, 101. Also see William F. Holmes, *The White Chief: James Kimble Vardaman* (Baton Rouge, La.: Louisiana State University Press, 1970), 113.

23. Lawrence M. Friedman, *A History of American Law* (New York: A Touchstone Book/ Simon & Schuster, 1985), 507.

24. Trotter, *The African American Experience*, 289.

25. Robert Muccigrosso, Ran Blazek, and Teri Maggio, *Term Paper Resource Guide to Twentieth-Century United States History* (Westport, Conn.: Greenwood Press, 1999), 32–34; Dorothy Schneider and Carl J. Schneider, *American Women in the Progressive Era, 1900–1920* (New York: Facts On File, 1993), 115–136.

26. George Coleman Osborn, *James Kimble Vardaman:*

Southern Commoner (Jackson, Miss.: Hederman Brothers, 1981), 50.

27. Barck and Blake, *Since 1900: A History of the United States in Our Times*, 5.

28. Robert Perkinson, "Between the Worst of the Past and the Worst of the Future: Reconsidering Convict Leasing in the South," *Radical History* 71 (Spring 1998): 209. For this era also see Pete Daniel, *The Shadow of Slavery: Peonage in the South, 1901–1969* (Urbana, Ill.: University of Illinois Press, 1990), 151–152.

29. Perkinson, "Between the Worst of the Past and the Worst of the Future: Reconsidering Convict Leasing in the South," 209.

30. *Ibid.*, 213. Also see David M. Oshinsky, *"Worse Than Slavery": Parchman Farm and the Ordeal of Jim Crow Justice* (New York: The Free Press, 1996), 1–2, 29, 37–67.

31. Joseph M. Hawes, *The Children's Rights Movement: A History of Advocacy and Protection* (Boston: Twayne Publishers, 1991), 192.

32. Stewart E. Tolnay and E. M. Beck, *A Festival of Violence: An Analysis of Southern Lynchings, 1882–1930* (Urbana, Ill.: University of Illinois Press, 1995), 46–47.

33. Thompson, "The Distribution of Lynch Victims in Mississippi, 1865–1966," 55, 69–70.

34. Tolnay and Beck, *A Festival of Violence*, 47.

35. NAACP, *Thirty Years of Lynching in the United States, 1889–1919* (New York: NAACP, April 1919), 1–30; Thompson, *Black Life in Mississippi*, 200–209.

36. NAACP, *Thirty Years of Lynching in the United States, 1889–1919*, 1–35.

37. Thompson, "The Distribution of Lynch Victims in Mississippi," 55.

38. *Ibid.*, 200–209.

39. *Ibid.*, 200–209. In 1901, two Italians were killed by a mob at Irwin, Mississippi; and in Washington, D.C., a protest and claim against the United States was presented to the Department of State. See Charles H. Watson, "Need of Federal Legislation in Respect to Mob Violence in Cases of Lynching of Aliens," *Yale Law Journal* 25, No. 7 (May 1916): 576–77.

40. Thompson, "The Distribution of Lynch Victims in Mississippi," 200–209.

41. Thompson, "The Distribution of Lynch Victims in Mississippi," 200–209. In 1900 the life expectancy of Americans stood at 47.3 years, but most lynching victims were killed in their twenties, thirties, and forties. See John F. Ross, "What You Didn't Know About Risk," *Reader's Digest*, 148, No. 888 (April 1996): 92; Julius E. Thompson, *Black Life in Mississippi: Essays on Political, Social and Cultural Studies in a Deep South State* (Lanham, Md.: University Press of America, 2001), 57–74, 191–221.

42. William Z. Foster, *The Negro People in American History* (New York: International Publishers, 1970), 456.

43. *The Fayette* (Miss.) *Chronicle*, October 3, 1902.

44. Henry Waring Ball Diaries, December 31, 1900–December 21, 1903 (Jackson, Miss.: Mississippi Department of Archives and History, Series 1, Box 1, Folder 5, Item 1).

45. Mary Church Terrell, "Lynching From A Negro's Point of View," *North American Review* 118 (June 1904): 854. Also see Dwyn M. Mounger, "Lynching in Mississippi" (M.A. Thesis, Mississippi State University, Starkville, 1961), 80.

46. *Collins Commercial* (Covington County, Miss.), November 2, 1906.

47. Harold Evans, with Gail Buckland and Kevin Baker, *The American Century* (New York: Alfred A. Knopf, 2000), 35.

48. Jack Temple Kirby, *Darkness at the Dawning: Race and Reform in the Progressive South* (Philadelphia, Pa.: J. B. Lippincott & Co., 1972), 33. Also see, "Mississippi Whitecappers Convicted," *The Voice of the Negro* 2, No. 2 (February 1905): 87. The consequences of racial sexual stereotypes is demonstrated in the following observation by historian Edward

Ayers on the late nineteenth and early twentieth centuries: "Just as white girls and women were raised to fear strange black men, so were black boys and men taught to avoid any situation where they might be falsely accused. For generations, young black men learned early in their lives that they could at any time be grabbed by a white woman in the wrong way, or merely being 'smart'—and dragged into the woods or a public street to be tortured, burned, mutilated. It was a poisoned atmosphere, one that permeated life far beyond those counties where a lynching had actually taken place, one that pervaded all the dealings each race had with the other." See Ayers, *The Promise of the New South*, 158.

49. See William F. Holmes, "Whitecapping: Agarian Violence in Mississippi, 1902–1906," *The Journal of Southern History* 35, No. 2 (May 1969): 267–274.

50. "The Life Saver Vardaman," *The Voice of the Negro* 1, No. 4 (April 1, 1904): 127–28.

51. On a few occasions Mississippians could also be arrested for a lynching, but as the *Lincoln County Times* notes, securing a conviction was another matter. The paper noted: "John Williams and Ed Hartzog, two white men residing near Prentiss, have been arrested on a charge of participating in the lynching of the negro Ambrose at that place on the 11th. It begins to look as if the pastime of 'lynching a nigger' is falling into disrepute in Mississippi. While no one has ever been convicted, arrests have been made in fifteen or twenty counties in the last few years, and the defendants put to considerable trouble and expense." See *The Lincoln County Times* (Brookhaven, Miss.), June 21, 1906.

52. Mississippi newspaper? No name; no date.

53. I. A. Newby, *Jim Crow's Defense: Anti-Negro Thought in America, 1900–1930* (Baton Rouge, La: Louisiana State University Press, 1965), 4–5.

54. Kenneth K. Bailey, *Southern White Protestantism in the Twentieth Century* (New York: Harper & Row, Publishers, 1964), 2–3; Ralph E. Luker, *The Social Gospel in Black and White: American Racial Reform, 1885–1912* (Chapel Hill, N.C.: The University of North Carolina Press, 1991), 5. An excellent example of white Mississippi attitudes toward blacks appeared in the *Hattiesburg Progress*, in 1903. According to this paper: "A Negro went to sleep on the Northeastern Railroad near Meridian the other day and was cut in two by a passing freight train. It may be a little dangerous to lie on the railroad track and go to sleep, but we can inform the Negroes of Hattiesburg that a man cannot get sweeter sleep any other way and advise them if they want sweet sleep and a long rest without apprehension of being disturbed go to some shady place on the track and there lie down and go sound asleep. A train will come along some time and you will wake up, perhaps after the train has passed, to find yourself in the New Jerusalem. At any rate give it a trial. It is good for your health and better for the community." See *Hattiesburg* (Miss.) *Progress*, June 21, 1902, July 29, 1903.

55. Marjorie Spruill Wheeler, *The New Women of the New South: The Leaders of the Woman Suffrage Movement in the Southern States* (New York: Oxford University Press, 1993), 108.

56. Mary Jane Brown, *Eradicating This Evil: Women in the American Anti-Lynching Movement, 1892–1940* (New York: Garland Publishing, 2000), 95.

57. Kevin K. Gaines, *Uplifting the Race: Black Leadership, Politics, and Culture in the Twentieth Century* (Chapel Hill, N.C.: The University of North Carolina Press, 1996), 85–88; "Ida B. Wells Barnett: The Reformer (1862–1931)," in: Henry Louis Gates, Jr., and Cornell West, *The African-American Century: How Black Americans Have Shaped Our Country* (New York: The Free Press, 2000), 37; Doris Weatherford, *American Women's History: An A to Z People, Organizations, Issues, and Events* (New York: Prentice Hall General Reference, 1994), 366–67; Gail Bederman, " 'Civilization,' The Decline of Middle-Class Manliness, and Ida B. Wells' Anti-Lynching Campaign (1892–94)," *Radical History* 52, (Winter 1992):

5–30; Carol Kort, *A to Z of American Women Writers* (New York: Facts On File, 2000), 231–232.

58. Bederman, " 'Civilization,' The Decline of Middle-Class Manliness, and Ida B. Wells' Anti-Lynching Campaign (1892–94)," 23–24. On the work of other black groups, outside of Mississippi, to focus public attention of the lynching problem, see: Trotter, *The African American Experience*, 340–41.

59. Seth M. Scheiner, "President Theodore Roosevelt and the Negro, 1901–1908," in Richard Resh, ed., *Black America: Confrontation and Accommodation in the Twentieth Century* (Lexington, Mass.: D.C. Heath & Co., 1969), 30.

60. Malcomson, *One Drop of Blood: The American Misadventure of Race*, 213.

61. John Hope Franklin and Alfred A. Moss, Jr., *From Slavery to Freedom: A History of African Americans* (Boston: McGraw Hill, 2000), 335–350.

62. Thomas G. Dyer, *Theodore Roosevelt and the Idea of Race* (Baton Rouge, La.: Louisiana State University Press, 1980), 89–90.

63. H. W. Brands, *T. R.: The Last Romantic* (New York: Basic Books, 1997), 496.

64. Lewis L. Gould, *The Presidency of Theodore Roosevelt* (Lawrence, Kansas: University Press of Kansas, 1991), 118.

65. Samuel R. Spencer, Jr., *Booker T. Washington and the Negro's Place in American Life* (Boston: Little, Brown & Co., 1955), 129–130. Also see Louis R. Harlan, *Booker T. Washington: The Making of a Black Leader, 1856–1901* (New York: Oxford University Press, 1972), 262–63.

66. Jay James, *Transcending the Talented Tenth: Black Leaders and American Intellectuals* (New York: Routledge, 1997), 46–47. See especially W. E. B. Du Bois, *The Souls of Black Folk* (Greenwich, Conn.: Fawcett Publications, 1968; reprint from the 1903 edition). Of course other national black leaders were also opposed to lynching. Among prominent leaders in the group were: Bishop McNeal Turner (1834–1915), a minister, political figure and important black nationalist; Representative George H. White (1852–1918), the last of the Reconstruction Era black legislators to serve in Congress (as a Republican from North Carolina, in 1897–1901); Charles W. Chesnutt (1858–1932), a leading black writer of the period; among others. See Deborah Gillon Straub, ed., *African American Voices*, Vol. 2: K-Z (New York: Gale Research, 1996), 349; Laverne McCain Gill, *African American Women in Congress: Forming and Transforming History* (New Brunswick, N.J.: Rutgers University Press, 1997), 250; Bradford Chambers, ed., *Chronicles of Negro Protest: A Background Book Documenting the History of Black Power* (New York: Parents' Magazine Press, 1968), 177–183; Historians have also noted the interest of journalists in social problems of this era, but Maurine Beasley argues that racism prevented many of them from really opposing lynching. See Maurine Beasley, "The Muckrakers and Lynching: A Case in Racism," *Journalism History* 9, Nos. 3–4 (Autumn-Winter 1982), 86–91. Likewise, some elements among white suffragists were fearful of attacking the issue of lynching because of their conceived need for the support of Southern white women in the struggle to secure the vote for women. See Geoffrey G. Ward, *Not for Ourselves Alone: The Story of Elizabeth Cady Stanton and Susan B. Anthony: An Illustrated History* (New York: Alfred A. Knopf, 1999), 188.

67. Hasia R. Diner, "Between Words and Deeds: Jews and Blacks in America, 1880–1935," in Jack Salzman and Cornell West, eds., *Struggles in the Promised Land: Toward a History of Black-Jewish Relations in the United States* (New York: Oxford University Press, 1997), 87–106.

68. Deborah Dash Moore, "Separate Paths: Blacks and Jews in the Twentieth-Century South," in Salzman and West, *Struggles in the Promised Land*, 276–77.

69. Paul Buhle and Robin D. G. Kelley, "Allies of a Different Sort: Jews and Blacks in the American Left," in: Salzman and West, *Struggles in the Promised Land*, 200. Also

see Hasia R. Diner, "Drawn Together By Self-interest: Jewish Representation of Race and Race Relations in the Early Twentieth Century," in V. P. Franklin, Nancy L. Grant, Harold M. Kletnick, and Genna Rae McNeil, eds., *African Americans and Jews in the Twentieth Century: Studies in Convergence and Conflict* (Columbia, Mo.: University of Missouri Press, 1998), 27–29.

70. Nance J. Weiss, "Long-Distance Runners of the Civil Rights Movement: The Contribution of Jews to the NAACP and the National Urban League in the Early Twentieth Century," in: Salzman and West, *Struggles in the Promised Land*, 123–152.

71. Joel R. Williamson, "C. Vann Woodward and the Origins of a New Wisdom," in: John Herbert Roper, ed., *C. Vann Woodward: A Southern Historian and His Critics* (Athens, Ga.: The University of Georgia Press, 1997), 203.

72. *Ibid.*, 218.

73. Philip S. Foner, *American Socialism and Black America: From the Age of Jackson to World War II* (Westport, Conn.: Greenwood Press, 1977), 127. On the establishment of African-American fraternities and sororities, during this period, which would have a major impact on black social development in the United States, see Lawrence C. Ross, Jr., *The Divine Nine: The History of African-American Fraternities and Sororities* (New York: Kensington Publishing Corp., 2000).

74. Robert Cook, *Sweet Land of Liberty?: The African American Struggle for Civil Rights in the Twentieth Century* (New York: Longman, 1998), 28–29.

75. Shamoon Zamir, *Dark Voices: W. E. B. Du Bois and American Thought, 1888–1903* (Chicago: The University of Chicago Press, 1995), 84–85.

76. Freidman, *A History of American Law*, 580. On the issue of lynching in other states during this period see: Alwyn Barr, *Black Texans: A History of African Americans in Texas, 1528–1995* (Norman, Okla.: University of Oklahoma Press, 1996), 84–85, 136–40; on South Carolina and North Carolina, see Benjamin E. Mays, *Born to Rebel: An Autobiography* (New York: Charles Scribner's Sons, 1971), 334–339; Jimmie Lewis Franklin, *Journey Toward Hope: A History of Blacks in Oklahoma* (Norman, Okla.: University of Oklahoma Press, 1982), 128–152, 233–35; Donald F. Tingley, *The Structuring of a State: The History of Illinois, 1899 to 1928* (Urbana, Ill.: The Board of Trustees of the University of Illinois, 1980), 290–305; Yohuru R. Williams, "Permission to Hate: Delaware, Lynching, and the Culture of Violence in America," *Journal of Black Studies* 32, No. 1 (September 2001): 3–29; Constance McLaughlin Green, *The Secret City: A History of Race Relations in the Nation's Capital* (Princeton, N.J.: Princeton University Press, 1967), 155–156; Sundiata Keita Cha-Jua, " 'Join Hands and Hearts with Law and Order': The 1893 Lynching of Samuel J. Bush and the Response of Decatur's African American Community," *Illinois Historical Journal* 83 (Autumn 1990): 187–200.

77. James Melvin Washington, ed., *Conversations With God: Two Centuries of Prayers by African Americans* (New York: Harper Collins Publishers, 1994), 87.

Chapter 6

1. W. D. Weatherford, *Present Forces in Negro Progress* (New York: Association Press, 1912), 77; U. S. Census, 1910; *Population Bulletin for Mississippi* (Jackson, Miss.: State of Mississippi, 1940), 1–2; Clara Sue Kidwell, *Choctaws and Missionaries in Mississippi, 1818–1918* (Norman, Okla.: University of Oklahoma Press, 1995), 196.

2. John N. Burrus, "Urbanization in Mississippi, 1890–1970," in Richard A. McLemore, ed., *A History in Mississippi, Volume II* (Hattiesburg, Miss.: University and College Press of Mississippi, 1973), 348.

3. Colin A. Palmer, *Passageways: An Interpretive History*

of Black America, Volume II: 1863–1965 (Fort Worth, Texas: Harcourt Brace and Co., 1998), 72.

4. Henry Bamford Parkers and Vincent P. Carossa, Recent America: A History, Book One, 1900–1933 (New York: Thomas Y. Crowell Co., 1963), 88.

5. Carole Marks, Farewell—We're Good and Gone: The Great Black Migration (Bloomington: Indiana University Press, 1989), 64.

6. The Voice (Mound Bayou, Miss.), July 12, 1970, 1–6; August Meier, "Booker T. Washington and the Town of Mound Bayou," Phylon 15, No. 4 (Fourth Quarter 1954) 396–401; John N. Ingham and Lynne B. Feldman, African-American Business Leaders: A Biographical Dictionary (Westport, Conn.: Greenwood Press, 1994), 724; Citizens of Color in Meridian, Mississippi (Meridian, Miss.: By John Barksdale, 1962), 1–27.

7. "Early Black Leaders Profiled," The Clarion-Ledger/Jackson Daily News, February 20, 1977, A-2; Clarion-Ledger, February 10, 1991, G-l. Between 1892 and 1914, black Mississippians created 14 banks. See Arthur James, Jimmie James, Jr., and Robert E. James, The Mississippi Black Bankers and Their Institutions (Jackson, Miss.: By the Authors, 1996), 8, 13–89.

8. Stewart E. Tolnay and E. M. Beck, "Racial Violence and Black Migration in the American South, 1910 to 1930," American Sociological Review 57 (February 1992): 104.

9. Ibid., 104; Marcus E. Jones, "Black Migration in the United States, with Emphasis on Selected Central Cities," (Ph.D. thesis, Department of Geography, Southern Illinois University at Carbondale, 1978), 44.

10. Malaika Adero, ed., Up South: Stories, Studies, and Letters of This Century's Black Migrations (New York: The New Press, 1993), 138–139.

11. Neil R. McMillen, Dark Journey: Black Mississippians in the Age of Jim Crow (Urbana, Ill.: University of Illinois Press, 1989), 272.

12. Ibid., 273. Readers may recall that some black Mississippians, as early as the 1890s to 1910s, had an interest in migrating to Africa, because of conditions in the state, where blacks were in "virtual slavery to the landowner and storekeeper." But even this possibility was surrounded with fear, for there was white opposition of a return to Africa, of even a few black Mississippians. One scholar notes, "A Mississippi black preacher reported that violence awaited any black man who talked of going to Africa. Of the seventy-two members of his proposed emigration group, the local whites 'caught two or three of the men and whipped them badly and talked about killing all of them that they could find out was going and they had all the colored people in Cohoma afraid to meet at my church.'" See Edwin S. Redkey, Black Exodus: Black Nationalist and Back-to-Africa Movements, 1890–1910 (New Haven, Conn.: Yale University Press, 1969), 9.

13. Gilbert C. Fite, Cotton Fields No More: Southern Agriculture, 1865–1980 (Lexington, Kentucky: The University Press of Kentucky, 1984), 238.

14. Neil Fligstein, Going North: Migration of Blacks and Whites From the South, 1900–1950 (New York: Academic Press, 1981), 37.

15. Ibid., 9.

16. Ibid., 21.

17. Estelle B. Freedman, No Turning Back: The History of Feminism and the Future of Women (New York: Ballantine Books, 2002), 80–81.

18. Melvin Drimmer, ed., Black History: A Reappraisal (Garden City, New York: Doubleday and Co., 1969), 325.

19. Jesse O. McKee, ed., Mississippi: A Portrait of an American State (Montgomery, Ala.: Clairmont Press, 1995), 126–128.

20. Loewen and Sallis, Mississippi: Conflict and Change, 195.

21. George M. Fredrickson, The Black Image in the White Mind: The Debate on Afro-American Character and Destiny, 1817–1914 (Middletown, Conn.: Wesleyan University Press, 1971), 271.

22. William Loren Katz, ed., Negro Population in the United States, 1790–1915 (New York: Arno Press and the New York Times, 1968), 420.

23. Thomas Jesse Jones, Negro Education: A Study of the Private and Higher Schools for Colored People in the United States, Volume I (Washington, D.C.: Government Printing Office, 1917), 37, 66, 382–83. Mississippi attitudes toward education are strikingly revealed in an observation by Joseph M. Hawes, who notes, "Massachusetts passed the first compulsory school attendance law in 1852; the last state to pass such a law was Mississippi in 1918." See Joseph M. Hawes, The Children's Rights Movement: A History of Advocacy and Protection (Boston: Twayne Publishers, 1991), 51.

24. Jones, Negro Education, 66.

25. "The Negro Since 1900: A Progress Report," in David Levering Lewis, ed., W. E. B. Du Bois: A Reader (New York: Henry Holt and Co., 1995), 412.

26. C. Eric Lincoln, "The Black Heritage in Religion in the South," in: Charles Reagan Wilson, ed., Religion in the South (Jackson, Miss.: University Press of Mississippi, 1985), 56–57.

27. The Jackson Advocate, December 9, 1982.

28. Ibid., May 3, 2001.

29. E. H. Beardsley, "Dedicated Servant or Errant Professional: The Southern Negro Physician Before World War II," in: Walter J. Fraser, Jr., and Wilfred B. Moore, Jr., eds., The Southern Enigma: Essays On Race, Class and Folk Culture (Westport, Conn.: Greenwood Press, 1983), 143–145.

30. Jessie Mosley, The Negro in Mississippi History (Jackson, Miss.: Helderman Bros., 1950), 95. Also see McMillen, Dark Journey: Black Mississippians in the Age of Jim Crow, 171–172.

31. Julius E. Thompson, The Black Press in Mississippi, 1865–1985 (Gainesville, Fla.: University Press of Florida, 1993), 11.

32. See William G. Jordan, Black Newspapers and America's War for Democracy, 1914–1920 (Chapel Hill, N.C.: The University of North Carolina Press, 2001), 110, 122–29.

33. The Jackson Advocate, December, 9, 1982.

34. J. Clay Smith, Jr., Emancipation: The Making of the Black Lawyer, 1844–1944 (Philadelphia: University of Pennsylvania Press, 1993), 294–298.

35. Benjamin Quarles, "The Morning Breaks: Black America, 1910–1935," in: Black Mosaic, Essays in Afro-American History and Historiography (Amherst: The University of Massachusetts Press, 1988), 143–144.

36. Pete Daniel, Standing at the Crossroads: Southern Life Since 1900 (New York: Hill and Wang, 1986), 29–30.

37. Arthur S. Link and William B. Catton, American Epoch: A History of the United States Since 1900 (New York: Alfred A. Knopf, 1973), 16.

38. Gabriel Kolko, Main Currents in Modern American History (New York: Harper and Row, Publishers, 1976), 307.

39. Paul Johnson, A History of the American People (New York: Harper Collins Publishers, 1999), 661.

40. Herbert Shapiro, White Violence and Black Response: From Reconstruction to Montgomery (Amherst: University of Massachusetts Press, 1988), 142.

41. Clarion-Ledger/Jackson Daily News, February 12, 1984. Neil R. McMillen notes the difficulties which came to some blacks in Mississippi for their NAACP activities. See McMillen, Dark Journey: Black Mississippians in the Age of Jim Crow, 31.

42. Robert Maccigrosso, Ron Blazek, and Teri Maggio, Term Paper Resource Guide to Twentieth-Century United States History (Westport, Conn.: Greenwood Press, 1999), 32–33.

43. McMillen, Dark Journey: Black Mississippians in the Age of Jim Crow, 303; Esmond Wright, The American Dream: From

Reconstruction to Reagan (Cambridge, Mass.: Blackwell Publishers, 1996), 586; Bernard C. Nalty, *Strength for the Fight: A History of Black Americans in the Military* (New York: The Free Press, 1986), 108.

44. Johnson, *A History of the American People*, 660–661.

45. William J. Cooper, Jr., and Thomas E. Terrill, *The American South: A History* (New York: Alfred A. Knopf, 1990), 547.

46. Nalty, *Strength for the Fight*, 124. African-American journalist Ted Poston noted the massive mistreatment of blacks as early as 1917: "During the first fourteen months of our participation in the World War I, 259 Negroes were lynched in the United States of America. And no Hun atrocity was half as revolting." See Kathleen A. Hauke, *Ted Poston: Pioneer American Journalist* (Athens, Ga.: University of Georgia Press, 1998). 15.

47. Gail Buckley, *American Patriots: The Story of Blacks in the Military From the Revolution to Desert Storm* (New York: Random House, 2001), 223.

48. McMillen, *Dark Journey: Black Mississippians in the Age of Jim Crow*, 30.

49. David M. Oshinsky, *"Worse Than Slavery": Parchman Farm and the Ordeal of Jim Crow Justice* (New York: The Free Press, 1996).

50. Biennial Report of the Board of Trustees, Superintendent and Other Officers of the Mississippi State Penitentiary, July 1, 1911, to July 1, 1913 (Jackson, Miss.: Tucker Printing House, 1913), 57.

51. Oshinsky, *"Worse Than Slavery": Parchman Farm and the Ordeal of Jim Crow Justice*, 137.

52. Pete Daniel, *The Shadow of Slavery: Peonage in the South, 1901-1969* (Urbana, Ill.: University of Illinois Press, 1990), 19.

53. Robert R. Moton, "The South and the Lynching Evil," *The South Atlantic Quarterly* 18, No. 3 (July 1919): 191; *Teacher's Resource Manual, The African American Experience: A History* (Englewood Cliffs, N.J.: Globe Book Co., 1992), 230; Vincent Tomkins, ed., 1899 (Detroit, Mich.: Gale, 1997), 559; NAACP, *Thirty Years of Lynching in the United States, 1889-1918* (New York: NAACP, 1919; reprint ed., New York: Negro Universities Press, 1969), 29, 32.

54. Leww Singelman and Susan Welch, *Black Americans' Views of Racial Inequality: The Dream Deferred* (New York: Cambridge University Press, 1991), 44–45.

55. Manning Marable, *Beyond Black and White: Transforming African-American Politics* (New York: Verso, 1995), 182.

56. Michael R. Belknap, *Federal Law and Southern Order: Racial Violence and Constitutional Conflict in the Post-Brown South* (Athens, Ga.: The University of Georgia Press, 1987), 3.

57. Daniel T. Williams, "The Lynching Records at Tuskegee Institute," in: *Eight Negro Bibliographies* (N.Y.: Krus Reprint Co., 1970), 6, 8, 11.

58. Thompson, "The Distribution of Lynch Victims in Mississippi," 62–66.

59. *Ibid.*, 68.

60. Tolnay and Beck, *A Festival of Violence*, 32–34, 142–149.

61. James S. Hirsch, *Riot and Remembrance: The Tulsa Race War and Its Legacy* (Boston: Houghton Mifflin Co., 2002), 51.

62. Johnson, *A History of the American People*, 661.

63. Robert J. Kelly, "The Ku Klux Klan: Recurring Hate in America," in: Robert J. Kelly and Jess Maghan, eds., *Hate Crime: The Global Politics of Polarization* (Carbondale, Ill.: Southern Illinois University Press, 1998), 60.

64. "Darkest Mississippi," *The Crisis* 18, No. 3 (July 1919): 142.

65. "The Civilization of Mississippi," *The Crisis* 7. No. 6 (April 1914): 285–286. For a further *Crisis* statement on this case, see *The Crisis* 8, No. 1 (May 1914): 20. It is noted that after Sam Petty was killed, "the burned bones and ashes were buried in the edge of the street in front of a colored barber shop." *Ibid.*, 20.

66. *New York Times*, January 21, 1915.

67. "Crime," *The Crisis* 11, No. 4 (February 1916): 168.

68. J. William Harris, "Etiquette, Lynching, and Racial Boundaries in Southern History: A Mississippi Example," *The American Historical Review* 100, No. 2 (April 1995): 407. For an NAACP story on this case, see NAACP, *Burning at Stake in the United States* (New York: NAACP, June 1919), 4–9.

69. The Shubuta Lynchings," *The Crisis* 18, No. 1 (May 1919): 24–25. Flint Kellogg notes an interesting twist on this case: "Upon receiving a letter of protest from the NAACP, signed by Shillady [Secretary of the NAACP], following the lynching of four Negroes at Shubata, Mississippi, Governor Theodore G. Bilbo was reported by the *Washington Bee* to have given a state official "advance information to the effect that I will tell them, in effect, to go to him." See Charles Flint Kellogg, *NAACP: A History of the NAACP, Volume I, 1909-1920* (Baltimore, Md.: The John Hopkins University Press, 1967), 231. According to the *Crisis*, when the NAACP protested another Mississippi lynching of March 21, 1919: "The Jackson, Miss. *Daily News* published the following anonymous reply to the telegram of the NAACP protesting to the Governor against the lynching of Eugene Green, at Belzonie, Miss.: 'The Governor is not in the city, and the telegram has not been answered. However, the National Association for the Advancement of Colored People need not remain in the dark concerning the fate of Green. He was 'advanced' all right from the end of a rope, and in order to save burial expenses his body was thrown into the Yazoo River. If this information does not suffice, we can give you the size of the rope and the exact location of where this coon was hung.'" See *The Crisis* 8, No. 1 (May 1919): 37.

70. McMillen, *Dark Journey: Black Mississippians in the Age of Jim Crow*, 232.

71. Mike Alexander, "Parish Street: A Neighborhood Built By Giants," *American Visions* 3, No. 4 (August 1988): 32–34.

72. *The Crisis* 17, No. 6 (April 1919): 289. The situation for black lawyers in Mississippi continued to be a complicated one in the 1910s. One writer notes that W. H. Mhoon "was one of about twenty-two black lawyers in Mississippi in 1909. Black lawyers had been barred from practicing in some countries in the latter part of the last century and the early part of this [the 20th] century." See Constance Baker Motley, *Equal Justice Under Law: An Autobiography* (New York: Farrar, Straus and Giroux, 1998), 74.

73. Karla F. C. Holloway, *Passed On: African American Mourning Stories, A Memorial* (Durham, N.C.: Duke University Press, 2002), 17–18.

74. Dewey W. Grantham, *The South in Modern America: A Region At Odds* (New York: Harper Collins Publishers, 1994), 85.

75. *The Crisis* 16., No. 4 (August 1918): 173; 17, No. 6 (April 1919): 1285.

76. *The Crisis* 18, No. 4 (August 1919): 189.

77. *The Crisis* 18, No. 5 (September 1919): 235.

78. *The Crisis* noted the personal efforts of a significant black doctor in Mississippi in the 1910s: "Dr. S. D. Redmond, a colored physician of Jackson, Mississippi, invited all the poor of the city to dine with him Christmas day." See *The Crisis* 11, No. 4 (February 1916): 167.

79. Thompson, *The Black Press in Mississippi, 1865-1985*, 14–15, 24; Julius E. Thompson, *The Black Press in Mississippi, 1865-1985: A Directory* (West Cornwall, Conn.: Locust Hill Press, 1988), 10–20.

80. Thompson, *The Black Press in Mississippi, 1865-1985*, 41; Julius E. Thompson, *Black Life in Mississippi: Essays on Political, Social and Cultural Studies in a Deep South State* (Lanham, Md.: University Press of America, 2001), 17–20.

81. Stewart E. Tolnay and E. M. Beck, "Rethinking the Role of Racial Violence in the Great Migration," in: Alferdteen Harrison, ed., *Black Exodus: The Great Migration From*

the *American South* (Jackson, Miss.: University Press of Mississippi, 1991), 22.

82. Eric Foner, *The Story of American Freedom* (New York: W. W. Norton and Co., 1998), 174. Roebuck "Pops" Staples (1914–?), born at Winona, Mississippi, notes that his family departed Mississippi in the middle of the Great Depression, "hoping to find a better life." See Alan Govenar, "Interview with Roebuck 'Pops' Staples," in: Alan Govenar, ed., *African American Frontiers: Slave Narratives and Oral Histories* (Santa Barbara, Calif.: ABC-Clio, Inc., 2000), 430–434.

83. Adero, *Up South: Stories, Studies, and Letters of This Century's Black Migrations*, 139.

84. *Ibid.*, 138.

85. Paul A. Gilje, *Rioting in America* (Bloomington, Ind.: Indiana University Press, 1996), 104–105.

86. Thomas Pearce Bailey, *Race Orthodoxy in the South and Other Aspects of the Negro Question* (New York: The Neale Publishing Co., 1914; reprint ed., New York: Negro Universities Press, 1969), 93.

87. Jordan, *Black Newspapers and America's War For Democracy, 1914-1920*, 130.

88. Dwyn M. Mounger, "Lynching in Mississippi, 1830–1930" (M.A. thesis, Department of History and Government, Mississippi State University, August 1961), 86.

89. Richard L. Watson, Jr., "From Populism Through the New Deal, Southern Political History," in: John B. Boles and Evelyn Thomas Nolen, eds., *Interpreting Southern History: Historiographical Essays in Honor of Sanford W. Higginbotham* (Baton Rouge. La.: Louisiana State University Press, 1987), 339–340.

90. See I. A. Newby, ed., *The Development of Segregationist Thought* (Homewood, Ill.: The Dorsey Press, 1968), 134.

91. *The Crisis* 17, No. l (November 1918): 9.

92. George M. Fredrickson, "The Triumph of Radical Racism—Joel Williamson's 'The Crucible of Race,'" in: *The Arrogance of Race: Historical Perspectives On Slavery, Racism, and Social Inequality* (Middletown, Conn.: Wesleyan University Press, 1988), 176.

93. On Taft see Paoloe Coletta, *The Presidency of William Howard Taft* (Lawrence: The University Press of Kansas, 1973), 266; James F. Vivian, ed., *William Howard Taft: Collected Editorials, 1917-1921* (New York: Praegar, 1990), 49–51. On Woodrow Wilson see: Kendrick A. Clements, *The Presidency of Woodrow Wilson* (Laurence: The University Press of Kansas, 1992), 45–46, 160; E. David Cronon, ed., *The Political Thought of Woodrow Wilson* (Indianapolis, Ind.: The Bobbs-Merrill Co., 1965), 395–97

94. Stacy L. Smith and Martha Soloman Watson, "William Edward Burghardt Du Bois (1868–1963), Professor, Editor, Civil Rights Leader," in: Richard W. Leeman, ed., *African-American Orators: A Bio-Critical Sourcebook* (Westport, Conn.: Greenwood Press, 1996), 99; David W. Southern, "The Crisis," in: John D. Buenker and Edward R. Kantowicz, eds., *Historical Dictionary of the Progressive Era, 1890-1920* (New York: Greenwood Press, 1988), 99.

95. Grace Elizabeth Hale, *Making Whiteness: The Culture of Segregation in the South, 1890-1940* (New York: Pantheon Books, 1998), 364.

96. William M. Banks, *Black Intellectuals: Race and Responsibility in American Life* (New York: W. W. Norton & Co., 1996), 276.

97. See "Monroe Nathan Work and His Contributions," *The Journal of Negro History* 34, No. 4 (October 1949): 449–451; Kevin K. Gaines, *Uplifting the Race: Black Leadership, Politics, and Culture in the Twentieth Century* (Chapel Hill, N.C.: The University of North Carolina Press, 1996), 85–88; Sigelman and Welch, *Black Americans' Views of Racial Inequality: The Dream Deferred*, 19; Hal W. Bochin, "Marcus Moziah Garvey (1887–1940), Black Nationalist," in: Leeman, *African-American Orators: A Bio-Critical Sourcebook*, 151–162; Deborah Gillon Straub, ed., *African American Voices, Volume 2: K–Z* (New York: Gale Research, 1996), 349; Carter G. Wood-

son, *The Negro in Our History* (Washington, D.C.: The Associated Publishers, 1947), 434–35; Tony Martin, *Marcus Garvey, Hero: A First Biography* (Dover, Mass.: The Majority Press, 1983). On the role of black fraternities and sororities see: Lawrence C. Ross, Jr., *The Divine Nine: The History of African American Fraternities and Sororities* (New York: Kensington Publishing Corp, 2002).

98. Abby Arthur Johnson and Ronald M. Johnson, "Away From Accommodation: Radical Editors and Protest Journalism, 1900–1910," *Journal of Negro History* 62, No. 4 (October 1977): 325–338.

99. Mark Ellis, "America's Black Press, 1914–18," *The Crisis* (September 1991): 20–27; Mary Frances Berry, *Black Resistance, White Law: A History of Constitutional Racism in America* (New York: Appleton-Century-Crofts, 1971), 142–143; *The Crusader Magazine* 1, No. 1 (September 1918): 12, 15–16, 31–32. On the negative treatment of some of the black press in the late 1910s see: Theodore Kornweibel, Jr., *"Seeing Red": Federal Campaigns Against Black Militancy, 1919-1925* (Bloomington, Ind.: Indiana University Press, 1998), 38–47; *The Messenger* 1, No. 11 (November 1917): 11.

100. Charles Harris Wesley, *The History of the National Association of Colored Women's Clubs: A Legacy of Service* (Washington, D.C.: National Association of Colored Women's Clubs, Inc., 1984), 528.

101. "Faith, Feminism, and the Future," in: Rosemary Skinner Keller and Rosemary Radford Ruether, eds., *In Our Own Voices: Four Centuries of American Women's Religious Writing* (San Francisco, Calif.: Harper San Francisco, 1995), 283.

102. *Ibid.*, 284.

103. Darryl Lytnan, *Great African-American Women* (New York: Gramercy Books, 1999), 215–217; "A Red Record," Ida B. Wells-Barnett, in: Gerda Lerner, ed., *Black Women in White America: A Documentary History* (New York: Pantheon Books, 1972), 196–199; Deborah E. McDowell, *"The Changing Same": Black Women's Literature, Criticism and Theory* (Bloomington, Ind.: Indiana University Press, 1995), 27–29; A'Lelia Bundles, *On Her Own Ground: The Life and Times of Madam C. J. Walker* (New York: Washington Square Press/Pocket Books, 2001), 180–83, 237–38, 270–72.

104. Thomas Harrison Baker, *The Memphis Commercial Appeal: The History of a Southern Newspaper* (Baton Rouge, La.: Louisiana State University Press, 1971), 206. As noted earlier, the muckrakers of the period 1890–1920 did not pay much attention to the conditions of blacks in American life, including the problem of lynching. See Maurine Beasley, "The Muckrakers and Lynching: A Case Study in Racism," *Journalism History* 9, Nos. 3–4 (Autumn-Winter 1982): 86–91.

105. "A Southern Protest Against Lynching," *The Outlook* 112 (January 19, 1916): 124- 125.

106. Dominic J. Capeci, Jr., "Commission On Interracial Cooperation," in: Buenker and Kantowicz, *Historical Dictionary of the Progressive Era, 1890-1920*, 84; Douglas L. Smith, *The New Deal in the Urban South* (Baton Rouge, La.: Louisiana State University Press, 1988), 246. On northern white women's interest in black affairs see: Bettina Aptheker, ed., *Lynching and Rape: An Exchange of Views by Jane Addams and Ida B. Wells* (New York: The American Institute for Marxist Studies, 1977), 1–41; Geoffrey C. Ward, *Not For Ourselves Alone: The Story of Elizabeth Cady Stanton and Susan B. Anthony, An Illustrated History* (New York: Alfred A. Knopf, 1999), 185; Carolyn Wedin, *Inheritors of the Spirit: Mary White Ovington and the Founding of the NAACP* (New York: John Wiley and Sons, 1998); Mary Jane Brown, *Eradicating This Evil: Women in the American Anti-Lynching Movement, 1892-1940* (New York: Garland Publishing, 2000), 95–116.

107. Scan Dennis Cashman, *America in the Twenties and Thirties: The Olympian Age of Franklin Delano Roosevelt* (New York: New York University Press, 1989), 272; David L. Porter, "Dyer Antilynching Bill," in: Editors of Salem Press, *The Civil Rights Movement*, Volume I (Pasadena, Calif: Salem Press, 2000), 215. For a hearing by the Committee on the

Judiciary, House of Representatives, on "To Protect Citizens of the United States Against Lynching In Default of Protection by the States," see: *Hearings Before the Committee on the Judiciary, Sixty-Fifth Congress, Second Session, on H.R. 11279 Serial 66* (Washington, D.C.: Government Printing Office, 1918), 1–27.

108. Nancy J. Weiss, "Long-Distance Runners of the Civil Rights Movement: The Contribution of Jews to the NAACP and the National Urban League in the Early Twentieth Century," in: Jack Salzman and Cornell West, eds., *Struggles in the Promised Land: Toward a History of Black-Jewish Relations in the United States* (New York: Oxford University Press, 1997), 123–124.

109. Paul Battle and Robin D. G. Kelley, "Allies of a Different Sort: Jews and Blacks in the American Left," in Salzman and West, *Struggles in the Promised Land*, 200.

110. Deborah Dash Moore, "Separate Paths: Blacks and Jews in the Twentieth-Century South," in Salzman and West, *Struggles in the Promised Land*, 285. (Years later, in 1984, Frank's conviction was overturned, by a posthumous pardon, by the Georgia Board of Pardons.) *Ibid.*, 285; Barton C. Shaw, "Leo Max Frank," in: Buenker and Kantowicz, *Historical Dictionary of the Progressive Era, 1890-1920*, 165. On this period also see Robert Seitz Frey and Nancy Thompson-Frey, *The Silent and the Damned: The Murder of Mary Phagan and the Lynching of Leo Frank* (Lanham, Md.: Madison Books, 1988).

111. W. Eugene Hoi Ion, *Frontier Violence: Another Look* (New York: Oxford University Press, 1974), 51.

112. Jimmie Lewis Franklin, *Journey Toward Hope: A History of Blacks in Oklahoma* (Norman, Okla.: University of Oklahoma Press, 1982), 131.

113. Dominic J. Capeci, Jr., *The Lynching of Cleo Wright* (Lexington, Ky.: The University Press of Kentucky, 1998), 176.

114. Yohuru R. Williams, "Permission to Hate: Delaware, Lynching, and the Culture of Violence in America," *Journal of Black Studies* 32, No. 1 (September 2001): 3–4.

115. Dennis B. Downey and Raymond M. Hyser, *No Crooked Death: Coatesville, Pennsylvania, and the Lynching of Zachariah Walker* (Urbana, Ill.: University of Illinois Press, 1991), 1–2.

Chapter 7

1. Ross Oregon, *Modern America, 1914 to 1945* (New York: Facts On File, 1995), 3–4; John N. Burrus, "Urbanization in Mississippi, 1890–1970," in: Richard A. McLemore, ed., *A History of Mississippi* Volume II (Hattiesburg: University and College Press of Mississippi, 1973), 348.

2. Charles S. Johnson, "The New Frontage On American Life," in: Alain Locke, ed., *The New Negro* (New York: Albert and Charles Boni, 1925; reprint ed., Touchstone Simon and Schuster, 1997), 280.

3. Gregory, *Modern America: 1914 to 1945*, 4. By 1910, Mississippi only had 1,253 Native Americans listed among its population base; this number would reach 1,458 by 1930. See Paul Stuart, *Nations Within a Nation: Historical Statistics of American Indians* (New York: Greenwood Press, 1987), 57.

4. David M. Kennedy, *Freedom From Fear: The American People in Depression and War, 1929-1945* (New York: Oxford University Press, 1999), 19.

5. Paul Johnson, *A History of the American People* (New York: Harper Collins Publishers, 1999), 529.

6. Gilbert C. Fite, *Cotton Fields No More: Southern Agriculture, 1865-1980* (Lexington: The University Press of Kentucky, 1984), 234–238.

7. Neil Fligstein, *Going North: Migration of Blacks and Whites From the South, 1900-1950* (New York: Academic Press, 1981), 16.

8. Sarah C. Campbell, "Black-Owned Banks Prospered Until Hard Times Closed Doors," *Clarion-Ledger*, February 10, 1991, G-l; Arthur James, Jimmie James, Jr., and Robert E. James, *The Mississippi Black Bankers and Their Institutions* (Jackson, Miss.: By the Authors, 1996), 21–30.

9. *Jackson Advocate*, December 9, 1982; John N. Ingham and Lynne B. Feldman, *African-American Business Leaders: A Biographical Dictionary* (Westport, Conn.: Greenwood Press, 1994), 724, 750.

10. Julius E. Thompson, *The Black Press in Mississippi, 1865-1985* (Gainesville: University Press of Florida, 1993), 15.

11. Pete Daniel, *Dee'n As It Come: The 1927 Mississippi River Flood* (New York: Oxford University Press, 1977), 7–11; Jesse O. McKee, ed., *Mississippi: A Portrait of an American State* (Montgomery, Ala.: Clairmont Press, 1995), 165.

12. James W. Loewen and Charles Sallis, eds., *Mississippi: Conflict and Change* (New York: Pantheon Books, 1974), 240.

13. Jerrold M. Packard, *American Nightmare: The History of Jim Crow* (New York: St. Martin's Press, 2002), 135.

14. I.A. Newby, *Jim Crow's Defense: Anti-Negro Thought in America, 1900-1930* (Baton Rouge: Louisiana State University Press, 1965), ix–x.

15. Langston Hughes, "Old Man River," in: Christopher C. Desantis, ed., *The Collected Works of Langston Hughes, Volume 10: Fight For Freedom and Other Writings on Civil Rights* (Columbia, Mo.: University of Missouri Press, 2001), 88–90.

16. Henry Allen Bullock, *A History of Negro Education in the South: From 1619 to the Present* (Cambridge, Mass.: Harvard University Press, 1967), 177–178, 180–181.

17. Jessie Mosley, *The Negro in Mississippi History* (Jackson, Miss.: Helderman Bros., 1950), 60–76; Cleopatra D. Thompson, *The History of the Mississippi Teachers Association* (Washington, D.C.: NBA Teacher Rights, and Jackson, Miss.: Mississippi Teachers Association, 1973), 164–172. The 1920s were a period of conflict on many black college campuses, including Alcorn College, which had a student strike in 1929. See Raymond Wolter, *The Negro on Campus: Black College Rebellions of the 1920s* (Princeton, N.J.: Princeton University Press, 1975), 277.

18. Bullock, *A History of Negro Education in the South*, 73.

19. *Ibid.*, 73–74.

20. Kennedy, *Freedom from Fear*, 19.

21. "Mississippi Medical and Surgical Association Celebrates 100 Years," *Jackson Advocate*, May 3, 2001, 3-A; Jim Rundles, "The Legend of Parish Street," *Jackson Advocate*, July 15, 1999, 8-A, and July 29, 1999, 2-B; Mike Alexander, "Parish Street: A Neighborhood Built by Giants," *American Visions* 3, No. 4 (August 1988): 32–37; E. H. Beardsley, "Dedicated Servants or Errant Professional: The Southern Negro Physician Before World War II," in: Walter J. Fraser, Jr., and Winfred B. Moore, Jr., eds., *The Southern Enigma: Essays on Race, Class, and Folk Culture* (Westport, Conn.: Greenwood Press, 1983), 143–152.

22. Neil R. McMillen, *Dark Journey: Black Mississippians in the Age of Jim Crow* (Urbana: The University of Illinois Press, 1989), 169–172.

23. Roger M. Valade, III, *The Essential Black Literature Guide* (Detroit: Visible Ink, 1996), 165–167; Gary D. Wintz, ed., *The Critics and the Harlem Renaissance* (New York: Garland Publishing, 1996).

24. Johnson, *A History of the American People*, 700.

25. Charles Shaar Murray, *Boogie Man: The Adventures of John Lee Hooker in the American Twentieth Century* (New York: St. Martin's Griffin, 2000), 14. Murray notes that "John Lee Hooker left the Mississippi Delta while still in the turbulence of adolescence. Nevertheless, Mississippi never left him." *Ibid.*, 14. It is believed that Hooker was born in 1917, perhaps at Clarksdale, Mississippi. *Ibid.*, 22.

26. Ralph Ellison, *Shadow and Act* (New York: The New American Library, 1964); Quoted in Deborah G. Felder, *The 100 Most Influential Women of All Time* (2001), 283.

27. Hazel Rowley, *Richard Wright: The Life and Times* (New York: Henry Holt & Co., 2001), 28–73.

28. Julius E. Thompson, "The Black Poet in Mississippi, 1900–1980," in: *Black Life in Mississippi: Essays on Political, Social, and Cultural Studies in a Deep South State* (Lanham, Md.: University Press of America, 2001), 93–95; James L. Conyers, Jr., ed., *African Studies: A Disciplinary Quest for Both Theory and Method* (Jefferson, N.C.: McFarland and Co., 1997), 209–211.

29. "African-Americans," in: June Melby Benowitz, ed., *Encyclopedia of American Women and Religion* (Santa Barbara, Calif.: ABC-Clio, 1998), 5. On the important issue of women as clergy, see: Barbara Brown Zikmund, Adair T. Lummis, and Patricia M. Y. Chang, *Clergy Women: An Uphill Calling* (Louisville, Ky.: Westminister John Knox Press, 1998), 5–7. On the importance of the blues and black religion see: Evelyn Brooks Higginbotham, "'Rethinking Vernacular Culture: Black Religion and Race Records in the 1920s and 1930s," in: Wahneema Lubiano, ed., *The House That Race Built: Black Americans, U.S. Terrain* (New York: Pantheon Books, 1997), 157–177.

30. Salley G. McMillen, *To Raise Up the South: Sunday Schools in Black and White Churches, 1865–1915* (Baton Rouge: Louisiana State University Press, 2001), 246.

31. John B. Skates, "Mississippi," in: David C. Roller and Robert W. Twyman, eds., *The Encyclopedia of Southern History* (Baton Rouge: Louisiana State University Press, 1979), 832–33.

32. *Ibid.*, 836.

33. McKee, *Mississippi: A Portrait of an American State*, 153.

34. William Archer, *Through Afro-America: An English Reading of the Race Problem* (Westport, Conn.: Negro Universities Press, 1970; originally published, London: Chapman and Hall, Ltd., 1910), 171.

35. Loewen and Sallis, *Mississippi: Conflict and Change*, 237.

36. Arthur M. Schlesinger, Jr., and John S. Bowman, eds., *The Almanac of American History* (New York: Barnes and Noble/Brompton Books Corp., 1993), 439. The editors note: "To educate women in the ways of politics, the National League of Women Voters is organized" in 1920. *Ibid.*, 439.

37. Dewey W. Grantham, *The South in Modern America: A Region at Odds* (New York: Harper Collins Publishers, 1994), 319.

38. Jerone G. Miller, *Search and Destroy: African-American Males in the Criminal Justice System* (New York: Cambridge University Press, 1996), 52.

39. Joe R. Feagin, *Racist America: Roots, Current Realities, and Future Reparations* (New York: Routledge, 2001), 147.

40. David M. Oshinsky, *"Worse Than Slavery": Parchman Farm and the Ordeal of Jim Crow Justice* (New York: The Free Press, 1996), 137.

41. *Ibid.*, 149. On the nature of peonage in Mississippi during the 1920s, see Pete Daniel, *The Shadow of Slavery: Peonage in the South, 1901–1969* (Urbana: University of Illinois Press, 1990), 161–168.

42. Oshinsky, *"Worse Than Slavery": Parchman Farm and the Ordeal of Jim Crow Justice*, 169.

43. Robert Perkinson, "Between the Worst of the Past and the Worst of the Future": Reconsidering Convict Leasing in the South," *Radical History Review* 71 (Spring 1998): 215.

44. Martin Gilbert, *History of the Twentieth Century* (New York: Harper Collins Publishers, 2001), 135.

45. David Chalmers, "The Hooded Knights Revive Rule by Terror in the Twenties," in: Frederick M. Binder and David M. Reimers, eds., *The Way We Lived: Essays and Documents in American Social History, Volume II: 1865–Present* (Lexington, Mass.: D. C. Heath & Co., 1996), 155.

46. Lenwood G. Davis and Janet L. Sims-Wood, *The Ku Klux Klan: A Bibliography* (Westport, Conn.: Greenwood

Press, 1984), 622–23; *Clarion-Ledger/Jackson Daily News*, February 12, 1984; Kenneth T. Jackson, *The Ku Klux Klan in the City, 1915–1930* (New York: Oxford University Press, 1967), 237. Three scholars note that "The Klan reached its peak in the mid–1920s. To millions of Americans it was a thing of terror. Exposés of its violent and illegal activities seemed to have no effect on its power. Finally, in November of 1925, the Klan's Grand Dragon, David C. Stephenson, was convicted on a charge of murder. This became a turning point for the Klan. By the following year, its membership was on the decline. By 1930 it had only about 9000 members." See Robert P. Green, Jr., Laura L. Becker, and Robert E. Coniello, *The American Tradition: A History of the United States* (Columbia, Ohio: Charles E. Merrill Publishing Co., 1986), 484.

47. Stewart E. Tolnay and E. M. Beck, *A Festival of Violence: An Analysis of Southern Lynchings, 1882–1930* (Urbana: University of Illinois Press, 1995), 47.

48. See Stewart E. Tolnay and E. M. Beck, "Racial Violence and Black Migration in the American South, 1910 to 1930," *American Sociological Review* 57 (February 1992): 103–116.

49. Michael D'Orso, *Like Judgment Day: The Ruin and Redemption of a Town Called Rosewood* (New York: Boulevard Books/The Berkley Publishing Group, 1996), 53. Dwyn M. Mounger quotes Beulah A. Ratliff, who lived in the Delta, on the various causes of lynchings in Mississippi: "While I was living in the Mississippi Delta I knew of Negroes being killed for the following causes: for the attacking [of] a white woman, 1; trying to enter a movie theater on the 'white side,' 1; trying to enter a 'white restaurant,' 1; house-breaking, 1; helping a Negro murderer to escape, 1; killing a white man, 1; shooting a white man, 4; drawing a gun on a white man, 1." See Dwyn M. Mounger, "Lynching in Mississippi, 1830–1930" (M.A. thesis, Mississippi State University, Department of History and Government, August 1961), 105; quoting Beulah A. Ratliff, "Mississippi: Heart of Dixie," *Nation* 64 (1922): 589.

50. *Negro Yearbooks, 1941–46 and 1947–51* (Durham, N.C.: Tuskegee Records, Microfilm edition, Duke University; and Southern Regional Papers, Microfilm edition, University of North Carolina).

51. Ralph Ginzburg, *100 Years of Lynchings* (New York: Lancer Books, 1962), 9; Thompson, *Black Life in Mississippi*, 213–214.

52. Thompson, *Black Life in Mississippi*, 213–214.

53. *Ibid.*, 213–214.

54. Linda Williams, *Playing the Race Card: Melodramas of Black and White From Uncle Tom to O. J. Simpson* (Princeton, N.J.: Princeton University Press, 2001), 346.

55. *Natchez Democrat*, January 2, 1923, 3–4.

56. *Southern Sentinel* (Ripley, Miss.), September 24, 1925, 1.

57. "Shame to Mississippi," *The Nation* 128, No. 3315 (January 16, 1929).

58. Robert Gordon, *Can't Be Satisfied: The Life and Times of Muddy Waters* (Boston: Little, Brown and Co., 2002), 10.

59. *The Crisis* 23, No. 4 (February 1922): 165–167; Thompson, *Black Life in Mississippi*, 44. 50, 57–74, 93, 112, 149–190; Thompson, *The Black Press in Mississippi, 1865–1985*, 11–16; *Delta Leader* (Greenville, Miss.), November 2, 1940, 1.

60. "Lynching," in: Susan Altman, ed., *The Encyclopedia of African-American Heritage* (New York: Facts On File, 1997), 151.

61. Mounger, "Lynching in Mississippi, 1830–1930," 109.

62. *Ibid.*, 110–112. Mounger noted further that "adjutant generals of the Mississippi National Guard during the 1920s generally showed a willingness and an ability to send out their units whenever they were called upon to prevent lynchings. In every instance from 1926 to 1930 when the militia was called out for the specific purpose of preventing a mob killing, the guardsmen were successful in their objective. At

times they employed machine guns, tear gas, and wire fences to protect prisoners from violence." *Ibid.*, 112. But local peace officers in Mississippi were not successful in preventing lynchings. According to Mounger: "In 1925 four lynch victims were taken from sheriffs or other peace officers in Mississippi. A mob took one of these from the courthouse itself, where he had just been acquitted of a murder charge. The following year one victim was taken from a jail and lynched, and another was killed in his cell. In 1927 three men were captured from Mississippi peace officers and murdered by mobs." *Ibid.*, 113.

63. Kenneth K. Bailey, *Southern White Protestantism in the Twentieth Century* (New York: Harper and Row, Publishers, 1964), 40.

64. Robert L. Zangrando, "The Organized Negro: The National Association for the Advancement of Colored People and Civil Rights," in: James C. Curtis and Lewis L. Gould, eds., *The Black Experience in America, Selected Essays* (Austin, Texas: University of Texas Press, 1970), 155.

65. *Ibid.*, 154.

66. *Ibid.*, 154; Carolyn Wedin, *Inheritors of the Spirit: Mary White Ovington and the Founding of the NAACP* (New York: John Wiley & Sons, 1998), 175–176; Michael E. Parrish, *Anxious Decades: America in Prosperity and Depression, 1920–1941* (New York: W. W. Norton & Co., 1992), 122; Carolyn Wedin Sylvander, *Jesse Redman Fauset: Black American Writer* (New York: The Whitston Publishing Co., 1981), 6–9; Melvin B. Tolson, "Walter White," in: Edward J. Mullen, ed., *The Harlem Group of Negro Writers* (Westport, Conn.: Greenwood Press, 2001), 77–82.

67. David L. Porter, "Dyer Antilynching Bill," in: *Editors of Salem Press, The Civil Rights Movement, Volume I* (Pasadena, Calif.: Salem Press, 2000), 215.

68. Thomas C. Holt and Elsa Barkley Brown, eds., *Major Problems in African-American History, Volume II: From Freedom to "Freedom Now," 1865–1990s* (Boston: Houghton Mifflin Co., 2000), 186–199.

69. James A. Emanuel and Theodore L. Gross, eds., *Dark Symphony: Negro Literature in America* (New York: The Free Press, 1968), 85–94.

70. Arnold Rampersad, *The Life of Langston Hughes, Volume 1: 1902–1941–I, Too, Sing America* (New York: Oxford University Press, 1986); Hal May, Deborah A. Straub, and Susan M. Trosky, eds., *Black Writers: A Selection of Sketches from Contemporary Authors* (Detroit: Gale Research, 1989), 124–128, 302; Alan Shucard, "Countee Cullen," in: Thadier Harris and Thadious M. Davis, eds., *Afro-American Writers From the Harlem Renaissance to 1940, Volume 51* (Detroit: Gale Research Co., 1987), 35–51; Houston A. Baker, Jr., *Afro-American Poetics: Revisions of Harlem and the Black Aesthetic* (Madison: The University of Wisconsin Press, 1988).

71. Carol P. Marsh-Lockett, ed., *Black Women Playwrights: Visions On the American Stage* (New York: Garland Publishing, 1999); Alain LeRoy Locke, *Race Contacts and Interracial Relations: Lectures on the Theory and Practice of Race* (Washington, D. C.: Howard University Press, 1992); Locke, *The New Negro; Sister Anthony Scally, "Woodson and the Genesis of ASALH," Negro History Bulletin* 40, No. 1 (January-February 1977): 635–55; Gary D. Wintz, *Black Culture and the Harlem Renaissance* (Houston: Rice University Press, 1988), 164–165; Chidi Ikonne, "Opportunity and Black Literature, 1923–33." *Phylon* 40, No. 1 (March 1979): 86–93; *The Messenger* 1, No. 9 (October 1920): 1020; Rayford W. Logan and Michael R. Winston, eds., *Dictionary of American Negro Biography* (New York: W. W. Norton & Co., 1982), 284–86, 347–48, 461–62, 614–16.

72. Mary Jane Brown, *Eradicating This Evil: Women in the American Anti-Lynching Movement, 1892–1940* (New York: Garland Publishing, 2000), 115.

73. David R. Roediger, ed., *Black On White: Black Writers On What it Means to be White* (New York: Schocken Books, 1998), 335.

74. Claude McKay, "The Lynching," in: *Selected Poems of Claude McKay* (New York: Twayne Publishers, Inc., 1953).

75. William Edward Eaton, *The American Federation of Teachers, 1916–1961: A History of the Movement* (Carbondale, Ill.: Southern Illinois University Press, 1975), 64–70; Jerone A. Chanes, "Who Does What?: Jewish Advocacy and Jewish Interest," in: L. Sandy Maisel, ed., *Jews in American Politics* (Lanham, Md.: Rowman and Littlefield Publishers, 2001), 105.

76. Estelle B. Freeman, *No Turning Back: The History of Feminism and the Future of Women* (New York: Ballantine Books, 2002), 84.

77. Richard Sherman, "The Harding Administration and the Negro: An Opportunity Lost," in: Richard Resh, ed., *Black America: Confrontation and Accommodation in the Twentieth Century* (Lexington, Mass.: D. C. Heath & Co., 1969), 64, 69. Also see Francis Russell, *The Shadow of Blooming Grove: Warren G. Harding in His Times* (New York: McGraw-Hill Book Co., 1968), 471–73.

78. Robert Sobel, *Coolidge: An American Enigma* (Washington, D. C.: Regnery Publishing, 1998). 249–250, 283.

79. Richard B. Sherman, *The Republican Party and Black America: From McKinley to Hoover, 1896–1933* (Charlottesville: University Press of Virginia, 1973), 248–49.

80. David L. Porter, "Dyer Antilynching Bill," in: Editors of Salem Press, *The Civil Rights Movement*, Volume 1 (Pasadena, Calif.: Salem Press, 2000), 215–216.

81. See Tony Martin, *Marcus Garney, Hero: A First Biography* (Dover, Mass.: The Majority Press, 1983), 161–163; C. Eric Lincoln and Lawrence H. Mamiya, *The Black Church in the African American Experience* (Durham, N.C.: Duke University Press, 1995), 382–404.

Chapter 8

1. Ross Gregory, *Modern America, 1914 to 1945* (New York: Facts On File, 1995), 3.

2. John N. Burrus, "Urbanization in Mississippi, 1890–1970," in Richard A. McLemore, ed., *A History in Mississippi, Volume II* (Hattiesburg: University and College Press of Mississippi, 1973), 348.

3. Gregory, *Modern America, 1914 to 1945*, 3.

4. James R. Grossman, *Land of Hope: Chicago, Black Southerners and the Great Migration* (Chicago: The University of Chicago Press, 1989), 18.

5. Joe R. Feagin, *Racial and Ethnic Relations* (Englewood Cliffs, N.J.: Prentice Hall, 1989), 225.

6. Pete Daniel, *Standing at the Crossroads: Southern Life Since 1900* (New York: Hill and Wang/Farrar, Straus and Giroux, 1986), 111. Peter Thompson writes of the era: "By 1933, 10,000 banks had failed or merged, and the value of their remaining assets had declined by 29%. The U. S. gross national product fell by over 25% between 1929 and 1933. Unemployment rose from 3.2% in 1929 to 25% in 1933. The Depression reached its nadir in 1933. In that year at least 30 million Americans were out of work." See Peter Thompson, *Dictionary of American History: From 1763 to the Present* (New York: Facts On File, 2000), 168.

7. John Ezell, *The South Since 1865* (Norman, Okla.: University of Oklahoma Press, 1982), 433. By 1930, the economic crisis could be seen in the fact that "in rural areas, food riots took place as farmers and their families looted village food shops and demonstrated against the local authorities." See Martin Gilbert, *History of the Twentieth Century* (New York: Harper Collins Publishers, 2001), 198.

8. Richard Wormser, *Hoboes: Wandering in America, 1870–1940* (New York: Walker and Co., 1994), 7. The author notes tragically that "an estimated 200,000 teenage hoboes wandered across America" in the 1930s. "On the trains many were killed." *Ibid.*, 107–114.

9. Charles Angoff and H. L. Mencken, "The Worst American State: Part III," *The American Mercury* 24, No. 95 (November 1931): 356. John Samuel Ezell later noted that this study listed "the four 'best' states [as] Massachusetts, Connecticut, New York, and (believe it or not) New Jersey, in that order." See John Samuel Ezell, "Summertime and the Livin' is Easy: Quality of Life in the South," in: *The South Since 1865* (Norman, Okla.: University of Oklahoma Press, 1982), 154.

10. Herald David Jaynes and Robin M. Williams, Jr., eds., *A Common Destiny: Blacks and American Society* (Washington, D.C.: National Academy Press, 1989), 57.

11. *Ibid.*, 59.

12. National data and surveys "show that most white Americans in 1939 thought blacks were less intelligent than whites (69 percent), and unambiguously endorsed segregated restaurants, neighborhoods, and schools (99, 97, and 98 percent of southerners and 62, 82, and 58 percent of northerners, respectively)." *Ibid.*, 60.

13. James T. Patterson, *Grand Expectations: The United States, 1945-1974* (New York: Oxford University Press, 1996), 381.

14. Ray Sprigle, *In the Land of Jim Crow* (New York: Simon and Schuster, 1949), 104-109.

15. Henry Allen Bullock, *A History of Negro Education in the South: From 1619 to the Present* (Cambridge, Mass.: Harvard University Press, 1967), 54-55, 132, 139-140.

16. Jaynes and Williams, 59.

17. Bullock, *A History of Negro Education in the South*, 139-140. In 1931, only 8.3 percent of Mississippi students were in high school. See Angoff and Mencken, "The Worst American State," 11.

18. Although historically black colleges in Mississippi also played a role in achieving black literacy (Alcorn College, Jackson State College, Rust College, Tougaloo College, and others), a special note must be made of the role of 10 historically private black educational institutions in Mississippi, in promoting black K-12 education. In 1931–32 these elementary and secondary schools were: (1) Christ's Missionary and Industrial College, Jackson, Holiness; (2) Delta Industrial Institute, Doddsville; (3) Girls' Industrial School, Moorhead, Congregational; (4) Johnson A. & M. High School, Stover, A. M. E. Zion; (5) Mary Holmes Seminary, West Point, Presbyterian; (6) Newton High School, Newton, Nonsect.; (7) Noxubee Industrial School, McLeod, Nonsect.; (8) St. Joseph's Academy, Meridian, Roman Catholic; (9) St. Mary's Catholic Institute, Vicksburg, Roman Catholic; and (10) Utica N. & I. Institute, Utica, Nonsect. See Monroe N. Work, *Negro Year Book, 1931-32* (Tuskegee, Ala.: Negro Year Book Publishing Co., 1932), 239.

19. *Jackson Advocate*, December 9, 1982.

20. *Simms' Blue Book and Directory*, 168.

21. Charles S. Johnson, *The Negro College Graduate* (College Park, Md.: McGrath Publishing Co., 1969, reprint ed.; originally published, Chapel Hill, N.C.: The University of North Carolina Press, 1938), 157.

22. *Jackson Advocate*, December 9, 1982.

23. *Simms' Blue Book and Directory*, 167-170.

24. Johnson, *The Negro College Graduate*, 156.

25. Richard Sterner, Lenore A. Epstein, Ellen Winston, and others, *The Negro's Share: A Study of Income Consumption, Housing and Public Assistance* (New York: Harper & Brothers, Publishers, 1943), 149.

26. See Clovis Semmes (aka Jabulani Kamau Makalani), *Racism, Health, and Post-Industrialism: A Theory of African-American Health* (Westport, Conn.: Praeger, 1996), 50–75.

27. Julius E. Thompson, *The Black Press in Mississippi, 1865-1985* (Gainesville, Fla.: University Press of Florida, 1993), 16–22.

28. *Jackson Advocate*, December 9, 1982.

29. Stephen W. Baskerville and Ralph Willett, eds., *Nothing Else to Fear: New Perspectives on America in the Thirties* (Dover, N.H.: Manchester University Press, 1985), 194–196.

30. *The 100 Most Influential Women*, 286.

31. Angela Y. Davis, *Blues Legacies and Black Feminism: Gertrude "Ma" Rainey, Bessie Smith, and Billie Holiday* (New York: Pantheon Books, 1998).

32. *Jackson Advocate*, May 23, 1991.

33. C. Eric Lincoln, "Knowing the Black Church: What It Is and Why," in: Janet Dewart, ed., *State of Black America* (New York: The National Urban League, 1989), 137–139; Edwin Scott Gaustad, *Historical Atlas of Religion in America* (New York: Harper & Row, Publishers 1962), 150–151.

34. Winthrop S. Hudson, *Religion in America: A Historical Account of the Development of American Religious Life* (New York: Charles Scribner's Sons, 1973), 351.

35. Flora Wilson Bridges, *Resurrection Song: African-American Spirituality* (Maryknoll, N.Y.: Orbis Books, 2001), 110–113; Ivory Phillips, *A Religion For Blacks in America* (Washington, D.C.: University Press of America, 1977), 1–4, 100.

36. See Marjorie Spruill Wheeler, *New Women of the New South: The Leaders of the Woman Suffrage Movement in the Southern States* (New York: Oxford University Press, 1993), 107–109, 122–123, 192–194.

37. *Clarion-Ledger/Jackson Daily News*, December 13, 1981; Jesse O. McKee, ed., *Mississippi: A Portrait of an American State* (Montgomery, Ala.: Clairmont Press, 1995), 354; Ralph McGill, *The South and the Southerner* (Boston: Little, Brown & Co., 1959), 119–121; Martha H. Swain, *Pat Harrison: The New Deal Years* (Jackson, Miss.: University Press of Mississippi, 1978), 200–206. A more moderate Mississippi politician of this period was Frank E. Smith, later a congressman from the state. See Frank E. Smith, *Congressman From Mississippi* (New York: Pantheon Books, 1964), 113.

38. John Skates, "Mississippi," in: David C. Roller and Robert W. Twyman, eds., *The Encyclopedia of Southern History* (Baton Rouge, La.: Louisiana Sate University Press, 1979), 833.

39. Donald R. Matthews and Jones W. Prothro, *Negroes and the New Southern Politics* (New York: Harcourt, Brace and World, 1966), 137–138.

40. Richard C. Cortner, *A 'Scottsboro' Case in Mississippi: The Supreme Court and Brown v. Mississippi* (Jackson, Miss.: University Press of Mississippi, 1986), from the book cover.

41. Katheryn K. Russell, *The Color of Crime: Racial Hoaxes, White Fear, Black Protectionism, Police Harassment, and Other Macroaggressions* (New York: New York University Press, 1998), 22.

42. *Ibid.*, 22.

43. David L. Cohn, *God Shakes Creation* (New York: Harper & Brothers, Publishers, 1935). 144-145.

44. Bryan Vila and Cynthia Morris, eds., *Capital Punishment in the United States: A Documentary History* (Westport, Conn.: Greenwood Press, 1997), 306.

45. David M. Oshinsky, *"Worse Than Slavery": Parchman Farm and the Ordeal of Jim Crow Justice* (New York: The Free Press, 1996), 122.

46. Pete Daniel, *The Shadow of Slavery: Peonage in the South, 1901-1969* (New York: Oxford University Press, 1973), 169.

47. David Pilgrim, "On the Resurgence of the Ku Klux Klan: A Theory of Schadenfrenden Socialization," in: David Pilgrim, ed., *On Being Black: An In-group Analysis* (Briston, Ind.: L. Wyndham Hall Press, 1989), 201–202; Martha Banta, "The Razor, the Pistol, and the Ideology of Race Etiquette," in: R. H. Ropers and Dan J. Pence, eds., *American Prejudice: With Liberty and Justice For Some* (New York: Insight Books/Plenum Press, 1995), 172–216; Stewart E. Tolnay and E. M. Beck, *A Festival of Violence: An Analysis of Southern Lynchings, 1882-1930* (Urbana, Ill.: University of Illinois Press, 1992), 47.

48. Ralph Ginzburg, *100 Years of Lynchings* (New York: Lancer Books, 1962), 50–70. Also see Robert L. Zangrando,

The NAACP Crusade Against Lynching, 1900–1950 (Philadelphia: Temple University Press, 1980).

49. Thompson, "The Distribution of Lynch Victims in Mississippi," 215–218.

50. Tolnay and Beck, *A Festival of Violence*, 32–34, 142–49.

51. James S. Hirsch, *Riot and Remembrance: The Tulsa Race War and Its Legacy* (Boston: Houghton Mifflin, 2002), 51–52.

52. J. Egerton, *Speak Now Against the Day: Negro Year Book*, 1941–46 and 1947–51 (Tuskegee, Ala.: Negro Year Book Publishing Co., 1947); Arthur F. Raper, *The Tragedy of Lynching* (Chapel Hill: The University of N.C. Press, 1938), 496. Raper notes, "Between 1889 and 1933, 3,745 people had been lynched in the United States—almost all in the southern states—ranging from a high of 255 in 1892 to a low of 8 in 1932; of this number, 2,954 had been black, 791 white; 1,406 of the victims had been accused of murder and 878 of rape or attempted rape (of white women, it should be noted, not black women), but 67 had been lynched merely for 'insult to whites.'..." *Ibid.*, 496.

53. Ginzburg, *100 Years of Lynching*, 53; quoting the *Knoxville* (Tenn.) *Journal*, July 23, 1933.

54. Jessie Daniel Ames, *The Changing Character of Lynching: Review of Lynching 1931–1941* (Atlanta, Ga.: Commission on Interracial Cooperation, July 1942); reprint, (New York: AMS Press, 1973), 42.

55. Ginzburg, *100 Years of Lynchings*, 217.

56. *Time*, March 26, 1934, 10.

57. Frank Shay, *Judge Lynch, His First Hundred Years*, 105; Ginzburg, *100 Years of Lynchings*, 227; *Clarion-Ledger*, June 23, 1935.

58. Shay, *Judge Lynch*, 248; *Newsweek*, April 24, 1937, 12. On April 13, 1937, a reporter from Jackson, Mississippi, wrote: "'We are justly proud of the fact that Mississippi has not had a lynching in fifteen months,' Governor Hugh White boasted in an address before the Farm Chemurgic Conference here this afternoon. A minute later he was called from the conference to learn from his secretary that two Negroes had just been lynched at Duck Hill." See *New York Times*, April 14, 1937.

59. Ginzburg, *100 Years of Lynchings*, 233. *The Philadelphia Tribune* reported on December 15, 1938: "An investigation by the NAACP proved, last week that Wilder McGowan, who was lynched in Wiggins, Miss., on November 21, was innocent of any crime. The lynching of McGowan, the NAACP reported, was the culmination of the 'pent-up-anger' of whites against an innocent Negro who had refused on numerous occasions in the past to accommodate himself to the attempt of white ruffians to frighten colored citizens. McGowen was lynched after members of a mob accused him of attacking an elderly white woman on Sunday, November 20. The woman said according to reports that she was attacked by a 'light-colored Negro with slick hair.' McGowen is a man of dark complexion and, the NAACP report said, was not in the vicinity when the alleged attack occurred." See Ginzburg, *100 Years of Lynching*, 233.

60. Jessie D. Ames, *The Changing Character of Lynching: Review of Lynching 1931–1941* (Atlanta, Ga.: Commission On Interracial Cooperation, July 1942), 27.

61. Langston Hughes, "Lynching Song," from *A New Song* (1938), in: Langston Hughes, ed., *The Collected Works of Langston Hughes*; Arnold Rampersad, Compiler, Volume I, *The Poems: 1921–1940* (Columbia, Mo.: University of Missouri Press, 2001), 149–150.

62. Thompson, *The Black Press in Mississippi, 1865–1985*, 16–22.

63. Neil R. McMillen, *Dark Journey: Black Mississippians in the Age of Jim Crow* (Urbana, Ill.: University of Illinois Press, 1989), 285, 293.

64. *Ibid.*, 302; Edwin N. Scott Gustad, *A Religious History of America* (New York: Harper & Row, Publishers, 1990), 239.

65. Hazel Rowley, *Richard Wright: The Life and Times* (New York: Henry Holt & Co., 2001), 110–111. The author notes that this story "was Wright's first publication in a book, and it was the first time he had been paid [$50.00] for his writing." *Ibid.*, 112.

66. Linda Metzger, ed., *Black Writers: A Selection of Sketches From Contemporary Authors* (Detroit: Gale Research, 1989), 351–52; David M. Tucker, *Lieutenant Lee of Beale Street* (Nashville, Tenn.: Vanderbilt University Press, 1971), 108–114.

67. Julius E. Thompson, "The Black Poet in Mississippi," in: *Black Life in Mississippi: Essays on Political, Social, and Cultural Studies in a Deep South State* (Lanham, Md.: University Press of America, 2001), 94–96.

68. Julius E. Thompson, *The Black Press in Mississippi, 1865–1985* (Gainesville, Fla.: University Press of Florida, 1993), 16–22.

69. Nickieann Fleener, " 'Breaking Down Buyer Resistance': Marketing the 1935 *Pittsburgh Courier* to Mississippi Blacks," *Journalism History* 13, Nos. 3–4 (Autumn-Winter 1986): 78–85. As early as 1925, journalist George Schuyler's first tour of Mississippi resulted in 10,000 subscriptions from the state. By 1935, at least 3,000 papers were still being distributed in the state. After Schuyler's second tour, in 1935, the subscriptions went back up to 10,000. *Ibid.*, 79, 84. Also see McMillen, *Dark Journey*, 174, 376–77.

70. Raymond Wolters, *The New Negro On Campus: Black College Rebellions of the 1920s* (Princeton, N.J.: Princeton University Press, 1975), 277. Also see Josephine McCann Posey, *Against Great Odds: The History of Alcorn State University* (Jackson, Miss.: University Press of Mississippi, 1994), 23–24.

71. Clarice T. Campbell and Oscar Allan Rogers, Jr., *Mississippi: The View from Tougaloo* (Jackson, Miss.: University Press of Mississippi, 1979), 148–149. Students at Jackson College began serious work and reflection in their vesper service programs during this period, and in the development of the *Blue and White Flash*, the student newspaper; the Dunbar Dramatic Club; and the student government council, which gave "them excellent opportunities for self-government, freedom of speech and action." See B. Baldwin Dansby, *A Brief History of Jackson College: A Typical Story of the Survival of Education Among Negroes in the South* (Jackson, Miss.: Jackson College, 1953), 148.

72. Robert S. McElvaine, *The Great Depression: America, 1929–1941* (New York: Three Rivers Press, 1993), 188.

73. John N. Burrus, "Urbanization in Mississippi, 1890–1970," 369.

74. McMillen, *Dark Journey*, 237.

75. *Ibid.*, 248.

76. McKee, *Mississippi: A Portrait of an American State*, 170–171; Wilson Jeremiah Moses, *Black Messiahs and Uncle Toms: Social and Literary Manipulations of a Religious Myth* (University Park, Pa.: The Pennsylvania State University Press, 1982), 165; Michael W. Fitzgerald, " 'We Have Found a Moses': Theodore Bilbo, Black Nationalism, and the Greater Liberia Bill of 1939," *The Journal of Southern History* LXIII, No. 2 (May 1997): 293–320; McElvaine, *The Great Depression*, 191.

77. Larry J. Griffin, "Narrative, Event-Structure Analysis and Casual Interpretation in Historical Sociology," *American Journal of Sociology* 98, No. 5 (March 1993): 1094–1133.

78. William M. Brewer, "Poor Whites and Negroes in the South Since the Civil War," *The Journal of Negro History* XV, No. 1 (January 1930): 26–37.

79. Julius Wayne Dadley, "A History of the Association of Southern Women for the Prevention of Lynching, 1930–1942" (Cincinnati, Ohio: Ph.D. diss., University of Cincinnati, 1979), 40, 48.

80. *Ibid.*, 73–74. In 1935, six white Mississippi women wrote Governor Sennett Conner of Mississippi in opposition to lynchings. They observed that "if local authorities continue indifferent in such cases, federal intervention will

be imperative." See "Women of Mississippi Urge Lynchers be Punished" (Atlanta, Ga.: Commission On Interracial Cooperation, July 26, 1935), 1.

81. Sean Dennis Cashman, *African-Americans and the Quest for Civil Rights, 1900-1990* (New York: New York University Press, 1991), 35.

82. Albert P. Blaustein and Robert L. Zangrando, eds., *Civil Rights and African-Americans: A Documentary History* (Evanston, Ill.: Northwestern University Press, 1991), 350–51.

83. *The Crisis* 42, No. 1 (January 1935): 16; David L. Lewis, *W.E.B. Du Bois: The Fight For Equality and the American Century, 1919-1963* (New York: Henry Holt and Co., 2000), 1–11, 336–37, 346.

84. *The Crisis* 44, No. 5 (May 1937): 129–158; Frances C. Locher, Martha G. Conway, Marie Evans, and David Versical, eds., *Contemporary Authors, Volume 104* (Detroit: Gale Research, 1982), 520–21; Roy Wilkins, with Tom Mathews, *Standing Fast: The Autobiography of Roy Wilkins* (New York: The Viking Press, 1982), 130–135.

85. *The Crisis* 1930–1939.

86. Sandra Kathryn Wilson, ed., *The Selected Writings of James Weldon Johnson, Volume 2: Social, Political, and Literary Essays* (New York: Oxford University Press, 1995), xi–xiiii; Walter F. White, *Rope and Faggot: A Biography of Judge Lynch* (New York: Knopf, 1929); *The Crisis* 46, No. 9 (September 1939): 268–70, 283, 286; B. Joyce Ross, *J. E. Spingarn and the Rise of the NAACP, 1911-1939* (New York: Atheneum, 1972), 44–47, 152–159.

87. Ross, *J. E. Spingarn and the Rise of the NAACP, 1911-1939*, 45. During 1930, the NAACP waged a special struggle to prevent Judge John J. Parker from gaining a seat on the U.S. Supreme Court, because of his conservative views. The association was successful in this campaign. See Kenneth W. Goings, *"The NAACP Comes of Age": The Defeat of Judge John J. Parker* (Bloomington: Indiana University Press, 1990), 1–72. In 1931, one of the most famous cases of the decade took place, the Scottsboro Boys of Alabama, in which nine young black men were accused of fighting with whites on board a train, and of raping two young white women. All were convicted, by all-white juries, and given the death sentence. Their cases became a national cause in the civil rights movement and left-wing groups, and the NAACP, although coming late to the case, was also forced to make a contribution for the defense of the men. The convictions were overturned on appeal to the Supreme Court. See James Goodman, *Stories of Scottsboro: The Rape Case That Shocked 1930s America and Revived the Struggle For Equality* (New York: Pantheon Books, 1994), xi–xiii; *Chicago Tribune*, April 3, 1994, 7.

88. Jacquelyn Dowd Hall, *Revolt Against Chivalry: Jessie Daniel Ames and the Women's Campaign Against Lynching* (New York: Columbia University Press, 1979), 159–164.

89. June Melby Benowitz, *Encyclopedia of American Women and Religion* (Santa Barbara, Calif.: ABC-Clio, 1998), 17–18.

90. Estelle B. Freedman, *No Turning Back: The History of Feminism and the Future of Women* (New York: Ballantine Books, 2002), 83. In Mississippi, six white women served as the organizing council of the ASWPL for the state. They were: Mrs. L. W. Alford, McComb; Mrs. A. L. Aven, Clinton; Mrs. T. D. Bratton, Jackson; and Mrs. Ernrest Moore, Clarksdale. See Jessie Daniel Ames, *Association of Southern Women for the Prevention of Lynching* (Atlanta. Ga.: ASWPL, 1932), 2.

91. Freedman, *No Turning Back*, 82–83.

92. Allida M. Black, ed., *Courage in a Dangerous World: The Political Writings of Eleanor Roosevelt* (New York: Columbia University Press, 1999), 6. Also see Blanche Wiesen Cook, *Eleanor Roosevelt, Volume Two: 1933-1938* (New York: Viking, 1999).

93. Cheryl Greenberg, "Negotiating Coalition: Black and Jewish Civil Rights Agencies in The Twentieth Century," in: Jackson Salzman and Cornell West, eds., *Struggles in the Promised Land: Toward a History of Black-Jewish Relations in the United States* (New York: Oxford University Press, 1997), 157; Jerone A. Chanes, "Who Does What?: Jewish Advocacy and Jewish Interest," in: L. Sandy Maisel, ed., *Jews in American Politics* (Lanham, Md.: Rowman & Littlefield Publishers, 2001), 105; Hasia R. Diver, *In the Almost Promised Land: American Jews and Blacks, 1915-1935* (Westport, Conn.: Greenwood Press, 1977), 90–92.

94. William Edward Eaton, *The American Federation of Teachers, 1916-1961: A History of the Movement* (Carbondale, Ill.: Southern Illinois University Press, 1975), 66.

95. Linda Reed, *Simple Decency and Common Sense: The Southern Conference Movement, 1938-1963* (Bloomington, Ind.: Indiana University Press, 1991), ix, xii.

96. John Egerton, *Speak Now Against the Day: The Generation Before the Civil Rights Movement in the South* (Chapel Hill, N.C.: The University of North Carolina Press, 1994), 360; Douglas L. Smith, *The New Deal in the Urban South* (Baton Rouge, La.: Louisiana State University Press, 1988), 246.

97. Gary Gerstle, *American Crucible: Race and Nation in the Twentieth Century* (Princeton, N.J.: Princeton University Press, 2001), 163.

98. Rayford W. Logan, *The Negro in the United States* (Princeton, N.J.: D. Vann Nostrand Co., 1957), 82. For this period also see: Mark Solomon, *The Cry Was Unity: Communists and African Americans, 1917-36* (Jackson, Miss.: University Press of Mississippi, 1998), 125; Bettina Aptheker, "Bibliographical Comment" [on Herbert Aptheker], in: Gary Y. Okihiro, ed., *In Resistance: Studies in African, Caribbean, and Afro-American History* (Amherst: The University of Massachusetts Press, 1986), 210–220; Robbie Lieberman, *"My Song Is My Weapon": People's Songs, American Communism, and the Politics of Culture, 1930-1950* (Urbana, Ill.: University of Illinois Press, 1989), 38–39.

99. Donald J. Lisio, *Hoover, Blacks, and Lily-Whites: A Study of Southern Strategies* (Chapel Hill, N.C.: The University of North Carolina Press, 1985), 256. Also see: Richard B. Sherman, *The Republican Party and Black America: From McKinley to Hoover, 1896-1933* (Charlottesville, Va.: University Press of Virginia, 1973), 224–251.

100. Donna L. Franklin, *Ensuring Inequality: The Structural Transformation of the African American Family* (New York: Oxford University Press, 1997), 64.

101. George C. Rable, "The South and the Politics of Antilynching Legislation, 1920–1940," *The Journal of Southern History* 51, No. 2 (May 1985): 209. Also see: Fred Greenbaum, "The Antilynching Bill of 1935: The Irony of 'Equal Justice—Under Law,'" *Journal of Human Relations* 5, No. 3 (1967): 72–85.

102. *Ibid.*, 217.

103. David L. Porter, "Dyer Antilynching Bill," in: Editors of Salem Press, *The Civil Rights Movement, Volume I* (Pasadena, Calif: Salem Press, 2000), 215. Two blacks served in Congress during the 1930s, Oscar DePriest (1871–1951), a Republican of Illinois, in 1929–1935; and Arthur W. Mitchell (1883–1968), a Democrat of Illinois, in 135–1942. DePriest was outspoken and the first black to serve in Congress since 1901; Mitchell was even more conservative, yet, in 1935, "he introduced H.R. 4457—an antilynching bill.... Troubled reactions followed primarily because of a common opinion about his introduction of a conflicting proposal: it would dilute the cause and thereby inflict significant damage to whatever chances there might be to enact a meaningful measure" [the Costigan-Wagner bill]. See Dennis S. Nordin, *The New Deal's Black Congressman: A Life of Arthur Wergs Mitchell* (Columbia, Mo.: University of Missouri Press, 1997), 88, 210; Laverne McCain Hill, *African American Women in Congress: Forming and Transforming History* (New Brunswick, N.J.: Rutgers University Press, 1997), 250.

104. Gary D. Wintz, *Black Culture and the Harlem Renais-*

sance (Houston, Texas: Rice University Press, 1988), 164–165; Roger M. Valade, III, *The Essential Black Literature Guide* (Detroit: Visible Ink, 1996), 165–167.

105. William L. Andrews, Frances Smith Foster, and Trudier Harris, eds., *The Concise Oxford Companion to African American Literature* (New York: Oxford University Press, 2001), 41–42, 53–55, 93–95, 207–08, 229–30, 282–83, 397–98; Arnold Rampersad, *The Life of Langston Hughes, Volume I, 1902–1941–I, Too, Sing America* (New York: Oxford University Press, 1986), 282–83; Wayne F. Cooper, *Claude McKay: Rebel Sojourner in the Harlem Renaissance, A Biography* (New York: Schocken Books, 1987), 100–101. A black Mississippi poet of note who emerged during this period was Jonathan Herdersori Brooks (1904–1945), a graduate of Tougaloo College, and author of *The Resurrection and Other Poems* (Dallas: Kaleidography Press, 1948), and other works. See Thadious M. Davis, "Southern Standard Bearers in the New Negro Renaissance," in: Louis D. Rubin, Jr., ed., *The History of Southern Literature* (Baton Rouge, La.: Louisiana State University Press, 1985), 295–96.

106. Leonard Harris, ed., *The Philosophy of Alain Locke, Harlem Renaissance and Beyond* (Philadelphia: Temple University Press, 1989), 293–309; Alain LeRoy Locke, *Race Contacts and Interracial Relations: Lectures on Theory and Practice of Race,* Jeffrey C. Stewart, ed., (Washington, D.C.: Howard University Press, 1992); Chidi Ikonne, "Opportunity and Black Literature, 1923–1933," *Phylon* 40, No. 1 (March 1979): 86–93.

107. Wintz, *Black Culture and the Harlem Renaissance,* 164–165; Dorothy Abbott, "Recovering Zora Neale Hurston's Work," *Frontiers* 12, No. 1 (1975): 175–181.

108. James V. Hatch and Ted Shine, eds., *Black Theatre USA: Plays by African Americans, 1847 to Today* (New York: The Free Press, 1996), 232; Robert C. Hart, "Black-White Literary Relations in the Harlem Renaissance," *American Literature* 44, No. 4 (January 1973): 612–628.

109. Kenneth Patchen, "Nice Day for a Lynching," in: Langston Hughes and Arna Bontemps, eds., *The Poetry of the Negro, 1746–1970: An Anthology* (Garden City, N.Y.: Doubleday and Co., 1970), 555. Also see Kenneth Patchen, *Collected Poems* (New York: New Directions Publishing, 1939).

110. Sister Anthony Scally, "The Carter Woodson Letters in the Library of Congress," *Negro History Bulletin* 38, No. 5 (June/July 1975): 419; Jacqueline Goggin, *Carter G. Woodson: A Life in Black History* (Baton Rouge, La.: Louisiana State University Press, 1993), 32–35, 55, 68–69, 84–85, 114–15, 125–27.

111. "William Leo Hansberry," in: Raymond W. Logan and Michael R, Winston, eds., *American Negro Biography* (New York: W. W. Norton and Co., 1982), 284–286.

112. W. E. B. Du Bois, *Black Reconstruction in America, 1860–1880* (New York: Russell & Russell, 1935); David Levering Lewis, *W.E.B. Du Bois: The Fight For Equality and the American Century, 1919–1963* (New York: Henry Holt & Co., 2000), 350–78.

113. Joseph J. Boris, ed., *Who's Who in Colored America, Volume I* (New York: Who's Who in Colored America Corp. Publishers, 1927), 217; Ann Allen Shockley and Sue P. Chandler, *Living Black American Authors: A Biographical Directory* (New York: R.R. Bowker Co., 1973), 168.

114. James A. Page, compiler, *Selected Black American Authors: An Illustrated Bio-Bibliography* (Boston, Mass.: G K. Hall and Co., 1977), 172–173.

115. G. Franklin Edwards, "'Edward Franklin Frazier," in: Rayford W. Logan and Michael R. Winston, eds., *American Negro Biography* (New York: W. W. Norton and Co., 1982), 241–44.

116. Vernon E. Jordan, Jr., "Eugene Kinckle Jones," in Logan and Winston, *American Negro Biography,* 304–66. Also see: Richard Robins, *Sidelines Activist: Charles S. Johnson and the Struggle for Civil Rights* (Jackson, Miss.: University Press of Mississippi, 1996), 102–103.

117. Ira E. Harrison and Faye Harrison, eds., *African American Pioneers in Anthropology* (Urbana, Ill.: University of Illinois Press, 1999), 9; Willie L. Baber, "St. Clair Drake: Scholar and Artist," in: *Ibid.,* 191–212.

118. "Ralph J. Bunche," in: Harry A. Ploski and Warren Mart, II, eds., *The Negro Almanac: A Reference Work on the Afro-American* (New York: The Bellwether Co., 1976), 346.

119. William A. Darity, Jr., "Abram Lincoln Harris, Jr.," in: Jack Salzman, David L. Smith, and Cornel West, eds., *Encyclopedia of African-American Culture and History,* Volume 3 (New York: Macmillan Library Reference, 1996), 1226–1227.

120. Joy James, *Transcending the Talented Tenth: Black Leaders and American Intellectuals* (New York: Routledge, 1997), 61–81; Alfreda M. Duster, ed., *Crusade For Justice: The Autobiography of Ida B. Wells* (Chicago: University of Chicago Press, 1970). Rounding out this list of key figures who influenced developments in the anti-lynching movement were: Father Divine [George Baker, Jr., 1879–1965], a religious leader; Clarence Mitchell, Jr. (1911–1984), a key lawyer of the era; Charles Hamilton Houston (1895–1950), an NAACP attorney and law professor at Howard University; Arthur Alfonso Schomburg (1874–1938), an important black book collector; Elijah Muhammad (1897–1975), a key leader in the Nation of Islam, a black nationalist organization; and Casper Holstein, an underworld numbers king in Harlem, who was very supportive of the Harlem Renaissance arts scene. See Mina A. Vaughn, "Father Divine, Religious Leader," in: Richard W. Leeman ed., *African-American Orators: A Bio-Critical Sourcebook* (Westport, Conn.: Greenwood Press, 1996), 71–81; Luther Brown, "Clarence M. Mitchell, Jr.: The 101st U.S. Senator," *Crisis* 105, No. 6 (December 1998): 10–13; Genna Rae McNeil, *Groundwork: Charles Hamilton Houston and the Struggle for Civil Rights* (Philadelphia: University of Pennsylvania Press, 1983), 24–25, 86–97; Elinor Des Verney Sinnette, *Arthur Alfonso Schomburg: Black Bibliophile and Collector* (Detroit, Mich: Wayne State University Press, 1989); Claude Andrew Clegg, III, *An Original Man: The Life and Times of Elijah Muhammad* (New York: St. Martin's Press, 1997), 285–287.

121. Angela Y. Davis, *Blues Legacies and Black Feminism: Gertrude "Ma" Rainey, Bessie Smith, and Billie Holiday* (New York: Pantheon Books, 1998), 181. Also see: Donald Clarke, *Wishing on the Moon: The Life and Times of Billie Holiday* (New York: Viking, 1994), 163–170.

122. Also see: David Margolick, *Strange Fruit: The Biography of a Song* (New York: Harper Collins Publishers, 2001).

123. David Margolick, "A Song That Reverberates in the American Soul," *New York Times,* July 2, 2000 B1, 27.

124. Thomas Kozikowski, "Paul Robeson," in: Hal May, Deborah A. Straub, and Susan M. Troskey, eds., *Black Writers: A Selection of Sketches from Contemporary Authors* (Detroit: Gale Research, 1989), 488–90.

125. Ronald Roach, "Giving the Duke His Due," *Black Issues in Higher Education* 16, No. 3 (April 1, 1999): 25–28, 38–39.

126. Donal Henahan, "When America Took a Big Step Against Bias," *The New York Times,* June 25, 1989, 25. For the period, also see: Samuel A. Floyd, Jr., ed., *Black Music in the Harlem Renaissance: A Collection of Essays* (New York: Greenwood Press, 1990). Readers should also remember that painters of the 1930s also worked on the lynching theme. Two examples are noted here: (1) Jose Clemente Orozco, a Mexican muralist who produced "The Hanged Man" (from the portfolio *The American Scene,* No. 1), in 1933–1934, lithograph; in the Museum of Modern Art, New York City, gift of Ahby Aldrich Rockefeller; and (2) an "Art Commentary on Lynching," an exhibition of at least 12 artists that ran for two weeks from February 15, 1935, at the Arthur U. Newton Galleries on East 57th St. in New York City. "This display of visual art was assembled specifically to draw attention to the need for a nationwide antilynching law under the sponsorship of the National Association For the Advance-

ment of Colored People and the College Art Association." See *The Image of America in Caricature and Cartoon* (Fort Worth, Texas: Amon Carter Museum of Western Art, 1976), 139; Margaret Rose Vendryes, "Hanging On Their Walls: An Art Commentary On Lynching, The Forgotten 1935 Art Exhibition," in: Judith Jackson Fossett and Jeffrey A. Tucker, eds., *Race Consciousness: African-American Studies for the New Century* (New York: New York University Press, 1997), 153–176.

127. Henry Warner Bowden, *Dictionary of American Religious Biography* (Westport, Conn.: Greenwood Press, 1993), 52–53; Melbourne S. Cummings, "Mary McLeod Bethune," in: Richard W. Leeman, ed., *African-American Orators: A Bio-Critical Sourcebook* (Westport, Conn.: Greenwood Press, 1996), 1–9.

128. Malu Halasa, *Mary McLeod Bethune: Educator* (New York: Chelsea House Publishers, 1989), 74–75.

129. *Ibid.*, 77.

130. Bowden, *Dictionary of American Religious Biography*, 52; Sarah Jane Deutsch, "From Ballots to Breadlines, 1920–1940," in: Nancy F. Cott, ed., *No Small Courage: A History of Women in the United States* (New York: Oxford University Press, 2000), 460. On the contributions of other black women during this era, such as Mrs. Daisy Lampkin, NAACP field secretary; Mrs. Charlotte Hawkins Brown; Miss Nannie Burroughs; and Mrs. Lugenia Hope, see: "How to Stop Lynchings: A Discussion," in: Gerda Lerner, ed., *Black Women in White America: A Documentary History* (New York: Vintage Books/Random House, 1992), 472–77. Also note the contributions to the anti-lynching work of the 1930s by such black women's sororities as Alpha Kappa Alpha, Delta Sigma Theta, Zeta Phi Beta, and others.

131. Paula Giddings, *When and Where I Enter: The Impact of Black Women on Race and Sex in America* (New York: Bantam Books, 1984), 206–207.

132. Brenda Gayle Plummer, *Rising Wind: Black Americans and U.S. Foreign Affairs, 1935–1960* (Chapel Hill, N.C.: University of North Carolina Press, 1969), 27.

133. Logan and Winston, *Dictionary of American Negro Biography*, 461–62, 614–16; Schomburg Center For Research in Black Culture/The New York Public Library, *African American Desk Reference* (New York: John Wiley & Sons, 1999), 14; Robert A. Hill, ed., George S. Schuyler, *Ethiopian Stories* (Boston: Northeastern University Press, 1994), vii–viii; George S. Schuyler, *Black and Conservative: The Autobiography of George S. Schuyler* (New Rochelle, N.Y.: Harlington House Publishers, 1966), 198–231; Kathleen A. Hauke, *Ted Poston: Pioneer American Journalist* (Athens: University of Georgia Press, 1998), 39; Leonard Ray Teel, "William Alexander Scott, II," in: Joseph P. McKerns, ed., *Biographical Dictionary of American Journalism* (New York: Greenwood Press, 1989), 632–33; Roland E. Wolseley, *The Black Press, USA* (Ames, Iowa: The Iowa State University Press, 1971), 30, 50. Black fraternities also gravitated to the cause of anti-lynching in the 1930s. Groups active in this effort were: Alpha Phi Alpha Fraternity, Inc.; Omega Psi Phi Fraternity, Inc.; Phi Beta Sigma Fraternity, Inc.; and Kappa Alpha Psi Fraternity, Inc. See Charles H. Wesley, *The History of Alpha Phi Alpha: A Development in College Life* (Washington, D.C.: The Foundation Publishers, 1957), 223; *The Oracle: Official Organ of Omega Psi Phi Fraternity* 64, No. 1 (Spring 1980): 61.

134. Quoted in David M. Kennedy, *Freedom From Fear: The American People in Depression and War 1929-1945* (New York: Oxford University Press, 1999), 19. For example, black registration in Mississippi for voting was only 850 at any given time between 1920 and 1930, yet the state had a population of 21-year-old and literate blacks of 290,782 in 1920. See Katherine Dupre Lumpkin, *The South in Progress* (New York: International Publishers, 1940), 211.

135. McElvaine, *The Great Depression: America, 1929-1941*, 194.

136. Joe R. Feagin, *Racist America: Roots, Current Realities, and Future Reparations* (New York: Routledge, 2001), 64.

137. Michael R. Belknap, *Federal Law and Southern Order: Racial Violence and Constitutional Conflict in the Post-Brown South* (Athens, Ga.: The University of Georgia Press, 1987), 8.

138. Certainly these issues were worldwide in the 1930s, especially with the holocaust against European Jews, Gypsies, and other groups waged largely by Germany. See Robert W. Kesting, "Forgotten Victims: Blacks in the Holocaust," *The Journal of Negro History* 77, No. 1 (Winter 1992): 30–36; Christopher Lehmann-Haupt, "Surviving in Germany, The Wrong Type at the Wrong Time," review of *An Underground Life: The Memoirs of a Gay Jew in Nazi Berlin*, in *The New York Times*, December 6, 1999, B-8.

Chapter 9

1. *Mississippi, America's State of Opportunity* (Jackson, Miss.: Mississippi State Board of Development, 1944), 17. Mississippi had 48 urban places in 1940, towns and cities with at least a population base of 2,500 people. See John N. Burrus, "Urbanization in Mississippi, 1890–1970," in: Richard A. McLemore, ed., *A History in Mississippi, Volume II* (Hattiesburg, Miss.: University and College Press of Mississippi, 1973), 348. Eighty percent of black Mississippians lived in rural areas in 1940, with 20 percent in urban areas. See Mark Lowry II, "Geographical Characteristics of a Bi-racial Society: The Mississippi Case" (Ph.D. diss., Syracuse University, 1973), 92.

2. Ronald Bailey, *Black Studies Program Booklet* (Oxford, Miss.: Black Studies Program, University of Mississippi, 1980), 2. Blacks in Mississippi represented about 8 percent of the national black population in 1940. The exact 1940 black population in Mississippi was 1,074,587, or 49.2 percent of the total for the state. There were 12,865,518 blacks in the United States in 1940. See Jessie Parkhurst Guzman, ed., *Negro Year Book, 1941-46* (Tuskegee, Ala.: The Tuskegee Institute Department of Records and Research, 1947), 2.

3. Vivian W. Henderson, "Religions, Race and Jobs," in: Arthur M. Ross and Herbert Hill, eds., *Employment, Race and Poverty* (New York: Harcourt, Brace and World. 1967), 83; Lewis M. Killian, *White Southerners* (Amherst, Mass.: The University of Massachusetts Press, 1985), 180.

4. Michael Barane, Richard E. Cohen, with Charles E. Cook, Jr., *The Almanac of American Politics 2002* (Washington, D.C.: National Journal Group, 2001), 853.

5. Charles P. Roland, *The Improbable Era: The South Since World War II* (Lexington, Ky.: The University Press of Kentucky, 1975), 25.

6. Gilbert C. Fite, *Cotton Fields No More: Southern Agriculture, 1865–1980* (Lexington, Ky.: The University Press of Kentucky, 1984), 187. Mississippi's major agricultural products during this period were cotton, corn, forest products, truck crops, cattle (beef and dairy), soybeans, and hay. See Lowry, "Geographical Characteristics of a Bi-racial Society: The Mississippi Case," 92.

7. Lowry, "Geographical Characteristics of a Bi-racial Society: The Mississippi Case," 150.

8. A. Robert Lee, *Designs of Blackness: Mapping in the Literature and Culture of Afro-America* (London: Pluto Press, 1998), 112.

9. Herbert B. Alexander, "New Black Professions," *Black and White* 2, No. 5 (June 1940): 15.

10. J. Clay Smith, Jr., *Emancipation: The Making of the Black Lawyer, 1844-1944* (Philadelphia, Pa.: University of Pennsylvania Press, 1993), 28, 299–300.

11. Charles V. Willie, ed., *Black/Brown/White Relations: Race Relations in the 1970s* (New Brunswick, N.J.: Transaction Books, 1977), 134–135. *Negro Digest* in March 1948 even listed Jackson, Mississippi, as one of "America's Ten Worst Cities for Negroes." Jackson came in at number five. In 1950, blacks

composed 40.9 percent of the city's population. See Charles M. Christian and Sari J. Bennett, *Black Saga: The African American Experience* (Boston: Houghton Mifflin Co., 1995), 377; *U.S. News and World Report* 52, No. 19, May 7, 1962, 53.

12. See Greta De Jong, in a review of R. Douglas Hurt, ed., *The Rural South Since World War II* (Baton Rouge, La.: Louisiana State University Press, 1998), *The Southern Quarterly* 38, No. 2 (Winter 2000): 164–165.

13. Quoted in Victoria E. Bynum, " 'White Negroes' in Segregated Mississippi: Miscegenation, Racial Identity, and the Law," *The Journal of Southern History* 64, No. 2 (May 1998): 247.

14. David R. Goldfield, *Black, White, and Southern: Race Relations and Southern Culture, 1940 to the Present* (Baton Rouge, La.: Louisiana State University Press, 1990), 2.

15. Florence O. Alexander, "The Education of Negroes in Mississippi," *Journal of Negro Education* 16 (1947): 375–376, 378.

16. Guzman, *Negro Year Book, 1941–1946*, 86. At private Rust College in Holly Springs, Mississippi, there were 16 teachers to instruct 134 students (19 males, and 115 females). At Tougaloo College, Tougaloo, Mississippi, near Jackson, there were 34 teachers to work with 195 students (28 males, and 178 females). *Ibid.*, 87.

17. Alexander, "The Education of Negroes in Mississippi," 376–377.

18. William Stuart Nelson, "Crucial Issues in America's Race Relations Today," in: William Stuart Nelson, ed., *The Christian Way in Race Relations* (New York: Harper & Brothers Publishers, 1948), 17. One scholar noted the major causes of death in Mississippi in 1940: heart; nephritis; pneumonia and influenza; intracranial lesions of vascular origin; accidents; cancer and other malignant tumors; tuberculosis; conditions peculiar to birth and infancy; syphilis; diarrhea. See John C. Belcher and Morton B. King, Jr., *Mississippi's People* (University, Miss.: Bureau of Public Administration, 1950), 32. On a black funded hospital, by the Mississippi Jurisdiction of the International Order of Twelve Knights and Daughters of Tabor, a fraternal group, in Mound Bayou, in 1942, see: David T. Beito, "Black Fraternal Hospitals in the Mississippi Delta, 1942–1967," *The Journal of Southern History* 65, No. 1 (February 1999): 109–136.

19. Walter White, *How Far the Promised Land?* (New York: The Viking Press, 1955), 162. One scholar notes just how difficult the health care issues were for blacks nationally in the forties: "In 1940 there were 3,430 Negro physicians and surgeons, 1,611 dentists and 7,192 trained nurses and student nurses in the United States. White physicians numbered 161,551. Stated in other terms there was one physician for every 743 persons in the general population as against one Negro physician for every 3.55 colored persons. These figures are significant in terms of Negro health." See Leslie S. Perry, "Patterns of Discrimination in Fundamental Human Rights," in: W. E. B. Du Bois, ed., *An Appeal to the World* (New York: NAACP, 1947), 81.

20. Julius E. Thompson, *The Black Press in Mississippi, 1865–1985* (Gainesville, Fla.: University Press of Florida, 1993), 23–24.

21. See Patrick S. Washburn, "J. Edgar Hoover and the Black Press in World War II," *Journalism History* 13, No. 1 (Spring 1986): 26, 33; Lee Finkle, *Forum For Protest: The Black Press During World War II* (Cranbury, N.J.: Associated University Presses, 1975), 1–50.

22. Jessie Mosley, *The Negro in Mississippi History* (Jackson, Miss.: Helderman Bros., 1950), 120.

23. Charles W. Tisdale, " 'Big Boy' Crudup: The Forgotten 'Blues' Hero," *Jackson Advocate*, February 21, 1980, C-5; "Blues For a Bluesman," *People's Weekly* 56, No. 12 (July 9, 2001): 60.

24. Black Mississippians were proud, like most of black America, when Jackie Robinson, in 1947, broke the color-line in baseball, when he joined the Brooklyn Dodgers team. See Robert Muccrgrosso, Ron Blazek, and Teri Maggio, *Term Paper Resource Guide To Twentieth-Century United States History* (Westport, Conn.: Greenwood Press, 1999), 155.

25. V. O. Key, Jr., and Alexander Heard, *Southern Politics in State and Nation* (New York: Alfred A. Knopf, 1949), 229.

26. Earl M. Lewis, "The Negro Voter in Mississippi," *Journal of Negro Education* 26 (1957): 334.

27. *Schomburg Center of African-American Reference Desk* (New York: John Wiley and Sons, 1999), 75.

28. *Ibid.*, 232. Also see "Oust Bilbo?" *The Crisis* 53, No. 10 (October 1946): 297. On the death of Bilbo, the *Crisis* noted: "He rose to high office and to power of a sort by disfranchising one-half the citizens of Mississippi who happened to be white. He remained in office by keeping the white citizens of his state in such depths of ignorance, poverty, and prejudice that although Mississippi was and is the last on the roll call of the 48 states in every important item of progress, they felt they were the honor guard of White Civilization and he their Knight in Armor. When he died on August 21, 1947, the white section of the human race lost a member who was more of an embarrassment than an ornament, and American Negroes lost an irritating but convenient and satisfying measuring rod of their progress." See the *Crisis* (September 1947): 265.

29. Patricia Sullivan, *Days of Hope: Race and Democracy in the New Era* (Chapel Hill, N. C.: The University of North Carolina Press, 1996), 137.

30. David R. Goldfield, *Black, White and Southern: Race Relations and Southern Culture: 1940 to the Present* (Baton Rouge, La.: Louisiana State University Press, 1990), 73.

31. Langston Hughes, "Pinning Down the Law," in: *The Collected Works of Langston Hughes, Volume 10: Fight For Freedom and Other Writings On Civil Rights*, ed., Christopher C. Desantis (Columbia, Mo.: University of Missouri Press, 2001), 119–120.

32. James W. Loewen and Charles Sallis, eds., *Mississippi: Conflict and Change* (New York: Pantheon Books, 1974), 239, 243; Jesse O. McKee, ed., *Mississippi: A Portrait of an American State* (Montgomery, Ala.: Clairmont Press, 1995), 173; Chester M. Morgan, *Redneck Liberal: Theodore G. Bilbo and the New Deal* (Baton Rouge, La.: Louisiana State University Press, 1985), 247–52.

33. John Egerton, *Speak Now Against the Day: The Generation Before the Civil Rights Movement in the South* (Chapel Hill: The University of N.C. Press, 1994), 400. Although smaller than in the 1920s, the Ku Klux Klan was still a presence in Mississippi during the 1940s. One study estimates that Klan membership in Mississippi for the period 1915–1944 stood at 15,000. See Kenneth T. Jackson, *The Ku Klux Klan in the City, 1915–1930* (New York: Oxford University Press, 1967), 237.

34. John Dittmer, *Local People: The Struggle For Civil Rights in Mississippi* (Urbana, Ill.: University of Illinois Press, 1994), 13. On a national case of importance, see Eric W. Rise, *The Martinsville Seven: Race, Rape, and Capital Punishment* (Charlottesville, Va.: University Press of Virginia, 1995). This case revolved around a charge in January 1949 by a thirty-two-year-old white woman in Martinsville, Virginia, that she had been raped by seven young black men. All were found guilty and received death sentences. In spite of an international and national outcry against the sentence, it was carried out in February 1951.

35. Neil R. McMillen, "Fighting For What We Didn't Have: How Mississippi's Black Veterans Remember World War II," in: Neil R. McMillen, ed., *Remaking Dixie: The Impact of World War II on the American South* (Jackson, Miss.: University Press of Mississippi, 1997), 93; Harvard Sitkoff, "African American Militancy in the World War II South: Another Perspective," in *Ibid.*, 73. Yet Sitkoff also notes that: "Two thousand African Americans went to prison for not complying with the Selective Service Act. Most were

members of the Ethiopian Pacific Movement, the Pacific Movement of the Eastern World, and the Nation of Islam. *Ibid.*, 73.

36. Phillip McGuire, ed., *Taps for a Jim Crow Army: Letters From Black Soldiers in World War II* (Lexington, Ky.: The University Press of Kentucky, 1993). IS7. Also see Alan M. Osur, *Blacks in the Army Air Forces During World War II: The Problem of Race Relations* (Washington, D. C.: Office of Air Force History). Neil A. Wynn, "Black Attitudes Toward Participation in the American War Effort, 1941–1945," *African-American Studies* 3, No. 1 (June 1972): 13–19.

37. *Jackson Advocate*, May 2, 1996; David M. Oshinsky, *"Worse Than Slavery": Parchman Farm and the Ordeal of Jim Crow Justice* (New York: The Free Press, 1996), 205–207. The problem of peonage continued during the 1940s in Mississippi. Herbert Aptheker observes the cases of "James Wiggins, a Negro worker of Clarksdale, Mississippi, [who] testified in January 1938 that he and his wife had been forced at gunpoint to work for one J. S. Decker. Upon attempting to escape and being caught, they were chained and offered for sale at $175.... The Washington office of the NAACP in April 1940 learned of another case of peonage from the lips of Claude B. Cistrunk, who escaped from Coleman and Kinch Watkins, operators of a sawmill in Mashulaville, Mississippi. Mr. Cistrunk received nothing but blows for fourteen months' labor at this mill" See Herbert Aptheker, "Peonage and Anti-peonage to World War I," in: *Afro-American History, The Modern Era* (New York: The Citadel Press, 1971), 194–195.

38. Oshinsky, *"Worse Than Slavery": Parchman Farm and the Ordeal of Jim Crow Justice*, 208. Blacks also seem to have been executed in large numbers on the national scene during the forties. One scholar noted, "Historically, blacks have been more likely to be executed than whites in proportion both to the general population and to the prison population. In the 1940s, for example, blacks made up less than 10 percent of the population, but more than 60 percent of prisoners executed were black. That's beginning to change, however. Since 1930, 51 percent of prisoners executed have been black, and since 1977, blacks constituted only 36 percent of executions, although they made up 48 percent of the prison population." See John U. Wright, ed., *The New York Times 2002 Almanac* (New York: Penguin Reference, 2001), 317.

39. Ross Gregory, *Almanacs of American Life: Modern America, 1914–1945* (New York: Facts On File, 1995), 384.

40. Arnold Rose, *The Negro In America: The Condensed Version of Gunnar Myrdal's An American Dilemma* (New York: Harper & Row Publishers, 1964), 186–187. Yet a new phenomenon emerged in the 1930s and 1940s called "secret" lynchings: "The decrease in lynching since World War II is somewhat misleading since legal and secret lynchings had by then replaced public lynchings. Unnecessary killings by police officers have taken many black lives. Secret attacks resulted in the deaths of hundreds of black or black and white civil rights workers in the South between the 1940s and the 1960s. Moreover, numerous white supremacy groups such as the ever-present Ku Klux Klan have periodically played an important role in violence directed against blacks in the 1970s and 1980s." See T. Alexander Smith and Lenahan O'Connell, *Black Anxiety, White Guilt and the Politics of Status Frustration* (Westport, Conn.: Praeger, 1997), 72.

41. The Lynching Records At Tuskegee Institute, 6–12.

42. *Equal Justice* (Winter 1941): 52. *Equal Justice* also noted, in 1941, that a year earlier "in Prentiss, Mississippi (Jan. 25, 1940), a double lynching of Hilton Fortenberry and Jerome Franklin, Negro prisoners, was averted only by the drawn bayonets of National Guardsmen sent in to protect them. The jail was 'held' with tear gas and riot guns." *Ibid.*, 53.

43. Madison S. Jones, Jr., Youth Director, Natchez, Mississippi, letter, November 7, 1942, to Walter White, Secretary, NAACP (Jackson, Miss.: Jackson State University

Archives); Office of War Information Bulletin, October 20, 1942.

44. George Lipsitz, *The Possessive Investment in Whiteness: How White People Profit From Identity Politics* (Philadelphia, Pa.: Temple University Press, 1998), 163.

45. "Racial: Trial and Terror," *Newsweek* 28, No. 19 (November 4, 1946), 33.

46. Crime of Lynching, Hearings Before a Subcommittee of the Committee On the Judiciary, U. S. Senate, Second Session on S42, SI352, and SI465 (Washington, D.C.: U.S. Government Printing Office, 1948), 101.

47. McComb, Mississippi, native Carroll Case (a white American), wrote an interesting book in 1998 called *The Slaughter*, which describes a major atrocity at Camp Van Dorn, Forrest County, Mississippi, during World War II: the death of 1,227 black soldiers at the hands of the U. S. military. A third of the book deals with facts; the rest is the author's fiction and interpretation. The case requires more investigation. See Herb Boyd, "New Book Uncovers Military Slaughter," *The New York Amsterdam News*, November 12, 1998, 36; Carroll Case, *The Slaughter: An American Atrocity* (Asheville, N.C.: FBC, Inc., 1998). [The author wishes to thank Dr. Harry B. Dunbar of New York for bringing Herb Boyd's article to my attention.]

48. Neil R. McMillen, *Dark Journey: Black Mississippians in the Age of Jim Crow* (Urbana, Ill.: University of Illinois Press, 1989), 197–253.

49. *A Monthly Survey of Events and Trends in Race Relations* 1, No. 1 (August 1943).

50. *Ibid.*, 1, No. 3 (September 1943): 5.

51. *Ibid.*, 1, No. 3 (October 1943): 6.

52. *Ibid.*, 1, No. 8 (April 1944): 8.

53. *Ibid.*, 1, No. 10 (June 1944): 6.

54. *Ibid.*, 2, Nos. 1 & 2 (August–September 1944): 16.

55. *Ibid.*, 2, No. 7 (February 1945): 191.

56. *Ibid.*, 2, No. 2 (April 1945): 258.

57. Lipsitz, *The Possessive Investment in Whiteness: How White People Profit From Identity Politics*, 163.

58. Another interesting case emerged in Mississippi in 1945, when a local black man, Willie McGee, was charged with raping a white woman. The case lasted throughout the 1940s. Scholar John Dittmer gives an excellent summary (see Chapter 10).

59. Julius E. Thompson, *Percy Greene and the Jackson Advocate: The Life and Times of a Radical Conservative Black Newspaperman, 1897–1977* (Jefferson, N.C.: McFarland & Co., Publishers, 1994), 25.

60. *Jackson Advocate*, October 20, 1942. Also see: Commission on Interracial Cooperation, "Triple Lynchings in Mississippi," (Atlanta, Ga.: Commission on Interracial Cooperation, Clip Sheet Number Eight, October 31, 1942), at Jackson State University Archives.

61. Thompson, *The Black Press in Mississippi, 1865-1985*, 23–39.

62. Dittmer, *Local People*, 29.

63. *Ibid.*, 29. Also see Jimmie Gates, "Mississippi NAACP Has Come A Long Way Since 1918 Founding," *Clarion Ledger/Jackson Daily News*, February 12, 1984, 1, 12A.

64. Dittmer, *Local People*, 26.

65. George Alexander Sewell, "Charles and Medger Evers: Leaders in Civil Rights," in: *Mississippi Black History Makers* (Jackson, Miss.: University Press of Mississippi, 1977), 331, 335.

66. Charles Evers and Andrew Szanton, *Have No Fear: The Charles Evers Story, A Black Man's Fight For Respect in America* (New York: John Wiley & Sons, 1997), 5–61.

67. Blyden Jackson, *The Waiting Years: Essays on American Negro Literature* (Baton Rouge, La.: Louisiana University Press, 1976), 203–204.

68. Harold Bloom, ed., *Richard Wright* (New York: Chelsea House Publishers, 1987), 229.

69. Julius E. Thompson, "The Black Poet in Mississippi,

1900–1980," in: *Black Life In Mississippi: Essays on Political, Social and Cultural Studies in a Deep South State* (Lanham, Md.: University Press of America, 2001), 97–99, 252–254.

70. Linda Metzger, ed., *Black Writers: A Selection of Sketches from Contemporary Authors* (Detroit: Gale Research, 1989), 351. See also David M. Tucker, *Lieutenant Lee of Beale Street* (Nashville, Tenn.: Vanderbilt University Press, 1971).

71. *Jackson City Directory*, 1945 (Jackson, Miss.: Tucker Printing House, 1945), 10–11; Alferdteen Harrison, *A History of the Most Worshipful Stringer Grand Lodge: Our Heritage is Our Challenge* (Jackson, Miss.: Most Worshipful Stringer Grand Lodge, 1977), 71–109.

72. *Jackson Advocate*, February 5, 1944, 1.

73. *Jackson Advocate*, January 27, 1983, January 16, 1992, 7-A. To this list of course, one adds the service contributions of Alpha Kappa Alpha, Zeta Phi Beta, and other groups.

74. *Commission on Interracial Cooperation*, Clip Sheet Number 8, October 31, 1942, 8–9; *Clarion Ledger*, October 21, 1942.

75. Monroe Lee Billington, *The American South: A Brief History* (New York: Charles Scribner's Sons, 1971), 344.

76. Wilson Jeremiah Moses, *Black Messiahs and Uncle Toms: Social and Literary Manipulations of a Religious Myth* (University Park, Pa.: The Pennsylvania State University Press, 1982), 165. Also see Kari Fredrickson, *The Dixiecrat Revolt and the End of the Solid South, 1932–1968* (Chapel Hill, N.C.: The University of North Carolina Press, 2001), 82–85.

77. McKee, *Mississippi: A Portrait of an American State*, 182. Also see Frank E. Smith, *Congressman From Mississippi* (New York: Pantheon Books, 1964), 111.

78. *Time* magazine, January 25, 1943, 24; *Clarion Ledger*, April 27, 1943; *New York Times*, April 20, 24, 1943; Thomas M. Leonard, *Day By Day: The Forties* (New York: Facts On File, 1977), 295. In another interesting development for the decade, on February 9, 1942, the Mississippi Supreme Court reversed a rape conviction (and thus death sentence) of Willie Upton. See the *Crisis* 49, No. 3 (March 1942): 79. In another case, in 1944, "A Mississippi jury freed the white lynchers of an aged Negro minister in a brief trial, though the lynchers were positively identified." See: *A Monthly Survey of Events and Trends in Race Relations* 2, No. 4 (November 1944): 90.

79. Jessie Daniel Ames, *Democratic Processes At Work in the South: Report of Commission on Interracial Cooperation, Inc., 1939–1941* (Atlanta. Ga.: Commission on Interracial Cooperation, Inc., October 1941), 14–15; *Could a Picture Like This be Taken in Your Town?* (Jackson, Miss.: Mississippi Council on Interracial Cooperation, 1940), 1–3.

80. Julius Wayne, "A History of the Association of Southern Women for the Prevention of Lynching, 1930–1942" (Ph.D. diss., University of Cincinnati, 1979), 1–110.

81. McKee, *Mississippi: A Portrait of an American State*, 157.

82. "Organizations Committed to a Program of Education to Prevent Lynching" (Atlanta, Ga.: Association of Southern Women for the Prevention of Lynching, October 1940), 3–4.

83. McKee, *Mississippi: A Portrait of an American State*, 213; Lyle Leverich, *Tom: The Unknown Tennessee Williams* (New York: Norton, 1997); Carol Kort, *A to Z of American Women Writers* (New York: Facts On File, 2000), 232.

84. Nan Elizabeth Woodruff, *Book Review of Robert L. Zangrando, The NAACP Crusade Against Lynching, 1909–1950* (Philadelphia, Pa.: Temple University Press, 1982), in: *Phyjon* (1983): 124.

85. A. Weinstein and F. O. Gatell, eds., *The Segregation Era, 1863–1954: A Modern Reader* (New York: Oxford University Press, 1970), 78.

86. Frances C. Locher, Martha G. Conway, Marie Evans, and David Versical, eds., *Contemporary Authors, Volume 104* (Detroit: Gale Research, 1982), 520–21; "Thurgood Marshall," in: Gene N. Landrum, *Profiles of Black Success: Thir-*

teen *Creative Geniuses Who Changed the World* (New York: Prometheus Books, 1997) 293; Trotter, *The African American Experience*, 443–492.

87. Two other national groups were also active in the 1940s, the National Urban League, active since 1911; and the Congress of Racial Equality, established in Chicago in 1942. Both groups supported the anti-lynching movement.

88. Frank Luther Mott, *American Journalism: A History, 1690–1960* (New York: The Macmillan Co., 1962), 794.

89. *Ibid.*, 795; Abby Arthur Johnson and Ronald Maberry Johnson, *Propaganda and Aesthetics: The Literary Politics of Afro-American Magazines in the Twentieth Century* (Amherst: The University of Massachusetts Press, 1979), 46–57, 110, 136.

90. Lee Finkle, *Forum for Protest: The Black Press During World War II* (Cranbury, N, J.: Fairleigh Dickinson University Press, 1975); *The Official Business and Professional Guide of Detroit 1946* (Detroit: Charlotte Perry, Publishers).

91. *Chicago Defender*, October 22, 1942.

92. *Pittsburgh Courier*, October 24, 1942.

93. Armistead S. Pride and Clint C. Wilson, II, *A History of the Black Press* (Washington, D. C.: Howard University Press, 1997), 127–156.

94. *Chicago Defender*, September 26, 1942.

95. "Mary McLeod Bethune," in: *Black Women in America* (New York: Macmillan Library Reference, 1999), 31–34.

96. Charles Harris Wesley, *The History of the National Association of Colored Women's Clubs: A Legacy of Service* (Washington, D. C.: National Association of Colored Women's Clubs, Inc., 1984), 528.

97. Rosalyn Terborg-Penn, "Discontented Black Feminists: Prelude and Postscript to the Passage of the Nineteenth Amendment," in: Darlene Clark Hine, Wilma King, and Linda Reed, eds., *"We Specialize in the Wholly Impossible": A Reader in Black Women's History* (Brooklyn, N.Y.: Carlson Publishing, Inc., 1995), 488. Readers should also note the varied interests of black women as expressed in such groups as Grand Temple, Daughters, Improved Benevolent Protective Order of Elks of the World; Imperial Court, Daughters of Isis; Eastern Star; Jack and Jill; National Association of Ministers' Women's Club; National Association of Ministers' Wives; National Association of Colored Graduate Nurses; National Association of Business and Professional Women's Clubs; and others. See Darlene Clark Hine and Kathleen Thompson, *A Shining Thread of Hope: The History of Black Women in America* (New York: Broadway Books, 1998), 180–81, 224, 245–48, 251–52.

98. *The Philadelphia Tribune*, September 24, 1946; Thomas Kozikowski, "Paul Robeson," in: May, Straub, and Trosky, *Black Writers: A Selection of Sketches from Contemporary Authors*, 488–90.

99. Eric Foner, book review of David L. Lewis, *W. E. B. Du Bois: The Fight For Equality and the American Century, 1919–1963* (New York: Henry Holt, 2000), *The Journal of Blacks in Higher Education* No. 30 (Winter, 2000/2001): 132.

100. Memorandum to Walter White from W. E. B. Du Bois. September 13, 1946, in: Herbert Aptheker, ed., *The Correspondence of W. E. B. Du Bois, Volume III: Selections, 1944–1963* (Amherst, Mass.: University of Massachusetts Press, 1978), 114–115.

101. William L. Patterson, *The Man Who Cried Genocide: An Autobiography* (New York: International Publishers, 1971), 156.

102. David Levering Lewis, *W. E. B. Du Bois: The Fight For Equality and the American Century, 1919–1963* (New York: Henry Holt and Co., 2000), 555. For this period also see Herbert Aptheker, *African-American History, The Modern Era*, for "The First Petition to the United Nations from the Afro-American People" (New York: The Citadel Press, 1971), 301–311.

103. Karl Evanzz, *The Messenger: The Rise and Fall of Elijah Muhammad* (New York: Pantheon Books, 1999), 131–132, 134–135.

104. C. Eric Lincoln, *The Black Muslims in America* (Grand Rapids, Mich.: William B. Eerdmans Publishing Co. and Trenton, N.J.: Africa World Press, 1994), 205–206. In 1907, Elijah Muhammad at age ten witnessed the aftermath of the lynching of an eighteen-year-old black man in Cordele, Georgia, who had been accused of raping a white woman. This event stayed with Muhammad for the rest of his life, and probably helps to explain his opposition to lynchings in general. See Claude Andrew Clegg III, *An Original Man: The Life and Times of Elijah Muhammad* (New York: St. Martin's Press, 1997), 10.

105. Mina A. Vaughn, "Father Divine (1879–1965), Religious Leader," in: Richard W. Leeman, ed., *African-American Orators: A Bio-Critical Sourcebook* (Westport, Conn.: Greenwood Press, 1996), 71–73. In 1933, the *New York Times* reported that Father Divine had twenty million followers in the United States and other countries, including European countries, Canada, and Australia. *Ibid.*, 73.

106. Robert Weisbrot, *Father Divine and the Struggle for Racial Equality* (Urbana, Ill.: University of Illinois Press, 1983), 157.

107. *Ibid.*, 158.

108. *Ibid.*, 158–159.

109. *Ibid.*, 161.

110. John B. Kirby, "Race, Class, and Politics: Ralph Bunche and Black Protest," in: Benjamin Rivlin, ed., *Ralph Bunche: The Man and His Times* (New York: Holmes and Meier, 1990), 29.

111. *Ibid.*, 33.

112. Esmond Wright, *The American Dream: From Reconstruction to Reagan* (Cambridge, Mass.: Blackwell, 1996), 606.

113. Hedda Garza, *African Americans and Jewish Americans: A History of Struggle* (New York: Franklin Watts/Grolier Publishing, 1995), 74. Eleanor Roosevelt continued to play a role, behind the scenes, in the 1940s. See Allida M. Black, ed., *What I Hope to Leave Behind: The Essential Essays of Eleanor Roosevelt* (Brooklyn, N.Y.: Carlson Publishing, 1995); Doris Kearns Goodwin, *No Ordinary Time: Franklin and Eleanor Roosevelt: The Home Front in World War II* (New York: Simon & Schuster, 1994), 162–165. It should be noted that national religious groups, such as the Baptists, Methodists, and others, also continued to be active in the anti-lynching cause during the 1940s. Readers should also be aware of the special concerns on the lynching issue held by the traditional black fraternities and sororities of this period. See George H. Schriver and Bill J. Leonard, eds., *Encyclopedia of Religious Controversies in the United States* (Westport, Conn.: Greenwood Press, 1997), 62–68.

114. Martin Gilbert, *History of the Twentieth Century* (New York: Harper Collins Publishers, 2001), 33.

115. Harvard Sitkoff, "Years of the Locust: Interpretations of the Truman Presidency Since 1965," in: Richard S. Kirkendall, ed., *The Truman Period as a Research Field: A Reappraisal* (Columbia, Mo.: University of Missouri Press, 1972), 102–103.

116. David McCullough, *Truman* (New York: A Touchstone Book/Simon & Schuster, 1992), 570.

117. Sean Dennis Cashman, *African-Americans and the Quest for Civil Rights, 1900–1990* (New York: New York University Press, 1991), 104.

118. *Time* (January 22, 1940): 19; *The Crisis* 47, No. 2 (February 1940): 49. Davis, *FDR: The War President, 1940–1943* (New York: Random House, 2000), 207, 745.

119. William Stuart Nelson, ed., *The Christian Way in Race Relations* (New York: Harper and Row, Publishers, 1948), 13.

120. C. Eric Lincoln and Lawrence H. Mamiya, *The Black Church in the African American. Experience* (Durham, N.C.: Duke University Press, 1990), 196–235; Wyatt Tee Walker, *"Somebody's Calling My Name": Black Sacred Music and Social Change* (Valley Forge, Pa.: Judson Press, 1992), 15–17, 20–21.

Nationally, American Jews remained supportive of anti-lynching efforts in this country during the 1940s. See Nancy J. Weiss, "Long-Distance Runners of the Civil Rights Movement: The Contribution of Jews to the NAACP and the National Urban League in the Early Twentieth Century," in: Jack Salzman and Cornel West, eds., *Struggles in the Promised Land: Toward a History of Black-Jewish Relations in the United States* (New York: Oxford University Press, 1997), 123–152.

121. Egerton, *Speak Now Against the Day*, 302–303.

122. Fred Hobson, *But Now I See: The White Southern Racial Conversion Narrative* (Baton Rouge, La.: Louisiana State University Press, 1999), 18.

123. *Ibid.*, 32. Overall, the southern press remained pro-segregationist during the 1940s, thus often an anti-black perspective prevailed in the pages of the press in the South. Conservative attitudes generally prevailed in the press outside of the South; but some papers, such as the *New York Times*, *Chicago Tribune*, and others, were supportive of anti-lynching efforts in the nation. See "The Southern White Press and the Negro" (Atlanta, Ga.: Commission on Interracial Cooperation, Inc., February 15, 1943) Vol. 2, No. 3, 1–6; Vol. 2, No. 4, February 27, 1943, 1–9; John B. Kirby, *Black American in the Roosevelt Era: Liberalism and Race* (Knoxville, Tenn.: University of Tennessee Press, 1980).

124. Nelson, *The Christian Way in Race Relations*, 11.

125. In reality, Mississippi's history from the long past to the 1940s places it in the company of major international events, especially the holocaust in Germany and Europe during the 1930s and World War II eras; the U. S. Government's "relocation" of 112,000 Japanese Americans to internment, or concentration camps, between 1942 and 1945; and the dropping of the atomic bombs on Hiroshima and Nagasaki in 1945 by the United States, making this country "the first nation to use the bomb, and that has had an effect on our culture." Of course, along with Mississippi, Georgia and Texas continued to be the other leading lynching states in the United States during this period. See Walter White, *Rope and Faggot: A Biography of Judge Lynch* (New York: Alfred A. Knopf, 1929), 234; Alwyn Barr, *Black Texans: A History of African Americans in Texas, 1528–1995* (Norman, Okla.: University of Oklahoma Press. 1996), 139–141. Also see: Jeffrey Shandler, *White American Watches: Televising the Holocaust* (New York: Oxford University Press, 1999), 23–26, 156–157, 230–233; Ralph Blumenthal, "Holocaust Children Who Did Not Grow Up," *The New York Times*, December 5, 1996, B-l-2; Michi Nishiura Weglyn, *Years of Infamy: The Untold Story of America's Concentration Camps* (Seattle, Washington: University of Washington Press, 1996), 4, 21; Robert Shaffer, "Cracks in the Consensus: Defending the Rights of Japanese Americans During World War II," *Radical History Review* 72 (Fall 1998): 84–120.

126. Fred Jerone, *J. Edgar Hoover's Secret War Against the World's Most Famous Scientist* (New York: St. Martin's Press, 2002), 83. Yet, one scholar notes that in 1945–1946, 56 blacks were lynched in the United States, "most of them returning veterans." *Ibid.*, 78.

127. Mildred Strunk, *Public Opinion, 1935–1946* (Princeton, N. J.: Princeton University Press, 1951), 151–152.

128. Robert L. Zangrando, "Lynching," in: *Dictionary of American History*, Vol. 4 (New York: Charles Scribner's Sons, 1976), 208.

Chapter 10

1. *Jackson Daily News*, July 27, 1977; *1950 U. S. Census.*

2. *Clarion-Ledger/Jackson Daily News*, July 1, 1984.

3. *U. S. News and World Report* 43 (May 7, 1962): 54; Lewis M. Killian, *White Southerners* (Amherst, Mass.: The University of Massachusetts Press, 1985), 181.

4. Julius E. Thompson, *The Black Press in Mississippi,*

1865-1985 (Gainesville, Fla.: University Press of Florida, 1993), 41. In 1950, there were 122,709 black farmers in Mississippi; by 1960 this number had been reduced to 55,174. See Gilbert C. Fire, *Cotton Fields No More: Southern Agriculture 1865-1980* (Lexington, Ky.: The University Press of Kentucky, 1984), 238.

5. Charles V. Willie, ed., *Black/Brown/White Relations, Race Relations in the 1970s* (New Brunswick, N.J.: Transaction Books, 1977), 135.

6. Claud Anderson, *Black Labor, White Wealth: The Search for Power and Economic Justice* (Edgewood, Md.: Duncan and Duncan, Publishers, 1994), 24–25.

7. John Dittmer, *Local People: The Struggle for Civil Rights in Mississippi* (Urbana, Ill.: University of Illinois Press, 1995), 20.

8. James L. Loewen and Charles Sallis, eds., *Mississippi: Conflict and Change* (New York: Pantheon Books, 1974), 249–250.

9. Andrew Barr, *Drink: A Social History of America* (New York: Carroll and Graf Publishers), 253.

10. *Jackson Advocate*, April 7, 1951.

11. *Jackson Advocate*, September 22, 1951.

12. Neil R. McMillen, *Dark Journey: Black Mississippians in the Age of Jim Crow* (Urbana, Ill.: University of Illinois Press, 1989), 169. There were also twenty-nine black dentists and eleven black pharmacists active in the state during the period. *Ibid.*, 170.

13. *Ibid.*, 170.

14. Dittmer, *Local People*, 34–35.

15. Richard Aubrey McLemore, "Higher Education in the Twentieth Century," in: R. A. McLemore, ed., *A History of Mississippi*, Volume II (Hattiesburg, Miss.: University and College Press of Mississippi, 1973), 440.

16. McMillen, *Dark Journey*, 90, 98–108.

17. *Chicago Tribune*, May 15, 1994.

18. Loewen and Sallis, *Mississippi: Conflict and Change*, 251.

19. Jesse O. McKee, ed., *Mississippi: A Portrait of an American State* (Montgomery. Ala.: Clairmont Press, 1995), 183. Also see: Numan V. Bartley, *The Rise of Massive Resistance: Race and Politics in the South During the 1950s* (Baton Rouge, La.: Louisiana State University Press, 1969), 76–77.

20. Earl Lewis, "The Negro Voter in Mississippi," *Journal of Negro Education* 26 (1957): 334–335; Charley S. Aiken, *The Cotton Plantation South Since the Civil War* (Baltimore, Md.: The Johns Hopkins University Press, 1998), 208. In 1958, Mississippi had registered 20,000 black voters. *Ibid.*, 208.

21. Dittmer, *Local People*, 79.

22. J. M. Miller, "A Dialogue with Aaron Henry," *Emerge* 2, No. 8 (November 1991): 12.

23. Dittmer, *Local People*, 48, 146.

24. Loewen and Sallis, *Mississippi: Conflict and Change*, 244–245.

25. Julius E. Thompson, *Percy Greene and the Jackson Advocate: The Life and Times of a Radical Conservative Black Newspaperman, 1897-1977* (Jefferson, N.C.: McFarland & Co., 1994), 44; Thompson, *The Black Press in Mississippi. 1865-1985*, 48–49.

26. Patterson, *Grand Expectations*, 25.

27. Ross Gregory, *Almanacs of American Life: Modern America, 1914 to 1945* (New York: Facts On File, 1995), 384.

28. Catherine Fisher Collins, *The Imprisonment of African American Women* (Jefferson, N.C.: McFarland & Co., Publishers, 1997), 64. The totals for the executions of American citizens stood at 717 for the years 1950–1959. See Bryan Vila and Cynthia Morris, eds., *Capital Punishment in the United States: A Documentary History* (Westport, Conn.: Greenwood Press, 1997), 309.

29. Dittmer, *Local People*, 45–46, 53, 69; John T. Elliff, *The United States Department of Justice and Individual Rights, 1937-1962* (New York: Garland Publishing, 1987), 159–160.

30. Dittmer, *Local People*, 45–46, 53, 59, 69; John T. Elliff,

The United States Department of Justice and Individual Rights, 1937-1962 (New York: Garland Publishing, 1987), 159–160.

31. *Ibid.*, 123.

32. David M. Oshinsky, *"Worse Than Slavery": Parchman Farm and the Ordeal of Jim Crow Justice* (New York: The Free Press, 1996), 205–208, 229.

33. *Jackson Advocate*, May 2, 1996.

34. Stewart E. Tolnay and E. M. Beck, *A Festival of Violence: An Analysis of Southern Lynchings, 1882-1930* (Urbana, Ill.: University of Illinois Press, 1995), 47.

35. Harry A. Ploski and James Williams, eds., *Reference Library of Black America, Volume I* (Detroit: Gale Research, 1990), 28.

36. Thompson, "The Distribution of Lynch Victims in Mississippi, 1865–1966," 219–220; Philip Dray, *At the Hands of Persons Unknown: The Lynching of Black America* (New York: Random House, 2002), 417–19, 422–32.

37. Ronald Bailey, *Remembering Medgar Evers ... For a New Generation* (Oxford, Miss: Heritage Publications, 1988), 10.

38. Dittmer, *Local People*, 79.

39. *Ibid.*, 21–22. Jessica Mitford was among a delegation of people sent to Mississippi by the Civil Rights Congress in mid–July 1950 to plead for the life of Willie McGee. Mitford found that "People were willing to discuss the McGee case in the privacy of their own homes, but refused to sign petitions or speak publicly in favor of the man. There were always a few who were a little ahead of the others on the race issue—this minority that reminded you of the whites who helped blacks escape on the underground railroad." She went on to note that the only vocal support in the state from a white person came from writer William Faulkner. See *Jackson Advocate*, July 27, 1950; the *Clarion-Ledger/Jackson Daily News*, December 16, 1979.

40. Walter Lowenfels, "Shoes That Walked for Willie McGee," *Freedomways* 2, No. 3 (Summer 1962): 243–44.

41. Jack Mendelsohn, *The Martyrs* (New York: Harper and Row, 1966), 2.

42. Herbert Shapiro, *White Violence and Black Response: From Reconstruction to Montgomery* (Amherst, Mass.: The University of Massachusetts Press, 1988), 411. On November 25, 1955, Gus Courts was shot in Belzoni, but survived the attack. No one was arrested in his case. See Mendelsohn, *The Martyrs*, 15–16.

43. *M is for Mississippi and Murder* (New York: NAACP, 1955), 5.

44. Susie Erenrich, ed., *Freedom is a Constant Struggle: An Anthology, Mississippi Civil Rights Movement* (Montgomery, Ala.: Black Belt: 1999), 4–5; also see Stephen J. Whitefield, *A Death in the Delta: The Story of Emmett Till* (New York: The Free Press, 1988).

45. Cleonara Hudson-Weems, *Emmett Till: The Sacrificial Lamb of the Civil Rights Movement* (Troy, Mich.: Bedford Publishers, 1994), 21. Also see Christopher Metress, ed., *The Lynching of Emmett Till: A Documentary Narrative* (Charlottesville, Va.: University of Virginia Press, 2002; Jolin W. Fountain, "Mamie Mobley is Dead at 81: Victim's Mother," *New York Times*, January 7, 2003, A-17. In the Spring of 2004, the United States Department of Justice reported that it was reopening the Emmett Till lynching case, with a new criminal investigation into the August 21, 1955 event. See *St. Louis Post-Dispatch*, May 11, 2004; *New York Times*, May 11, 12, 2004.

46. James A. Emanuel, "Emmett Till," in: Arnold Adoff, ed., *Celebrations: A New Anthology of Black American Poetry* (Chicago: Follett Publishing).

47. Jere Nash, "'Blood Justice': They Had Already Lynched the Legal System," The *Clarion-Ledger/Jackson Daily News*, September 21, 1986, 3-F; on this case also see Howard Smead, *Blood Justice: The Lynching of Mack Charles Parker* (New York: Oxford University Press, 1986).

48. Keith E. Baird, "Poplarville II," *Freedomways* 2, No. 2 (Spring 1962): 172.

49. Read Massengill, *Portrait of a Racist: The Man Who*

Killed Medgar Evers (New York: St. Martin's Press, 1994), 96; Dittmer, *Local People*, 54; *New York Times*, May 21, 1997.

50. Massengill, *Portrait of a Racist*, 96.

51. *Ibid.*, 96; Bailey, *Remembering Medgar Evers...For a New Generation*, 6–8.

52. Bailey, *Remembering Medgar Evers ... For a New Generation*, 5.

53. Dittmer, *Local People*, 32.

54. *Ibid.*, 33.

55. *Prospectus of the First Annual Meeting of the Mississippi Regional Council of Negro Leadership* (Mound Bayou, Miss.: Mississippi Regional Council of Negro Leadership, May 2, 1952), 1–18. The Mississippi Council of Negro Leadership stated its objectives as being: "To guide our people in their civic responsibilities regarding health, education, religion, registration and voting, law enforcement, tax paying, the preservation of property, the value of saving and to guide us in all things which will make us stable, qualified, conscientious citizens which will lead us to first-class citizenship in all things." *Ibid.*, 1.

56. Clay Lyle, *Organizational Activities of Rural Negroes in Mississippi* (State College, Miss.: Mississippi State College, Agricultural Experiment Station, Circular 192, December 1953), 1–15.

57. See Nicholas Lemann, *The Promised Land: The Great Black Migration and How It Changed America* (New York: Alfred A Knopf. 1991); Marcus E. Jones, *Black Migration in the United States with Emphasis on Selected Central Cities* (Ph.D. diss., Department of Geography, Southern Illinois University at Carbondale, August 1978), 39, 44, 75–80; Paul Geib, "From Mississippi to Milwaukee: A Case Study of the Southern Black Migration to Milwaukee, 1940–1970." *Journal of Negro History* 83, No. 4 (Fall 1998): 229–248.

58. Thompson, *The Black Press in Mississippi, 1865–1985*, 41.

59. *Ibid.*, 40–57.

60. *Ibid.*, 51.

61. Dittmer, *Local People*, 30.

62. See Cleopatra D. Thompson, *The History of the Mississippi Teachers Association* (Washington, D. C.: NET Rights and Mississippi Teachers Association, 1973), 119–150. The official organ of black teachers in Mississippi, the *Mississippi Educational Journal for Teachers in Colored Schools*, was established at Jackson in 1927. *Ibid.*, 106–108.

63. Dittmer, *Local People*. 35–36, Also see Constance Baker Motley, *Equal Justice ... Under Law: An Autobiography* (New York: Farrar, Straus and Giroux, 1998), 75. In March 1957, the student body at Alcorn College staged a protest over a series of eight articles in the segregationist *State Times* of Jackson by Alcorn professor Clennon King, who criticized the NAACP and supported the segregation system in Mississippi. For their protests against professor King, at least seven Alcorn students were expelled from the institution. The NAACP helped the students to enter college at Central State College, Xenia, Ohio, and Virginia Union University, Richmond, Virginia. *The Crisis* noted: "It was this mass act of defiance by Negro students against the symbol of Mississippi power and authority—the all white board of directors— that shook the very foundations of white supremacy and the Jim Crow system in that state." See *The Crisis* 64, No. 6 (June-July, 1957): 349; *Ibid.*, 64 (May 1957): 290–91, 295.

64. Harold Bloom, ed., *Richard Wright* (New York: Chelsea House Publishers, 1987), 229–30; Hazel Rowley, *Richard Wright: The Life and Times* (New York: Henry Holt and Co., 2001), 213–528.

65. Julius E. Thompson, "The Black Poet in Mississippi," in: James L. Conyers, Jr., ed., *Africana Studies: A Disciplinary Quest for Both Theory and Method* (Jefferson, N.C.: McFarland & Co., 1997), 214.

66. See Mabel H. Pittman, "Literature: Its Contribution to Education in Mississippi," in: *Mississippi Mind Scape: Education* (Jackson, Miss.: Committee for the Humanities, 1986), 10–12.

67. Eileen Southern, *The Music of Black Americans: A History* (New York: W. W. Norton & Co., 1983), 336–337, 422–27, 493–96.

68. On the impact of black radio and disk jockeys, such as Early Wright of Clarksdale, see Peter Applebome, "An Institution in Mississippi Radio," *The New York Times*, June 28, 1989, A-14. Also see Richard Sorrell and Carl Francese, *From Tupelo to Woodstock: Youth, Race and Rock and Roll in America, 1954–1969* (Dubuque, Iowa: Kendall/Hunt Publishing Co., 1995).

69. Earl Black, *Southern Governors and Civil Rights: Racial Segregation as a Campaign Issue in the Second Reconstruction* (Cambridge, Mass.: Harvard University Press, 1976), 40–42.

70. *Ibid.*, 60.

71. James Dickerson, *Dixie's Dirty Secret: The True Story of How the Government, the Media, and the Mob Conspired to Combat Integration and the Vietnam Antiwar Movement* (Armonk, New York: M. E. Sharpe, 1998), 16–17.

72. *Clarion-Ledger*, April 8, 1996.

73. Dickerson, *Dixie's Dirty Secret*, 16; Loewen and Sallis, *Mississippi: Conflict and Change*, 243.

74. Dittmer, *Local People*, 45.

75. Bartley, *The Rise of Massive Resistance*, 83, 86.

76. Dittmer, *Local People*, 70.

77. *Ibid.*, 48.

78. Philip Dray, *At Hands of Persons Unknown: The Lynching of Black America* (New York: Random House, 2002). On the Ku Klux Klan during this period see John George and Laird Wilcox, *Nazis, Communists, Klansmen, and Others on the Fringe* (Buffalo, New York: Prometheus Books, 1992), 394–95. This study notes: "Between 1 January 1956 and 1 June 1963, for instance, there were 138 cases of dynamitings in the South associated with the Klan.... Among all the rubble were Negro homes, churches, and integrated schools." *Ibid.*, 395. Also see Francis M. Wilhoit, *The Politics of Massive Resistance* (New York: George Braziller, 1973), 104–106.

79. Thompson, *The Black Press in Mississippi, 1865–1985*, 44. Also see Thompson, *Percy Greene and the Jackson Advocate*, 83. A moderate politician who can be added to this list is Congressman Frank E. Smith. See Frank E. Smith, *Congressman from Mississippi* (New York: Pantheon Books, 1964).

80. Noel E. Polk and James R. Scafidel, eds., *An Anthology of Mississippi Writers* (Jackson, Miss.: University Press of Mississippi, 1979), 194–195.

81. "Eudora Welty," in: Dorothy Abbott, ed., *Mississippi Writers, Volume II: Non-Fiction* (Jackson, Miss.: University Press of Mississippi, 1986), 731–32; "Eudora Welty," in Carol Kort, *A to Z of American Women Writers* (New York: Facts On File, 2000), 232; "Tennessee Williams," in: Abbott, *Mississippi Writers*, 733; "Race, Class, and Redemption in Walker Percy's *The Last Gentlemen*," in : Jeffrey J. Folks, *From Richard Wright to Toni Morrison: Ethics in Modern and Postmodern American Narrative* (New York: Peter Lang, 2001), 107–120. Two other Mississippi groups had some interest in the lynching problem of the period, but for different reasons. Some white Mississippi women, as in the past, were opposed to lynching as a social problem, including members of the Mississippi Federated Clubs, active in Mississippi since 1898. Select members among white Mississippi business persons were opposed to lynching because of its negative impact on business and future investments in the state. See *Clarion-Ledger*, May 26, 1968; Charles Sallis and John Quincy Adams, "Desegregation in Jackson, Mississippi," in: Elizabeth Jacoway and David R. Colburn, eds., *Southern Businessmen and Desegregation* (Baton Rouge, La.: Louisiana State University Press, 1982), 236–256.

82. Dray, *At the Hands of Persons Unknown*, 420.

83. Curt Gentry, *J. Edgar Hoover: The Man and His Secrets* (New York: W. W. Norton & Co., 1991), 441.

84. Lee Sigelman and Susan Welch, *Black Americans' Views of Racial Inequality: The Drama Deferred* (New York: Cambridge University Press, 1991), 19.

85. Armistead S. Pride and Glint C. Wilson II, *A History of the Black Press* (Washington, D. C.: Howard University Press, 1997), 141–156, 185–197.

86. Julius E. Thompson, "The Social Backgrounds of Four Major Twentieth-Century African American Intellectuals: St. Clair Drake (1911–1990), Rayford W. Logan (1897–1982), Benjamin E. Mays (1894–1984), and Benjamin Quarles (1904–1996): Traditions and Hope from One Generation to the Next," in: James L. Conyers, Jr., ed., *Black American Intellectualism and Culture: A Social Study of African American Social and Political Thought* (Stanford, Conn.: JAI Press, Inc., 1999), 11–24.

87. Alan Draper, *Conflict of Interests: Organized Labor and the Civil Rights Movement in the South, 1954–1968* (Ithaca, New York: ILR Press, 1994), 158–159; Timothy N. Thurber, *The Politics of Equality: Hubert H. Humphrey and the African American Freedom Struggle* (New York: Columbia University Press, 1999), 70–71, 93–95; Robbie Lieberman, "*My Song is My Weapon: People's Songs, American Communism, and the Politics of Culture, 1930–50* (Urbana: University of Illinois Press, 1989), 7–8, 109–10, 124–25, 155; Manning Marable, *Race, Reform and Rebellion: The Second Reconstruction in Black America, 1945–1982* (Jackson. Miss.: University Press of Mississippi, 1984). On attempts by Hollywood to deal with lynching in American films during the 1950s see: James Naremore, *More Than Might: Film Noir in its Contexts* (Berkeley, Calif.: University of California Press, 1998), 126–127. On the concerns of American religious groups on violence and lynching see: James F. Findlay, Jr., *Church People in the Struggle: The National Council of Churches and the Black Freedom Movement, 1950–1970* (New York: Oxford University Press, 1993); Michael B. Friedland, *Lift Up Your Voice Like a Trumpet: White Clergy and the Civil Rights and Antiwar Movements, 1954–1973* (Chapel Hill, N.C.: The University of North Carolina Press, 1998).

88. The lynching of Harry T. Moore (1906–1951), of the NAACP and Progressive Voters' League, took place in Florida during this period and had national implications. Ben Green notes, "On Christmas night in 1951, in a small orange grove in tiny Mims, Florida, a bomb placed under a bed ended Harry Moore's life. Although his daughters, Peaches and Evangeline, survived, his wife, Harriette, died of her wounds a week later. Unjustly neglected until now, Moore's death stands at the first in what was to be a long and tragic line of assassinations in the civil rights movement." See Ben Green, *Before His Time: The Untold Story of Harry T. Moore, America's First Civil Rights Martyr* (New York: The Free Press, 1999), from the cover, 22–23, 44–47, 176–177.

89. Neil R. McMillen, *Dark Journey: Black Mississippians in the Age of Jim Crow* (Urbana: University of Illinois Press, 1989), 317.

Chapter 11

1. Julius E. Thompson, *The Black Press in Mississippi, 1865–1985* (Gainesville, Fla.: The University Press of Florida, 1993), 59–60. Conditions in agriculture continued to decline for Mississippi, and especially so for blacks. Jesse O. McKee points out: "As recently as 1950, 40 percent of the work force in Mississippi was engaged in agriculture. By 1960, the percentage had dropped to 21. The percentage has continued to decline: 7.6 percent in 1970, 4 percent in 1980, and less than 4 percent in the 1990s. The number of agricultural workers has fallen from over 300,000 in 1950 to less than 40,000 in 1990." See Jesse O. McKee, ed., *Mississippi: A Portrait of an American State* (Montgomery, Ala.: Clairmont Press, 1995), 278.

2. James W. Silver, *Mississippi: The Closed Society* (New York: Harcourt, Brace & World, 1966), vii–xxii.

3. Etheridge Knight, "A Poem For Myself (or Blues for a Mississippi Black Boy)," in: John Oliver Killens and Jerry W. Ward, Jr., eds., *Black Southern Voices: An Anthology of Fiction, Poetry, Drama, Non-Fiction, and Critical Essays* (New York: Penguin Group, 1992), 246–47.

4. Howard Zinn, *SNCC: The New Abolitionists* (Boston: Beacon, 1964), 64.

5. Julius E. Thompson, *Percy Greene and the Jackson Advocate: The Life and Times of A Radical Conservative Black Newspaperman, 1897–1977* (Jefferson, N.C.: McFarland & Co., Publishers, 1994), 98–99.

6. John Dittmer, *Local People: The Struggle For Civil Rights in Mississippi* (Urbana: University of Illinois Press, 1994), 118–119.

7. Dittmer, *Local People*, 116–193; *The New York Times*, May 21, 1997; Richard J. Jensen and Jon C. Hammerball "Robert Parris Moses (1935–), Civil Rights Activist, Social Activist, Professor," in: Richard W. Leeman, ed., *African-American Orators: A Bio-Critical Sourcebook* (Westport, Conn.: Greenwood Press, 1996), 261–269; "Fannie Lou Hamer, 1917–1977," in: Jessie Carney Smith, ed., *Epic Lives: One Hundred Black Women Who Made a Difference* (Detroit: Visible Ink Press, 1993), 235–239; Eric Burner, *And Gently He Shall Lead Them: Robert Parris Moses and Civil Rights in Mississippi* (New York: New York University Press, 1994), 28–29; "Annie Devine, 88, Right's Advocate in Mississippi," *New York Times*, September 1, 2000.

8. Marcus D. Pohlman, *Black Politics in Conservative America* (New York: Longman, 1990), 40–41; Leslie Burl McLemore, "Mississippi Freedom Democratic Party," *The Black Politician* 3, No. 2 (October 1971): 19–22.

9. "Police Tactics in Mississippi," in: Alan F. Westin, ed., *Freedom Now! The Civil Rights Struggle in America* (New York: Basic Books, Publishers, 1964), 205–210.

10. Dittmer, *Local People*, 82–34 (7), 96–97; David M. Oshinsky, "*Worse Than Slavery*": *Parchman Farm and the Ordeal of Jim Crow Justice* (New York: The Free Press, 1996), 229–36.

11. Schomburg Center For Research in Black Culture, *African American Desk Reference: A Stonesong Press Book* (New York: John Wiley & Sons, 1999), 317; Julius E. Thompson, "The Distribution of Lynch Victims in Mississippi, 1865–1966," in: *Black Life in Mississippi: Essays on Political, Social and Cultural Studies in a Deep South State* (Lanham, Md.: University Press of America, 2001), 69–71, 220–221.

12. Dittmer, *Local People*, 109–110, 165–66, 171–173, 247; Fred Powledge, *Free At Last?: The Civil Rights Movement and the People Who Made It* (New York: Harper Collins Publishers, 1991), 462–79.

13. Stewart E. Tolnay and E. M. Beck, *A Festival of Violence: An Analysis of Southern Lynchings, 1882–1930* (Urbana, Ill.: University of Illinois Press, 1995), 32–34, 142–149, 251.

14. Jack Mendelsohn, *The Martyrs* (New York: Harper and Row, 1966), 29–30.

15. *Ibid.*, 31. Herbert Lee's killer, E. H. Hurst, told a *New York Times* reporter that "he and Lee had been involved in a real estate deal. Lee was supposed to pay him $500 but refused to do so, Hurst said." *Ibid.*, 31.

16. Charles M. Payne, *I've Got the Light of Freedom: The Organizing Tradition and the Mississippi Freedom Struggle* (Berkeley: University of California Press, 1995), 288–89.

17. Ralph E. Luker, *Historical Dictionary of the Civil Rights Movement* (Lanham, Md.: The Scarecrow Press, 1997), 84.

18. Athan G. Theohara, with Tony G. Poveda, Susan Rosenfeld, and Richard Gid Powers, *The FBI: A Comprehensive Reference Guide* (Phoenix, Arizona: The Oryx Press, 1999), 70–71.

19. Reed Massengill, *Portrait of a Racist: The Man Who Killed Medgar Evers* (New York: St. Martin's Press, 1994), 146–147.

20. Thompson, *Black Life in Mississippi: Essays On Political, Social and Cultural Studies in a Deep South State*, 91–120, 123–140, 143–144, 223–275; William L. Andrews, Frances Smith Foster and Trudier Harris, eds., *The Concise Oxford Companion to African American Literature* (New York: Oxford University Press, 2001), 35–38, 146–147, 159–60, 248–249,

272–73, 437–438, 453–456; Betsy Spratt," 'Mississippi Delta' Author Talks About Her Life and Career," *The Michigan Chronicle*, December 9, 1989, 1-B.

21. Steven F. Lawson, *Running For Freedom: Civil Rights and Black Politics in America Since 1941* (New York: The McGraw-Hill Co., 1997), 95–98, 121–122, 150–151; "Fannie Lou Hamer, 1917–1972, From Sharecropper to Shining Light," in: Amy Alexander, *Fifty Black Women Who Changed America* (Secaucus, N.J.: A Birch Lane Press Book, Carol Publishing Group, 1999), 128–133.

22. Frank R. Parker, *Black Votes Count: Political Empowerment in Mississippi, After 1965* (Chapel Hill, N.C.: The University of North Carolina Press, 1990), 31.

23. Ibid., 32; Davis, "Blacks' Political Representation in Rural Mississippi," 149–159.

24. Mississippi's black professional groups continued to play a role in the advancement struggles of black Mississippians. However, their total numbers still remained small in the 1960s, and this had an impact on their ability to be very progressive on social and political issues. For instance, in 1950, there were 34 black dentists in the state, but by 1960, this number had decreased to 30, or one African American dentist per 30,525 black Mississippians. See Editors of *Ebony, The Negro Handbook* (Chicago: Johnson Publishing Co., 1966), 324.

25. Thompson, *Percy Greene and the* Jackson Advocate, 100.

26. Silver, *Mississippi: The Closed Society*, 20.

27. Francis M. Wilhoit, *The Politics of Massive Resistance* (New York: George Braziller, 1973), 88.

28. Ibid., 89.

29. Anonymous, *The Sovereignty Files: The Real Story* (Jackson, Miss.: Town Square Books, 1999), 195–264.

30. Thompson, *The Black Press in Mississippi, 1865-1985*, 64, 66.

31. See Statement of Rev. William P. Davis, Mississippi Baptist Seminar, in *Hearings Before the U. S. Commission on Civil Rights, Volume II: Administration of Justice* (Jackson, Miss.: Hearings Held in Jackson, Mississippi, February 1965), 397–415; Walker Percy, "Mississippi: The Fallen Paradise," in: Jon Meacham, ed., *Voices In Our Blood: America's Best on the Civil Rights Movement* (New York: Random House, 2001), 318–328; Jesse O. McKee, ed., *Mississippi: A Portrait of an American State* (Montgomery, Ala.: Clairmont Press, 1995), 206–213, 229; Frank E. Smith, *Congressman From Mississippi: An Autobiography* (New York: Capricorn Books, 1967); Mary E. Best, *Seventy Septembers* [a history of the work of the Holy Spirit Missionary Sisters of Mississippi and Arkansas], (Jackson, Miss.: Holy Spirit Missionary Sisters, 1988).

32. Joe Williams Trotter, Jr., *The African American Experience* (Boston: Houghton Mifflin Co., 2001), 531–37, 539–44, 561.

33. Diarmuid Jeffreys, *The Bureau: Inside the Modern FBI* (Boston: Houghton Mifflin Co., 1995). 66. Also see Jackson O'Dell, "The FBI's Southern Strategies," in: Bud Schultz and Ruth Schultz, eds., *It Did Happen Here: Recollection of Political Repression in America* (Berkeley: University of California Press, 1989), 279–288.

34. See "Negro Justice vs. White Justice," *The Crisis* 68, No. 3 (March 1961): 154–158, "Mississippi Meeting," 68, No. 5 (May 1961): 291–293, "Probe Mississippi Shooting," 70, No. 4 (April 1963): 218–220; "Medgar W. Evers," 70, No. 6 (June-July 1963): 324–325; "On Medgar Evers' Murder," 70, No. 6 (June-July 1963): 326–328, "Medgar Evers' Legacy," 71, No. 6 (June-July 1964): 370–374, "Report of the Special Mississippi Investigation Committee of the National Board of Directors of the NAACP," 71, No. 9 (November 1964): 581–593, "Victims of White Supremacy, 1951–1965," 72, No. 4 (April 1965): 244–246, "Aid Mississippi Murder Attempt Victim [in Natchez, Miss.]," 72, No. 9 (November 1965): 586–587.

35. Martin Luther King, Jr., *Strength To Love* (New York: Harper and Row, 1963); Clayborne Carson, *In Struggle:*

SNCC and the Black Awakening of the 1960s (Cambridge: Harvard University Press, 1981); Talmadge Anderson, *Introduction To African American Studies: Cultural Concepts and Theory* (Dubuque, Iowa: Kendall/Hunt Publishing Co., 1993), 104; August Meier and Elliott Rudwick, *CORE: A Study in the Civil Rights Movement 1942-1968* (New York: Oxford University Press, 1973), 101–408; James Farmer, *Lay Bare the Heart: An Autobiography of the Civil Rights Movement* (New York: Arbor House, 1985), 185–305. On an influential African intellectual, from Nigeria, Wole Soyinka (1934–), who has spoken widely on African-American affairs, see: Eldred Durosimi Jones, *The Writing of Wole Soyinka* (London: James Currey Ltd., and Portsmouth, N.H.: Heinemann, 1988).

36. "How Negroes Rank Their Leaders," *Newsweek* (August 22, 1966): 22, 34.

37. Cleve McDowell, age 21, in June, 1963, was the second known African American, after James Meredith, to attend the University of Mississippi; he was a student at the institution's law school. See *The Crisis*, 70, No. 6 (June-July 1963): 373; David M. Halbfinger, "40 Years After Infamy, Ole Miss Looks to Reflect and Heal," *New York Times*, September 27, 2001, 1, 20-A.

38. Martin Luther King, Jr., *Why We Can't Wait* (New York: New American Library, 1964); David Levering Lewis, *King: A Biography* (Urbana: University of Illinois Press, 1978); Claiborne Carson, ed., *The Autobiography of Martin Luther King, Jr.* (New York: Intellectual Properties Management and Warner Books, 1998), 246–331; Michael Eric Dyson, *Making Malcolm: The Myth and Meaning of Malcolm X* (New York: Oxford University Press, 1995).

39. Langston Hughes, ed., *New Negro Poets: USA* (Bloomington, Ind.: Indiana University Press, 1964), 13–14, 34–35, 41, 96; Dudley Randall, ed., *The Black Poets: A New Anthology* (New York: Bantam Books, 1971), 81, 90–91, 123–132, 151, 158–160, 170–172, 181, 207, 240, 323; Darlen Clark Hine and Kathleen Thompson, *A Shining Thread of Hope: The History of Black Women in America* (New York: Broadway Books, 1998), 266–294.

40. Langston Hughes, "Mississippi," in: *The Panther and the Lash: Poems of Our Times* (New York: Alfred A. Knopf, 1969), 43; Primus St. John, "Lynching and Burning," in: Arnold Adoff, ed., *The Poetry of Black America: Anthology of the 20th Century* (New York: Harper and Row, Publishers, 1973), 349; Sam Greenlee, "Lynch Parties," *Ammunition: Poetry and Other Raps* (London: Bogle-L'Ouverture Publications, Ltd., 1975), 39.

41. Also see Onwuchekwa Jemie, "Or Does It Explode?" in: Henry Louis Gates, Jr., and K. A. Appiah, eds., *Langston Hughes: Critical Perspectives: Past and Present* (New York: Amistad, 1993), 135–171.

42. Loften Mitchell, *Black Drama: The Story of the American Negro in the Theatre* (New York: Hawthorn Books, 1967), 103–105, 180–182, 185–186, 188–190, 197–199, 200–205, 209–10, 213; Christina Davis, "Interview with Toni Morrison," in: Henry Louis Gates, Jr., and K. A. Appiah, eds., *Toni Morrison: Critical Perspectives, Past and Present* (New York: Amistad, 1993), 412; Margaret Croyden, "Toni Morrison Tries Her Hand at Playwriting," in: Danille Taylor-Guthrie, ed., *Conversations With Toni Morrison* (Jackson, Miss.: University Press of Mississippi, 1994), 218–222.

43. Samuel A. Hay notes the special roles of eleven major coalitions of theatre companies in the United States during and after the Black Arts Movement: "the Organization of Black American Culture in Chicago (1967), the Black Theatre Alliance of New York (1971), the Coalition of Black Revolutionary Artists of Chicago (1972), the Southern Black Cultural Alliance (1972), the Black Theatre Alliance of Chicago (1974), the Audience Development Committee of New York (1973), the Midwest Afrikan-American Theatre Alliance (1976), the Black Arts Council of Dallas (1984), the Black Theatre Collective of New York (1986), the San Francisco Area Multi-Cultural Production Fund (1988), and the

African Continuum Theatre Coalition (Act Co) in Washington, D. C. (1989). See Samuel A. Hay, *African American Theatre: A Historical and Critical Analysis* (New York: Cambridge University Press, 1994), 263.

44. William Ferris, *Blues From the Delta* (Garden City, New York: Anchor Books, 1979); Paul Oliver, *The Story of the Blues* (Radnor, Pa.: Chilton Book Co., 1975); Kerran Sanger, "When the Spirit Says Sing": *The Role of Freedom Songs in the Civil Rights Movement* (New York: Garland Publishing, 1995).

45. Nina Simone, "Mississippi Goddam," (Santa Monica, Calif.: Sam Fox Publishing Co., Inc., 1964); Guy and Candie Carawan, eds., *Sing For Freedom: The Story of the Civil Rights Movement Through Its Songs* (Bethlehem, Pa.: A Sing Out Publication, 1990), 188–193.

46. Nina Simone with Stephen Cleary, *I Put a Spell on You: The Autobiography of Nina Simone* (New York: Pantheon Books, 1991), 90.

47. Molly Askin, "The Endless Freedom Summer," *Chicago Tribune*, February 19, 1989, 4: Doug McAdam, *Freedom Summer* (New York: Oxford University Press, 1989); Clayborne Carson, *In Struggle: SNCC and the Black Awakening of the 1960s* (Cambridge: Harvard University Press, 1981).

48. Mary Aickin Rothschild. "White Women Volunteers in the Freedom Summers: Their Life and Work in a Movement for Social Change," *Feminist Studies* 5, No.3 (Fall 1979): 466–495. On the role of Jewish activists, organizations, and especially Mississippi Freedom Summer volunteers, see Liz McMillen, "'Straight Talk' about Blacks and Jews," *The Chronicle of Higher Education* 42, No. 35 (May 10, 1996): A12.

49. See Betsy Bowden, *Performed Literature: Words and Music by Bob Dylan* (Lanham, Md.: University Press of America, 2001), 8–13.

50. Florence Halpern, *Survival: Black/White* (New York: Pergamon Press, 1973), 9–10.

51. Alphonso Pinkney, *The Committed: White Activists in the Civil Rights Movement* (New Haven, Conn.: College and University Press, Publishers, 1968), 90. Also see "Victims of 'White Supremacy,' 1951–1965." *The Crisis* 72, No. 4 (April 1965): 244–246.

52. Adam Fairclough, *Better Day Coming: Blacks and Equality, 1890-2000* (New York: Viking, 2001), 256–262; Charles Marsh, *God's Long Summer: Stories of Faith and Civil Rights* (Princeton, N.J.: Princeton University Press, 1997), 24–25, 32, 39, 44–45, 57–58, 89–104. One study notes data from the Department of Justice for 1964 and violence against Mississippi blacks:

1. February 15, 1964—Adams County. A Negro man, Winston, was attacked and beaten by masked and armed men asking if he was a member of the NAACP.
2. February 16, 1964—Adams County. Two Negro men, Curtis and Jackson, were beaten by armed men wearing white hoods down to their waists. The men questioned the two Negroes about their membership in the NAACP.
3. February 18, or 25, 1964—Lincoln County. A 28year-old Negro man was beaten by a group of four white men who stopped his car while he was returning home from work. He was accused of following a white lady, taken out into the county, and both his eyes were blackened.
4. March 25, 1964—Hinds County. The plate glass windows in the grocery store belonging to a Negro active in the civil rights work in Jackson, Rev. Smith, were broken. A Klan pamphlet was discovered in the debris.
5. Panola County. West Camp Church was broken into and its windows were smashed and chairs inside the church were damaged. This church has been used for voter registration purposes every other week.
6. April 4, 1964—Neshoba County. A dozen crosses were burned at various spots throughout the county.
7. April 5, 1964—Adams County. Richard Joe Butler, Negro, was stopped outside Natchez by a group of white men

wearing hoods. He was shot several times and seriously wounded, requiring hospitalization.
8. April 9, 1964—Jones County. Two crosses allegedly burned at the home of Ollie Cole and the home of Sam Merrill, both Negro employees of the Masonite Corporation in Laurel.
9. April 24, 1964—Statewide. Crosses were burned across the state. The Highway Patrol received reports of 71 crosses being burned in 61 areas of Mississippi including Jackson, Hattiesburg, Vicksburg, Utica, Crystal Springs, Greenwood, Natchez, Greenville, Meridian, Fayette, and Winona.
10. June 4, 1964—Hinds County. Ethel Jordan and Alvin Higgins, both Negroes, were beaten on their way home after they stopped to assist a white man in a car that appeared to be disabled. Jordan suffered a fractured rib and a tremendously swollen left side of the head, and a severely contused hand.
11. June 6, 1964—Amite County. Roland Sleeper, a Negro, was taken from his home near Liberty, Mississippi, and whipped by four white men who also threatened to kill him. He was asked if any NAACP people were staying at his home.
12. June 11, 1964—Pike County. Ivey Gutter, a Negro male who resides near Summit, was beaten by unknown white males who were armed and wore black hoods.

See Marsh, *God's Long Summer: Stories of Faith and Civil Rights*, 57–58.

53. "Mississippi: Then and Now," *The Crisis* 72, No. 3 (March 1965): 185.

54. George H. Gallup, *The Gallup Poll: Public Opinion, 1935-1971, Volume 3, 1959-1971* (New York: Random House, 1972), 1970.

55. D. Eric Lincoln, *The Black Muslims in America* (Grand Rapids, Mich.: W. B. Eerdmans Publishing Co./Trenton, N.J.: Africa World Press, 1994), 254–276, DeCaro, *On the Side of My People: A Religious Life of Malcolm X*, 271–93.

56. Claude Andrew Clegg, III, *An Original Man: The Life and Times of Elijah Muhammad* (New York: St. Martin's Press, 1997), 23–25, 35–40, 78–276.

57. Marvin X, "Did You Vote Nigger?" in: Ahmed Alhamisi and Harun Kofi Wangara, eds., *Black Arts: An Anthology of Black Creations* (Detroit: Black Arts Publications, 1969), 139–140.

58. Vincent Harding, *Hope and History: Why We Must Share the Story of the Movement* (Maryknoll, New York: Orbis Books, 1990), 5, 19, 34–35.

59. W. Fitzhugh Brundage, ed., *Under Sentence of Death: Lynching in the South* (Chapel Hill, N.C.: The University of North Carolina Press, 1997), 1; Tolnay and Beck, *A Festival of Violence*, 271–272. Readers may wish to consult Thompson, *Black Life in Mississippi: Essays On Political, Social and Cultural Studies in a Deep South State*, for a listing of lynching victims in Mississippi for the period 1889–1966, pages 191–221.

Epilogue

1. Jesse O. McKee, ed., *Mississippi: A Portrait of an American State* (Montgomery, Ala.: Clairmont Press, 1994), 258.

2. Michael Barane and Richard E. Cohen, with Charles E. Cook, Jr., *The Almanac of American Politics 2002* (Washington, D.C.: National Journal Group, 2001), 862. On two significant minority groups see: "Delta Lotus: Quan Relates Inside Story of Chinese Culture in Delta," The *Clarion-Ledger/Jackson Daily News*, August 15, 1982, G-1; and "Choctaws Move From Reservation to Dealer's Lot," *The New York Times*, May 14, 2002, C-1–2.

3. Julius E. Thompson, *The Black Press in Mississippi, 1865-1985* (Gainesville, Fla.: University Press of Florida, 1993), 113.

4. *Jackson Advocate*, May 30, 2002, 16-A.

5. On the economic crisis in the Delta see: Robert M. Press, "In Mississippi, A Look at One Town's Progress," *Christian Science Monitor*, September 1, 1982; Ronald Smothers, "Hope as Seen for Poor of 7-State Delta," *New York Times*, November 21, 1989; Jason DeParle, "Tunica Journal: The Shacks Disappear, but the Poverty Lives On,'" *New York Times*, March 10, 1991; Russ Rymen, "Hope In Mississippi," *Health* 7, No. 2 (March/April 1993): 80–86; Michael Tisserand, "Mississippi Delta Still in Dark," *USA Today*, March 1, 1994.

6. *Clarion-Ledger*, December 16, 1979.

7. *Clarion-Ledger*, February 23, 1997, 57. Also see David Firestone, "Mississippi Farmers Return to Roots of Cotton," *New York Times*, July 16, 2001, A-1, 9. By 2001, Mississippi had assumed the position as the number three leading cotton producing state in the United States. *Ibid.*

8. McKee, *Mississippi: A Portrait of an American State*, 279. On an interesting case of greater state efforts to bring more manufacturing jobs to Mississippi (Nissan), and black landowners' refusal to sell their land for the project in Canton, Mississippi, see "Black Landowners Hold Ground in Mississippi," *New York Times*, September 10, 2001. A1, 20.

9. John W. Wright, ed., *The New York Times 2002 Almanac* (New York: Penguin Reference, 2001), 186. Economic change in Mississippi is represented by the rising standard of living of the Mississippi Band of Choctaw Indians. In 1962, this minority group in Mississippi had a per capita income of only $995; by 1982, this figure increased to $3,176; and by 1997, to $9,023. See *New York Times*, May 14, 2002.

10. "Distribution of Black Physicians in the United States," U.S. Department of Health, Education, and Welfare, Availability Data on Minorities and Women (Washington, D. C.: Office for Civil Rights, June 1973); *Black Resource Guide* (Washington, D. C.: Black Resource Guide, Inc., 1982), 63.

11. "Pity the Poor White Male," *The Journal of Blacks in Higher Education* 12 (Summer 1996): 13; Gerry Everding, "Racism A 'Male Thing,' Suggests Study of Small Group," *Jackson Advocate*, October 24, 1996), 4-B.

12. "New Poll Finds Widespread Misperceptions About Race Among Whites," *St. Louis Post-Dispatch*, July 11, 2001, A-4.

13. John Dittmer, *Local People: The Struggle for Civil Rights in Mississippi* (Urbana, Ill.: University of Illinois Press, 1994), 427.

14. The state's lawmakers even officially ended slavery in Mississippi in 1995. The *New York Times* noted for its readers: "This Just In: Mississippi Abolishes Slavery": "One hundred and thirty years after the rest of the nation, Mississippi today ratified the constitutional amendment that formally outlawed slavery in the United States. Without debate, the Mississippi House of Representatives approved a resolution ratifying the 13th amendment; the State Senate had approved it earlier. No action by Gov. Kirk Fordice is required. The state will notify Congress, and the action will be noted in Congressional records. When Lincoln's Emancipation Proclamation went into effect on Jan. 1, 1863, at the height of the Civil War, it freed, 'all persons held as slaves in areas still in rebellion.' The 13th amendment, ratified on Dec. 18, 1865, eight months after the war ended, abolished slavery throughout the United States. But Mississippi, whose lawmakers were angry because slave owners had not been reimbursed for the value of freed slaves, refused to ratify the amendment, even though its provisions applied in Mississippi as elsewhere. This year State Senator Hillman Frazier, Democrat of Jackson, persuaded his fellow lawmakers that it was time for Mississippi to formally close its book on slavery." See *New York Times*, March 17, 1995, A-8.

15. Charles C. Bolton, "The Last Stand of Massive Resistance: Mississippi Public School Integration, 1970," *The Journal of Mississippi History* 61, No. 4 (Winter 1999): 341.

16. *Ibid.*, 348–349.

17. Laurence H. Fuchs, *The American Kaleidoscope: Race, Equality, and the Civic Culture* (Hanover, N.H.: Wesleyan University Press/University Press of New England, 1990), 297–298. Two other educational issues must be noted here. First, Mississippi teachers have historically received low salaries. In 2001, Governor Ronnie Musgrove recommended a salary increase "from $31,892 now to $41,445 by 2005, slightly above the projected 2005 Southeastern average salary of $41,199." See "Mississippi Teacher Salaries," *New York Times*, July 24, 2001, A-22. Secondly, black Mississippians have sought relief for historically black higher educational institutions (Alcorn State, Jackson State, and Mississippi Valley State, among others), since the 1970s, in a federal district court suit known as the Ayers case. In 1995, the state of Mississippi agreed to seek $35.8 million from the state legislature to promote improvements for the state's black public colleges. For the black community, the question now centers on: what will be the future of black colleges in the state and will they ever be "equal" to their historically white sister institutions (University of Mississippi, Mississippi State University, University of Southern Mississippi, Delta State University, etc.)? See Scott Jaschik, "Ruling in Mississippi," *The Chronicle of Higher Education* 41, No. 27 (March 17, 1995): A-23–27; Ivory Phillips, "Conditions That Led to Ayers Still Alive," *Jackson Advocate*, August 31, 2000, 4-A.

18. Joe Atkins, "Mississippi's Rich Cultural Heritage Can Be A Source of Pride, Wealth," *Clarion-Ledger*, March 1, 1992, 3-G; Newsletter, *The Jacqueline House Museum* (Vicksburg, Miss.: The Jacqueline House Museum, 2002); *Project Southern Cross*, letter (Natchez, Miss.: Project Southern Cross, September 2, 1996); Charles A. Taylor, ed., *Guide to Multicultural Resources 1993–1994* (Fort Atkinson, Wis.: Praxis Publications, 1994), 42. On the continuing significance of the work of black writers and artists, such as Dr. Endesha Ida Mae Holland and C. Leigh McInnis, see: "From the Mississippi Delta is a Tale of Victory Seized," *The New York Times*, November 24, 1991; Endesha Ida Mae Holland, *From the Mississippi Delta: A Memoir* (New York: Simon & Schuster, 1997); *Black Magnolias, A Journal* (Jackson, Miss.) Vol. 1, No. 2 (Spring 2002): 1.

19. Barbara Omolade, *The Rising Song of African American Women* (New York: Routledge, 1994), 214–221, 230–245; James L. Conyers, Jr., "African American Males: Memory, Culture, and Ethos," *Journal of African American Men* 4, No. 4 (February 2000), 19–36.

20. Paul Johnson, *A History of the American People* (New York: Harper Collins Publishers, 1999), 972.

21. Darlene Clark Hine and Kathleen Thompson, *A Shining Thread of Hope: The History of Black Women in America* (New York: Broadway Books, 1998), 311–13; Lerone Bennett, Jr., "The 10 Biggest Myths About the Black Family," *Ebony* 41, No. 10 (August 1986): 123–32.

22. John J. Dilulio, Jr., "Black Churches and the Inner-City Poor," in: Christopher H. Foreman, Jr., ed., *The African American Predicament* (Washington, D.C.: Brookings Institution Press, 1999), 123.

23. See Laurie Goodstein, "Most Americans See Benefits in Religion, A Poll Shows," *New York Times*, January 10, 2001, A-13; C. Eric Lincoln and Lawrence H. Mamiya, *The Black Church in the African American Experience* (Durham, N.C.: Duke University Press, 1990), 173, 183–185.

24. See "Black Church Fires," *USA Today*, June 28, 1996, 3-A.

25. *USA Today*, June 12, 1996, 3-A, June 28, 1996, 1-A, July 1, 1996, 1, 5-A; *Columbia* (Mo.) *Daily Tribune*, June 18, 1996, 10-A; *Jackson Advocate*, June 27, 1996, 5-A; *New York Times*, June 25, 1996, A-9.

26. Manning Marable, "Why the Churches Burn?" *The St. Louis American*, August 8, 1996, A-7.

27. *New York Times*, June 8, 16, 20, 1996; *St. Louis Post-Dispatch*, June 19, 1996; *The Kansas City Star*, July 9, 1996; Joe Maxwell, "Racial Healing in the Land of Lynching,"

Christianity Today, 38, No. 1 (January 10, 1994): 24–26. Yet segregation in American religious institutions is also a fact of life. See "Blacks, Whites Attend Separate Churches," *USA Today*, June 14, 1996, 2-A.

28. Michael Hirsley, "U. S. Muslims Search for Understanding," *Chicago Tribune*, February 11, 1994, 1, 8-A. One study notes that "by 2000, America had roughly one thousand mosques and many national Islamic organizations, including the Muslim Students Association (established in 1963) and the Islamic Society of North America (1981)." See Stephen Prothero, "Islam," in: P. S. Beyer, ed., *The Oxford Companion to U. S. History* (New York: Oxford University Press, 2001), 396.

29. Peter T. Kilborn, "Black Americans Trailing Whites in Health, Studies Say," *New York Times*, January 26, 1998, A-16; "Deaths From AIDS Will Soar in Next 20 Years, Report Says," *St. Louis Post-Dispatch*, July 3, 2002, A-8; *Jackson Advocate*, November ?, 1991, 11-A.

30. Paul Farmer, "Women, Poverty, and AIDS," in Paul Farmer, Margaret Connors, and Janie Simmons, eds., *Women, Poverty, and AIDS: Sex, Drugs, and Structural Violence* (Monroe, Maine: Common Courage Press, 1996), 21. Other national problems which also impact on black Mississippians are increasing suicides among blacks and other mental health issues; and the problem of hunger among very poor blacks. See Alvin F. Poussaint and Amy Alexander, *Lay My Burden Down: Unraveling Suicide and the Mental Health Crisis Among African-Americans* (Boston: Beacon Press, 2000), 12–153; Doris Witt, *Black Hunger: Food and the Politics of U.S. Identity* (New York: Oxford University Press, 1999), 32–33, 74, 230–32, 238.

31. Glenn C. Loury, *The Anatomy of Racial Inequality* (Cambridge, Mass.: Harvard University Press, 2002), 182.

32. Howard Zinn, *The Twentieth Century: A People's History* (New York: Harper Collins Publishers, 1998), 425.

33. On the significance of the black press in Mississippi during this period see: Thompson, *The Black Press in Mississippi, 1865–1985*, 81–150.

34. Richard Hofstadter and Beatrice K. Hofstadter, eds., *Great Issues in American History: From Reconstruction to the Present Day, 1864–1981* (New York: Vintage Books/Random House, 1982), 439.

35. Byron D'Andra Orey, "Black Legislative Politics in Mississippi," *Journal of Black Studies* 30, No. 6 (July 2000): 795.

36. Ibid., 796–97. Also see Robert C. Smith, *We Have No Leaders: African Americans in the Post–Civil Rights Era* (Albany, N.Y.: SUNY Press, 1996), 271–72.

37. Ibid., 807.

38. Ibid., 809. Yet, black representation continues to grow in Mississippi. Orey notes that "in 1992, the black membership in the state legislature increased from 12% to 24%." Ibid., 811. This factor has increased the political power of blacks in the Mississippi legislature.

39. Dewey M. Clayton, *African Americans and the Politics of Congressional Redistricting* (New York: Garland Publishing, 2000), 175; Schomburg Center, *African American Reference Desk* (New York: John Wiley and Sons, 1999), 78; Thompson, *Black Life In Mississippi*, 147.

40. Tom Dent, *Southern Journey: A Return to the Civil Rights Movement* (New York: William Morrow, 1997), 296. Statewide and nationally, the NAACP still maintains a position of great influence among historically civil rights organizations. In fact, by the mid–1990s, the NAACP had over 500,000 members in 1,800 chapters in the United States (2,200 branches in 2000), while the chapters in Mississippi have had over 15,000 members since 1959. See Charles M. Payne, *I've Got the Light of Freedom: The Organizing Tradition and the Mississippi Freedom Struggle* (Berkeley: University of California Press, 1995), 60.

41. "Blacks, Hispanics Report Higher Rate of Police Threats, Agency Says," *St. Louis Post-Dispatch*, March 12, 2001, A-5.

42. Michael C. Dawson, "Globalization, the Racial Divide, and a New Citizenship," in: Rodolfo D. Torres, Louis F. Miron, and Jonathan Xavier Inda, eds., *Race, Identity, and Citizenship: A Reader* (Maiden, Mass.: Blackwell Publishers, 1999), 379.

43. "National Poll Ranks State 50th in Fair Legal Climate," *Jackson Advocate*, March 21, 2002, 3-A.

44. Roi D. Townsey, "The Incarceration of Black Men," in: Lawrence Gary, ed., *Black Men* (Beverly Hills, Ca.: Sage Publications, 1981), 233.

45. Dennis Camire, "Jail Overcrowding Strains Lawmakers' Resolve," *Clarion-Ledger Jackson Daily News*, February 14, 1982, 3, 6-A; Alphonso C. Chester II, "Health Care Crisis at Parchman," *Jackson Advocate*, May 9, 2002, 13-A; Emily Wilkerson, "AIDS is Major Cause of Deaths in Prison," *St. Louis Post-Dispatch*, May 5, 1994. One recent author notes that in 1995, Parchman Prison "was home to sixty-eight hundred prisoners, meaning that roughly one Mississippian in thirty was imprisoned there.... The prison's population had exploded over the past decade.... Eighty-five percent of [the] inmates are black." See Richard Rubin, *Confederacy of Silence: A True Tale of the New Old South* (New York: Atria Books, 2002), 316–24.

46. "More Than Million Inmates Doing Time in U. S. Prisons," *The Clarion-Ledger*, October 28, 1994, 5-A. By this late date (1994), Mississippi held 10,691 prisoners convicted of state and federal crimes. Ibid.

47. Loury, *The Anatomy of Racial Inequality*, 81.

48. "Data on Teenage Black Men Show Rise in Suicide by Gun," *New York Times*, March 21, 2002, A-30; Earl Ofari Hutchinson, "Growing Suicide Rate Among Black Males," *Jackson Advocate*, May 28, 1998, 5-A; Paul Hampel, "Suicides and Casting a Shadow Over the Already Dark World of our Area's Jails," *St. Louis Post-Dispatch*, July 2, 2000, B-1, 5. The nature of this crisis is reflected in this statement: "The facts are, that 25 percent of black males 15–25 are in prison or on probation, the majority of which comes from single parent families." See *St. Louis American*, October 10, 1996. A-7.

49. Robert Brent Toplin, "Violence and Culture: The United States," in: Kuman Rupesinghe and Marcial Rubio, eds., *The Culture of Violence*, (New York: United Nations University Press, 1994), 245. Black women have also suffered greatly in terms of higher imprisonment rates since the 1970s. In 1980, there were 78,000 American women incarcerated in the United States [and] 1.1 million men. One study notes: "Drug offenses alone account for 66 percent of all women in federal prisons and 33 percent of women in state penitentiaries." See Nina Siegal, "Women in Prison," *Ms* 9, No. 2 (September/October 1998): 65, 67.

50. *New York Times*, June 12, 24, 2000; *Jackson Advocate*, August 13, 1998, A-A.

51. *Jackson Advocate*, March 20, 1997, 1-A; Stewart E. Tolnay and E. M. Beck, *A Festival of Violence: An Analysis of Southern Lynchings, 1882–1930* (Urbana, Ill.: University of Illinois Press, 1995), 47.

52. Leonard J. Moore, "Ku Klux Klan," in: Beyer, *The Oxford Companion to U. S. History*, 425.

53. Scott Clifford, "Murder and Homicide," in: *Ready Reference, American Justice, Volume II* (Pasadena, Calif.: Salem Press, 1996), 532.

54. Arthur M. Schlesinger, Jr., and John S. Bowman, eds., *The Almanac of American History* (New York: Barnes and Noble/Brompton Books, 1993), 576. On other incidents of this nature note the May 15, 1970, "Death Valley," at Jackson State University, when two young black men were killed by 'sniper fire.' See *Jackson Daily News*, December 29, 1970, 1, 16-A; and "Youth Slain at Moorhead Vacant House," on an alleged break-in at a private house. See *Jackson Daily News*, September 21, 1972, 1, 16-A. CBS Reports noted in 1995 that Louisiana, a neighboring state of Mississippi, was the most dangerous state to live in in the United States. Louisiana also had the highest murder rate in the country, with many of

its prisoners housed at Angola Prison. See CBS Reports, January 26, 1995.

55. *New York Times*, August 18, 1998, A-10; *Jackson Advocate*, June 8, 2000, 1, 8-A; Evers, *For Us, The Living*, 378; Thompson, *Black Life in Mississippi*, 71; Marable, *Speaking Truth to Power*, 29; *Columbia Missourian*, July 13, 2000, 7-A; *St. Louis Post-Dispatch*, June 28, 2000, A-5; *Jackson Advocate*, July 6, 2000, 1-A, 8-A; *USA Today*, June 30, 2000, 3-A.

56. Thompson, *Black Life in Mississippi*, 70–71.

57. Marable, *Speaking Truth to Power*, 29; *Jackson Advocate*, January 13, 1994, 1-A; Alton Hornsby, Jr., and Deborah Gillen Straub, *African American Chronology, Volume 2, 1973–1993* (New York: UXL/Gale Research, 1994), 343; *USA This Week*, March 1, 1994, 10–12.

58. Wright, *The New York Times 2002 Almanac*, 314–15.

59. *Ibid.*, 317. Nationally, the United States has executed 598 individuals between 1977 and 2001. *Ibid.*, 317. The execution of black men for the crime of rape remains a national disgrace. One author notes: "From 1930 to 1981, 455 men were executed for rape; of that number, 405 were black men. They were put to death on the flimsiest evidence, mostly the word of white women. It was nice and legal then, and it still is today." See Earl Ofari Hutchinson, *The Assassination of the Black Male Image* (New York: Simon & Schuster, 1996), 73.

60. Paul Delaney, "A New South For Blacks," in: John B. Boles, ed., *Dixie Dateline: A Journalistic Portrait of the Contemporary South* (Houston, Texas: Rice University Studies, 1983), 41, 44.

61. B. B. King, with David Pitz, *Blues All Around Me: The Autobiography of B. B. King* (New York: Avon Books, 1996), 233.

62. Clenora Hudson-Weems, "Resurrecting Emmett Till: The Catalyst of the Modern Civil Rights Movement," *Journal of Black Studies* 29, No. 2 (November 1998): 179.

63. Cloyte Murdock Larsson, "Land of the Till Murder Revisited," *Ebony* 41, No. 5 (March 1986): 53, 57–58.

64. Pauli Murray, "For Mack C. Parker," in: Arnold Adoff, ed., *The Poetry of Black America: Anthology of the 20th Century* (New York: Harper Collins Publishers, 1973), 110.

65. For other contemporary views see: C. Leigh McInnis, "The New African American Writers of Mississippi," *Art Changes/In Motion Magazine* (February 28, 2000): 1–8; Maxwell, "Racial Healing in the Land of Lynching," 24–26; and "Black Woman Who Lived Nearby Gives $150,000 to [University of Southern Mississippi]," *The Chronicle of Higher Education* 41, No. 48 (August 11, 1995): A-31.

66. Frederick M. Wirt, *"We Ain't What We Was": Civil Rights in the New South* (Durham, N. C.: Duke University Press, 1997), 208. Also see Richard Morin, "A Distorted Image of Minorities: Poll Suggests that What Whites Think They See May Affect Beliefs," *The Washington Post*, October 8, 1995, A-1, 27; R. G. Grant, *Racism, Changing Attitudes, 1900–2000* (Austin, Texas: Raintree Steck-Vaughn Publishers, 2000), 20–21, 42–43.

67. See Hugh B. Price, "The White-Collar Ku Klux Klan," *The Jackson Advocate*, January 28, 1999, 5-A; Milton Kleg, *Hate, Prejudice and Racism* (Albany, N.Y.: SUNY Press, 1993), 14–15; On the historical significance of the term "Nigger" and its impact on American race relations, see: Randall Kennedy, *Nigger: The Strange Career of a Troublesome Word* (New York: Pantheon Books, 2002), 172–176.

68. David Firestone, "Mississippi Votes by Wide Margin to Keep State Flag that Includes Confederate Emblem," *The New York Times*, April 18, 2001, A-12.

69. Katie Blount, "Sovereignty Commission Records Open," *Newsletter of the Mississippi Department of Archives & History* (Jackson, Miss.: MDAH, March 17, 1998), 1; *Mississippi History Newsletter*, "Sovereignty Commission Papers Scheduled for March 17 Opening," *MDAH*, February 1998, 1.

70. Payne, *I've Got the Light of Freedom: The Organizing Tradition and the Mississippi Freedom Struggle*, 391–441; C. Gerald Fraser, "'60 s Voices: Reflections on Civil Rights Movement." *New York Times*, April 18, 1988, B-3.

71. *Perspectives* 36, No. 5 (May 1998): 3; "NAACP Rebuilding," *Clarion-Ledger*, October 20, 1996, 6-A.

72. *Jackson Advocate*, June 15, 2000, 2-A. On the issue of police violence, especially such cases as the alleged murder of Amadou Diallo by four white New York City police officers, see *The New York Times*, February 2, 2000, A-23, and March 1, 2000, A-23.

73. Jacob U. Gordon, *Black Leadership for Social Change* (Westport, Conn.: Greenwood Press, 2000), 213.

74. Certainly the freedom struggles in Southern Africa received inspiration and encouragement from the U. S. civil rights movement, as have protest struggles in many other lands, including Ireland. See Edward Bever, *Africa: International Government and Politics Series* (Phoenix, Arizona: The Oryx Press, 1996), 259–260; Diane McWhorter, *Carry Me Home, Birmingham, Alabama: The Climactic Battle of the Civil Rights Revolution* (New York: Simon & Schuster, 2001), 464–465; "Remember the Martyrs of the Movement," *Ebony* (February 1990): 58, 60–61.

75. Vernon E. Jordan, Jr., with Annette Gordon-Reed, *Vernon Can Read: A Memoir* (New York: Public Affairs/Perseus Book Group, 2001), 169, 172. On the modern black religious condition see: Christopher H. Foreman, Jr., ed., *The African American Predicament* (Washington, D. C.: Brookings Institution Press, 1999), 129–136; "Inmates Ask Author [Taylor Branch] All About Dr. King," *New York Times*, January 7, 1989, 13; Manning Marable, "Black Fundamentalism: Farrakhan and Conservative Black Nationalism," *Race & Class* 39, No. 4 (April–June 1998), 1–22; *Columbia Missourian*, March 13, 2002, 7-A.

76. *New York Times*, November 10, 1998; Jacqueline Johnson, *Stokely Carmichael: The Story of Black Power* (Englewood Cliffs, N.J.: Silver Burdett Press, 1990), 124.

77. *St. Louis American*, February 13, 1997, C-1, 9; March 13, 1997, 2-B. On a giant among American actors in film history see: Sidney Portier, *The Measure of a Man: A Spiritual Autobiography* (San Francisco, Ca.: Harper Collins Publishers, 2000), 107, 117–118, 201. On a critical assessment of Hollywood's attempts to portray blacks on film, and especially "Mississippi Burning," which examines certain aspects of the Civil Rights Movement in Mississippi, see: Sundiata K. Cha-Jua, "Mississippi Burning: The Burning of Black Self-Activity," *Radical History Review* 45 (1989): 125–136. On a second film, "Ghosts of Mississippi," which seeks to explore the Medgar Evers case, see: DeWayne Wickham, "Black Hero Missing in Movie," *USA Today*, December 24, 1996, 13-A; Thomas Gibson, "Ghosts of Mississippi Doesn't Stand a Ghost of a Chance to Impress," *St. Louis American*, January 9, 1997, 11.

78. See Frances I. Cress Welsing, "Build A World Without Racism," *Integrated Education: Minority Children in Schools* 13, No. 1 (January-February 1975): 20–26; Cornel West, "American Radicalism," in: Peter Osborne, ed., *A Critical Sense: Interviews With Intellectuals* (New York: Routledge, 1996), 126–142; *The Philadelphia Inquirer*, June 16, 1996, B-l, 4; Jesse Jackson, *Summit on Violence By Rainbow Coalition*, C-Span, January 7–9, 1994; "The Case of Mumia Abu-Jamal," (Hyattsville, Md.: A Project of the Quixote Center, April 1995), 1–4; Mumia Abu-Jamal, "Father Figures," in *These Times* 24, No. 8 (March 20, 2002), 28–29; Salim Muwakkil, "Mumia's Last Chance," *In These Times* 24, No. 1 (December 12, 1999): 22–23. Among new literary groups that helped to raise cultural issues in the 1990s and beyond is the Richard Wright Circle, which publishes a biannual newsletter. This organization, devoted to exploring and promoting the works and life of Richard Wright, was founded in 1991 by Margaret Walker Alexander, Samuel Allen, Ralph Ellison, Michel Fabre, Maryemma Graham, Jerry W. Ward, Jr., and Julia Wright. See *The Richard Wright Newsletter* 6, No. 2 (Spring/Summer 1998): 1–3.

79. Bakari Kitwana, *The Hip Hop Generation: Young Blacks and the Crisis in African American Culture* (New York: Basic

Civitas Books, 2002), from the cover. Also see: Jamilah Eve-lyn, "Hip-Hop: Are Today's Faculty and Administrators Sim-ply Out of Touch? Or Has Today's Popular Music Truly Corrupted the Minds of a Whole Generation?" *Black Issues in Higher Education* 17, No. 21 (December 7, 2000), 24–29.

80. See Dan Dulin, "Rhyme and Reason: Poet Maya Angelou Tells ... Why She Never Lets a Chance To Talk About AIDS Pass," *America's AID Magazine, Issue 75* (Janu-ary 2001): 47–48, 50–52; B. Andrew Plant, "Moving For-ward: Coretta Scott King Tells ... Why the Civil Rights Movement is Important to AIDS Activism," *America's AID Magazine* 10, No. 11 (November 2001): 30–33. Also see: "Looking for America: The Coretta Scott King Award (Now 30 Years Old, Has Changed the Heart of Our Nation)," *School Library Journal* 45, No. 5 (May 1999): 29–31.

81. Richard Reeves, *President Nixon Alone in the White House* (New York: Simon & Schuster, 2001), 511; Robert R. Detlefson, *Civil Rights Under Reagan* (San Francisco, Ca.: Institute For Contemporary Studies, 1991), 4–5; Haynes Johnson, *The Best of Times: America in the Clinton Years* (New York: A James H. Silverman Book, Harcourt, 2001), 134–37, 530–31. DeWayne Wickham, *Bill Clinton and Black America* (New York: Ballantine Books, 2002), 1.

82. On the issue of hate groups and anti-black attitudes of the national level since 1966, see: Eduardo Bonilla-Silva, *White Supremacy and Racism in the Post-Civil Rights Era* (Boul-der, Colorado: Lynne Rienner Publishers, 2001), 1–119; Bar-bara Perry, *In the Name of Hate: Understanding Hate Crimes* (New York: Routledge, 2001), 43, 138–139. On more liberal thinking among white Americans see: Dorothy Dawson Burlage, *Deep In Our Hearts: Nine White Women in the Free-dom Movement* (Athens, Ga.: The University of Georgia Press, 2000); Gary Murrell, "On Herbert Aptheker and His Side of History: An Interview with Eric Foner," *Radical History Review* 78, No. 6 (2000): 7–26. Tolnay and Beck, *A Festival of Violence*, 37. Mississippi must also be measured against the general violence of the 20th century, one of the crudest in world history. See Harry Levins, "Here's Looking at a Bloody, Boisterous 20th Century," *St. Louis Post-Dispatch*, December 31, 2000, 1, 8-A.

83. Neil R. McMillen, *Dark Journey, Black Mississippians in the Age of Jim Crow* (Urbana, Ill.: University of Illinois Press, 1989), 229–230.

84. See James B. Jacobs and Kimberly Potter, *Hate Crimes: Criminal Law and Identity Politics* (New York: Oxford Univer-sity Press, 1998), 58–138; Matt Milner, "Hate Crimes on the Increase in the U. S.," *The Boonville (Mo.) Daily News*, August 13, 1999, 1-A; "FBI's Hate Crime Data Show Race is Primary Motivation for Attacks," *Columbia Missourian*, November 6, 1996, 4-A; "Study of 100 Rampage Slayings Reveals They Are Well-Planned, With No Way Out for the Killers," *St. Louis Post-Dispatch*, April 9, 2000, A-10; Jane Kenway, Lindsay Fitz-clarence, and Lindsay Hasluck, "Toxic Shock: Understand-ing Violence Against Young Males in the Work Place," *The Journal of Men's Studies* 8, No. 2 (Winter 2000): 131–152; Leighton C. Whitaker, *Understanding and Preventing Violence: The Psychology of Human Destructiveness* (New York: CRC Press, 2000), 7–122.

85. Margaret D. Canio, *The Encyclopedia of Violence: Ori-gins, Attitudes, Consequences* (New York: Facts On File, 1993), 109–128.

86. Curt Gentry, *J. Edgar Hoover: The Man and the Secrets* (New York: W. W. Norton & Co., 1991), 563.

87. See Larry Copeland, "From a Whisper to a Shout: Museums Teach Black History," *USA Today*, (2001), 1–2A.

88. David R. Goldfield, *Black, White, and Southern: Race Relations and Southern Culture, 1940 to the Present* (Baton Rouge, La.: Louisiana State University Press, 1990), 273.

89. *New York Times*, June 25, 2000, 16-D.

90. This is true of all groups. See Scott Berg, "Remem-bering the Past, Looking to the Future: American Indian

Heritage Month [November of each year] Marks a Time to Reflect Upon the History, Struggles and Culture of our Nation's Earliest Inhabitants," *Columbia Missourian*, Novem-ber 16, 1999, 5-A.

91. "Time Heals Few Wounds for Emmett Till's Mother," *Jet* 66, No. 5 (April 9, 1984): 54–56.

92. "Chicago's 71st Street is Renamed for Emmett Till," *Jet* 80, No. 17 (August 12, 1991): 4–5.

93. Goldfield, *Black, White and Southern: Race Relations and Southern Culture, 1940 to the Present*, 273.

94. On the regional implications of these issues see: W. Fitzhugh Brundage, ed., *Where These Memories Grow: History, Memory, and Southern Identity* (Chapel Hill, N.C.: The Uni-versity of North Carolina Press, 2000).

95. "Death By Lynching," *New York Times*, March 16, 2000, A-30. Also see Roberta Smith, "An Ugly Legacy Lives On, Its Glare Unsoftened by Age," *New York Times*, January 13, 2000, B-l, 8; Brent Staples, "The Perils of Growing Com-fortable With Evil," *New York Times*, April 9, 2000, 16-D; Clarence Page, " 'Without Sanctuary': Lynchings Were a Part of U. S, History," *St. Louis Post-Dispatch*, March 19, 2000, B-7; Keith A. Owens, "The Truth Shall Make Us Ill," *Metro-times* (Detroit, Mich.), August 9, 2000, 9.

96. James Allen, Hilton Als, John Lewis, and Leon F. Litwack, *Without Sanctuary: Lynching Photography in America* (Santa Fe, N. M.: Twin Palms Publishers, 2000). This work and others helps to expand human understanding of a key topic in history. As we have seen with the holocaust in Euro-pean history, each generation must fight to access, analyze, and promote the study of the past. See: "Defending Holo-caust History" *Ideas: Columbia* (Mo.) *Magazine of Issues and Insight*, April 13, 1997, 2–3; Michael Sherman and Alex Grobman, *Who Says the Holocaust Never Happened and Why Do They Say It?* (Berkeley, Ca.: University of California Press, 2000); Tara Bahrampour, "History That's Painful to Re-call, Impossible Not to Feel," *New York Times*, May 3, 2000, A-25.

97. David G. Myers, *The American Paradox: Spiritual Hunger in an Age of Plenty* (New Haven, Conn.: Yale Univer-sity Press, 2000), 111–114.

98. Joel R. Williamson, "C. Vann Woodward and the Origins of a New Wisdom," in: John Herbert Roper, ed., *C. Vann Woodward: A Southern Historian and His Critics* (Athens, Ga.: The University of Georgia Press, 1997), 218. Such a heroic effort will also help Americans to focus better on such modern problems as the Scottsboro Boys case of 1931, or even of the internment of American citizens of Japanese ancestry during World War II. See Dinitia Smith, "Scotts-boro 70 Years Later, Still Notorious, Still Painful," *New York Times*, March 29, 2001, B-1, 7; Alice Yang Murray, ed., *What Did the Internment of Japanese Americans Mean?* (Boston, Mass.: Bedford/St. Martin's Press, 2000).

99. Randall Robinson, *The Debt: What America Owes to Blacks* (New York: Dutton/ Penguin Group, 2000), 201.

100. See Andrew Rigby, *Justice and Reconciliation: After the Violence* (Boulder, Colorado: Lynne Bienner Publishers, 2001), 1–136. Blacks and whites have called for reparations for blacks and their descendants who lost everything in the Tulsa Race Riot of 1921. See "Riot and Remembrance: The Tulsa Race War and Its Legacy," *Jackson Advocate*, March 28, 2002, 7-A.

101. See Tom Lutz, *Crying: The Natural and Cultural His-tory of Tears* (New York: W. W. Norton & Co., 1999); D. J. Enright, ed., *The Oxford Book of Death* (New York: Oxford University Press, 1987), 43–82, 101–122, 123–146, 313–332.

102. See Bob Blauner, *Still the Big News: Racial Oppression in America* (Philadelphia, Pa,; Temple University Press, 2001), 24–38.

103. Richard Polenberg, *One Nation Divisible: Class, Race, and Ethnicity in the United States Since 1938* (New York: The Viking Press, 1980), 15–109.

Bibliography

Abbott, Dorothy. "Recovering Zora Neale Hurston's Work." *Frontiers* 12, No. 1 (1975): 175–181.

Adamson, Christopher R. "Punishment After Slavery: Southern State Penal Systems, 1865–1890." *Social Problems* 30, No. 5 (June 1983): 555–569.

Adero, Malaika, ed. *Up South: Stories, Studies, and Letters of This Century's Black Migrations.* New York: The New Press, 1993.

Adoff, Arnold, ed. *Celebrations: A New Anthology of Black American Poetry.* Chicago: Follett Publishing, 1977.

____. *The Poetry of Black America: Anthology of the 20th Century.* New York: Harper and Row, Publishers, 1973.

Aiken, Charley S. *The Cotton Plantation South, Since the Civil War.* Baltimore, Md.: The Johns Hopkins University Press, 1998.

Akin, Edward N. *An Illustrated History.* Northridge, Calif.: Windsor Publications, 1987.

Alexander, Amy. *Fifty Black Women Who Changed America.* Secaucus, N.J.: A Birch Lane Press Book, Carol Publishing Group, 1999.

Alexander, Florence O. "The Education of Negroes in Mississippi." *Journal of Negro Education* 16 (1947): 3–5, 380.

Alexander, Herbert B. "The New Black Professions," *Black and White* 2, No. 5 (June 1940) 15–1."

Alexander, Mike. "Farish Street: A Neighborhood Built by Giants." *American Visions* 3, No. 4 (August 1988) 32–3."

Alhamisi, Ahmed, and Harun Kofi Wangara, eds. *Black Arts: An Anthology of Black Creations.* Detroit: Black Arts Publications, 1969.

Altman, Susan, ed. *The Encyclopedia of African-American Heritage.* New York: Facts On File, 1997.

Ames, Jessie Daniel. *The Changing Character of Lynching: Review of Lynching 1931–1941.* Atlanta, Ga.: Commission on Interracial Cooperation, July 1942; reprint ed., New York: AMS Press, 1973.

____. *Democratic Processes at Work in the South: Report of Commission on Interracial Cooperation, Inc., 1939–1941.* Atlanta, Ga.: Commission on Interracial Cooperation, Inc., October, 1941.

Anderson, Cloud. *Black Labor, White Wealth: The Search for Power and Economic Justice.* Edgewood, Md.: Duncan and Duncan, Publishers, 1994.

Andrews, William L., Frances Smith Foster, and Trudier Harris, eds. *The Concise Oxford Companion to African American Literature.* New York: Oxford University Press, 2001.

Angoff, Charles, and H.L. Mencken. "The Worst American State: Part III." *The American Mercury* 24, No. 95 (November 1931): 355–371.

Appiah, Kwame Anthony, and Henry Louis Gates, Jr., eds. *Africana: The Encyclopedia of the African and African-American Experience.* New York: Basic Civitas Books, 1999.

Aptheker, Bettina, ed. *Lynching and Rape: An Exchange of Views by Jane Adams and Ida B. Wells.* New York: The American Institute for Marxist Studies, 1977.

____. *Woman's Legacy: Essays on Race, Sex, and Class in American History.* Amherst: The University of Massachusetts Press, 1982.

Aptheker, Herbert. *Afro-American History, The Modern Era.* New York: The Citadel Press, 1971.

____. *To Be Free: Pioneering Studies in Afro-American History.* New York: International Publishers, 1968.

____, ed. *The Correspondence of W. E. B. Du Bois, Volume III: Selections, 1944–1963.* Amherst: University of Massachusetts Press, 1978.

____. *A Documentary History of the Negro People in the United States, 1910–1932, Volume 3.* Secaucus, N.J.: The Citadel Press, 1977.

Archer, William. *Through Afro-America: An English Reading of the Race Problem.* Westport, Conn.: Negro Universities Press, 1970; originally published, London: Chapman and Hall, Ltd., 1910.

Athearn, Robert G. *In Search of Canaan: Black Migration to Kansas, 1879–80.* Lawrence: The Regents of Kansas, 1978.

Ayers, Edward L. *The Promise of the New South: Life After Reconstruction.* New York: Oxford University Press, 1992.

____. *Vengeance and Justice: Crime and Punishment in the 19th Century American South.* New York: Oxford University Press, 1984.

Bailey, Kenneth K. *Southern White Protestantism in the Twentieth Century*. New York: Harper and Row, Publishers, 1964

Bailey, Ronald. *Remembering Medgar Evers ... For a New Generation*. Oxford, Miss.: The Civil Rights Documentation Project, 1988.

Bailey, Thomas Pearce. *Race Orthodoxy in the South and Other Aspects of the Negro Question*. New York: The Neale Publishing Co., 1914; reprint ed.: New York: Negro Universities Press, 1969.

Baird, Keith E. "Poplarville II." *Freedomways* 2, No. 2 (Spring 1962): 172.

Baker, Houston, A., Jr. *Afro-American Poetics: Revisions of Harlem and the Black Aesthetic*. Madison: The University of Wisconsin Press, 1988.

Bakersville, Stephen W., and Ralph Willett, eds. *Nothing Else to Fear: New Perspectives on America in the Thirties*. Dover, N.H.: Manchester University Press, 1985.

Barane, Michael, Richard E. Cohen, and Charles E. Cook, Jr. *The Almanac of American Politics 2002*. Washington, D.C.: National Journal Group, 2001.

Barck, Oscar Theodore, Jr., and Nelson Manfred Blake. *Since 1900: A History of the United States in Our Times*. New York: Macmillan Publishing Co., 1974.

Barksdale, John. *Citizens of Color in Meridian, Mississippi*. Meridian, Miss.: By John Barksdale, 1962.

Barr, Alwyn. *Black Texans: A History of African-Americans in Texas, 1528–1995*. Norman: University of Oklahoma Press, 1996.

Barr, Andrew. *Drink: A Social History of America*. New York: Carroll and Graf Publishers, 1999.

Bartley, Numan V. *The Rise of Massive Resistance: Race and Politics in the South During the 1950s*. Baton Rouge: Louisiana State University Press, 1969.

Beasley, Maurine. "The Muckrackers and Lynching: A Case Study in Racism." *Journalism History* 9, Nos. 3–4 (Autumn-Winter 1982): 86–91.

Beck, E. M., and Stewart E. Tolnay. "The Killing Fields of the Deep South: The Market for Cotton and the Lynching of Blacks, 1882–1930." *American Sociological Review* 55 (August 1990): 526–239.

Bederman, Gail. "'Civilization,' The Decline of Middle-Class Manliness, and Ida B. Wells' Anti-Lynching Campaign (1892–94)." *Radical History* 52 (Winter 1992): 5–30.

_____. *Manliness and Civilization: A Cultural History of Gender and Race in the United States, 1880–1917*. Chicago: The University of Chicago Press, 1995.

Beito, David T. "Black Fraternal Hospitals in the Mississippi Delta, 1942–1967." *The Journal of Southern History* 65, No. 1 (February 1999):109–136.

Belcher, John C., and Morton B. King, Jr. *Mississippi's People*. University, Miss.: Bureau of Public Administration, 1950.

Belknap, Michael R. *Federal Law and Southern Order: Racial Violence and Constitutional Conflict in the Post-Brown South*. Athens: The University of Georgia Press, 1987.

Bennett, Lerone, Jr. *Before the Mayflower: A History of the Negro in America, 1619–1964*. Baltimore, Md.: Penguin Books, 1966.

Benowitz, June Melby, ed. *Encyclopedia of American Women and Religion*. Santa Barbara, Calif.: ABC-Clio, 1998.

Berry, Mary Frances. *Black Resistance, White Law: A History of Constitutional Racism in America*. New York: Allen Lane/The Penguin Press, 1994.

Biennial Report of the Board of Trustees, Superintendent and Other Officers of the Mississippi State Penitentiary, July 1, 1911, to July 1, 1913. Jackson, Miss.: Tucker Printing House, 1913.

Billington, Monroe Lee. *The American South: A Brief History*. New York: Charles Scribner's Sons, 1971.

Binder, Frederick M., and David M. Reamers, eds. *The Way We Lived: Essays and Documents in American Social History*. Volume II: 1865–Present. Lexington, Mass.: D. C. Heath and Co., 1996.

Black, Allida M., ed. *Courage in a Dangerous World: The Political Writings of Eleanor Roosevelt*. New York: Columbia University Press, 1999.

Black, Earl. *Southern Governors and Civil Rights: Racial Segregation as a Campaign Issue in the Second Reconstruction*. Cambridge, Mass.: Harvard University Press, 1976.

Black Women in America. New York: Macmillan Library Reference, 1999.

Blassingame, John. *The Slave Community: Plantation Life in the Antebellum South*. New York: Oxford University Press, 1979.

Blaustein, Albert P., and Robert L. Zangrando, eds. *Civil Rights and African-Americans: A Documentary History*. Evanston, Ill.: Northwestern University Press, 1991.

Bloom, Harold, ed. *Richard Wright*. New York: Chelsea House Publishers, 1987.

Boles, John B., and Evelyn Thomas Nolen, eds. *Interpreting Southern History: Historigraphical Essays in Honor of Sanford W. Higginbotham*. Baton Rouge: Louisiana State University Press, 1987.

Boris, Joseph J., ed. *Who's Who in Colored America, Volume I*. New York: Who's Who in Colored America Corp., Publishers, 1927.

Bowden, Betsy. *Performed Literature: Words and Music by Bob Dylan*. Lanham, Md.: University Press of America, 2001.

Bowden, Henry Warner. *Dictionary of American Religious Biography*. Westport, Conn.: Greenwood Press, 1993.

Boyd, Melba Joyce. *Discarded Legacy: Politics and Poetics in the Life of Frances E. W. Harper, 1825–1911*. Detroit: Wayne State University Press, 1994.

Brammer, Dana B. "Mississippi." *Encyclopedia Americana, Volume 19*. Danbury, Conn.: Grolier, 1981.

Brands, H. W. *T.R.: The Last Romantic*. New York: Basic Books, 1997.

Branham, Robert James, and Philip Toney, eds. *Lift Every Voice: African American Oratory, 1789–1900*. Tuscaloosa: The University of Alabama Press, 1998.

Brawley, Benjamin. *The Negro Genius*. New York: Dodd, Mead and Co., 1937.

Brewer, William M. "Poor Whites and Negroes in the South Since the Civil War." *The Journal of Negro History* 15, No 1 (January 1930): 26–37.

Bridges, Flora Wilson. *Resurrection Song: African-American Spirituality*. Maryknoll, New York: Orbis Books, 2001.

Brodsky, Alyn. *Grover Cleveland: A Study in Character*. New York: St. Martin's Press, 2000.

Brown, Luther. "Clarence M. Mitchell. Jr.: The 101st U.S. Senator." *Crisis* 105, No. 6 (December 1998): 10–13.

Brown, Mary Jane. *Eradicating This Evil: Women in the American Anti-Lynching Movement, 1892–1940*. New York: Garland Publishing, 2000.

Brown, Maxwell Richard. *Strain of Violence: Historical Studies of American Violence and Vigilantism*. New York: Oxford University Press, 1975.

Brundage, W. Fitzhugh, ed. *Under Sentence of Death: Lynching in the South*. Chapel Hill: The University of North Carolina Press, 1997.

Buckley, Gail. *American Patriots: The Story of Blacks in the Military: From the Revolution to Desert Storm*. New York: Random House, 2001.

Buenker, John, and Edward R. Kantowicz, eds. *Historical Dictionary of the Progressive Era, 1890–1920*. New York: Greenwood Press, 1988.

Bullock, Henry Allen. *A History of Negro Education in the South: From 1619 to the Present*. Cambridge, Mass.: Harvard University Press, 1967.

Bundles, A'Lelia. *On Her Own Ground: The Life and Times of Madam C. J. Walker*. New York: Washington Square Press/Pocket Books, 2001.

Burner, Eric. *And Gently He Shall Lead Them: Robert Parris Moses and Civil Rights in Mississippi*. New York: New York University Press, 1994.

Bynum, Victoria. "'White Negroes' in Segregated Mississippi: Miscegenation, Racial Identity, and the Law." *The Journal of Southern History* 64, No. 2 (May 1998): 247–276.

Campbell, Clarice T., and Oscar Allan Rogers, Jr. *Mississippi: The View from Tougaloo*. Jackson: University Press of Mississippi, 1979.

Capeci, Dominic J., Jr. *The Lynching of Cleo Wright*. Lexington: The University Press of Kentucky, 1998.

Carawan, Guy, and Candi Carawan, eds. *Sing for Freedom: The Story of the Civil Rights Movement through Its Songs*. Bethlehem, Pa.: A Sing Out Publication, 1990.

Carson, Clayborne. *In Struggle: SNCC and the Black Awakening of the 1960s*. Cambridge, Mass.: Harvard University Press, 1981.

Case, Carroll. *The Slaughter: An American Atrocity*. Asheville, N.C.: FBC, Inc., 1998.

Cashman, Sean Dennis. *African-Americans and the Quest for Civil Rights, 1900–1990*. New York: New York University Press, 1991.

_____. *America in the Twenties and Thirties: The Olympian Age of Franklin Delano Roosevelt*. New York: New York University Press, 1989.

Cha-Jua, Sundiata Keita. "'Join Hands and Hearts with Law and Order': The 1893 Lynching of Samuel J. Bush and the Response of Decatur's African American Community." *Illinois Historical Journal* 83 (Autumn, 1990): 187–200.

Chalmers, David M. *Hooded Americanism: The History of the Ku Klux Klan*. Chicago: Quadrangle Books, 1965.

Chambers, Bradford, ed. *Chronicles of Negro Protest: A Background Book Documenting the History of Black Power*. New York: Parents' Magazine Press, 1968.

Christina, Bennett, and Sari J. Bennett. *Black Saga: The African American Experience*. Boston: Houghton Mifflin Co., 1995.

The Civil Rights Movement, Volume 2. Pasadena, Calif.: Salem Press, 2000.

"The Civilization of Mississippi." *The Crisis* 7, No. 6 (April 1914): 285–286.

Clarke, Donald. *Wishing on the Moon: The Life and Times of Billie Holiday*. New York: Viking, 1994.

Clegg, Claude Andrew, III. *An Original Man: The Life and Times of Elijah Muhammad*. New York: St. Martin's Press, 1997.

Clements, Kendrick A. *The Presidency of Woodrow Wilson*. Lawrence: The University Press of Kansas, 1992.

Clowes, W. Laird. *Black America: A Study of the Ex-Slave and His Late Master*. London: Cassell and Co., Limited, 1891; reprint ed.: Westport, Conn.: Negro Universities Press, 1970.

Cohen, William. *At Freedom's Edge: Black Mobility and the Southern White Quest for Racial Control, 1861–1915*. Baton Rouge: Louisiana State University Press, 1991.

Cohn, David L. *God Shakes Creation*. New York: Harper and Brothers, Publishers, 1935.

Coletta, Paoloe. *The Presidency of William Howard Taft*. Lawrence: The University Press of Kansas, 1973.

Collins, Catherine Fisher. *The Imprisonment of African American Women*. Jefferson, N.C.: McFarland, 1997.

Conyers, James L., ed. *Africana Studies: A Disciplinary Quest for Both Theory and Method*. Jefferson, N.C.: McFarland, 1997.

Cook, Blanche Wiesen. *Eleanor Roosevelt, Volume Two: 1933–1938*. New York: Viking, 1999.

Cook, Robert. *Sweet Land of Liberty: The African-American Struggle for Civil Rights in the Twentieth Century*. New York: Longman, 1998.

Cooper, Arnold. "The Tuskegee Machine in Action: Booker T. Washington's Influence on Utica Institute, 1903–1915." *The Journal of Mississippi History* 58, No. 4 (November 1986): 283–295.

Cooper, Wayne F. *Claude McKay: Rebel Sojourner in the Harlem Renaissance, A Biography*. New York: Schocken Books, 1987.

Cooper, William, and Thomas E. Terrill. *The American South: A History*. New York: Alfred A. Knopf, 1990.

_____. *The American South: A History, Volume II*. New York: The McGraw-Hill Co., 1996.

Cott, Nancy F., ed. *No Small Courage: A History of Women in the United States*. New York: Oxford University Press, 2000.

Coulter, E. Merton. *The South During Reconstruction, 1865–1877*. Baton Rouge: Louisiana State University Press, 1941.

Courtner, Richard C. *A "Scottsboro" Case in Mississippi: The Supreme Court and Brown v. Mississippi*. Jackson: University Press of Mississippi, 1986.

Couto, Richard A. *Ain't Gonna Let Nobody Turn Me Round: The Pursuit of Racial Justice in the Rural South*. Philadelphia, Pa.: Temple University Press, 1991.

Crime of Lynching, Hearings Before a Subcommittee of the Committee on the Judiciary, U.S. Senate, Second Session on S42, SI352, and SI465. Washington, D.C.: U. S. Government Printing Office, 1948.

Cronon, E. David., ed. *The Political Thought of Woodrow*

Wilson. Indianapolis, Ind.: The Bobbs-Merrill Co., 1965.

Cruden, Robert. *The Negro in Reconstruction*. Englewood Cliffs, N.J.: Prentice Hall, 1969.

Culberson, William C. *Vigilantism: Political History of Private Power in America*. New York: Greenwood Press, 1990.

Currie, James T. "From Slavery to Freedom in Mississippi's Legal System." *The Journal of Negro History* 65, No. 2 (Spring 1980): 112–125.

Curtis, James C., and Lewis L. Gould, eds. *The Black Experience in America: Selected Essays*. Austin: University of Texas Press, 1970.

Dadley, Julius Wayne. "A History of the Association of Southern Women for the Prevention of Lynching. 1930–1912" (Cincinnati, Ohio: Ph.D. diss., University of Cincinnati, 1979).

Daniel, Pete. *Dee'n as It Come: The 1927 Mississippi River Flood*. New York: Oxford University Press, 1977.

_____. *The Shadow of Slavery: Peonage in the South, 1901–1969*. New York: Oxford University Press, 1973.

_____. *Standing at the Crossroads: Southern Life Since 1900*. New York: Hill and Wang, 1986.

Dansby, B. Baldwin. *A Brief History of Jackson College: A Typical Story of the Survival of Education Among Negroes in the South*. Jackson, Miss.: Jackson College, 1953.

Davis, Allen F., and Harold D. Woodman, eds. *Conflict and Consensus in Modern American History*. Lexington, Mass.: D.C. Heath and Co., 1980.

Davis, Angela Y. *Blues Legacies and Black Feminism: Gertrude "Ma" Rainey, Bessie Smith, and Billie Holiday*. New York: Pantheon Books, 1998.

Davis, Kenneth S. *FDR: The War President, 1940–1943*. New York: Random House, 2000.

Davis, Lenwood G., and Janet L. Sims-Wood. *The Ku Klux Klan: A Bibliography*. Westport, Conn.: Greenwood Press, 1984.

DeSantis, Christopher C., ed. *The Collected Works of Langston Hughes. Volume 10: Fight for Freedom and Other Writings on Civil Rights*. Columbia: University of Missouri Press, 2001.

Dewart, Janet, ed. *The State of Black America*. New York: The National Urban League, 1989.

Dickerson, James. *Dixie's Dirty Secret: The True Story of How the Government, the Media, and the Mob Conspired to Combat Integration and the Vietnam Antiwar Movement*. Armonk, New York: M. E. Sharpe, 1998.

Dictionary of American History. New York: Charles Scribner's Sons, 1976.

Dittmer, John. *Local People: The Struggle for Civil Rights in Mississippi*. Urbana: University of Illinois Press, 1994.

Doenecke, Justus D. *The Presidencies of James A. Garfield and Chester A. Arthur*. Lawrence: The University Press of Kansas, 1981.

D'Orso, Michael. *Like Judgment Day: The Ruin and Redemption of a Town Called Rosewood*. New York: Boulevard Books/The Berkley Publishing Group, 1996.

Douglass, Frederick. "Lynch Law in the South." *The North American Review* 155, No. 428 (1892): 17–24.

Downey, Dennis B., and Raymond M. Hyser. *No Crooked Death: Coatesville, Pennsylvania, and the Lynching of Zachariah Walker*. Urbana: University of Illinois Press, 1991.

Draper, Alan. *Conflict of Interests: Organized Labor and the Civil Rights Movement in The South, 1954–1968*. Ithaca, New York: ILR Press, 1994.

Dray, Philip. *At the Hands of Persons Unknown: The Lynching of Black America*. New York: Random House, 2002.

Drimmer, Melvin, ed. *Black History: A Reappraisal*. Garden City, New York: Doubleday and Co., 1969.

Driver, Hasia. *In the Almost Promised Land: American Jews and Blacks, 1915–1935*. Westport, Conn.: Greenwood Press, 1977.

Du Bois, W. E. B. *Black Reconstruction in America*. New York: Russell and Russell, 1935.

_____. *Dusk of Dawn: An Essay Toward an Autobiography of a Race Concept*. New York: Harcourt, Brace and World, 1940, 1968.

_____. *The Negro Church*. Atlanta, Ga.: Atlanta University Press, 1903; reprint ed., New York: Octagon Books, 1968.

_____. *The Souls of Black Folk*. Greenwich, Conn.: Fawcett Publications, 1968.

_____, ed. *An Appeal to the World*. New York: NAACP, 1947.

Dulaney, W. Marvi. *Black Police in America*. Bloomington: Indiana University Press, 1996.

Dunbar, Paul L. *The Complete Poems of Paul L. Dunbar*. New York: Dodd, Mead and Co., 1913.

Dunham, Melerson Guy. *Centennial History of Alcorn A. & M. College*. Hattiesburg: University and College Press of Mississippi, 1971.

Dunn, Martin. *The Black Press (1827–1890): The Quest for National Identity*. New York: G. P. Putnam's Sons, 1971.

Duster, Alfreda M., ed. *The Autobiography of Ida B. Wells*. Chicago: University of Chicago Press, 1970.

Dyer, Thomas G. *Theodore Roosevelt and the Idea of Race*. Baton Rouge: Louisiana State University Press, 1980.

Eagles, Charles, ed. *Is There a Southern Political Tradition?* Jackson: University Press of Mississippi, 1996.

Eaton, William Edward. *The American Federation of Teachers, 1916–1961: A History of the Movement*. Carbondale, Ill.: Southern Illinois University Press, 1975.

Egerton, John. *Speak Now Against the Day: The Generation Before the Civil Rights Movement in the South*. Chapel Hill: The University of North Carolina Press, 1994.

Eleazer, R. B. *Understanding Our Neighbors: An Educational Approach to America's Major Race Problems*. Atlanta, Ga.: Conference on Education and Race Relations, 1940.

Elliff, John T. *The United States Department of Justice and Individual Rights, 1937–1962*. New York: Garland Publishing, 1987.

Ellis, Mark. "America's Black Press, 1914–18." *The Crisis* (September 1991): 20–27.

Ellison, Ralph. *Shadow and Act*. New York: Random House, 1964.

Emanuel, James A., and Theodore L. Gross, eds. *Dark Symphony: Negro Literature in America*. New York: The Free Press, 1968.

Emeka, Mauris Porter. *Black Banks: Past and Present.* Kansas City, Mo.: Mauris L. P. Emeka, 1971.

Encyclopedia International. New York: Grolier, 1971.

Erenrich, Susie, ed. *Freedom Is a Constant Struggle: An Anthology of the Mississippi Civil Rights Movement.* Montgomery, Ala.: Black Belt Press, 1999.

Escort, Paul D., and David R. Goldfields, eds. *Major Problems in the History of the American South, Volume II: The New South.* Lexington, Mass.: D. C. Heath and Co., 1990.

Evans, Harold, with Gail Buckland and Kevin Baker. *The American Century.* New York: Alfred A. Knopf, 2000.

Evans, Maurice S. *Black and White in the Southern States: A Study of the Race Problem in the United States, from a South African Point of View.* London: Hongmans, Green and Co., 1915.

Evanzz, Karl. *The Messenger: The Rise and Fall of Elijah Muhammad.* New York: Pantheon Books, 1999.

Evers, Charles, and Andrew Szanton. *Have No Fear: The Charles Evers Story: A Black Man's Fight for Respect in America.* New York: John Wiley and Sons, 1997.

Ezell, John. *The South Since 1865.* Norman: University of Oklahoma Press, 1982.

Fairclough, Adam. *Better Day Coming: Blacks and Equality, 1890–2000.* New York: Viking, 2001.

Feagin, Joe R. *Racial and Ethnic Relations.* Englewood Cliffs, N.J.: Prentice Hall, 1989.

_____. *Racist America: Roots, Current Realities, and Future Reparations.* New York: Routledge, 2001.

Findlay, James F. *Church People in the Struggle: The National Council of Churches and the Black Freedom Movement, 1950–1970.* New York: Oxford University Press, 1993.

Fink, Leon, ed. *Major Problems in the Gilded Age and the Progressive Era: Documents and Essays.* Lexington, Mass.: D.C. Heath and Co., 1993.

Finkle, Lee. *Forum for Protest: The Black Press During World War II.* Cranbury, N.J.: Associated University Presses, 1975.

Fite, Gilbert C. *Cotton Fields No More: Southern Agriculture, 1865–1980.* Lexington: The University Press of Kentucky, 1984.

Fitzgerald, Michael W. "'We Have Found a Moses': Theodore Bilbo, Black Nationalism, and the Greater Liberia Bill of 1939." *The Journal of Southern History* 63, No. 2 (May 1997): 293–320.

Fleener, Nickieann. "'Breaking Down Buyer Resistance': Marketing the 1935 Pittsburgh Courier to Mississippi Blacks." *Journalism History* 13, Nos. 3–4 (Autumn-Winter 1986): 78–85.

Flexner, Eleanor. *Century of Struggle: The Woman's Rights Movement in the United States.* Cambridge, Mass.: The Belknap Press of Harvard University Press, 1975.

Fligstein, Neil. *Going North: Migration of Blacks and Whites From the South, 1900–1950.* New York: Academic Press, 1981.

Foner, Eric. *Freedom's Lawmakers: A Directory of Black Office Holders During Reconstruction.* New York: Oxford University Press, 1993.

_____. *Reconstruction: America's Unfinished Revolution, 1863–1887.* New York: Harper and Row, Publishers, 1988.

_____. *The Story of American Freedom.* New York: W. W. Norton & Co., 1998.

Foner, Philip S. *American Socialism and Black America: From the Age of Jackson to World War II.* Westport, Conn.: Greenwood Press, 1977.

Fossett, Judith Jackson, and Jeffrey A. Tucker, eds. *Race Consciousness: African American Studies for the New Century.* New York: New York University Press, 1997.

Foster, William Z. *The Negro People in American History.* New York: International Publishers, 1970.

Frankel, Noralee. *Freedom's Women: Black Women and Families in Civil War Era Mississippi.* Bloomington: Indiana University Press, 1999.

Franklin, Donna L. *Ensuring Inequality: The Structural Transformation of the African-American Family.* New York: Oxford University Press, 1997.

Franklin, Jimmie Lewis. *Journey Toward Hope: A History of Blacks in Oklahoma.* Norman: University of Oklahoma Press, 1982.

Franklin, John Hope, and Alfred A. Moss, Jr. *From Slavery to Freedom: A History of African Americans.* New York: McGraw-Hill, 2000.

Franklin, V. P., Nancy L. Grant, Harold M. Kletnick, and Genna Rae McNeil, eds. *African Americans and Jews in the Twentieth Century: Studies in Convergence and Conflict.* Columbia: University of Missouri Press, 1998.

Fraser, Walter J., and Winfred B. Moore, Jr., eds. *The Southern Enigma: Essays on Race, Class and Folk Culture.* Westport, Conn.: Greenwood Press, 1983.

Frederickson, Kair. *The Dixiecrat Revolt and the End of the Solid South, 1932–1968.* Chapel Hill: The University of North Carolina Press, 2001.

Fredrickson, George M. *The Arrogance of Race: Historical Perspectives on Slavery, Racism, and Social Inequality.* Middletown, Conn.: Wesleyan University Press, 1988.

_____. *The Black Image in the White Mind: The Debate on Afro-American Character and Destiny, 1817–1914.* Middletown, Conn.: Wesleyan University Press, 1971.

Freedman, Estelle B. *No Turning Back: The History of Feminism and the Future of Women.* New York: Ballantine Books, 2002.

Frey, Robert Seitz, and Nancy Thompson-Frey. *The Silent and the Damned: The Murder of Mary Phagan and the Lynching of Leo Frank.* Lanham, Md.: Madison Books, 1988.

Friedland, Michael B. *Lift Up Your Voice Like a Trumpet: White Clergy and the Civil Rights and Antiwar Movements, 1954–1973.* Chapel Hill: The University of North Carolina Press, 1998.

Friedman, Lawrence. *A History of American Law.* New York: A Touchstone Book/Simon and Schuster, 1985.

Gaines, Kevin K. *Uplifting the Race: Black Leadership, Politics, and Culture in the Twentieth Century.* Chapel Hill: The University of North Carolina Press, 1996.

Gallup, George H. *The Gallup Poll: Public Opinion, 1935–1971, Volume 3, 1959–1971.* New York: Random House, 1970.

Garner, James W. *Reconstruction in Mississippi.* New York: The Macmillan Co., 1901; reprint ed., Gloucester, Mass.: Peter Smith, 1964.

Garza, Hedda. *African Americans and Jewish Americans: A History of Struggle*. New York: Franklin Watts/Grolier Publishing, 1995.

Gates, Henry Louis, Jr., and K. A. Appiah, eds. *Langston Hughes: Critical Perspectives, Past and Present*. New York: Amistad, 1993.

_____. *Toni Morrison: Critical Perspectives, Past and Present*. New York: Amistad, 1993.

Gates, Henry Louis, Jr., and Cornell West. *The African-American Century: How Black Americans Have Shaped Our Country*. New York: The Free Press, 2000.

Gatewood, Willard B. *Aristocrats of Color: The Black Elite, 1880–1920*. Bloomington: Indiana University Press, 1990.

Gaustad, Edwin Scott. *Historical Atlas of Religion in America*. New York: Harper and Row, Publishers, 1962.

George, John, and Laird Wilcox. *Nazis, Communists, Klansmen, and Others on the Fringe*. Buffalo, New York: Prometheus Books, 1992.

Gerstle, Gary. *American Crucible: Race and Nation in the Twentieth Century*. Princeton, N.J.: Princeton University Press, 2001.

Gibson, J. W., and W. H. Crogman. *Progress of a Race*. Miami, Fla.: Mnemosyne Publisher, 1902.

Giddings, Paula. *When and Where I Enter: The Impact of Black Women on Race and Sex in America*. New York: William Morrow and Co., 1984.

Gilbert, Martin. *History of the Twentieth Century*. New York: HarperCollins Publishers, 2001.

Gilje, Paul W. *Rioting in America*. Bloomington: Indiana University Press, 1996.

Gill, Laverne McCain. *African American Women in Congress: Forming and Transforming History*. New Brunswick, N.J.: Rutgers University Press, 1997.

Ginzburg, Ralph. *100 Years of Lynchings*. Baltimore, Md.: Black Classic Press, 1988.

Goggin, Jacqueline. *Carter G. Woodson: A Life in Black History*. Baton Rouge: Louisiana State University Press, 1993.

Goings, Kenneth W. *"The NAACP Comes of Age": The Defeat of Judge John J. Parker*. Bloomington: Indiana University Press, 1990.

Goldfield, David R. *Black, White, and Southern: Race Relations and Southern Culture, 1940 to the Present*. Baton Rouge: Louisiana State University Press, 1990.

Gordon, Robert. *Can't Be Satisfied: The Life and Times of Muddy Waters*. Boston: Little, Brown and Co., 2002.

Gossett, Thomas F. *Race: The History of an Idea in America*. Dallas, Texas: Southern Methodist University Press, 1963.

Gottesman, Ronald, and Richard Maxwell Brown, eds. *Violence in America: An Encyclopedia*. New York: Charles Scribner's Sons, 1999.

Gound, Lewis L. *The Presidency of William McKinley*. Lawrence: The Regents Press of Kansas, 1980.

Govenar, Alan, ed. *African American Frontiers: Slave Narratives and Oral Histories*. Santa Barbara, Calif.: ABC-Clio, 2000.

Grant, Donald L. *The Anti-Lynching Movement: 1883–1937*. San Francisco, Calif.: R and E Research Associates, 1975.

Grantham, Dewey W. *The South in Modern America: A Region at Odds*. New York: Harper Collins Publishers, 1994.

_____. *Southern Progressivism: The Reconciliation of Progress and Tradition*. Knoxville: The University of Tennessee Press, 1983.

Green, Ben. *Before His Time: The Untold Story of Harry T. Moore, America's First Civil Rights Martyr*. New York: The Free Press, 1999.

Green, Constance McLaughlin. *The Secret City: A History of Race Relations in the Nation's Capital*. Princeton, N.J.: Princeton University Press, 1967.

Green, Robert P., Jr., Laura L. Becker, and Robert E. Coviello. *The American Tradition: A History of the United States*. Columbia, Ohio: Charles E. Merrill Publishing Co., 1986.

Greenbaum, Fred. "The Antilynching Bill of 1935: The Irony of 'Equal Justice—Under Law.'" *Journal of Human Relations* 5, No. 3 (1967): 72–85.

Greenlee, Sam. *Ammunition: Poetry and Other Raps*. London: Bogle-L'Ouverture Publications, Ltd., 1975.

Gregory, Ross. *Modern America, 1914 to 1945*. New York: Facts On File, 1995.

Griffin, Larry J. "Narrative, Event-Structure Analysis and Causal Interpretation in Historical Sociology." *American Journal of Sociology* 98, No. 5 (March 1993): 1094–1133.

_____, and Don H. Doyle, eds. *The South as an American Problem*. Athens: The University of Georgia Press, 1995.

Griffin, Paul R. *Seeds of Racism in the Soul of America*. Cleveland, Ohio: The Pilgrim Press, 1999.

Grimshaw, Allen D. "Lawlessness and Violence in America and Their Special Manifestations in Changing Negro-White Relationships." *The Journal of Negro History* 44, No. 1 (January 1959): 52–72.

_____. *Racial Violence in the United States*. Chicago: Aldine Publishing Co., 1969.

Grossman, James R. *Land of Hope: Chicago, Black Southerners and the Great Migration*. Chicago: The University of Chicago Press, 1989.

Gustad, Edwin N. Scott. *A Religious History of America*. New York: Harper and Row, Publishers, 1990.

Guzman, Jessie Parkhurt, ed. *Negro Year Book, 1941–46*. Tuskegee, Ala.: The Tuskegee Institute Department of Records and Research, 1947.

_____. *1952 Negro Year Book: A Review of Events Affecting Negro Life*. New York: Wm. H. Wise and Co., 1952.

Halasa, Malu. *Mary McLeod Bethune: Educator*. New York: Chelsea House Publishers, 1989.

Hale, Grace Elizabeth. *Making Whiteness: The Culture of Segregation in the South, 1890–1940*. New York: Pantheon Books, 1998.

Hall, Jacquelyn Dowd. *Revolt Against Chivalry: Jessie Daniel Ames and the Women's Campaign Against Lynching*. New York: Columbia University Press, 1979.

Hall, Kermit L., ed. *The Oxford Companion to American Law*. New York: Oxford University Press, 2002.

Halpern, Florence. *Survival: Black/White*. New York: Pergamon Press, 1973.

Harlan, Louis R. *Booker T. Washington: The Making of a*

Black Leader, 1856-1901. New York: Oxford University Press, 1972.

Harlan, Louis, S. B. Kaufman, and R. W. Smock, eds. *The Booker T. Washington Papers, 1889-1895.* Urbana: University of Illinois Press, 1989.

Harris, J. William. "Etiquette, Lynching, and Racial Boundaries in Southern History: A Mississippi Example." *The American Historical Review* 100, No. 2 (April 1995): 387–410.

Harris, Leonard, ed. *The Philosophy of Alain Locke, Harlem Renaissance and Beyond.* Philadelphia: Temple University Press, 1989.

Harris, Thaider, and Thadious M. Davis, eds. *Afro-American Writers from the Harlem Renaissance to 1940, Volume 51.* Detroit: Gale Research Co., 1987.

Harris, William C. *The Day of the Carpetbagger: Republican Reconstruction in Mississippi.* Baton Rouge: Louisiana State University Press, 1979.

_____. "James Lynch: Black Leader in Southern Reconstruction." *The Historian* 34, No. 1 (November 1971): 40–61.

Harrison, Alferdteen. *A History of the Most Worshipful Stringer Grand Lodge: Our Heritage Is Our Challenge.* Jackson, Miss.: Most Worshipful Stringer Grand Lodge, 1977.

_____. ed. *Black Exodus: The Great Migration from the American South.* Jackson: University Press of Mississippi, 1991.

Harrison, Ira E., and Faye Harrison, eds. *African American Pioneers in Anthropology.* Urbana: University of Illinois Press, 1999.

Hatch, James V., and Ted Shine, eds. *Black Theatre USA: Plays by African Americans, 1847 to Today.* New York: The Free Press, 1996.

Hauke, Kathleen A. *Ted Poston: Pioneer American Journalist.* Athens: University of Georgia Press, 1998.

Hawes, Joseph M. *The Children's Rights Movement: A History of Advocacy and Protection.* Boston: Twayne Publishers, 1991.

Haws, Robert, ed. *The Age of Segregation: Race Relations in the South, 1890-1945.* Jackson: University Press of Mississippi, 1978.

Hays, Samuel A. *African American Theatre: A Historical and Critical Analysis.* New York: Cambridge University Press, 1994.

Hearings Before the United States Commission on Civil Rights, Volume II: Administration of Justice. Jackson, Miss: Hearings Held in Jackson, Miss., February 16–20, 1965.

Helm, Mary. *The Upward Path: The Evolution of a Race.* New York: Eaton and Mains, 1909.

Hemmingway, Theodore. "Booker T. Washington in Mississippi: October, 1908." *The Journal of Mississippi History* 96, No. 1 (February 1984): 29–42.

Hermann, Janet Sharp. *The Pursuit of a Dream.* New York: Oxford University Press, 1981.

Higginbotham, Evelyn Brooks. *Righteous Discontent: The Women's Movement in the Black Baptist Church, 1880-1920.* Cambridge, Mass.: Harvard University Press, 1993.

Hill, Lavrne McCain. *African American Women in Congress: Forming and Transforming History.* New Brunswick, N.J.: Rutgers University Press, 1997.

Hill, Robert A., ed. *George S. Schuyler, Ethiopian Stories.* Boston: Northeastern University Press, 1994.

Hine, Darlene Clark, and Kathleen Thompson. *A Shining Thread of Hope: The History of Black Women in America.* New York: Broadway Books, 1998.

Hirsch, James S. *Riot and Remembrance: The Tulsa Race War and Its Legacy.* Boston: Houghton Mifflin, 2002.

Hobson, Fred. *But Now I See: The White Southern Racial Conversion Narrative.* Baton Rouge: Louisiana State University Press, 1999.

Hodes, Martha. *White Women, Black Men: Illicit Sex in the Nineteenth-Century South.* New Haven, Conn.: Yale University Press, 1997.

Hofstadter, Richard, and Beatrice K. Hofstadter, eds. *Great Issues in American History: From Reconstruction to the Present Day, 1864-1981.* New York: Vintage Books/Random House, 1982.

Holland, Endesha Ida Mae. *From the Mississippi Delta: A Memoir.* New York: Simon and Schuster, 1997.

Hollon, W. Eugene. *Frontier Violence: Another Look.* New York: Oxford University Press, 1974.

Holloway, Karla F.C. *Passed On: African American Mourning Stories: A Memorial.* Durham, N.C.: Duke University Press, 2002.

Holmes, William F. "The Leflore County Massacre and the Demise of the Colored Farmers' Alliance." *Phylon* 4, No. 3 (1973): 267–274.

_____. *The White Chief: James Kimble Vardaman.* Baton Rouge: Louisiana State University Press, 1970.

_____. "Whitecapping: Agrarian Violence in Mississippi, 1902–1906." *The Journal of Southern History* 35, No. 2 (May 1969): 267–274.

Holtclaw, Robert Fulton. *Black Magnolias: A Brief History of the Afro-Mississippian, 1865-1980.* Shaker Heights, Ohio: The Keeble Press, 1984.

_____. "The Negro in the Reconstruction of Mississippi." (M.A. thesis, History Department, Howard University, June, 1936).

"How Negroes Rank Their Leaders." *Newsweek* (August 22, 1966): 22, 34.

Hudson, Winthrop S. *Religion in America: An Historical Account of the Development of American Religious Life.* New York: Charles Scribner's Sons, 1973.

Hudson-Weems, Clenora. *Emmett Till: The Sacrificial Lamb of the Civil Rights Movement.* Troy, Mich.: Bedford Publishers, 1994.

_____. "Resurrecting Emmett Till: The Catalyst of the Modern Civil Rights Movement." *Journal of Black Studies* 29, No. 2 (November 1998): 179–188.

Hughes, Langston. *The Collected Works of Langston Hughes.* Ed., Arnold Rampersad *Volume l: The Poems, 1921-1940.* Columbia, Mo.: University of Missouri Press, 2001.

_____. *The Collected Works of Langston Hughes.* Ed., Christopher C. Desantis. *Volume 10: Fight for Freedom and Other Writings on Civil Rights.* Columbia, Mo.: University of Missouri Press, 2001.

_____, ed. *New Negro Poets: USA.* Bloomington, Ind.: Indiana University Press, 1964.

_____. *The Panther and the Lash: Poems of Our Times.* New York: Alfred A. Knopf, 1969.

_____, and Arna Bontemps, eds. *The Poetry of the Negro,*

1746–1970: An Anthology. Garden City, N.Y.: Doubleday and Co., 1970.

Hutchinson, Earl Ofari. *The Assassination of the Black Male Image.* New York: Simon and Schuster, 1996.

Ingham, John N., and Lynne B. Feldman. *African-American Business Leaders: A Biographical Dictionary.* Westport, Conn.: Greenwood Press, 1994.

Jackson, Blyden. *The Waiting Years: Essays on American Negro Literature.* Baton Rouge: Louisiana State University Press, 1976.

Jackson, Kenneth T. *The Ku Klux Klan in the City, 1915–1930.* New York: Oxford University Press, 1967.

Jacobs, James B., and Kimberly Potter. *Hate Crimes: Criminal Law and Identity Politics.* New York: Oxford University Press, 1998.

Jacoway, Elizabeth, and David R. Colburn, eds. *Southern Businessmen and Desegregation.* Baton Rouge: Louisiana State University Press, 1982.

James, Arthur, Jimmie James, Jr., and Robert E. James. *The Mississippi Black Bankers and Their Institutions.* Jackson, Miss.: By the Authors, 1996.

James, Joy. *Transcending the Talented Tenth: Black Leaders and American Intellectuals.* New York: Routledge, 1997.

Jaynes, Herald David, and Robin M. Williams, Jr., eds. *A Common Destiny: Blacks and American Society.* Washington, D.C.: National Academy Press, 1989.

Jeffreys, Diarmuid. *The Bureau: Inside the Modern FBI.* Boston: Houghton Mifflin Co., 1995.

Jenkins, Robert L. "The Development of Black Higher Education in Mississippi (1865–1920)" *The Journal of Mississippi History* 45, No. 4 (November 1983): 276–280.

Jerome, Fred. *The Einstein File: J. Edgar Hoover's Secret War Against the World's Most Famous Scientist.* New York: St. Martin's Press, 2002.

Johannsen, Robert W., ed. *Reconstruction, 1865–1877.* New York: The Free Press, 1970. Johnson, Charles S. *The Negro College Graduate.* Chapel Hill: The University of North Carolina Press, 1938; reprint ed., College Park, Md.: McGrath Publishing Co., 1969.

Johnson, Edward A. *A School History of the Negro Race in America from 1619 to 1890.* Philadelphia: Sherman and Co., 1893.

Johnson, Haynes. *The Best of Times: America in the Clinton Years.* New York: A James H. Silverman Book, Harcourt, 2001.

Johnson, Jacqueline. *Stokely Carmichael: The Story of Black Power.* Englewood Cliffs, N.J.: Silver Burdett Press, 1990.

Johnson, Paul. *A History of the American People.* New York: HarperCollins Publishers, 1999.

Jones, Beverly W. "Mary Church Terrell and the National Association of Colored Women, 1896 to 1901." *The Journal of Negro History* 67, No. 1 (Spring 1982): 20–33.

Jones, LeRoi [Amiri Baraka]. *Blues People: Negro Music in White America.* New York: William Morrow and Co., 1963.

Jones, Marcus E. "Black Migration in the United States, with Emphasis on Selected Central Cities." (Ph.D. thesis, Department of Geography, Southern Illinois University at Carbondale, 1978).

Jones, Thomas Jesse. *Negro Education: A Study of the Private and Higher Schools for Colored People in the United States, Volume I.* Washington, D.C.: Government Printing Office, 1917.

Jordan, Vernon, Jr., with Annette Gordon-Reed. *Vernon Can Read: A Memoir.* New York: Public Affairs/ Perseus Book Group, 2001.

Jordan, William G. *Black Newspapers and America's War for Democracy, 1914–1920.* Chapel Hill: The University of North Carolina Press, 2001.

Juguo, Zhang. *W. E. B. Du Bois: The Quest for the Abolition of the Color Line.* New York: Routledge, 2001.

Katz, William Oren, ed. *Negro Population in the United States, 1790–1915.* New York: Arno Press and the New York Times, 1968.

Keller, Rosemary Skinner, and Rosemary Redford Ruether, eds. *In Our Own Voices: Four Centuries of American Women's Religious Writing.* San Francisco, Calif.: Harper San Francisco, 1995.

Kellogg, Charles Flint. *NAACP, A History of the NAACP, Volume I: 1909–1920.* Baltimore, Md.: The Johns Hopkins University Press, 1967.

Kelly, Robert J. and Jess Maghan, eds. *Hate Crime: The Global Politics of Polarization.* Carbondale, Ill.: Southern Illinois University Press, 1998.

Kennedy, David M. *Freedom from Fear: The American People in Depression and War, 1929–1945.* New York: Oxford University Press, 1999.

Kennedy, Randall. *Nigger: The Strange Career of a Troublesome Word.* New York: Pantheon Books, 2002.

_____, ed. *From Slavery to Sharecropping: White and Black Labor in the Rural South, 1865–1900.* New York: Garland Publishing, 1994.

Kennedy, Stetson. *After Appomattox: How the South Won the War.* Gainesville: University of Florida Press, 1995.

Kesting, Robert W. "Forgotten Victims: Blacks in the Holocaust." *The Journal of Negro History* 77, No. 1 (Winter 1992): 30–36.

Key, V. O., Jr., and Alexander Heard. *Southern Politics in State and Nation.* New York: Alfred A. Knopf, 1949.

Keyssar, Alexander. *The Right to Vote: The Contested History of Democracy in the United States.* New York: Basic Books/Perseus Books Group, 2000.

Kidwell, Clara Sue. *Choctaws and Missionaries in Mississippi, 1818–1918.* Norman: University of Oklahoma Press, 1995.

Killens, John Oliver, and Jerry W. Ward, Jr., eds. *Black Southern Voices: An Anthology of Fiction, Poetry, Drama, Non-Fiction, and Critical Essays.* New York: Penguin Group, 1992.

Killian, Lewis M. *White Southerners.* Amherst: The University of Massachusetts Press, 1985.

King, B. B., with David Pitz. *Blues All Around Me: The Autobiography of B. B. King.* New York: Avon Books, 1996.

King, Martin Luther, Jr. *Strength to Love.* New York: Harper and Row, 1963.

Kirby, Jack Temple. *Darkness at the Dawning: Race and Reform in the Progressive South.* Philadelphia: J. B. Lippincott and Co., 1972.

Kirkendall, Richard S., ed. *The Truman Period as a*

Research Field: A Reappraisal. Columbia: University of Missouri Press, 1972.

Kitiwana, Bakari. *The Hip Hop Generation: Young Blacks and the Crisis in African American Culture.* New York: Basic Civitas Books, 2002.

Klenke, Karin. *Women and Leadership: A Contextual Perspective.* New York: Springer Publishing Co., 1996.

Klinkner, Philip A., and Rogers M. Smith. *The Unsteady March: The Rise and Decline of Racial Equality in America.* Chicago: The University of Chicago Press, 1999.

Knopke, Harry J., Robert J. Norrell, and Ronald W. Rogers, eds. *Opening Doors: Perspectives on Race Relations in Contemporary America.* Tuscaloosa: The University of Alabama Press, 1991.

Kolko, Gabriel. *Main Currents in Modern American History.* New York: Harper and Row, Publishers, 1976.

Kornweibel, Theodore, Jr. *"Seeing Red": Federal Campaigns Against Black Militancy, 1919–1925.* Bloomington: Indiana University Press, 1998.

Kort, Carol. *A to Z of American Women Writers.* New York: Facts On File, 2000.

Kousser, J. Morgan. *The Shaping of Southern Politics: Suffrage Restriction and the Establishment of the One-Party South, 1880–1910.* New Haven, Conn.: Yale University Press, 1974.

Landrum, Gene N. *Profiles of Black Success: Thirteen Creative Geniuses Who Changed the World.* New York: Prometheus Books, 1997.

Larsson, Clotye Murdock. "Land of the Till Murder Revisited." *Ebony* 4, No. 5 (March 1986).

Lawson, Steven F. *Running for Freedom: Civil Rights and Black Politics in America Since 1941.* New York: The McGraw-Hill Co., 1997.

Lee, A. Robert. *Designs of Blackness: Mapping in the Literature and Culture of Afro-America.* London: Pluto Press, 1998.

Leeman, Richard W., ed. *African-American Orators: A Bio-Critical Sourcebook.* Westport, Conn.: Greenwood Press, 1996.

Leonard, Thomas M. *Day by Day: The Forties.* New York: Facts On File, 1977.

Lerner, Gerda, ed. *Black Women in White America: A Documentary History.* New York: Pantheon Books, 1972.

Leverich, Lyle. *Tom: The Unknown Tennessee Williams.* New York: Norton, 1997.

Lewis, David Levering. *W. E. B. Du Bois: Biography of a Race, 1868–1919.* New York: Henry Holt and Co., 1993.

_____. *W. E. B. Du Bois: The Fight for Equality and the American Century, 1919–1963.* New York: Henry Holt and Co., 2000.

_____, ed. *W. E. B. Du Bois: A Reader.* New York: Henry Holt and Co., 1995.

Lewis, Earl M. "The Negro Voter in Mississippi." *Journal of Negro Education* 26 (1957): 329–50.

Lieberman, Robbie. *"My Song Is My Weapon": American Communism, and the Politics of Culture, 1930–1950.* Urbana: University of Illinois Press, 1989.

Lincoln, C. Eric. *The Black Muslims in America.* Grand Rapids, Mich.: William B. Eerdmans Publishing Co. and Trenton, N.J.: Africa World Press, 1994.

_____, and Lawrence H. Mamiya. *The Black Church in*

the African American Experience. Durham, N.C.: Duke University Press, 1990.

Link, Arthur, and William B. Catton. *American Epoch: A History of the United States Since 1900.* New York: Alfred Knopf, 1973.

Lipsitz, George. *The Possessive Investment in Whiteness: How White People Profit from Identity Politics.* Philadelphia, Pa.: Temple University Press, 1998.

Lisio, Donald J. *Hoover, Blacks, and Lily-Whites: A Study of Southern Strategies.* Chapel Hill: The University of North Carolina Press, 1985.

Lloyd, R. Grann. *White Supremacy in the United States: An Analysis of its Historical Background, with Special Reference to the Poll Tax.* Washington, D.C.: Annals of American Research, 1952.

Locher, Frances C., Martha G. Conway, Marie Evans, and David Versical, eds. *Contemporary Authors, Volume 104.* Detroit: Gale Research, 1982.

Locke, Alain Leroy, ed. *The New Negro.* New York: Albert and Charles Boni, 1925; reprint ed., New York: Touchstone/Simon and Schuster, 1997.

_____. *Race Contacts and Interracial Relations: Lectures on the Theory and Practice of Race,* ed., Jeffrey C. Stewart. Washington, D.C.: Howard University Press, 1992.

Loewen, James. *The Mississippi Chinese: Between Black and White.* Cambridge, Mass.: Harvard University Press, 1971.

_____, and Charles Sallis, eds. *Mississippi: Conflict and Change.* New York: Pantheon Books, 1974.

Lofgren, Charles A. *The Plessy Case: A Legal-Historical Interpretation.* New York: Oxford University Press, 1987.

Logan, Frenise A. *The Negro in North Carolina, 1876–1894.* Chapel Hill: The University of North Carolina Press, 1964.

Logan, Rayford W. *The Betrayal of the Negro: From Rutherford B. Hayes to Woodrow Wilson.* New York: Da Capo Press, 1997.

_____. *The Negro in the United States.* Princeton, N.J.: D. Vann Nostrand Co., 1957.

_____, and Michael R. Winston, eds. *Dictionary of American Negro Biography.* New York: W. W. Norton and Co., 1982.

Logan, Shirley Wilson. *"We Are Coming": The Persuasive Discourse of Nineteenth-Century Black Women.* Carbondale: Southern Illinois University Press, 1999.

Loury, Glenn C. *The Anatomy of Racial Inequality.* Cambridge, Mass.: Harvard University Press, 2002.

Lowenfels, Walter. "Shoes That Walked for Willie McGee." *Freedomways* 2, No. 3 (Summer 1962): 243–44.

Lowry, Mark, II. "Geographical Characteristics of a Bi-Racial Society: The Mississippi Case." (Ph.D. diss., Syracuse University, 1973).

Lubiano, Wahneema, ed. *The House That Race Built: Black Americans, U.S. Terrain.* New York: Pantheon Books, 1997.

Luedtke, Luther S., ed. *Making America: The Society and Culture of the United States.* Chapel Hill: The University of North Carolina Press, 1992.

Luker, Ralph E. *Historical Dictionary of the Civil Rights Movement.* Lanham, Md.: The Scarecrow Press, 1997.

_____. *The Social Gospel in Black and White, American Racial Reform, 1885–1912*. Chapel Hill: The University of North Carolina Press, 1991.

Lumpkin, Katharine Dupre. *The South in Progress*. New York: International Publishers, 1940.

Lyle, Clay. *Organizational Activities of Rural Negroes in Mississippi*. State College: Mississippi State College, Agricultural Experiment Station, Circular 192, December 1953.

Lyman, Darryl. *Great African-American Women*. New York: Gramercy Books, 1999.

Lynch, John Roy. *Reminiscences of an Active Life: The Autobiography of John Roy Lynch*. Ed, John Hope Franklin. Chicago: The University of Chicago Press, 1970.

Malcomson, Scott L. *One Drop of Blood: The American Misadventure of Race*. New York: Farrar, Straus, Giroux, 2000.

Mankiller, Wilma, ed. *The Reader's Companion to U.S. Women's History*. Boston: Houghton Mifflin, 1998.

Marable, Manning. *Beyond Black and White: Transforming African-American Politics*. New York: Verso, 1995.

Martin, Tony. *Marcus Garvey, Hero: A First Biography*. Dover, Mass.: The Majority Press, 1983.

Martin, Waldo E. *The Mind of Frederick Douglass*. Chapel Hill: The University of North Carolina Press, 1984.

Massengill, Read. *Portrait of a Racist: The Man Who Killed Medgar Evers*. New York: St. Martin's Press, 1994.

Matthews, Donald R. and Jones W. Porothro. *Negroes and the New Southern Politics*. New York: Harcourt, Brace and World, 1966.

Maxwell, Richard. *Brown, Strain of Violence: Historical Studies of American Violence and Vigilantism*. New York: Oxford University Press, 1975.

McElvaine, Robert S. *The Great Depression: America, 1929–1941*. New York: Three Rivers Press, 1993.

McGuire, Philip, ed. *Taps for a Jim Crow Army: Letters from Black Soldiers in World War II*. Lexington: The University Press of Kentucky, 1993.

McKay, Claude. *Selected Poems of Claude McKay*. New York: Twayne Publishing, 1953.

McKee, Jesse O., ed. *Mississippi: A Portrait of an American State*. Montgomery, Ala.: Clairmont Press, 1995.

McKitrick, Eric L. *Andrew Johnson and Reconstruction*. Chicago: The University of Chicago Press, 1960.

McLemore, R. A., ed. *A History of Mississippi*, 2 volumes. Hattiesburg: University and College Press of Mississippi, 1973.

McMillen, Neil R. *Dark Journey: Black Mississippians in the Age of Jim Crow*. Urbana: University of Illinois Press, 1989.

_____, ed. *Remaking Dixie: The Impact of World War II on the American South*. Jackson: University Press of Mississippi, 1997.

McPherson, James M. *The Negro's Civil War*. New York: Vintage Books, 1965.

Meier, August. *Negro Thought in America, 1880–1915: Racial Ideologies in the Age of Booker T. Washington*. Ann Arbor: The University of Michigan Press, 1966.

Metzger, Linda, ed. *Black Writers: A Selection of Sketches from Contemporary Authors*. Detroit: Gale Research, 1989.

Millen, Jerone G. *Search and Destroy: African-American Males in the Criminal Justice System*. New York: Cambridge University Press, 1996.

Mollison, Irvin C. "Negro Lawyers in Mississippi." *The Journal of Negro History* XV, No. 1 (January 1930): 38–71.

Morrison, Samuel Eliot. *The Oxford History of the American People*. New York: Oxford University Press, 1965.

Mosely, Jessie. *The Negro in Mississippi History*. Jackson, Miss.: Helderman Bros., 1950.

Moses, Wilson Jeremiah. *Black Messiahs and Uncle Toms: Social and Literary Manipulations of a Religious Myth*. University Park: The Pennsylvania State University Press, 1982.

Motley, Constance Baker. *Equal Justice Under Law: An Autobiography*. New York: Farrar, Straus and Giroux, 1998.

Moton, David R., Jr. "Southern Violence: An Analysis of Lynching in the South-Central Region of the United States, 1889 to 1918." (M.A. thesis, Department of Sociology, Northern Illinois University, Dekalb, 1986.)

Mott, Frank Luthern. *American Journalism: A History, 1690–1960*. New York: MacMillan, 1962.

Mounger, Dwyn M. "Lynching in Mississippi, 1830–1930." (M.A. thesis, Department of History and Government, Mississippi State University, August, 1961.)

Mungazi, Dickson A. *The Journey to the Promised Land: The African American Struggle for Development Since the Civil War*. Westport, Conn.: Praeger, 2001.

NAACP. *Burning at Stake in the United States*. New York: NAACP, June 1919.

_____. *Thirty Years of Lynching in the United States, 1889–1918*. New York: NAACP, 1919.

Nalty, Bernard C. *Strength for the Fight: A History of Black Americans in the Military*. New York: The Free Press, 1986.

The Negro Handbook. Chicago: Johnson Publishing Co., 1966.

Nelson, William Stuart. *The Christian Way in Race Relations*. New York: Harper and Brothers, Publishers, 1948.

Newby, I. A. *Jim Crow's Defense: Anti-Negro Thought in America, 1900–1930*. Baton Rouge: Louisiana State University Press, 1965.

_____, ed. *The Development of Segregationist Thought*. Homewood, Ill.: The Dorsey Press, 1968.

Newkirk, Pamela. *Within the Veil: Black Journalists, White Media*. New York: New York University Press, 2000.

Newton, Michael, and Judy Ann Newton. *The Ku Klux Klan: An Encyclopedia*. New York: Garland Publishers, 1991.

Nieman, Donald G., ed. *African-Americans and Non-Agricultural Labor in the South, 1865–1900*. New York: Garland Publishing, 1994.

Noble, Stuart Grayson. *Forty Years of the Public Schools in Mississippi, with Special Reference to the Education of the Negro*. New York: Teachers College, Columbia University, 1918.

Nordholt, J. W. Schulte. Translated by M. B. Van Wijngaarden. *The People That Walk in Darkness*. New York: Ballantine Books, 1956.

Nordin, Dennis S. *The New Deal's Black Congressman: A Life of Arthur Wergs Mitchell.* Columbia: University of Missouri Press, 1997.

Okihiro, Gary Y., ed. *In Resistance: Studies in African, Caribbean, and Afro-American History.* Amherst: The University of Massachusetts Press, 1986.

Olson, James. *The Ethnic Dimension in American History.* New York: St. Martin's Press. 1994.

Omolade, Barbara. *The Rising Song of African American Women.* New York: Routledge, 1994.

Orey, Byron D'Andra. "Black Legislative Politics in Mississippi." *Journal of Black Studies* 30, No. 6 (July 2000): 791–814.

"Organizations Committed to a Program of Education to Prevent Lynching." Atlanta, Ga.: Association of Southern Women for the Prevention of Lynching, October, 1940.

Osbom, George Coleman. *James Kimble Vardaman: Southern Commoner.* Jackson, Miss.: Helderman Bros., 1981.

Oshinsky, David M. *"Worse Than Slavery": Parchman Farm and the Ordeal of Jim Crow Justice.* New York: The Free Press, 1996.

Osofsky, Gilbert, ed. *The Burden of Race: A Documentary History of Negro-White Relations in America.* New York: Harper and Row, Publishers, 1967.

Osur, Alan M. *Blacks in the Army Air Force During World War II: The Problem of Race Relations.* Washington, D.C.: Office of Air Force History, 1977.

Ownby, Tom. *American Dreams in Mississippi: Consumers, Poverty and Culture, 1830–1998.* Chapel Hill: The University of North Carolina Press, 1999.

Page, James A., compiler. *Selected Black American Authors: An Illustrated Bio-Bibliography.* Boston: G. K. Hall and Co., 1977.

Painter, Nell Irvin. *Exodusters: Black Migration to Kansas After Reconstruction.* New York: Alfred A. Knopf, 1977.

_____. *Standing at Armageddon: The United States, 1877–1919.* New York: W.W. Norton and Co., 1987.

Pairish, Michael E. *Anxious Decades: America in Prosperity and Depression, 1920–1941.* New York: W. W. Norton and Co., 1992.

Parker, Frank R. *Black Votes Count: Political Empowerment in Mississippi, After 1965.* Chapel Hill: The University of North Carolina Press, 1990.

Parkes, Henry Bamford and Vincent P. Carossa. *Recent America: A History, Book One: 1900–1933.* New York: Thomas Y. Crowell Co., 1963.

Patchen, Kenneth. *Collected Poems.* New York: New Directions Publishing, 1939.

Patterson, Martha H. "Recovering the Work of American Clubs Women.": *American Quarterly* 51, No. 1 (March 1999): 221–227.

Patterson, William L. *The Man Who Cried Genocide: An Autobiography.* New York: International Publishers, 1971.

Payne, Charles M. *I've Got the Light of Freedom: The Organizing Tradition of the Mississippi Freedom Struggle.* Berkeley: University of California Press, 1995.

Perkinson, Robert. "Between the Worst of the Past and the Worst of the Future: Reconsidering Convict Leasing in the South." *Radical History* 71 (Spring 1998).

Phillips, Ivory. *A Religion for Blacks in America.* Washington, D.C.: University Press of America, 1977.

Pierce, Neal R. *The Deep South States of America: People, Politics, and Power in the Seven Deep South States.* New York: W. W. Norton and Co., 1904.

Pilgrim, David, ed. *On Being Black: An In-Group Analysis.* Bristol, Ind.: Wyndham Hall Press, 1989.

Pinkney, Alphonso. *The Committed: White Activists in the Civil Rights Movement.* New Haven, Conn.: College and University Press, Publishers, 1968.

Ploski, Harry A. and James Williams, eds. *Reference Library of Black America.* Detroit: Gale Research, 1990.

Plummer, Brenda Gayle. *Rising Wind: Black Americans and U.S. Foreign Affairs, 1935-1960.* Chapel Hill: University of North Carolina Press, 1969.

Pohlman, Marcus D. *Black Politics in Conservative America.* New York: Longman, 1990.

Poitier, Sidney. *The Measure of a Man: A Spiritual Autobiography.* San Francisco, Calif.: HarperCollins Publishers, 2000.

Polenberg, Richard. *One Nation Divisible: Class, Race, and Ethnicity in the United States Since 1938.* New York: The Viking Press, 1980.

Polk, Noel E., and James R. Scafidel, eds. *An Anthology of Mississippi Writers.* Jackson: University Press of Mississippi, 1979.

Population Bulletin for Mississippi. Jackson: State of Mississippi, 1940.

Posey, Josephine McCann. *Against Great Odds: The History of Alcorn State University.* Jackson: University Press of Mississippi, 1994.

Poussint, Alvin F., and Amy Alexander. *Lay My Burden Down: Unraveling Suicide and the Mental Health Crisis Among African-Americans.* Boston: Beacon Press, 2000.

Powledge, Fred. *Free At Last?: The Civil Rights Movement and the People Who Made It.* New York: HarperCollins Publishers, 1991.

Pride, Armistead Scott. "The Names of Negro Newspapers." *American Speech* 29, No. 2 (May 1954): 114–118.

_____, and Clint C. Wilson, II. *A History of the Black Press.* Washington, D.C.: Howard University Press, 1997.

Prospectus of the First Annual Meeting of the Mississippi Regional Council of Negro Leadership. Mound Bayou, Miss.: Mississippi Regional Council of Negro Leadership, May 2, 1952.

Quarles, Benjamin. *Black Mosaic: Essays in Afro-American History and Historiography.* Amherst: The University of Massachusetts Press, 1988.

Rabinowitz, Howard N., ed. *Southern Leaders of the Reconstruction Era.* Urbana: University of Illinois Press, 1982.

Rable, George C. "The South and the Politics of Antilynching Legislation, 1920–1940." *The Journal of Southern History* 51, No. 2 (May 1985).

Rampersad, Arnold. *The Life of Langston Hughes, Volume I: 1902–1941–I, Too, Sing America.* New York: Oxford University Press, 1986.

_____. *Volume II: 1941-1967, I Dream a World.* New York: Oxford University Press. 1988.

Randall, Dudley, ed. *The Black Poets: A New Anthology.* New York: Bantam Books, 1971.

Randell, William Peirce. *The Ku Klux Klan: A Century of Infamy.* Philadelphia: Chilton Books, 1965.

Ratliff, Beulah A. "Mississippi: Heart of Dixie." *Nation* 114 (1922).

Ready Reference, American Justice, Volume II. Pasadena, Calif.: Salem Press, 1996.

Redkey, Edwin S. *Black Exodus: Black Nationalist and Back-to-Africa Movements, 1890–1910.* New Haven, Conn.: Yale University Press, 1969.

Reed, Linda. *Simple Decency and Common Sense: The Southern Conference Movement, 1938–1963.* Bloomington: Indiana University Press, 1991.

Reeves, Richard. *President Nixon Alone in the White House.* New York: Simon and Schuster, 2001.

Resh, Richard, ed. *Black America: Confrontation and Accommodation in the Twentieth Century.* Lexington, Mass.: D. C. Heath and Co., 1969.

Rice, Eric W. *The Martinsville Seven.* Charlottesville: University Press of Virginia, 1995.

Rigby, Andrew. *Justice and Reconciliation: After the Violence.* Boulder, Co.: Lynne Bienner Publishers, 2001.

Rivlin, Benjamin, ed. *Ralph Bunche: The Man and His Times.* New York: Holmes and Meier, 1990.

Roach, Ronald. "Giving the Duke His Due." *Black Issues in Higher Education* 16, No. 3 (April 1, 1999): 25–28, 38–39.

Robins, Richard. *Sidelines Activist: Charles S. Johnson and the Struggle for Civil Rights.* Jackson: University Press of Mississippi, 1996.

Robinson, Randall. *The Debt: What America Owes to Blacks.* New York: Dutton/Penguin Group, 2000.

Roediger, David R., ed. *Black on White: Black Writers on What It Means to Be White.* New York: Schocken Books, 1998.

Roland, Charles P. *The Improbable Era: The South Since World War II.* Lexington: The University Press of Kentucky, 1975.

Roller, David C., and Robert W. Twyman, eds. *The Encyclopedia of Southern History.* Baton Rouge: Louisiana State University Press, 1979.

Roper, John Herbert, ed. *C. Vann Woodward: A Southern Historian and His Critics.* Athens: The University of Georgia Press, 1997.

Ropers, R. H., and Dan J. Pence, eds. *American Prejudice: With Liberty and Justice for Some.* New York: Insight Books/Plenum Press, 1995.

Rose, Arnold. *The Negro in America: The Condensed Version of Gunnar Myrdal's An American Dilemma.* New York: Harper and Row, Publishers, 1964.

Rosenbaum, Tommye Hague. *A History of the Mississippi Federation of Women's Clubs, 1898–1998.* Jackson: Mississippi Federation of Women's Clubs, 1998.

Ross, Arthur M., and Herbert Hill, eds. *Employment, Race and Poverty.* New York: Harcourt, Brace and World, 1967.

Ross, B. Joyce. *J. E. Spingarn and the Rise of the NAACP, 1911–1939.* New York: Atheneum. 1972.

Ross, Job F. "What You Didn't Know about Risk." *Reader's Digest* 148, No. 888 (April 1996): 55–58

Ross, Lawrence C., Jr. *The Divine Nine: The History of*

African-American Fraternities and Sororities. New York: Kensington Publishing Corp, 2002.

Rothschild, Mary Aickin. "White Women Volunteers in the Freedom Summers: Their Life and Work in a Movement for Social Change." *Feminist Studies* 5, No. 3 (Fall 1979): 466–495.

Rowells American Newspaper Directory. New York: The Printers' Ink Publishing Co., 1905.

Rowley, Hazel. *Richard Wright: The Life and Times.* New York: Henry Holt and Co., 2001.

Rubin, Louis D. Jr., ed. *The History of Southern Literature.* Baton Rouge: Louisiana State University Press, 1985.

Rubin, Richard. *Confederacy of Silence: A True Tale of the New Old South.* New York: Atria Books, 2002.

Runnion, James B. "The Negro Exodus." *The Atlantic Monthly* 46, No. 162 (August 1879): 222–223.

Rupesinghe, Kuman, and Marcial Rubio, eds. *The Culture of Violence.* New York: United Nations University Press, 1994.

Russell, Francis. *The Shadow of Blooming Grove: Warren G. Harding in His Times.* New York: McGraw-Hill Book Co., 1968.

Russell, Katheryn K. *The Color of Crime: Racial Hoaxes, White Fear, Black Protectionism, Police Harassment and Other Macroaggressions.* New York: New York University Press, 1998.

Sachs, Moshe Y., ed. *World Mark Encyclopedia of the States.* New York: World Mark Press and John Wiley and Sons, 1986.

Salzman, Jack, ed. *The African-American Experience.* New York: Macmillan Library Reference, 1998.

____, and Cornell West, eds. *Struggles in the Promised Land: Toward a History of Black-Jewish Relations in the United States.* New York: Oxford University Press, 1997.

____, David Lionel Smith and Cornell West, eds. *Encyclopedia of African-American Culture and History, Volume 3.* New York: Macmillan Library Reference/ Simon and Schuster Macmillan, 1996.

Sansing, David G. *Mississippi: Its People and Culture.* Minneapolis: T. S. Denison and Co., 1981.

Sarba, Jonathan, ed. *Minority Faiths and the American Protestant Mainstream.* Urbana: University of Illinois Press, 1998.

Scally, Anthony Sister. "The Carter Woodson Letters in the Library of Congress." *Negro History Bulletin* 38, No. 5 (June/July 1975).

____. "Woodson and the Genesis of AS ALH." *Negro History Bulletin* 40, No. 1 (January-February 1977): 653–55.

Schlesinger, Arthur M., Jr., and John S. Bowman, eds. *The Almanac of American History.* New York: Barnes and Noble/Brompton Books Corp, 1993.

Schneider, Dorothy, and Carl J. Schneider. *American Women in the Progressive Era, 1900–1920.* New York: Facts On File, 1993.

Schomburg Center for Research in Black Culture/The New York Public Library. *African American Desk Reference.* New York: John Wiley and Sons, 1999.

Schriverer, George H., and Bill J. Leonard, eds. *Encyclopedia of Religious Controversies in the United States.* Westport, Conn.: Greenwood Press, 1997.

Schultz, Bud, and Ruth Schultz, eds. *It Did Happen*

Here: Recollections of Political Repression in America. Berkeley: University of California Press, 1989.

Schuyler, George S. *Black and Conservative: The Autobiography of George S. Schuyler.* New Rochelle, N.Y.: Arlington House Publishers, 1966.

Schweninger, Loren. *Black Property Owners in the South, 1790-1915.* Urbana: University of Illinois Press, 1990.

Seemes, Clovis [aka Jabulani Kamau Makalani]. *Racism, Health and Post-Industrialism: A Theory of African-American Health.* Westport, Conn.: Praeger, 1996.

Sewell, George Alexander, and Margaret L. Dwight. *Mississippi Black History Makers.* Jackson: University Press of Mississippi, 1984.

Shapiro, Herbert. *White Violence and Black Response: From Reconstruction to Montgomery.* Amherst: The University of Massachusetts Press, 1988.

Sherman, Richard B. *The Republican Party and Black America: From McKinley to Hoover, 1896-1933.* Charlottesville: University Press of Virginia, 1973.

Shockley, Ann Allen, and Sue P. Chandler. *Living Black American Authors: A Biographical Directory.* New York: R. R. Bowker Co., 1973.

"The Shubuta Lynchings." *The Crisis* 18, No. 1 (May 1919): 24-25.

Siegal, Nina. "Women in Prison." *Ms.* 9, No. 2 (September/October 1998).

Silver, James W. *Mississippi: The Closed Society.* New York: Harcourt, Brace and World, 1966.

Simkins, Francis Butler. *A History of the South.* New York: Alfred A. Knopf, 1961.

Simone, Nina. "Mississippi Goddam." Santa Monica, Calif.: Sam Fox Publishing Co., Inc., 1964.

_____, with Stephen Deary. *I Put a Spell on You: The Autobiography of Nina Simone.* New York: Pantheon Books, 1991.

Singelman, Leww, and Susan Welch. *Black Americans' Views of Racial Inequality: The Dream Deferred.* New York: Cambridge University Press, 1991.

Sinnette, Elinor Des Verney. *Arthur Alfonso Schomburg: Black Bibliophile and Collector.* Detroit: Wayne State University Press, 1989.

Smead, Howard. *Blood Justice: The Lynching of Mack Charles Parker.* New York: Oxford University Press, 1986.

Smith, Douglass L. *The New Deal in the Urban South.* Baton Rouge: Louisiana State University Press, 1988.

Smith, Frank E. *Congressman from Mississippi.* New York: Pantheon Books, 1964.

Smith, J. Clay. *Emancipation: The Making of the Black Lawyer, 1844-1944.* Philadelphia: University of Pennsylvania Press, 1993.

Smith, Jessie Carney, ed. *Epic Lives: One Hundred Black Women Who Made a Difference.* Detroit: Visible Ink Press, 1993.

Smith, John David, ed. *Emigration and Migration Proposals: Solutions to "The Negro Problem."* New York: Garland Publishing, 1993.

Smith, Robert C. *We Have No Leaders: African Americans in the Post–Civil Rights Era.* Albany: State University of New York Press, 1996.

Smith, T. Alexander, and Lenahan O'Connell. *Black Anxiety, White Guilt, and the Politics of Status Frustration.* Westport, Conn.: Praeger, 1997.

Smith, Theophus H. *Conjuring Culture: Biblical Formations of Black America.* New York: Oxford University Press, 1994.

Sobel, Robert. *Coolidge: An American Enigma.* Washington, D.C.: Regnery Publishing, 1998.

Solomon, Mark. *The Cry Was Unity: Communists and African-Americans, 1917-36.* Jackson: University Press of Mississippi, 1998.

Southern, Eileen. *The Music of Black Americans: A History.* New York: W. W. Norton and Co., 1983.

"A Southern Protest Against Lynching." *The Outlook* 112 (January 19, 1916): 124-125.

"The Southern White Press and the Negro." Atlanta, Ga.: Commission on Interracial Cooperation, Inc., February 15, 1943.

The Sovereignty Files: The Real Story. Jackson, Miss.: Town Square Books, 1999.

Spencer, Samuel R., Jr. *Booker T. Washington and the Negro's Place in American Life.* Boston: Little, Brown and Co., 1955.

Sprigle, Ray. *In the Land of Jim Crow.* New York: Simon and Schuster, 1949.

Standford, P. Thomas. *The Tragedy of the Negro in America.* Boston: By the Author, 1898.

Steelman, John R. "A Study of Mob Action in the South." (Ph.D. diss., Department of Sociology, the University of North Carolina, Chapel Hill, 1928).

Sterner, Richard, Lenore A. Epstein, Ellen Winston, and Others. *The Negro's Share: A Study of Income Consumption, Housing and Public Assistance.* New York: Harper and Brothers, Publishers, 1943.

"The Story of Charles Caldwell." Bolton, Miss.: Bolton Bicentennial Project, 1975.

Straub, Deborah Gillon, ed. *African American Voices, Volume 2: K-Z.* New York: Gale Research, 1996.

Strunk, Mildred. *Public Opinion, 1935-1946.* Princeton, N. J.: Princeton University Press, 1951.

Stuart, Paul. *Nations within a Nation: Historical Statistics of American Indians.* New York: Greenwood Press, 1987.

Sullivan, Patricia. *Days of Hope: Race and Democracy in the New Deal Era.* Chapel Hill: The University of North Carolina Press, 1996.

Swain, Martha H. *Pat Harrison: The New Deal Years.* Jackson: University Press of Mississippi, 1978.

Swint, Henry Lee. *The Northern Teacher in the South, 1862-1870.* New York: Octagon Books, 1967.

Sylvander, Carolyn Wedin. *Jessie Redmon Fauset: Black American Writer.* New York: The Whitston Publishing Co., 1981.

Taylor, Arnold H. *Travail and Triumph: Black Life and Culture in the South Since the Civil War.* Westport, Conn.: Greenwood Press, 1976.

Taylor-Guthrie, Danille, ed. *Conversations with Toni Morrison.* Jackson: University Press of Mississippi, 1994.

Teacher's Resource Manual. *The African American Experience: A History.* Englewood Cliffs, N.J.: Glove Book Co., 1992.

Terrell, Mary Church. "Lynching from a Negro's Point of View." *North American Review* 118 (June 1904): 853-868.

Theohara, Athan G., Tonny G. Poveda, Susan Rosenfeld, and Richard Gid Powers. *The FBI: A Compre-*

hensive Reference Guide. Phoenix, Arizona: The Oryx Press, 1999.

Thompson, Cleopatra D. *The History of the Mississippi Teachers Association.* Washington, D.C.: NEA Teachers Rights and Mississippi Teachers Association, 1973.

Thompson, Julius E. *Black Life in Mississippi: Essays on Political, Social and Cultural Studies in a Deep South State.* Lanham, Md.: University Press of America, 2001.

____. *The Black Press in Mississippi, 1865–1985.* Gainesville: University Press of Florida, 1993.

____. *Hiram R. Revels, 1827–1901: A Biography.* New York: Arno Press, 1982.

____. *Percy Greene and the Jackson Advocate: The Life and Times of a Radical Conservative Black Newspaperman, 1897–1977.* Jefferson, N.C.: McFarland, 1994.

Thompson, Patrick H. *The History of Negro Baptists in Mississippi.* Jackson, Miss.: The R. W. Bailey Printing Co., 1898.

Thompson, Peter. *Dictionary of American History, From 1763 to the Present.* New York: Facts On File, 2000.

Thornbrough, Emma Lou. "American Negro Newspapers, 1880–1914." *Business History Review* 40, No. 4 (Winter 1966): 467–490.

Thurber, Timothy N. *The Politics of Equality: Hubert H. Humphrey and the African American Freedom Struggle.* New York: Columbia University Press, 1999.

Tingley, Donald F. *The Structuring of a State: The History of Illinois, 1899 to 1928.* Urbana: The Board of Trustees of the University of Illinois, 1980.

Tolnay, Stewart E. *A Festival of Violence: An Analysis of Southern Lynchings, 1882–1930.* Urbana: University of Illinois Press, 1992.

____, and E. M. Beck. "Racial Violence and Black Migration in the American South, 1910 to 1930." *American Sociological Review* 57 (February 1992).

Tomkins, Vincent, ed. *America Eras: Development of the Industrial United States.* Detroit: Gale, 1997.

Torres, Rodolfo, Louis F. Miron, and Jonathan Xavier Inda, eds. *Race, Identity, and Citizenship: A Reader.* Maiden, Mass.: Blackwell Publishers, 1999.

Trefousee, Hans L. *The Radical Republicans: Lincoln's Vanguard for Racial Justice.* New York: Alfred A. Knopf, 1969.

Trelease, Allen W. *Reconstruction: The Great Experiment.* New York: Harper and Row, Publishers, 1971.

____. *White Terror: The Ku Klux Klan, Conspiracy and Southern Reconstruction.* Westport, Conn.: Greenwood Press, 1971.

Tristano, Richard M. "Holy Family Parish: The Genesis of an African-American Catholic Community in Natchez, Mississippi." *The Journal of Negro History* 73, No. 4 (Fall 1998): 258–283.

Trotter, Joe William, Jr. *The African American Experience.* Boston: Houghton Mifflin Co.

Tucker, David M. *Lieuenan: Lee of Beale Street.* Nashville, Tenn.: Vanderbilt University Press, 1971.

Tyrack, David. *Nobody Knows: Black Americans in the Twentieth Century.* New York: The Macmillan Co., 1969.

Valde, Roger M. III. *The Essential Black Literature Guide.* Detroit: Visible Ink, 1996.

Vila, Byran, and Cynthia Morris, eds. *Capital Punishment in the United States: A Documentary History.* Westport, Conn.: Greenwood Press, 1997.

Vivian, James F., ed. *William Howard Taft, Collected Editorials, 1917–1921.* New York: Praeger, 1990.

Walker, Wyatt Tee. *"Somebody's Calling My Name": Black Sacred Music and Social Change.* Valley Forge, Pa.: Judson Press, 1992.

Ward, Geoffrey C. *Not for Ourselves Alone: The Story of Elizabeth Cady Stanton and Susan B. Anthony, An Illustrated History.* New York: Alfred A. Knopf, 1999.

Washburn, Patrick S. "J. Edgar Hoover and the Black Press in World War II." *Journalism History* 13, No. 1 (Spring 1986): 26–33.

Washington, Booker T. "A Cheerful Journey Through Mississippi." *World's Work* (February 1908): 11278–82.

____. *The Story of the Negro: The Rise of the Race from Slavery.* New York: The Outlook Co., 1909; reprint ed., New York: Double Day, Doran and Co., 1940; reprinted, Gloucester, Mass.: Peter Smith, 1969.

Washington, James Melvin, ed. *Conversations with God: Two Centuries of Prayers by African Americans.* New York: HarperCollins Publishers, 1994.

Watson, Charles H. "Need of Federal Legislation in Respect to Mob Violence in Cases of Lynching of Aliens." *Yale Law Journal* 25, No. 7 (May 1916).

Weatherford, Doris. *American Women's History: An A to Z of People, Organizations, Issues, and Events.* New York: Prentice-Hall General Reference, 1994.

Weatherford, W. D. *Present Forces in Negro Progress.* New York: Association Press, 1912.

Wedin, Carolyn. *Inheritors of the Spirit: Mary White Ovington and the Founding of the NAACP.* New York: John Wiley and Sons, 1998.

Weghyn, Michi Nishiurai. *Years of Infamy: The Untold Story of America's Concentration Camps.* Seattle: University of Washington Press, 1996.

Weinstein, Allen, and F. O. Gatell, eds. *The Segregation Era, 1863–1954: A Modern Reader.* New York: Oxford University Press, 1970.

Weisbrot, Robert. *Father Divine and the Struggle for Racial Equality.* Urbana: University of Illinois Press, 1983.

Wells, Samuel J., and Roseanna Tubby, eds. *After Removal: The Choctaw in Mississippi.* Jackson: University Press of Mississippi, 1986.

Wells-Barnett, Ida B. *Mob Rule in New Orleans: Robert Charles and His Fight to the Death.* Chicago: Ida B. Wells-Barnett, 1892.

____. *A Red Record: Tabulated Statistics and Alleged Causes of Lynchings in the United States, 1892–1893–1894.* Chicago: Donohue and Henneberry, 1895.

Wesley, Charles Harris. *The History of the National Association of Colored Women's Clubs: A Legacy of Service.* Washington, D.C.: National Association of Colored Women's Clubs, 1984.

Westin, Alan F., ed. *Freedom Now!: The Civil Rights Struggle in America.* New York: Basic Books, Publishers, 1964.

Wharton, Vernon Lane. *The Negro in Mississippi, 1865–1890.* New York: Harper and Row, 1965.

Wheeler, Marjorie Spruill. *New Women of the New South: The Leaders of the Woman Suffrage Movement in the Southern States.* New York: Oxford University Press, 1993.

White, Deborah Gray. *Too Heavy a Load: Black Women in Defense of Themselves, 1894–1994.* New York: W. W. Norton & Co., 1999.

White, Walter. *How Far the Promised Land?* New York: The Viking Press, 1955.

_____. *Rope and Faggot: A Biography of Judge Lynch.* New York: Alfred A. Knopf, 1929.

Whitefield, Stephen J. *A Death in the Delta: The Story of Emmett Till.* New York: The Free Press, 1988.

Wickham, Dewayne. *Bill Clinton and Black America.* New York: Ballantine Books, 2002.

Wilhoit, Francis M. *The Politics of Massive Resistance.* New York: George Braziller, 1973.

Wilkins, Roy, with Tom Mathews. *Standing Fast: The Autobiography of Roy Wilkins.* New York: The Viking Press, 1982.

Williams, Daniel T. "The Lynching Records at Tuskegee Institute." In: *Eight Negro Bibliographies.* New York: Krus Reprint Co., 1970.

Williams, Gilbert Anthony. *The Christian Recorder, Newspaper of the African Methodist Episcopal Church.* Jefferson, N.C.: McFarland, 1996.

Williams, Linda. *Playing the Race Card: Melodramas of Black and White: From Uncle Tome to O.J. Simpson.* Princeton, N.J.: Princeton University Press, 2001.

Williams, Yohura R. "Permission to Hate: Delaware, Lynching, and the Culture of Violence in America." *Journal of Black Studies* 32, No. 1 (September 2001): 3–29.

Willie, Charles V., ed. *Black/Brown/White Relations: Race Relations in the 1970s.* New Brunswick, N.J.: Transaction Books, 1977.

Willis, Gregory A. *Democratic Religion: Freedom, Authority, and Church Discipline in the Baptist South, 1785–1900.* New York: Oxford University Press, 1997.

Willis, John Charles. *On the New South Frontier: Life in the Yazoo-Mississippi Delta, 1865–1920.* (Ph.D. diss., University of Virginia, 1991).

Wilson, Charles Reagan, ed. *Religion in the South.* Jackson: University Press of Mississippi, 1985.

Wilsonson, Sandra Kathryn, ed. *The Selected Writings of James Weldon Johnson, Volume 2: Social, Political, and Literary Essays.* New York: Oxford University Press, 1995.

Wintz, Gary D. *Black Culture and the Harlem Renaissance.* Houston, Texas: Rice University Press, 1988.

Wirt, Frederick M. *"We Ain't What We Was": Civil Rights in the New South.* Durham, N.C.: Duke University Press, 1997.

Wish, Harvey, ed. *The Negro Since Emancipation.* Englewood Cliffs, N.J.: Prentice-Hall, 1964.

Witt, Doris. *Black Hunger: Food and the Politics of United States Identity.* New York: Oxford University Press, 1999.

Wolseley, Roland E. *The Black Press, U.S.A.* Ames: Iowa State University Press, 1990.

Wolters, Raymond. *The New Negro on Campus: Black College Rebellions of the 1920s.* Princeton, N.J.: Princeton University Press, 1975.

"Women of Mississippi Urge Lynchers Be Punished." Atlanta, Ga.: Commission on Interracial Cooperation, July 26, 1935.

Woodson, Carter G. *A Century of Negro Migration.* Washington, D.C.: The Association for the Study of Negro Life and History, 1918.

_____. *The Negro in Our History.* Washington, D.C.: The Associated Publishers, 1947.

Woodward, C. Vann. *The Strange Career of Jim Crow.* New York: Oxford University Press, 1974.

Woodward, D. W. *Negro Progress in a Mississippi Town: Being a Study of Conditions in Jackson, Mississippi.* Cheyney, Pa.: The Biddle Press, 1908.

Wormser, Richard. *Hoboes: Wandering in America, 1870–1940.* New York: Walker and Co., 1994.

Wright, Esmond. *The American Dream: From Reconstruction to Reagan.* Cambridge, Mass.: Blackwell, 1996.

Wright, John, ed. *The New York Times 2002 Almanac.* New York: Penguin Reference, 2001.

Wynn, Neil A. "Black Attitudes Toward Participation in the American War Effort, 1941–1945." *Afro-American Studies* 3, No. 1 (June 1972): 13–19.

Yates, Gayle Graham. *Mississippi Mind: A Personal Cultural History of an American State.* Knoxville: The University of Tennessee Press, 1990.

Young, N. Clifford. "A Case Study of the Tarboro Lynching." (M.A. thesis, Department of Sociology, University of North Carolina at Chapel Hill, 1931).

Zamir, Shamoon. *Dark Voices: W. E. B. Du Bois and American Thought, 1888–1903.* Chicago: The University of Chicago Press, 1995.

Zangrando, Robert. *The NAACP Crusade Against Lynching.* Philadelphia: Temple University Press, 1980.

Zikmund, Barbara Brown, Adair T. Lummis, and Patricia N. Y. Chang. *Clergy Women: An Uphill Calling.* Louisville, Ky.: Westminster John Knox Press, 1998.

Zinn, Howard. *The New Abolitionists.* Boston: Beacon, 1964.

_____. *The Twentieth Century: A People's History.* New York: HarperCollins Publishers, 1998.

Index

Black Community (National) 5, 7,
8, 12; anti-lynching efforts 130–
31; brutality 79–80, 87, 90, 91;
campaign against abuse 126–28;
concerns and actions 16, 24, 27,
32, 41, 47, 57, 73, 75, 88; of daily
lives 107, 114, 144, 154; general
conditions 108, 114, 155; hardships 92, 94, 95, 101, 105 106;
institutional racism 115–16; medical crisis 139, 181; membership
in NAACP 127; in Mississippi 3,
9, 10, 11, 30, 55, 57, 71, 72; in
the 1960s 156; psychological and
physical wounds 125, 137–38; voting efforts 118
Black Convention Movement 26,
41
Black experience: problems of 172
Black farmers 29, 37, 60, 78, 99,
104; Twelfth Annual Negro
Farmer's Conference 71
Black history 87, 90, 111
Black intellectuals 90, 110, 133, 154,
188
Black-Jewish relations 76
Black labor (workers) 59–60, 116,
190; agricultural focus 138; black
women 115, 138; during the Great
Depression 114; Mississippi's loss
of 137
Black lawyers (1890–1899) 17, 29,
30, 37; decline of 62, 71, 78, 92,
93, 139; in Mississippi 59; treatment of, in Mississippi courts
115; in the United States 92
Black lynch mobs 55
Black middle class 9, 17, 18, 29, 30,
59; activities of in 1950s 139; contemporary 176; in Mississippi 78,
92
Black-on-black crime 97
Black physicians 29, 45, 59, 78, 79,
81, 92; decline 93, 139; number
61, 71; services 117, 176; World
War II era 115
Black press, in Mississippi 13, 18,
30, 40, 61; circulation 113; cover-
age of lynchings 25–26, 37, 41,
72, 74, 78, 89, 130, 149–50, 154;
impact of white terror 137;
strength 90, 93, 119; World War
II concerns 117, 130–31
Black protests 105, 132, 140–41,
186; migration 149
"Black Shirts" organizations 114
Black teachers, harsh treatment of
150; decline of 177
Black troops (also Colored soldiers)
13, 71, 117, 130; abuse 133;
attempt at voting 118; killing
119–20, 126, 141
Black voting (voters): campaigns
157; as courageous act 127–28;
dangers 118, 142–43, 146, 149;
efforts to stop 118; potential 140;
reduction 32, 60, 62, 72, 76, 81,
95; support 149
Black women: college women's
groups 131; in prison 96;

response to lynching crisis 56,
60, 75, 110; as victims of lynching
38, 49–50, 66, 99, 122
Black Women's Clubs (organiza-
tions) 8, 18; activities 46, 150;
against lynching 113, 131
Black writers (1940–2000) 167–69
Blake, Nelson M. 47
Blauner, Bob 191
Blues see music
B'nai B'rith 89, 109
Bond, Julian 187
Bontemps, Arna 89, 110, 111, 150
Bowers, Sam 164, 190
Boycotts 105, 169, 178
Brady, Jim 72
Braun, Carol Moseley 187
Bromfield, W.H. 93
Brooks, Gwendolyn 150, 154
Brooks, Jonathan Henderson 106
Brown, Joseph Clinton 106
Brown, R. Jess 150
Brown, Sterling A. 110, 150
Brown vs. Board of Education 139,
151–52
Brown vs. Mississippi (court case) 95
Bruce, Blanche K. 5, 8, 13, 14
Bruce, John Edward 74
Brumfield, Eli 158
Brundage, Fitzhugh 6
Bryant, Roy 147
Buckley, Gail 63
Bullock, Henry Allen 79
Bunche, Ralph 112, 131–33, 154,
171
Bureau of the Census 81
Bush, George W. (president) 189
Business, black achievements in 17,
29, 30, 44–45, 59–60, 71, 78, 93,
106

Caldwell, Charles 11, 12
Caldwell, Sam 11, 12
Calhoun, Charles 182
Campbell, David Scott 185
Capeci, Dominic J., Jr. 76
Carmichael, Stokely (Kwame Toure)
171, 188
Carter, Hodding 134
Carter, Hodding, Jr. 153, 170
Carter, Hodding, III 152
Carter, Jimmy 189
Carter, Robert 150
Carthan, Nancy Jane 147
Cashman, Scan Dennis 75
Catton, William B. 62
Censorship 106, 117
Chain gangs 10
Chalmers, David 82
Chaney, James 159, 164–165, 189
Chappie, Levye 106
Chicago Black Women's Clubs 56
Chicago Defender 60, 72, 80; cover-
age of lynchings 106, 113, 130,
154; pledge against segregation
131
Chicago's Negro Fellowship League
56
Children's Defense Fund 177
Childress, Alice 172

Christian, C.B. 93
Civil rights 89, 107, 109, 114, 148,
149
Civil Rights Act of 1875 18–19
Civil rights activists 157; lynching
of 160, 162, 183; violence against
157, 160
Civil Rights Commission (U.S.)
149
Civil Rights Congress 132, 145
Civil rights legislation (bills) 165,
174
Civil rights movement 147, 151,
155, 176; opposition 160–161
Civil Rights Movement (Missis-
sippi), activities of 169
Civil rights organizations 154, 157,
166, 170–171
Civil War 3, 5, 6, 13, 18, 31, 36, 78,
97; Mississippi Flag as relic of
186
Clark, Robert 180
Clinton, Bill (U.S. president) 180,
189
"The Closed Society" 156
Cohen, Williams 21
Cohn, David Lo 95
Cold War 117, 131, 148, 154
Coldwater River (Mississippi) 104
Coleman, J.P. (Mississippi governor)
140, 148, 151
Coleman, T.B. 93
Collins, Malachi 71
Commercial Appeal (Memphis) 75
Commission on Interracial Cooper-
ation 75, 95, 109, 113
Committee of One Hundred 72,
106
Communist Party 145, 152–153
Confederate Memorial Day 76
Confederates (Confederacy) 3, 5,
18, 133, 186
Congress (U.S. government) 1, 13,
14, 81, 118, 140; actions on lynch-
ing 15, 75, 89, 90, 107, 108, 110,
130, 154; blocking of legislation
133, 148; refusal to pass lynch law
136, 153, 170
Congress on Racial Equality
(CORE) 154, 157, 159, 166, 170,
187
Convict-lease system 19, 20, 29, 47,
48
Conyers, John 191
Cooke, Sam 151
Coolidge, Calvin 89
Cooper, Anna Julia 75
Cooper, P.O. 92
Cortner, Richard C. 95
Cosey, Dr. A.A. 128
Costigan, Edward C. 110
Costigan-Wagner, Bill 110
Cotton 9, 17, 29, 78, 91, 94, 96,
115, 176
Council of African Affairs 131
Council of Federated Organizations
(COFO) 157
Couto, Richard A. 42
Criminal executions 97; capital
punishment 120, 140–141